THE CRUSADE OF FREDERI

Crusade Texts in Translation

Editorial Board

Malcolm Barber (Reading), Peter Edbury (Cardiff),
Bernard Hamilton (Nottingham), Norman Housley (Leicester),
Peter Jackson (Keele)

Titles in the series include

Peter Jackson
The Seventh Crusade, 1244–1254
Sources and Documents

Malcolm Barber and Keith Bate
Letters from the East
Crusaders, Pilgrims and Settlers in the 12th–13th Centuries

Bernard S. Bachrach and David S. Bachrach
The *Gesta Tancredi* of Ralph of Caen
A History of the Normans on the First Crusade

Colin Imber
The Crusade of Varna, 1443-45

Carol Sweetenham
Robert the Monk's History of the First Crusade
Historia Iherosolimitana

Damian J. Smith and Helena Buffery
The Book of Deeds of James I of Aragon
A Translation of the Medieval Catalan *Llibre dels Fets*

The Crusade of Frederick Barbarossa
The History of the Expedition of the Emperor Frederick and Related Texts

Translated by

G. A. LOUD
University of Leeds, UK

ASHGATE

Published by
Ashgate Publishing Limited
Wey Court East
Union Road
Farnham
Surrey, GU9 7PT
England

Ashgate Publishing Company
Suite 420
101 Cherry Street
Burlington
VT 05401-4405
USA

www.ashgate.com

British Library Cataloguing in Publication Data
The Crusade of Frederick Barbarossa: The History of the Expedition of the Emperor
    Frederick and Related Texts. – (Crusade Texts in Translation)
    1. Frederick I, Holy Roman Emperor, ca. 1123–1190. 2. Crusades--Third, 1189-1192–
    Sources. 3. Germany – History – Frederick I, 1152–1190 – Sources. I. Series
    II. Magnus, of Reichersberg. III. Otto, von St. Blasien, d. 1223. IV. Loud, G. A.
    943'.024-dc22

Library of Congress Cataloging-in-Publication Data
Frederick I, Holy Roman Emperor, ca. 1123–1190.
    [Historia de expeditione Frederici Imperatoris. English]
    The Crusade of Frederick Barbarossa: The History of the expedition of the Emperor
    Frederick and related texts / [translated and annotated by] G.A. Loud.
        p.   cm. – (Crusade Texts in Translation)
    Includes bibliographical references and index.
    1. Frederick I, Holy Roman Emperor, ca. 1123–1190. 2. Frederick I, Holy Roman
    Emperor, ca. 1123–1190 – Death and burial. 3. Crusades – Third, 1189–1192 – Early
    works to 1800. 4. Holy Roman Empire – History – Frederick I, 1152–1190 – Early
    works to 1800. 5. Crusades – Third, 1189–1192 – Sources. I. Loud, G. A. II. Title.
    D163.A3F74 2009
    956'.014–dc22   2009053574

ISBN 9780754665755 (hbk)
ISBN 9781472413963 (pbk)
ISBN 9781409406815 (ebk-PDF)
ISBN 9781409480907 (ebk-ePUB)

Printed and bound in Great Britain
by MPG PRINTGROUP

Contents

Preface   *vii*
Maps   *ix*
Genealogical Charts   *xi*
Abbreviations   *xv*

Introduction   1

The History of the Expedition of the Emperor Frederick   33

The History of the Pilgrims   135

The Chronicle of Magnus of Reichersberg   149

A Letter Concerning the Death of the Emperor Frederick   169

The Chronicle of Otto of St Blasien 1187–1197   173

An Account of the Seaborne Journey of the Pilgrims Heading
to Jerusalem Who Captured Silves in 1189   193

Frederick I's Imperial 'Land Peace' (issued at Nuremberg,
29 December 1188)   209

Bibliography   *213*
Index   *223*

Preface

From the time of Sir Walter Scott onwards, discussion of the Third Crusade of 1189-92 has tended to focus on Richard the Lionheart and the Anglo-Norman Crusade. Much more recently, the publication of English translations of primary sources in this same series by Peter Edbury and Helen Nicholson has allowed students also to study the siege of Acre in depth from its beginnings in the autumn of 1189. In comparison, the German expedition led by the Emperor Frederick I, which in contrast to those of the kings of France and England took the 'traditional' overland route through the Balkans and Asia Minor, has been neglected, despite its great intrinsic interest. The death of the emperor, drowned while crossing, or bathing in, a river in Armenia, tends to be seen as rendering the expedition a fiasco, although it is argued here that this was very far from being the case. My own interest in this subject has stemmed directly from my teaching in the University of Leeds of both Crusader history and more recently that of medieval Germany. It has been the latter, in particular, which has encouraged me to investigate the sources and the background to Frederick's expedition, and my thanks must go to the students who over the last three years have taken what was a pretty experimental module. A number of others have made substantial contributions to this project. My publisher John Smedley encouraged me to turn the brief extracts that I had translated for my students into a book, and one of the series editors, Bernard Hamilton, has read and commented on the entire manuscript, some of it more than once. Professor John Davies of the University of Liverpool helped me with the translation of some of the more problematic passages in the *Historia de Expeditione*, during what was otherwise an entirely social occasion. I have also benefited from extensive help from two of my colleagues at Leeds, Alan Murray and Ian Moxon, both of whom have shown that (contrary to popular stereotypes) Scots can be the most generous of friends. Alan has shared his knowledge of Crusader and German history, and of German geography, and has furnished me with copies of his articles and copious bibliographical advice. Both he and Ian have also read drafts of the introduction. Ian meanwhile has done his best to remedy the defects of my classical education. Time and again he has abandoned whatever he was then doing to assist me with Latin passages where I was hopelessly confused or in error. I hope that he will forgive some of my more free or colloquial renditions, painful as they must be to his austere respect for the Latin language. I have striven to render these translations as accurate as possible, but any translator must tread a fine line between accuracy and intelligibility. Similarly, I have tried to be consistent with regard to place and personal names, but when in doubt have tended to use the forms most familiar to Anglophone readers. Needless to say, none of those named above bear any responsibility for any flaws in the finished product; although without their assistance there would have been far more than there now are.

Finally there are the two dedicatees of this book. My wife Kate has helped with the maps and genealogical charts, and coped with the fallout from the expiry of my laptop halfway through the writing of this book, as well as patiently suffering my obsession with the distant past interfering with matters domestic. The other dedicatee, my former collaborator and close friend Thomas Wiedemann, is sadly no longer here to read this. A brilliant classicist who died far too young, he would have particularly encouraged my new concern with the history of the country where he was born, not least because his father had as a student gone to the lectures of the great Heidelberg medievalist Karl Hampe, the historian of the Salian and Staufen emperors. Thomas's last gift to me, his father's copy of one of the most famous works of medieval German history, Kantorowicz's *Friedrich der Zweite*, sits on my bookshelf as I write these words.

Leeds and Lyme Regis, September 2009.

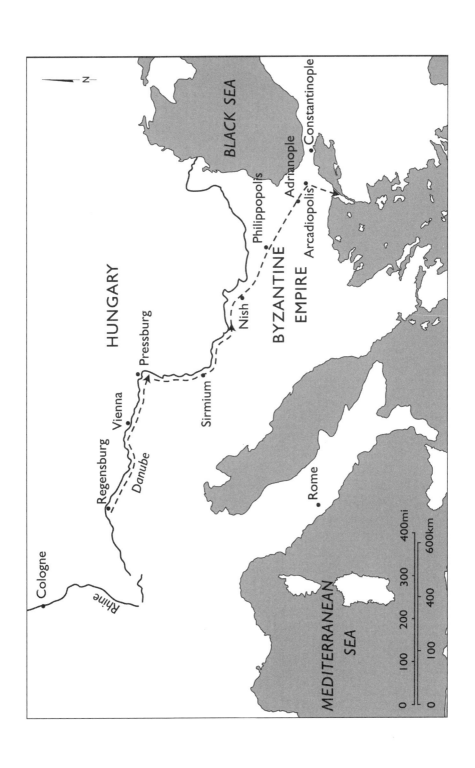

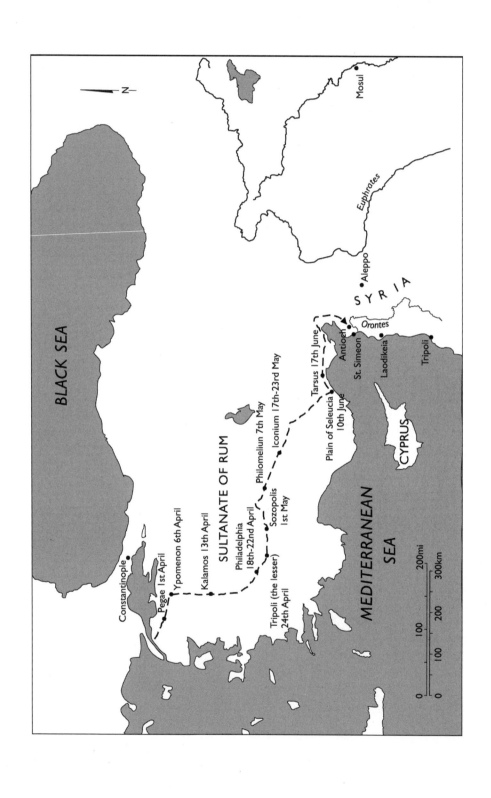

Genealogical Charts

The Staufen Imperial Family

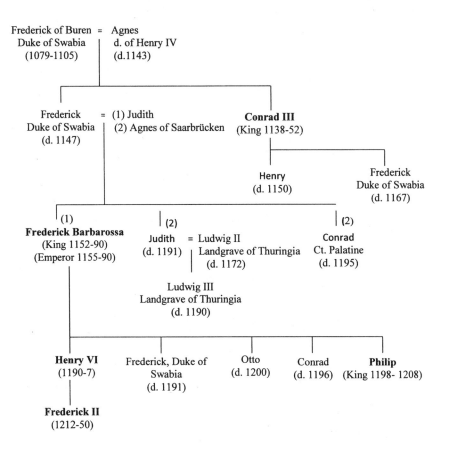

The Babenberger Dukes of Austria

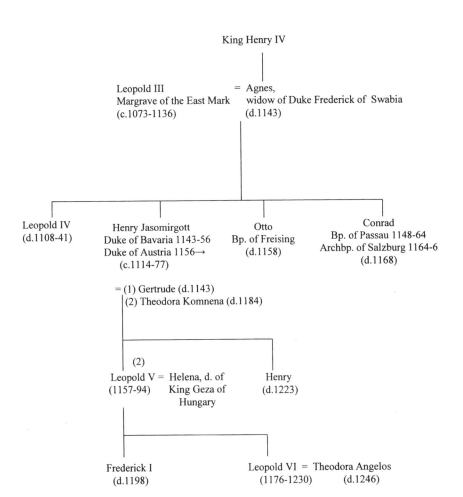

King Henry IV

Leopold III = Agnes,
Margrave of the East Mark   widow of Duke Frederick of Swabia
(c.1073-1136)   (d.1143)

Leopold IV
(d.1108-41)

Henry Jasomirgott
Duke of Bavaria 1143-56
Duke of Austria 1156→
(c.1114-77)

Otto
Bp. of Freising
(d.1158)

Conrad
Bp. of Passau 1148-64
Archbp. of Salzburg 1164-6
(d.1168)

= (1) Gertrude (d.1143)
  (2) Theodora Komnena (d.1184)

(2)
Leopold V = Helena, d. of
(1157-94)   King Geza of
            Hungary

Henry
(d.1223)

Frederick I
(d.1198)

Leopold VI = Theodora Angelos
(1176-1230)   (d.1246)

The Seljuk Sultans of Iconium

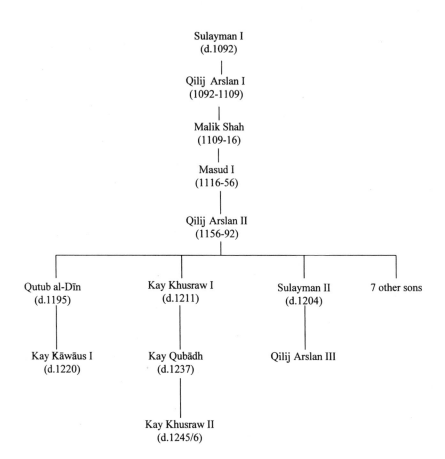

Sulayman I
(d.1092)

Qilij Arslan I
(1092-1109)

Malik Shah
(1109-16)

Masud I
(1116-56)

Qilij Arslan II
(1156-92)

Qutub al-Dīn   Kay Khusraw I   Sulayman II   7 other sons
(d.1195)   (d.1211)   (d.1204)

Kay Kāwāus I   Kay Qubādh   Qilij Arslan III
(d.1220)   (d.1237)

Kay Khusraw II
(d.1245/6)

Abbreviations

Clementi, 'Calendar'	D.R. Clementi, 'Calendar of the diplomas of the Hohenstaufen Emperor Henry VI concerning the kingdom of Sicily', *Quellen und Forschungen aus italienischen Archiven und Bibliotheken* 35 (1955), 86–225.
Dipl. Fred. I	*Die Urkunden Friedrichs I*, ed. Heinrich Appelt (5 vols, MGH Diplomatum Regum et Imperatorum Germaniae, x, Hannover 1975–90).
Itinerarium Peregrinorum	*Itinerarium Peregrinorum*, in Hans Eberhard Mayer, *Das Itinerarium Peregrinorum. Eine zeitgenössiche englische Chronik zum dritten Kreuzzug in ursprünglicher Gestalt* (MGH Schriften 18: Stuttgart 1962), pp. 243–357.
Mainzer Urkundenbuch ii(2)	*Mainzer Urkundenbuch* ii *Die Urkunden seit dem Tode Erzbischof Adalberts I (1137) bis zum Tode Erzbischofs Konrads (1200), Teil II, 1176–1200*, ed. Peter Acht (Darmstadt 1978).
MGH	Monumenta Germania Historica, following the usual conventions (SRG = Scriptores Rerum Germanicarum; SS = Scriptores, etc.).
Quellen	*Quellen zur Geschichte des Kreuzzuges Kaiser Friedrichs I.*, ed. Anton Chroust (MGH SRG, n.s. V, Berlin 1928).
Reg. Henry VI	*Die Regesten des Kaiserreiches unter Heinrich VI. 1165–(1190)–1197*, ed. Gerhard Baaken, after J.F. Böhmer (Regesta Imperii IV(3), Cologne 1972).
Urkunden HL	*Die Urkunden Heinrichs des Löwen, Herzogs von Sachsen und Bayern*, ed. Karl Jordan (MGH, Weimar 1949).
Urkundenbuch für Niederrheins	*Urkundenbuch für die Geschichte des Niederrheins*, ed. Theodor J. Lacomblet (4 vols, Düsseldorf 1840–58).

Introduction

Although the Crusade of Frederick Barbarossa has been, to some extent anyway, neglected by Anglophone historians, the contemporary sources for that expedition are surprisingly full. We are indeed much better informed, especially from German sources, about this expedition to assist the Holy Land than we are about the corresponding one led by Frederick's uncle, Conrad III, some 40 years earlier, in which the later Emperor Frederick had taken part as a young man.[1] However, all three of the principal contemporary sources describing Barbarossa's Crusade must be treated with some caution. Neither their composition nor their transmission is entirely straightforward, and the interrelationship between the three texts is complex. In this respect, the German sources for the Third Crusade resemble the equally complex and interrelated Anglo-Norman texts that describe this same Crusade.

The longest, richest and most important of these three sources is the *Historia de Expeditione Friderici Imperatoris*. This is a strictly contemporary text, completed c. 1200 at the latest, and quite possibly earlier. Parts of this account survive in two very early manuscripts, one written at the Benedictine monastery of St Lamprecht in Styria c. 1200, the other at the Praemonstratensian abbey of Mühlhausen in Bohemia (now Milevsko in the Czech Republic), probably before 1221. Unfortunately, neither of these manuscripts is complete; indeed, the Styrian one contains only about a third of the text, while the Mühlhausen one, although fuller, still has substantial omissions. We are dependent for our knowledge of the complete text, or at least as complete a text as now survives, on two copies made in Moravia, presumably from a different archetype, during the mid-eighteenth century under the supervision of Josef Bonaventura Piter (1708–

---

[1]   The most detailed modern account is by Ekkehard Eickhoff, *Friedrich Barbarossa im Orient. Kreuzzug und Tod Friedrichs I.* (Tübingen 1977). This is particularly useful for its careful analysis of the route followed by the expedition. There is also a full and interesting discussion, especially valuable for the preparations for the expedition, by Rudolf Hiestand, '"*Precipua tocius christianismi columpna*". Barbarossa und der Kreuzzug', in *Friedrich Barbarossa. Handlungsspielräume und Wirkungsweisen des Staufischen Kaisers*, ed. Alfred Haverkamp (Vorträge und Forschungen 40: Sigmaringen 1992), pp. 51–108. By contrast, Edgar N. Johnson, 'The Crusades of Frederick Barbarossa and Henry VI', in *A History of the Crusades*, ed. Kenneth Setton, ii *The Later Crusades, 1189–1311*, ed. R.L. Wolff and H.W. Hazard (Madison 1969), 87–122, offers little more than a summary and paraphrase of the *Historia de Expeditione*. For a more general context, see Rudolf Hiestand, 'Kingship and Crusade in twelfth-century Germany', in *England and Germany in the High Middle Ages: in Honour of Karl J. Leyser*, ed. Alfred Haverkamp and Hanna Vollrath (Oxford 1996), pp. 235–65.

64), noted antiquarian and Abbot successively of the monasteries of Brewnov and Raigern (now Rajhrad, not far from Brno). One of these manuscripts indeed has corrections in the abbot's own hand.[2]

The authorship of this account is similarly problematic, and more so than might seem at first sight. The Mühlhausen manuscript has a title heading, written by Gerlach, Abbot of that monastery 1187–1221, which describes the text as 'The History of the Expedition of the Emperor Frederick, written by an Austrian cleric who was present on this same'.[3] A later thirteenth-century hand has then added 'called Ansbert' (*nomine Ansberte*). But while some later historians have accepted this identification, and identified the author of the *Historia de Expeditione* as Ansbert, this identification cannot be unequivocally accepted. One might in default of other evidence still be cautious in following such a later, even if only somewhat later, attribution, but this is not the principal reason why one should be sceptical. More to the point, the *Historia de Expeditione* is undoubtedly a composite text, which is the work of more than one author. The bulk of the History is indeed a contemporary, and at first sight an eyewitness account of the Crusading expedition of 1189–90, after a brief preface describing the fall of Jerusalem and the calling of the Crusade. But appended to this is an account (only a quarter as long) of the later consequences and ramifications of the Crusading expedition as these affected the German empire. These include the attempts of Barbarossa's son and successor the Emperor Henry VI to conquer the kingdom of Sicily, ultimately successful in December 1194; the capture and subsequent ransoming and liberation of Richard the Lionheart; the death of Duke Leopold of Austria after a riding accident, also in December 1194; and the various plans made by Henry VI for a new expedition to the east. The work concludes with a brief account of his attempts to transform Germany into a hereditary monarchy; the last event mentioned is his departure for Italy in the summer of 1196. This section would appear to have been finished before Henry's sudden death in September 1197: he is throughout referred to as though still alive.

Not only is the focus of these two parts very different, but they are also embellished in subtly different styles at the ends of phrases, and especially of sentences, with one or another of the main accentual *clausulae* that became fashionable during the twelfth century, and that were known to contemporaries as the *cursus*. More than half of the account of the Crusade itself employs the *cursus velox* style (seven syllable units, stress on first, fourth and sixth syllables, thus óoo ‖ óoóo) and just under 30 percent the so-called *tritrochaeus* or *cursus trispondaicus* rhythm (six syllable units, stress on first and fifth syllables: óoo ‖ oóo). However, in the later part, these proportions are more or less exactly

---

[2]   *Quellen zur Geschichte des Kreuzzuges Kaiser Friedrichs I.*, ed. Anton Chroust (MGH SRG, n.s. 5, Berlin 1928; reprint Munich 1989), pp. ix–xiv.

[3]   Gerlach quoted a few brief passages from the *Historia de Expeditione* in his continuation of the annals of Vincent of Prague, *Continuatio Gerlaci Abbatis Milovicensis*, MGH SS xvii.706.

reversed. Matters are admittedly further complicated by two small sections: the page of introduction, which relies far more than the rest of the text on the *cursus tardus* (six syllable units, stress on first and fourth syllables: óoo ‖ óoo), and the brief account of the death of the Emperor Frederick, which like the later section relies primarily on the *tritrochaeus*.[4] Whatever quibbles one might make as to the exact significance of these stylistic details, the conclusion is clear: these variations in the prosody surely point to more than one authorial hand at work. The *Historia de Expeditione* would thus appear to be based upon, or a combination of, different works, and not necessarily all written at the same time. And as for the 'certain Austrian cleric', whether or not he be called Ansbert, one should note that while a letter to Duke Leopold of Austria was included at the start of the *Historia*, in the account of the Crusade itself the duke was only mentioned once, and that not by name, for although he had taken the Cross he did not accompany the main expedition. Indeed, this account said nothing at all about the expedition's brief stay in Vienna, whereas the later *Historia Peregrinorum* praised Duke Leopold's generosity there.[5] However, in the last part of the *Historia de Expeditione*, Leopold played a central role, and indeed was to a considerable extent the hero of this section. Thus, if 'a certain Austrian cleric' may have put the text, as it now stands, together, he almost certainly only wrote the last part, which one is tempted to style 'the appendix', himself.

Not only this, but behind a significant part of the text, the narrative of the Crusade once it had crossed into Asia Minor, there lies another, and even more strictly contemporary, account, by one who did indeed participate in the Crusade. The narrative of the *Historia de Expeditione* draws heavily upon a record of the Crusade, described as a *memoria*, but which is effectively a diary, written by a Bavarian cleric, Tageno, dean of the cathedral of Passau, who took part in the expedition and who died at Tripoli in the autumn of 1190 (his death was noted in passing in the later text).[6] For a substantial section, covering the three and a half weeks until the eve of the death of the Emperor Frederick (16 May to 9 June 1190), the *Historia de Expeditione* copies the diary of Tageno more or less verbatim.[7]

However, the relationship between the 'diary' of Tageno and the *Historia de Expeditione* is, in fact, more complicated than this brief summary suggests.

---

[4] *Quellen*, pp. xix–xxi.

[5] *Quellen*, p. 130 [and see below, p. 147].

[6] Below, p. 118. Tageno became dean of Passau in 1187, having previously been a minor member of the clergy of the cathedral, *Die Regesten der Bischöfe von Passau* i *731–1206*, ed. Egon Boshof and Franz-Reiner Erkens (Munich 1992), 273–4 no. 893 (July 1183), 278–9 no. 915 (1172 x 1187), 279 no. 916.

[7] Ferdinand Güterbock, 'Il Diario di Tageno e altre fonti della terza Crociata', *Bullettino dell'Istituto Storico Italiano per le Medio Evo* 55 (1941), 223–69; here at 254–60. The early pages of Güterbock's study conveniently summarise the arguments of an older generation of German-language study of these texts.

First, Tageno's diary does not survive as an independent text, but as a series of insertions in the chronicle of Magnus of Reichersberg, which was probably compiled contemporaneously, and certainly before the death of Magnus in 1195.[8] Magnus recorded that a copy of this text had been sent back to him from the Holy Land. Second, although the sections within the chronicle of Magnus that were derived from Tageno's narrative appear to be readily identifiable, it is by no means clear that the text reproduced there corresponds exactly with what Tageno originally wrote. For one thing, the account of the Crusaders' activities is sometimes, although not invariably, presented in the third person. Hence, while, for example, on 13 May 1190 'when it was the holy day of Pentecost, God spared us' (*pepercit nobis Deus*), earlier, at the end of March, we read that 'they set off on their journey with pack animals, and for two days they had an extremely difficult march, beset by shortage' (*cum sagmis aggressi sunt et per duas dies valde laboriosam et penuriosam viam habuerunt*). It is possible that Tageno cast some of his account in the third person, but it is more probable that Magnus, writing from his monastery in Bavaria, altered the text, particularly since the *Historia de Expeditione* consistently used the first person 'we', including in the long section where Tageno's account was plagiarised without significant change apart from this.

Furthermore, this may not be the only way in which the text that Magnus copied of Tageno's diary may have been altered, for it has been plausibly suggested that not only did he draw on the dean's narrative but he also used the *Historia de Expeditione*, although in an earlier redaction than the one now extant.[9] Three conclusions may therefore be derived from this. First, the text of Tageno's diary, as we now possess it transmitted by Magnus, is corrupt and some way from the original; second, the close correspondence between the narratives of Tageno and the *Historia* may not simply be due to the author of the latter using, and frequently plagiarising the former; and, finally, the first draft of the main part of the *Historia de Expeditione* must date from before 1195, even though the appendix section clearly does not. That Tageno's original text was some way from what was reproduced by Magnus is also suggested by the survival of a variant version in the work of an early sixteenth-century humanist, Aventinus, although it is a good question how far the differences between this and the version of Magnus were due to the original text or to the humanist himself. That these differences are more matters of style than substance suggests the latter. Furthermore, was

---

[8]　*Chronicon Magni Presbiteri*, ed. Wilhelm Wattenbach, MGH SS xvii.509–17 [full text of this work, MGH SS xvii.476–523]. Reichersberg was a house of Augustinian canons in the diocese of Salzburg. The death of Magnus is recorded at the start of a continuation to his chronicle, ibid., 523.

[9]　Güterbock, 'Il Diario di Tageno', 248–52.

Aventinus using Tageno's original text at all, or a version (perhaps different from the one we now possess) of the Reichersberg chronicle?[10]

One should not, therefore, exaggerate the indebtedness of the *Historia de Expeditione* to Tageno. Indeed, the two narratives of the earlier stages of the Crusade, until the crossing of the Bosphorus, are independent, and much of Magnus's account of the earlier part of the expedition's time in the Balkans actually comprises the text of a letter from Bishop Diepold of Passau, which is not reproduced or used by the author of the *Historia*. It was only when describing the events from 29 March 1190, when the German army began its march on the Asian shore of the Bosphorus, that the latter began to use Tageno's diary.[11] Even then, to begin with the two accounts are not identical; it was only from mid-May, for a period of just over three weeks, that the texts we now possess of Tageno–Magnus and the *Historia de Expeditione* are all but the same, and, as has been suggested above, this may represent a two-way process.

This limited use of the diary of Tageno also points to a further aspect of the composition of the *Historia de Expeditione*. While there is a clear distinction between the main text and the subsequent appendix, the former is itself a composite text. Apart from the stylistic contrasts between the preface, the account of the emperor's death and the rest of the main text (discussed above), which may or may not be significant, this main part of the text would seem to fall into four distinct sections. First, there is the news of the fall of Jerusalem and the calling of the Crusade, which relies to a considerable extent on documents incorporated within it, above all Gregory VIII's bull *Audita Tremendi*, but including also a widely distributed letter to the Master of the Italian Hospitallers Archembald describing the battle of Hattin, also copied by Magnus,[12] and another letter from Hermenger, the steward (*provisor*) of the Hospital at Jerusalem, to the Duke of Austria, dating from August or September 1188, describing Saladin's further conquests of that year, principally in northern Syria. But, in addition, Chroust, the modern (1928) editor of the text, suggests that the account of the expedition itself is divided into three distinct sections of unequal length: (1) from the departure of the Crusade in May 1189 until the middle of November in that year; (2) from the arrival of the army in Adrianople on 22 November 1189 until the crossing of the Bosphorus at Easter 1190; and (3) from the army setting out into Asia Minor until the death of the emperor in June. The first section concluded with the emperor sending back envoys with news to his son and designated successor

---

[10]   Güterbock, 'Il Diario di Tageno', 225–30. The work of Aventinus, now extremely rare, and which I have not used directly, was first published in 1522.

[11]   *Quellen*, pp. lviii–lxiii; Güterbock, 'Il Diario di Tageno', 234–6.

[12]   *Chronicon Magni Presbiteri*, MGH SS xvii.508–9. Magnus also included the text of an even more widely distributed letter, from Terricus, the preceptor of the Temple, one of the survivors of Hattin, copied by, among others, Roger of Howden (not included here, but translated by Malcolm Barber, *The New Knighthood. A History of the Order of the Temple* (Cambridge 1994), pp. 115–16).

Henry VI and to the King of Hungary, and indeed may have been based on a version of the newsletter (if such it was) sent back to Germany then (clearly this must have been considerably fuller than the text of the letter from Frederick to Henry which is reproduced in the 'history'). The second section may also have been based upon a similar contemporary report: certainly, as Chroust suggested, the reference to Tokili, the envoy of the Sultan of Iconium, as 'a wise and sensible man, who according to human judgment feared the Lord', was surely not written after the end of April 1190, when despite the previous negotiations for a peaceful passage through the sultan's lands, the Crusader army came under heavy attack from the Turks – in the words of the *Historia*, 'The Turks showed themselves not as friends, but as most savage enemies.'[13] The Pisan envoys (from a traditionally pro-imperial city), with whom the emperor had been in contact while his army waited to cross from Gallipoli, would have been one obvious means of sending a further report back to Germany. Furthermore, there is a near-contemporary reference to such a report being sent back to Henry VI after the crossing of the Bosphorus.[14] In addition, it was only in the third section that the *Historia de Expeditione* depended upon the diary of Tageno, suggesting therefore that this was compiled separately. Subsequently, the compiler of the *Historia*, or of the main part of that account (as opposed to the 'appendix'), stitched together these various separate sections and reworked them.[15] But that they were reworked is clear, both because of the stylistic unity of the *cursus* employed throughout the account of the expedition's progress, and through a number of retrospective references that reveal some element of hindsight. While some of these, such as the critical remarks about as yet unsuspected Greek treachery, may stem from the reports sent back from the expedition itself, others would seem to be later insertions. Thus, for example, during the account of the preparations of the Crusade, Bishop Gottfried of Würzburg was described as 'a man of noble birth, who was at this time (*tunc temporis*) most highly regarded for his knowledge of letters and his eloquent speech'. Chroust suggested, surely rightly, that this was only written after the bishop's death in July 1190.[16] One might also point to the quotation, during the first section of the account of the expedition proper, of a passage from the work of Otto of Freising, to describe the Hellespont, as a clear example of later reworking.[17] On the other hand, such reworking was by no means comprehensive: thus, after listing those who took part in the expedition, the account continued to mention disparagingly those who 'violated their vow'

---

[13]   *Quellen*, p. xlii. See below, pp. 92, 100.

[14]   *Chronicon Montis Sereni*, MGH SS xxiii.161 (from the Saxon monastery of Lauterberg). For the continued significance of newsletters as sources for medieval chroniclers, see John Taylor, *English Historical Literature in the Fourteenth Century* (Oxford 1986), pp. 229–30.

[15]   *Quellen*, pp. xxvi–lvii.

[16]   *Quellen*, pp. xxvii. See below, pp. 43–4.

[17]   *Quellen*, pp. xxxvi, 48. See below, pp. 76–7.

and 'abandoned the way of Christ'. Yet this list included the kings of France and England, as well as Count Philip of Flanders and Bishop Roger of Cambrai, all of whom ultimately did go on Crusade; the latter two both died during the siege of Acre in 1191. This section was thus clearly written before then, and almost certainly before September 1190 when Count Philip left Flanders to embark on the Crusade.[18] It is therefore part of the strictly contemporary material embedded in the account.

Since, if the later reference to 'Ansbert' was in any way correct, he was more likely to have been the writer of the concluding section of the work, we do not know the name of the author, or more properly the compiler, of the majority of the *Historia de Expeditione*. Whoever he was, he appears to have been familiar with the formulae and intitulature of the imperial chancery, and of course to have had access to the text of such documents as the treaty between Barbarossa and Isaac Angelos in February 1190.[19] The compiler may possibly have come from the Passau region, on the Bavarian–Austrian border: certainly he emphasised the role of men from this region, as for example Frederick of Berg, the advocate of the church of Passau, whose bravery was mentioned on a number of occasions, and whom he described as 'always quite ferocious in fighting the enemies of the army of the Holy Cross'. The valiant actions of Bishop Diepold of Passau were also mentioned several times, and the only German abbot to be mentioned, Isenrich of Admont, who died in Bulgaria, was from the same diocese.[20] That the compiler was from Passau would also explain how he had access to the diary of Tageno, and how Magnus of Reichersberg (from the neighbouring diocese of Salzburg) may in turn have used an early draft of the *Historia de Expeditione*.

The third related text to give an account of the Crusade is the *Historia Peregrinorum*. This work, which survives only in a single early thirteenth-century manuscript from the Cistercian monastery of Salem (Salmansweiler) on Lake Constance, is probably also a very early one, perhaps written before the death of Henry VI, or possibly c. 1200.[21] Although this treatise is only about half the length of the *Historia de Expeditione*, it too seems to be a composite text, comprising three distinct sections: describing the conquest of Palestine by Saladin, the preparations for a new Crusade and (by far the longest section) the expedition itself. It ends abruptly while describing the emperor's death, and the manuscript appears to be incomplete, although it may only be missing a few sentences. The

---

[18]   *La Chronique de Gislebert de Mons*, ed. Léon Vanderkindere (Brussels 1904), p. 248 [= Gilbert of Mons, *Chronicle of Hainaut*, trans. Laura Napran (Woodbridge 2005), p. 136].

[19]   *Quellen*, pp. xliv–xlvii.

[20]   *Quellen*, pp. l–li.

[21]   For this abbey, see for example Frederick I's diploma of confirmation and protection of June 1183, which comments on the change of name: *id est locum . qui olim Salmanneswilare nuncupabatur, nunc autem mutuo nomine Salem dicitur, Dipl. Fred. I,* iv,66–8 no. 847, quoted from p. 67.

tract is early, but not an eyewitness account, and indeed the author made extensive use of an early recension of the *Historia de Expeditione*. He did not follow this latter text slavishly, however, and sometimes altered or confused its chronology; there are also a number of instances where the *Historia Peregrinorum* differs from, contradicts or adds to the earlier account. A few of the additions would appear to reflect eyewitness testimony or written report unknown to the author of the *Historia de Expeditione*. The author was also on occasion prepared to be mildly critical of the emperor, generally for being 'credulous' in believing what he was told by Turkish or Greek envoys, although he also lamented that the east was 'a land of scorpions' where treachery and backstabbing was the norm.[22] The first part of the *HP* may also have used a brief tract, or newsletter, concerning Conrad of Montferrat's deeds in the Holy Land; certainly it highlights his defence of Tyre, which the *Historia de Expeditione* did not even mention. (Conrad came from a family who were distantly related to the Staufen, and his father had been one of Frederick's most reliable allies during his Italian campaigns.[23]) By contrast to the author/compiler of the *Historia de Expeditione*, the author of the *HP* was probably from Swabia, and he may indeed have been a monk of Salem. For example, in his account of the battle outside Philomelium, on 7 May 1190, while the *Historia de Expeditione* refers only to the leadership of the dukes of Swabia and Merania, the *HP* highlights the valour of Ulrich of Lutzelenhard, a Swabian nobleman.[24] Furthermore, the account in the *HP* of the courts held at Strassburg in December 1187 and Mainz in March 1188 is so similar to that in the (Swabian) Marbach Annals that they may both have derived this from the same source.[25] Because the *HP* does make extensive, if only occasionally verbatim, use of the *Historia de Expeditione*, and often presents a very similar account, only the first (independent) part of the text has been translated below, although the footnotes to the *Historia de Expeditione* draw attention to contradictions and additional information in the *Historia Peregrinorum*, and provide translations of passages which significantly add to the account of the earlier text.

Four further texts translated here are independent ones that differ greatly from one another. The brief tract entitled *Letter About the Death of the Emperor Frederick* [*Epistola de Morte Friderici Imperatoris*] is a strictly contemporary text, a newsletter giving a very brief account of the Crusade's passage through Asia Minor, written immediately after the drowning of the emperor, and before

---

[22]   *Quellen*, pp. 128, 151–2 [see below, pp. 93n.249, 146].

[23]   Marcel Pacaut, *Frederick Barbarossa* (London 1970), pp. 86–7, 99, 144. The Margrave had fought on the emperor's side at the battle of Legnano, and then entertained him at Christmas 1176, *Annales Magdeburgenses*, MGH SS xvi.194, *Annales Pegavienses*, ibid., 261.

[24]   *Quellen*, pp. 79, 160.

[25]   *Quellen*, pp. 122–3. *Annales Marbacenses qui dicuntur*, ed. Hermann Bloch (MGH SRG, Hanover 1907), pp. 58–60. For the above paragraph, see Chroust's discussion, *Quellen*, pp. lxxi–xcv.

the expedition arrived at Antioch. The author may have been Bishop Gottfried of Würzburg, who (as noted above) died at Antioch in July 1190. If he was the author, his hope expressed at the end of the letter for better times ahead 'through the mercy of God' strikes one as poignant indeed, given that the bishop would have written this only a month before his own end. This text survives in two early thirteenth-century manuscripts, in one of which it serves as an appendix to the *Deeds of Frederick* by Otto of Freising and Rahewin.[26] While there is no evidence that this account was directly used by the author/compiler of the *Historia de Expeditione*, this was precisely the sort of text that lies behind the constituent parts of this History. (The letter of Diepold of Passau copied by Magnus was another such.)

By contrast, the account of the Crusade and its aftermath from the Chronicle of Otto of St Blasien forms part of a more general chronicle-history, written c. 1209–10 at the monastery of St Blasien in the Black Forest. Otto, who died as Abbot of this monastery in 1223, was one of the principal historians of early thirteenth-century Germany, and his portrayal of Frederick's Crusade, the subsequent capture of Richard the Lionheart and the abortive German expedition to the Holy Land of 1197, which might be considered as a continuation of the unfinished business of the earlier Crusade, provides a vivid picture of how this was viewed retrospectively, 20 years later, but by a historian who was sympathetic to the Staufen dynasty and more generally to imperial authority.

The penultimate text translated presents a contrast of a different sort. This account, another strictly contemporary one, does not deal directly with the expedition of Frederick Barbarossa at all, but rather with a seaborne expedition that set off from Germany as part of his Crusade, but in the event campaigned in Portugal, where it captured the town of Silves in the Algarve in September 1189. However, since it was the intention of these Crusaders from north Germany to continue to Jerusalem (like the English and Flemish who helped to capture Lisbon in 1147), and since the only surviving manuscript of the work also contains one of the only two copies of the *Epistola de Morte*, it seems appropriate to add this work to our collection.[27] It does after all deal with another part of the German Crusade of 1189–92, and the expedition that took Silves then continued on to Acre, where it provided a substantial and very welcome reinforcement to the

---

[26] *Quellen*, pp. xcvi–xcix.

[27] The manuscript, now in Turin, was purchased by an Italian scholar, Costanzo Gazzera, in a market in Aix-en-Provence in 1837. It was published by Chroust, *Quellen*, 179–96, but not entirely satisfactorily, since he relied on a colleague to make the transcription, which contains a number of dubious readings. I have therefore translated the text from the superior edition of C.W. David, *Narratio de Itinere Navali Peregrinorum Hierosolymam Tendentium et Silviam Capientium*, in the *Proceedings of the American Philosophical Society* 81 (1939), 591–676. For David's comments on Chroust's edition, ibid., 607–8.

exiguous forces that had begun the siege in August 1189.[28] The text describing the capture of Silves was the work of a member of this expedition, and would appear to have been written very soon after the events it described, and certainly before the recapture of Silves by the Almohad ruler al-Mansūr in July 1191 (the Algarve was only finally conquered by the Portuguese in 1249).

Finally, as an appendix, Barbarossa's German land peace of 1188 has been translated. Although the date of this edict has been disputed, and surviving versions carry the date 29 December 1187, Burchard of Urspberg, who copied the full text of the decree into his chronicle, written in the 1220s, says that it was issued after the emperor had taken the Cross, which he did in March 1188.[29] The land peace should therefore be seen as one of the measures that Frederick took to secure the domestic tranquillity of Germany during his absence (discussed in more detail below), and as a text proceeding directly from his decision to undertake the Crusade.

* * * *

The accounts translated here are the principal, but by no means the only, contemporary or near-contemporary accounts of the German Crusade of 1189–90. The march of the German army and the tragic death of the emperor at the moment when he had almost succeeded in leading his army to Syria naturally excited the interest of contemporary writers, and not just within the German *Reich*. Other accounts, in more or less detail, include a short text written in Italy during the 1190s, called 'The Deeds of the Emperor Frederick on the Holy Expedition', which in each of the two surviving manuscripts has been appended to an earlier, and more substantial, history of Frederick's campaigns in northern Italy in the 1150s and 1160s, written soon after the peace treaty between the emperor and Lombard League negotiated in 1177. Both these texts were in turn copied and adapted by several later Italian writers. However, this brief account of the Crusade contributes little or nothing original, although it confirms the broad outlines of the story in the *History of the Expedition* and the *History of the Pilgrims*.[30] More problematic is whether the author of this text had access to any of the other accounts of the Crusade. There are undoubtedly some resemblances; for example, the description of the Turkomans of Asia Minor: 'They are wild Turks, who are subject to no rule and possess no places, but dwell in the countryside,' which

---

[28]   *Itinerarium Peregrinorum*, I.27, p. 309 = *Chronicle of the Third Crusade. A Translation of the* Itinerarium Peregrinorum et Gesta Regis Ricardi, trans. Helen J. Nicholson (Crusader Texts in Translation 3: Aldershot 1997), p. 74.

[29]   *Burchardi Praepositi Urspergensis Chronicon*, ed. Oswald Holder-Egger and Bernhard von Simson (MGH SRG, Hanover 1916), pp. 65–9.

[30]   *Gesta Federici I. Imperatoris in Expeditione Sacra*, in *Gesta Federici I. Imperatoris in Lombardia*, ed. Oswald Holder-Egger (MGH SRG, Hanover 1892), pp. 74–98.

is similar, although not identical, to a passage in the *Historia Peregrinorum*.[31] Given the limited distribution of this text, and of the *Historia de Expeditione*, direct use of these two would at first sight appear unlikely, although the author of the Italian account may have used some of the same sources (probably, as has been suggested, letters about the expedition). On the other hand, the *Historia Peregrinorum* was used, during the later thirteenth century, by the Franciscan Salimbene of Parma, and perhaps also by the earlier chronicler Bishop Sicard of Cremona, writing in the early 1200s, so it is not impossible that the author of 'The Deeds of the Emperor Frederick' may also have seen it.[32]

More important, however, than 'The Deeds of the Emperor Frederick' for our knowledge of Barbarossa's Crusade are two secondary (that is not eyewitness) accounts from Germany, the first contained within the so-called 'Royal Chronicle of Cologne', written at the monastery of St Pantaleon in that city, and the other in the important north German 'Chronicle of the Slavs' by Arnold, Abbot of the monastery of St John at Lübeck, written, or at least completed, c. 1209–10. (This section of the Cologne chronicle was completed soon after 1199, when the account of the recension in question breaks off.) These two texts add some details to the accounts translated here, although once again without significantly contradicting what we are told by Tageno and the author of the *History of the Expedition*. Points of interest from these two accounts will be noted in the footnotes.[33] Arnold, in particular, displayed a lively interest in the affairs of the Holy Land; his chronicle also described the pilgrimage of Duke Henry the Lion of Saxony to Jerusalem in 1172, and gives the fullest contemporary account of the later German expedition of 1197, which was brought to an abrupt end by news of the death of Henry VI.[34] There is also a surprisingly full account of Barbarossa's expedition in the 'Itinerary of the Pilgrims', written by an English participant in the Third Crusade. Much of his information must have come from German survivors of the Crusade who later took part in the siege of Acre; interestingly, his view of the emperor's dealings with the Greeks and Turks was similar to that of the *HP* author: 'Caesar was too credulous, for he thought other people were as highly principled as he.'

---

[31]   *Gesta Federici I. Imperatoris*, p. 86; *Historia Peregrinorum*, p. 155 [see below, p. 100].

[32]   *Quellen*, p. xciii. *Chronicon Fratris Salimbene de Adam*, ed. Oswald Holder-Egger (MGH SS xxii, Hanover 1905–13), pp. 9–12. That Sicard used the *HP* directly is much less certain – he says very little about the expedition itself, and his information about Conrad of Montferrat may have come from the same source used by the author of the *HP*.

[33]   *Chronica Regia Coloniensis*, ed. Georg Waitz (MGH SRG, Hanover 1880), pp. 136–52; *Arnoldi Chronica Slavorum*, ed. J.M. Lappenberg (MGH SRG, Hanover 1868), IV.6–15, pp. 126–44 [Arnold's chronicle can also be found in MGH SS xxi.115–250].

[34]   For the latter, *Chronica Slavorum*, V.26–9, pp. 197–212.

This probably reflected popular feeling among the German participants in the expedition whom the author encountered during his stay at Acre.[35]

News of the fall of Jerusalem reverberated around Christendom, as the wide distribution of the various letters announcing the disaster, two of which were copied in the *History of the Expedition,* shows. The lamentation over these events in a wide variety of contemporary sources shows its impact.[36] The Cologne account of the subsequent Crusade was probably based on newsletters or reports sent back to Germany and distributed there, as was much of the *History of the Expedition.*[37] The use of the same, or very similar, sources may indeed explain why most of the German accounts of the Crusade are broadly alike.[38] Yet while, in addition to the various texts already mentioned, a variety of other annalistic sources also discussed the expedition of Frederick Barbarossa, these accounts are usually brief, and surprisingly by no means all the historians of the next generation took much notice of it. A case in point is one author already mentioned, Burchard, provost of the Praemonstratensian abbey of Urspberg, near Augsburg, from 1215 until his death c. 1231, whose chronicle, intended as a continuation of that of Otto of Freising, is one of our most important sources for Germany at the end of the twelfth century. Burchard reproduced the text of Frederick's peace edict of 1188 (as translated here), but otherwise what he said about the Crusade was drawn from another brief text circulating about the fall of Jerusalem and the siege of Acre, in which the expedition and death of the emperor was dismissed in a couple of brief paragraphs.[39] This suggests that for all the widespread participation in the Crusade, its memory may not have been very well preserved. Yet we should also note that while many clerics still kept annals in German monasteries during the twelfth and thirteenth centuries, such sources were usually very parochial, and if patrons or neighbours, or great men from the region, had not been directly involved in the expedition, both sources of information and interest may have been slight. And while the tradition of recording the *Gesta Episcoporum* continued in a number of German sees into the early thirteenth century (notably Halberstadt, Lausanne, Liège, Magdeburg, Trier and Utrecht), only one of those prelates took part in the 1189–90 expedition. Furthermore, the brief and unsympathetic biography of Bishop Rudolf of Liège, written almost 60 years after the event, contributes little

---

[35]   Nicholson, *Chronicle of the Third Crusade,* pp. 49–67 (quotation, p. 59 = *Itinerarium Peregrinorum,* I.22, p. 295).

[36]   That in the *Annales Pegavienses* [Pegau Annals], *Continuatio Secunda,* MGH SS xvi.266, is a case in point, but cf. also Arnold of Lübeck, *Chronica Slavorum,* IV.7, p. 127.

[37]   *Chronica Regia Coloniensis,* introduction, p. xiii.

[38]   We may compare with this the complex network of interrelationship that linked German accounts of the genesis of the First Crusade, recently examined by Eva Haverkamp, 'What did the Christians know? Latin reports of the persecution of the Jews in 1096', *Crusades* 7 (2008), 59–86, especially pp. 64–70.

[39]   *Burchardi Praepositi Urspergensis Chronicon,* pp. 59–64; Frederick's expedition is mentioned on pp. 61–2.

to our knowledge of the Crusade, apart from the allegation that the bishop took the Cross 'because of the sharp pricking of his conscience about his own sin'.[40]

What, however, the other contemporary German sources do provide for us, which is missing in the direct accounts of the Crusade, is some sense of the political background and preparations for the expedition. The *History of the Expedition* and the *History of the Pilgrims* concentrate upon the preaching of the Crusade, and especially the great council at Mainz, the *curia Christi* or *curia Dei* as they variously describe it, but say nothing about the more directly political measures that the emperor needed to take to ensure the stability of his realm in his absence, and to ensure the smooth succession of his eldest son Henry should he fail to return, as of course was the case. Admittedly, Frederick had taken steps some years earlier to ensure the continuance of his dynasty on the imperial throne. Henry had been crowned king while still a small child in 1169.[41] He was now (in March 1188) 22, and with his heir an adult Frederick was in a stronger situation than Conrad III had been in 1147, when his eldest son had been only ten.[42] Henry's status as king and heir had been further enhanced more recently when he and his brother Frederick had been knighted, amid great ceremony, at a court held at Mainz at Whitsun in 1184, an assembly at which the ceremonial and chivalric elements of rulership in Germany had reached their apogee. Henry's marriage to the heiress of the kingdom of Sicily, celebrated at Milan in January 1186 'with the most magnificent splendour and royal pageantry', had performed much the same function for the kingdom of Italy, as well as confirming earlier peace settlements with the towns of the Lombard League. The Lenten assembly at Mainz in 1188, while summoned to prepare the Crusading expedition and thus more overtly religious in tone, and without the tournament that was part of the 1184 gathering, was also another ceremonial affirmation of Staufen rule, with Frederick now the *gloriosus signifer* of the army of the Cross.[43] But the

---

[40]   Giles of Orval, *Gesta Episcoporum Leodensium*, c. 46, MGH SS xxv.113.

[41]   *Chronica Regia Coloniensis*, p. 120. See Peter Csendes, *Heinrich VI* (Darmstadt 1993), pp. 35–41.

[42]   Hiestand, 'Kingship and Crusade', 253–5, suggests that the need to provide for the succession in the ruler's absence actively encouraged the hereditary nature of German kingship. Henry had been born in or about November 1165, at Nymwegen, Gerhard Baaken, 'Die Altersfolge der Söhne Friedrich Barbarossas und die Königsherbung Heinrichs VI', *Deutsches Archiv für Erforschung des Mittelalters* 33 (1977), 435–72, especially 458.

[43]   Josef Fleckenstein, 'Friedrich Barbarossa und das Rittertum. Zur Bedeutung der großen Mainzer Hoftage von 1184 und 1188', in *Festschrift für Heinrich Heimpel zum 70. Geburtstag 1971* (3 vols, Göttingen 1972), ii.1023–41; Heinz Wolter, 'Der Mainzer Hoftage von 1184 als politische Fest', in *Feste und Feiern im Mittelalter*, ed. Detlef Altenburg, Jörg Jarnut and Hans-Hugo Steinhof (Sigmaringen 1991), pp. 193–9, who stresses the significance of this first meeting for imperial control of Lower Lotharingia. Quotations from *Ottonis de Sancto Blasio Chronica*, p. 39, and the *Historia de Expeditione*, (*Quellen*, p. 15), below p. 45. According to the *Annales Marbacenses*, p. 58, more than 70 *principes regni* attended the 1184 court. For Frederick's settlement of disputes with Milan, see also

purpose of the 1188 council was more than merely ceremonial, and as well as the emperor's assumption of the Cross, and encouragement of others to do the same, and measures to protect the Jewish community (always vulnerable when a Crusade was called), he also sought to secure domestic peace within his realm through the resolution of disputes and the reconciliation of enemies.[44] First and foremost the emperor himself sought a solution to his long-standing dispute with Archbishop Philip of Cologne (an issue to which the *History of the Expedition* made brief reference, but without recording the result).[45] Bishop Baldwin of Utrecht was also reconciled with his inveterate opponent Count Otto of Geldern, something which according to the Cologne chronicler 'nobody had been able to do previously', and some of those involved in this dispute then 'joyfully took the Cross'.[46] Similarly, the emperor and his eldest son attempted to resolve another long-standing dispute in Lower Lotharingia, between Count Henry of Namur and his nephew Count Baldwin V of Hainaut, albeit with only temporary success.[47] The Land Peace issued at Nuremberg in the last days of December 1188 was part of that process, even if its terms sought to regulate and limit feuds and their impact rather than to prevent them entirely – a sign of how much more limited the emperors' control over their realm was than, for example, that of the Anglo-Norman or Sicilian kings. Even as the expedition was about to set off in the spring of 1189, the emperor continued to seek a resolution to disputes, notably an internal quarrel within the Wettin family that had led the elderly Margrave Otto of Meissen to be imprisoned by his own son Albrecht, although in the event this

---

Dipl. Fred. I, nos 896 (February 1185) and 941 (June 1186, establishing peace between Cremona and Milan).

[44]   The importance of dispute settlement is stressed by Hiestand, 'Barbarossa und der Kreuzzug', pp. 55–7. See also Robert Chazan, 'Emperor Frederick I, the Third Crusade and the Jews', *Viator* 8 (1977), 83–93.

[45]   The *Annales Marbacenses*, p. 58, indeed suggested that the emperor would have taken the Cross at the Strassburg council of December 1187, but for his dispute with the Archbishop of Cologne. The best contemporary account of the origins of the quarrel is by Arnold of Lübeck, *Chronica Slavorum*, III.17–18, pp. 102–6, but see also *Chronica Regia Coloniensis*, pp. 135–6. Frederick had earlier in that year tried to enlist the Saxon nobility against the archbishop, whom he accused of gross ingratitude towards him, while the archbishop was in turn making alliances with other opponents of the emperor, such as the Count of Flanders. Meanwhile Henry VI and Archbishop Conrad of Mainz, among others, were working for a reconciliation; *Die Jüngere Hildesheimer Briefsammlung*, ed. Rolf de Kegel (MGH Die Briefen der deutschen Kaiserzeit vii, Munich 1995), pp. 113–4 no. 65, 118–20 no. 69, 184–5 no. 126, 187–8 no. 129.

[46]   *Chronica Regia Coloniensis*, p. 139; cf. *Mainzer Urkundenbuch* ii(2).828–30 no. 508. Otto of Geldern was noted by the *Historia de Expeditione* as one of those who went to the Holy Land by sea [below, p. 57]. The work of reconciliation was also noted, in more general terms, by Arnold of Lübeck, *Chronica Slavorum*, IV.7, p. 128.

[47]   *Le Chronique de Gislebert de Mons*, pp. 207–9 [Gilbert of Mons, *Chronicle of Hainaut*, pp. 113–15].

familial quarrel was far from settled, and required further intervention from King Henry after Frederick's expedition had departed.[48]

By far the most significant problem facing the emperor was what to do about his most notable domestic opponent Henry the Lion, the former Duke of Saxony and Bavaria, whom the emperor had deprived of his titles, outlawed and exiled in 1180. Having lost both his duchies and the lands that he had held in fief from the empire, Henry's material power had been greatly diminished, but he still retained his allodial land around Brunswick and at least some of his vassals, and his alliance with the King of England, whose daughter Matilda he had married in 1168, ensured that he remained a figure of European significance. Furthermore, one of his most important local opponents, Count Adolf III of Holstein, had enlisted in the Crusade and would thus be removed from Saxony. Barbarossa summoned both Henry and his successor as duke, Bernhard of Anhalt, to a meeting at Goslar at the end of July 1188. He reconciled the two men, but then gave Henry a choice, albeit a decidedly unappealing one: he could be restored to some of his lands and rights if he agreed to abandon any claim to the rest; he could take part in the Crusade at the emperor's expense, at the end of which he would be more fully restored; or he and his eldest son could go into exile for three years. Henry chose exile, although in the event he soon returned once Frederick was gone, and Henry VI had to launch a punitive expedition against him in the winter of 1189. Peace was only finally established in July 1190.[49]

In addition to these political concerns, which were ignored by the compiler of the *History of the Expedition*, the emperor also launched a considerable diplomatic effort to facilitate his expedition. This is discussed to some extent by the direct accounts of the Crusade, though more so by the *Historia Peregrinorum* than by the *Historia de Expeditione*, in which mention of some of this diplomacy, notably the envoy dispatched to Qilij Arslan of Iconium, emerges almost by accident as the account proceeds. Apart from the embassy to Saladin of Count Henry of Diez, to which the *HP* refers, but of which the emperor cannot have had much hope of success, this diplomatic activity comprised three, or possibly four, other elements. First, soon after the Mainz council in the spring of 1188, Archbishop Conrad of Mainz was sent to Hungary to arrange routes and the provision of supplies for the army.[50] Relations between Barbarossa and King Bela III were already good, although a project for a daughter of the former to marry a son of the latter had been brought to naught by the girl's death in 1184.[51] However,

---

[48]   *Annales Pegavienses, Continuatio Secunda*, MGH SS xvi.267 ; *Chronicon Montis Sereni*, MGH SS xxiii.161; *Cronica Reinhardsbrunnensis*, MGH SS xxx(1).543–4.

[49]   Arnold, *Chronica Slavorum*, IV.7, V.1–3, pp. 128, 147–50. Frederick was at Goslar between 25 July and 8 August 1188, *Dipl. Fred. I*, nos 974–5. See Karl Jordan, *Henry the Lion* (Oxford 1986), pp. 187–92, and Csendes, *Heinrich VI*, pp. 75–6.

[50]   *Chronica Regia Coloniensis*, p. 139.

[51]   *Annales Marbacenses*, p. 55; *Monumenta Erphesfurtensia, saec. XII, XIII, XIV*, ed. Oswald Holder-Egger (MGH SRG, Hanover 1899), p. 193.

Barbarossa's cousin and ally Duke Leopold of Austria was married to a sister of the Hungarian king, who had welcomed him and a large escort when Leopold had travelled on pilgrimage to Jerusalem in 1182, although relations between these two had recently become cooler.[52] Second, Gottfried of Wiesenbach, described as a *probus miles*, was sent to negotiate with Qilij Arslan for an unopposed passage through Turkish Asia Minor. This was not as unlikely a possibility as it might appear at first sight. On his return from pilgrimage to Jerusalem in 1172, Henry the Lion had travelled peacefully through the sultan's dominions, and the latter had provided him with an escort, met him in person and showered him with presents, including two leopards.[53] An embassy from the sultan had also come to the imperial court in 1179.[54] The contemporary accounts suggest that the emperor had reason to hope that he would be granted safe conduct, and certainly the presence of Turkish envoys at Nuremberg in the last days of 1188 gave him encouragement in these hopes. Negotiations continued as the expedition passed through the Byzantine Empire, and an envoy from the sultan reached the army in February 1190 as it prepared to cross the Bosphorus. While the subsequent attacks on the Crusading army by the Turks led the westerners to assume that these negotiations had from the first been conducted in bad faith, this was not necessarily the case. The problem was rather the fragmenting authority of the elderly sultan, whose control over the Turkomans within his dominions had always been limited, and whose sons, and especially his eldest son Qutb al-Dīn, were now seeking to displace him.[55] Third, Frederick also sought to secure the passage of his army through the Byzantine Empire.

Here he was following in the footsteps of the first two Crusades, in the second of which he himself had as a young man taken part. Frederick appears to have sent a legation to Byzantium in the summer of 1188, on a mission very similar to that of the Archbishop of Mainz to Hungary, to request free passage through the empire and the provision of supplies. In response, envoys from the Emperor Isaac

---

[52]   *Annales Mellicenses*; *Continuatio Zwetlensis Altera*, both ed. Wilhelm Wattenbach, MGH SS ix. 505, 542, 544. Karl Lechner, *Die Babenberger, Markgrafen und Herzoge von Österreich 976–1246* (6th ed., Vienna 1996), p. 184 [See below, p. 120].

[53]   Arnold, *Chronica Slavorum*, I.9, pp. 23–5. For Gottfried, *Chronica Regia Coloniensis*, p. 141, and below, pp. 75, 92, 103.

[54]   *Ottonis de Sancto Blasio Chronica*, ed. Adolf Hofmeister (MGH SRG, Hanover 1912), p. 37. Otto's story that the sultan offered to become a Christian if he could marry one of Frederick's daughters is extremely unlikely (and he was writing 30 years later). But this does not therefore cast doubt on the reality of the embassy.

[55]   According to the somewhat later account of Ibn al-Athir, Qilij Arslan used the rebellion of his sons as an excuse when he explained to Saladin why he had been unable to stop the Crusaders crossing Asia Minor; here the sultan was being somewhat disingenuous, [*The*] *Chronicle of Ibn al-Athīr for the Crusading Period, from al-Kāmil fi'l-ta'rīkh*, Part 2, *The Years 541–589/1146–1193: The Age of Nur al-Din and Saladin*, translated by D.S. Richards (Aldershot 2007), p. 376.

Angelos, led by the Logothete of the Drome (effectively foreign minister) John Dukas, travelled to Germany and were present at Nuremberg over the New Year of 1188/9.[56] In the spring of 1189, Frederick dispatched a further, and more high-powered, embassy, headed by Bishop Herman of Münster and Count Rupert III of Nassau (the latter one of the emperor's most loyal and long-standing supporters), to precede his army and confirm arrangements for its passage through Byzantine territory, not least for the provision of food supplies and markets. The subsequent tribulations of this embassy at the hands of the Byzantine emperor were discussed at length by the *Historia de Expeditione* and other contemporary sources. The problems here were threefold. First, Isaac Angelos had already concluded an alliance with Saladin, and had promised the latter to obstruct the passage of the German expedition.[57] Second, the emperor was afraid that Barbarossa's expedition would further weaken the Byzantine overlordship over the Balkans, already endangered through the revolt of Bulgaria in 1186, and his envoys had almost certainly told him that there had previously been contacts between Barbarossa and the Serb zupan Stephen Nemanja, envoys from whom had also been present at Nuremberg at the end of 1188.[58] Third, the Byzantines suspected that Frederick, with whom they had long had frosty diplomatic relations, may well have harboured ambitions to conquer their empire itself. Indeed, Arnold of Lübeck recognised this, when he reported that the Governor of Branchevo had sent back a message to Isaac: 'You should know that if they [the Germans] shall enter your land, they will drive you from your throne and will seize your empire.'[59] The consequence was that Barbarossa's army fought a series of actions with Byzantine troops and occupied a number of towns in Thrace, and it was only the threat of force that eventually secured passage over the Bosphorus. But, as both the emperor himself proclaimed, and as was recognised by several contemporary commentators, not all of them German, he was in reality only interested in Byzantium insofar as it lay between him and his objective, the kingdom of Jerusalem.[60]

In addition, it is possible that Frederick also made efforts to contact the rulers of Cilician Armenia, the Christian enclave in the mountainous southeast of Asia Minor, through which his army would need to travel to reach Antioch, and of Antioch itself. The evidence for this is inconclusive, although Armenian

---

[56]   *O City of Byzantium: Annals of Niketas Choniates*, translated H.P. Magoulias (Detroit 1984), p. 221.

[57]   See here Charles M. Brand, 'The Byzantines and Saladin: opponents of the Third Crusade', *Speculum* xxxvii (1962), 167–181.

[58]   *Chronica Regia Coloniensis*, p. 142. Hiestand, 'Barbarossa und der Kreuzzug', p. 93; Peter Munz, *Frederick Barbarossa. A Study in Medieval Politics* (London 1969), p. 389.

[59]   *Chronica Slavorum*, IV.9, p. 132.

[60]   See below, p. 84, and compare *Historia Peregrinorum*, p. 149, and the French continuation of William of Tyre, *Estoire d'Eracles*, c. 90, translated in Peter W. Edbury, *The Conquest of Jerusalem and the Third Crusade* (Aldershot 1996), p. 85.

envoys had earlier been present when the emperor met Pope Lucius III at Verona in 1184, and a further Armenian embassy had arrived at the papal Curia in the spring of 1189. At the very least, Clement III must then have informed them, and through them their homeland, of the forthcoming expedition, but an Armenian source suggests that he also entrusted letters for Prince Leo of Armenia and the Catholicos (the spiritual leader of the Armenian Church) to Bishop Herman of Münster.[61] Whether Frederick was at this time already contemplating the creation of an Armenian client kingdom, as sanctioned by his son Henry VI in 1197, is impossible to say – one would tend to think that this was a project that grew out of the Crusade itself.[62] But, as will be discussed below, one consequence of the expedition was that Bohemond III of Antioch became a vassal of the empire, and it is at least feasible, and perhaps even probable, that the imperial court had been in touch with Archbishop Albert of Tarsus, the prince's chancellor and envoy to the west, during the months in which the expedition was in preparation.[63] However, this was another part of the preparations for the Crusade that the German accounts of the expedition ignore.

The third aspect of the preparations for the Crusade that is ignored or only briefly touched upon by the sources translated here is the matter of finance. Such an expedition required a major investment, both by the participants and by the emperor. Admittedly, the German emperors and their subjects had extensive experience of expeditions to Italy, of which there had been no fewer than six during Barbarossa's reign. The arrangements for the organisation and financing of such expeditions were well established. But an expedition to the east was a matter of an altogether larger scale, and there would be no possibility there of levying the *fodrum*, a local tax specifically for the support of the emperor's army, or for troops to serve for a limited period and then return home, to be replaced by others, as could happen in Italy, especially for extended operations, as for example the 1174–8 campaign there. We are told that Barbarossa ordered that those involved were to prepare, and have the resources, for a two-year expedition, and that the rank-and-file participants were to have at least three marks for their expenses – those who could not furnish themselves with this were not to come, 'for he did not wish the army to be hampered by a crowd of unsuitable people'. He also sent home a number of those who did turn up when the expedition mustered but

---

[61]   Gérard Dédéyan, 'De la prise de Thessalonique par les Normands (1185) á la croisade de Frédéric Barbarousse (1189–90) : le revirement politico-religieux des pouvoirs arméniens', in *Chemins d'Outre-Mer. Études sur la Méditerranée médiévale offertes à Michel Balard* (Paris, 2004), i.183–96, at p. 192. Renewed persecution by the Greeks after 1180 had encouraged the Armenians to seek closer relations with Rome.

[62]   Hiestand, 'Barbarossa und der Kreuzzug', pp. 94–5.

[63]   Rudolf Hiestand, 'Antiochia, Sizilien und das Reich am Ende des 12. Jahrhunderts', *Quellen und Forschungen aus italienischen Archiven und Bibliotheken* 73 (1993), 109–13.

were deemed unsuitable, either through lack of resources or lack of discipline.[64] Clearly the emperor had learned from the Second Crusade of 1147–8, where the German army had been severely hampered by a horde of noncombatants, among whom casualties had been disproportionately high. But the expenses for the nobles and knights on the expedition would have been much higher than those of the common soldiers: the so-called *Längeres Kölner Dienstrecht* suggests that a knight needed a minimum of one mark a month to maintain himself and his dependents on campaign in Italy during the later twelfth century, as well as a much more substantial sum to prepare and equip himself for such an expedition.[65] Given a total force of perhaps 12,000–15,000 men, including around 3,000 knights (this perhaps a conservative estimate), the complete expedition would have required funds in the region of 90,000 marks, most of which it would have to bring with it.[66] While some provisions would be acquired through plunder and foraging, this was hardly desirable in potentially friendly territory, where it was important not to alienate the inhabitants if this could be avoided. Furthermore, 'friendly territory' included not just Hungary and the Byzantine lands, but in the event of securing an agreement for peaceful passage also those of the Sultan of Iconium.

---

[64]   *Historia Peregrinorum*, p. 126; Otto of St Blasien, *Chronica*, p. 45 [translated below, pp. 144, 176]; Arnold of Lübeck, *Chronicon Slavorum*, IV.8, p. 129.

[65]   This text recorded the customs of the *ministeriales* (unfree knights) of the archbishop of Cologne, c. 1165. 'Those who have benefices worth five marks or more, if the archbishop so wishes, shall go on this expedition without any excuse [being accepted], and the archbishop shall give ten marks to each of them to make their preparations, and 40 ells of the cloth which is called *schorlot,* so that he may clothe his servants, and for every two knights one packhorse with a saddle and all that pertains to the saddle, and two saddlebags with a cover, which is called a *dekhut,* and four horseshoes with 23 nails. When he has arrived at the Alps, each knight must be given one mark for every month thereafter from the archbishop's chamber for his expenses.' *Quellen zur deutschen Verfassungs-, Wirtschafts- und Sozialgeschichte bis 1250,* ed. L. Weinrich (Darmstadt 1977), pp. 266–78 no. 70, c. 4, at pp. 268–9.

[66]   Alan V. Murray, 'Finance and logistics of the Crusade of Frederick Barbarossa', *In Laudem Hierosolymitani: Studies in Crusades and Material Culture in Honour of Benjamin Z. Kedar*, ed. I. Shagrir, R. Ellenblum and J. Riley-Smith (Aldershot 2007), pp. 357–68, especially 358–61. For the possible size of the army, Eickhoff, *Friedrich Barbarossa im Orient*, p. 47; Hiestand, 'Barbarossa und der Kreuzzug', p. 69. Contemporary estimates were, of course, usually much larger, as for example the '90,000 armed warriors' of the *Gesta Federici I. Imperatoris in Expeditione Sacra*, p. 78, the '100,000 well armed men, not counting the common people' of the *Chronicon Montis Sereni*, MGH SS xxiii.161, or even the 600,000 men at arms claimed by the *Annales Stadenses*, MGH SS xvi.351. More realistically, the Cologne chronicle said that there were '30,000 men, among whom were 15,000 picked knights', *Chronica Regia Coloniensis*, p. 144, but even this figure is too big.

Alan Murray has rightly drawn our attention to the physical problems of transportation that such huge sums of coinage created, especially once the army began to lose pack animals at an alarming rate, as it did after it entered Turkish territory.[67] However, there is also the question of how this money was raised in the first place. Most participants were expected to fund themselves, if necessary, through the sale or mortgaging of property, as indeed was also the case, at least in the first instance, for expeditions to Italy. Thus the Count of Duras in Lower Lotharingia (modern Belgium) sold both the castle from which his title was derived and the advocacy of the church of St Trond to the Duke of Louvain for 800 marks to finance his participation in the expedition.[68] However, the emperor still needed to pay for his own following, including his *ministeriales* such as the Marshal Henry of Kalden, who played a prominent part in the campaign, and Frederick of Hausen (who was killed in May 1190),[69] and he would have to be prepared to assist other members of the Crusade should their funds run low, as in some cases they inevitably would. Yet, as Rudolf Hiestand has pointed out, there is no evidence that the so-called 'Saladin tithe' raised in the kingdoms of France and England was levied in Germany. Levies were presumably made (the evidence is limited) from the German towns, perhaps from Italy, and from churchmen, at least those who did not take part in the expedition themselves – 11 bishops did march with the emperor, and the Archbishop of Bremen subsequently went by sea. In addition, the process of peacekeeping, reconciliation and settlement of claims that preceded the Crusade was not only politically necessary for the emperor, but also offered a chance to raise money. Thus, Archbishop Philip of Cologne contributed 2,000 marks, as part of the process of recovering the emperor's grace, and Count Baldwin of Hainault 1,150 marks for the recognition of his claims to Namur. Presumably those who were granted privileges in the 18 months during which the expedition was planned and prepared also paid handsomely for these.[70]

---

[67]   Murray, 'Finance and logistics', pp. 361–4.

[68]   *Chronique de Gislebert*, p. 240 [Gilbert of Mons, *Chronicle of Hainaut*, p. 131], in this case the count may have been more than usually prepared to make an outright sale, because he and his brothers were childless, and the advocacy was in dispute. Hiestand, 'Barbarossa und der Kreuzzug', 86–7, draws attention to two other such transactions, in one of which the Archbishop of Cologne purchased property from the Landgrave of Thuringia, who travelled to the Holy Land by sea, for 400 marks. For another, in which Count Engelbert of Berg loaned money in return for a mortgage in 1189, *Urkundenbuch für die Geschichte des Niederrheins*, i.364 nos 520–1. For imperial expeditions to Italy, Karl-Friedrich Krieger, 'Obligatory military service and the use of mercenaries in imperial military campaigns under the Hohenstaufen Emperors', in *England and Germany in the Middle Ages* [above, note 1], 151–68, especially 158–60.

[69]   Frederick was specifically identified as a *ministerialis*, along with other prominent members of this class, by Gilbert of Mons, *Le Chronique de Gislebert de Mons*, p. 232. The translation by Napran, *The Chronicle of Hainaut*, p. 126, obscures this, by translating *ministerialis* as 'official'.

[70]   Hiestand, 'Barbarossa und der Kreuzzug', pp. 87–8.

But the major source of finance for the emperor must have been the resources of his own lands, both 'imperial' property and the extensive family lands of the Staufen, which Frederick had by the end of his reign greatly enhanced.[71] Some years later his youngest, and by then last surviving, son, Philip of Swabia, justifying his own claims to the German throne, could boast that: 'among all the princes of the empire there was at that time [*1198*] none richer, more powerful or more glorious than ourselves. For we had very ample and widespread possessions, and we [also] had very many castles, strongly fortified and impregnable. We had so many *ministeriales* that we could scarcely number them with any certainty. We had castles, towns, manors and very wealthy burgesses. We had an enormous sum of money in gold and silver, and a hoard of precious stones.'[72] These were the resources that financed the emperor's Crusade. Furthermore, during the expedition further sources of cash or precious metal also became available, with tribute from the Byzantines and the booty from the sack of Iconium. As the Crusaders approached the friendly territory of Cilician Armenia, they may well have been quite well endowed financially, if desperately short of food, water and baggage animals to carry their loot.[73]

While the narrative texts describing the Crusade, and especially the *Historia de Expeditione* that is the centrepiece of this collection, tend to neglect much of this background and preliminary organisation, with the partial exception of the diplomacy, they are, however, of great value and interest for the expedition itself. Three features of the *Historia de Expeditione* stand out. First, there is the detailed list of the principal men who took part in the expedition, some 70 in number, including 12 bishops (one from Hungary), the dukes of Swabia and Dalmatia, two margraves and 26 counts.[74] Whereas for most Crusading expeditions the personnel involved, even those of exalted social rank, has to be painstakingly (and incompletely) reconstructed from scattered references in the texts, for the Crusade of Frederick Barbarossa we can analyse the recruitment, composition and structure of the army in considerable detail. We can also compare the involvement of the German nobility in the Crusade with that in the various Italian expeditions of the emperor. The significant role of the episcopate in these earlier expeditions is an obvious point of comparison. Thus, in the emperor's fifth, and most prolonged, Italian expedition of 1174–8, four of the German archbishops and no fewer than 15 bishops had played a part, although nearly all were present for some rather than all the time. This reminds us that Barbarossa

---

[71]   For this, see especially Karl Leyser, 'Frederick Barbarossa and the Hohenstaufen polity', *Viator* 19 (1988), 153–76 [reprinted in K.J. Leyser, *Communications and Power in Medieval Europe. The Gregorian Revolution and Beyond* (London 1994), pp. 115–42].

[72]   *Regestum Innocentii III Papae super Negotio Romani Imperii*, ed. Friedrich Kempf (Rome 1947), pp. 317–20 no. 136; older edition in MGH *Constitutiones*, ed. L. Weiland (Hanover 1896), ii.11–12 no. 10.

[73]   Murray, 'Finance and logistics', 366–7.

[74]   Below, pp. 48–55.

still exercised a significant level of control over the German Church, and indeed retained considerable influence over the appointment of prelates. Furthermore, most German bishops had significant secular and military resources.[75] That more than a quarter of the *Reich*'s episcopate took part in the 1189–90 Crusade is therefore hardly surprising. Four of these bishops, Diepold of Passau, Martin of Meissen, Herman of Münster and Conrad of Regensburg, had also been with the emperor in Italy during his most recent expedition south of the Alps in 1184–6.[76] So too had Gottfried, the imperial chancellor, who was subsequently chosen as Bishop of Würzburg and played a prominent role on the Crusade.[77] Another of the prelates on the Crusade, Arnold of Osnabrück, had taken part in the previous Italian expedition in 1176–7 and been one of the imperial delegation at the Venice peace conference in the summer of 1177.[78] There was also one further bishop, Otto of Bamberg, who took the Cross, joined the expedition and accompanied it as far as Pressburg, but then returned to Germany, who had also taken part in the early stages of the 1184–6 Italian expedition.[79] Bishops Otto and Gottfried had also been sent by the emperor to conduct negotiations with Pope Urban III at Verona in the early months of 1187.[80] Since the *Historia de Expeditione* did not include Otto of Bamberg among those who failed to fulfil their vow, one might conclude that his return from the Crusading expedition was because of imperial,

---

[75]   Bernhard Töpfer, 'Kaiser Friedrich I. Barbarossa und der deutsche Reichsepiskopat', in *Friedrich Barbarossa: Handlungsspielräume und Wirkungsweisen des staufischen Kaisers* [see above, note 1], pp. 389–433, especially 422–7 for the Italian expeditions. Töpfer suggests, ibid., p. 413, that the emperor was directly involved in at least a third of the episcopal appointments in Germany during his reign. For the military capabilities and proclivities of the episcopate, Benjamin Arnold, 'German bishops and their military retinues in the medieval Empire', *German History* 7 (1989), 161–83; and Timothy Reuter, '*Episcopi cum sua militia*: the prelate as warrior in the early Staufen era', in *Warriors and Churchmen in the High Middle Ages. Essays Presented to Karl Leyser* (London 1992), pp. 79–94. Archbishop Rainald of Cologne had, for example, led more than 500 knights on the Italian expedition of 1161, *Das Geschichtswerk des Otto Morena und seiner Fortsetzer*, ed. Ferdinand Güterbock (MGH SRG, Berlin 1930), p. 135; and his successor Philip was accompanied by 400 men at the peace of Venice in 1177, *Historia Ducum Veneticorum*, MGH SS xiv.84.

[76]   *Dipl. Fred. I*, nos 868 (October 1184), 903 (May 1185), 933–5 (March 1186), 945 (June 1186).

[77]   *Dipl. Fred I*, nos 872–3, 875 (October 1184), 935 (March 1186), 938, 940 (May 1186), 941–6 (June 1186).

[78]   *Dipl. Fred. I*, nos 653 (July 1176), 670 (May 1177), 685 (July 1177); *Historia Ducum Veneticorum*, c. 12, MGH SS xiv.85. The *Continuatio Zwetlensis Altera*, MGH SS ix.541, suggested that Diepold of Passau may also have been in Italy in 1177, but this is not confirmed by any charter evidence.

[79]   *Dipl. Fred. I*, nos 866 (Sept. 1184), 868, 876–7 (October 1184), 879, 881, 883–6 (all November 1184).

[80]   *Annales Magdeburgenses*, MGH SS xvi.195.

or perhaps papal, instructions rather than owing to any personal reluctance to continue.[81]

However, in addition to these bishops, we may also note the prominent role taken in these earlier Italian expeditions by several of the lay nobles who joined the Crusade, notably Count Florenz III of Holland, counts Henry of Diez and Rupert of Nassau, both of whom were from Hesse, and the Franconians Count Simon of Spanheim, Count Poppo of Henneberg and Adalbert of Hildenburg, also Conrad the Burgrave of Nuremberg, as well as by the fathers of other participants such as Duke Berthold (V) of Merania, Count Henry of Saarbrücken and Adalbert of Grumbach.[82] Some of these were especially closely tied to the emperor. Berthold (IV) of Merania (who died on 14 November 1188), for example, owed his promotion to the emperor, first to be Margrave of Istria in 1173, on the death without direct heir of the last Spanheimer margrave, and then his promotion to ducal rank in 1180 in the wake of Henry the Lion's fall. He had been captured while fighting for the emperor at the battle of Legnano in 1176.[83] His son's participation in Frederick's Crusade thus reflected this family's continued alliance with the Staufen. Gilbert of Mons considered the counts of Nassau and Diez to be among the particular associates (*familiares*) of the emperor.[84] Henry the elder of Diez, who was sent to carry Barbarossa's challenge to Saladin, had been one of the emperor's most trusted associates for almost 30 years, having for example been one of his envoys to the King of Hungary as far back as 1164.[85] He had taken part in the 1167 Italian expedition, and been present at the peace of Venice in 1177, and was one of those who swore on the emperor's behalf that he would observe the terms of the Treaty of Konstanz with the Lombard cities in 1183. (Four other future Crusaders also swore to this: Bishop Herman of Münster, Gottfried the chancellor and later Bishop of Würzburg, Berthold V of Merania and Margave Herman of Baden.[86]) Count Engelbert of Berg, an elderly man who died while the expedition was still in the Balkans, was another who had been closely tied to Barbarossa for many years. He had taken part in the siege of Milan in 1160, was a recipient of imperial patronage, a regular witness of

[81]   That he did not continue on the Crusade is shown by his witnessing a diploma of Henry VI at Cologne on 25 March 1190, *Urkundenbuch für Niederrheins*, i.365–6 no. 524. Another reason for this may have been his involvement in the process of canonisation for his predecessor, Otto I, Bishop of Bamberg 1102–39, the 'apostle of Pomerania', which was under way during the summer of 1189, *Germania Sacra*, iii(3), ed. Albert Brackmann (Berlin 1935), 280–1.

[82]   See below, pp. 49–50, 55.

[83]   Ralph of Diceto, *Opera Historica*, ed. William Stubbs (2 vols, London: Rolls Series 1876), i.409.

[84]   *Le Chronique de Gislebert de Mons*, p. 272 [*The Chronicle of Hainaut*, p. 150].

[85]   *Die Admonter Briefsammlung*, ed. Gunther Hödl and Peter Classen (MGH Die Briefe der deutschen Kaiserzeit vi, Munich 1983), pp. 178–81 nos 20, 22.

[86]   *Dipl. Fred. I*, nos 694–5, 699, 848.

Frederick's charters, including the so-called 'Gelnhausen charter' of April 1180 that confirmed the downfall of Henry the Lion, and had helped to fund others to take part in the Italian expeditions (to his own considerable profit).[87] When Adalbert of Hildenburg died during the siege of Acre he was buried next to the emperor's son Duke Frederick of Swabia.[88] Landgrave Ludwig III of Thuringia, who travelled to the Holy Land by sea and died there, was the emperor's nephew and another particularly close ally, who had been with him in Italy both in 1176–7 and 1184–5, and had been one of his chief supporters in the overthrow of Henry the Lion.[89] Thus, the *Historia de Expeditione* is an important source not just for the Crusade, but also for the relationship of the Staufen emperor with the German aristocracy. However, while the participants on the Crusade included a core of nobles with close connections to the emperor, we must not assume that this was the only reason for participation, or that all those who joined the Crusade were his allies or close supporters. There were others, especially from more peripheral regions, who rarely if ever attended his court or witnessed his *diplomata*.[90] Two of the counts from Lower Lotharingia who took part in the expedition, Henry of Sayn and Henry of Kuick, later (after 1198) supported the claims of the Welf candidate for the throne, Otto IV, rather than those of Barbarossa's son Philip, as did one of those who went by sea, the Saxon Count Simon of Tecklenburg.[91] On the other hand, one of those participants who seems to have had little connection with the imperial court under Barbarossa, the long-lived Count Ulrich of Kyburg (d. 1227),

---

[87]   Frederick confirmed grants of fiefs in June 1169 and February 1174, *Dipl. Fred. I*, nos 553, 612; charters he witnessed included ibid., nos 580 (Sept. 1171), 614, 618–19 (March, May 1174), 795–6 (Gelnhausen, April 1180). Archbishop Philip of Cologne mortgaged estates to him to fund his participation in the fifth Italian expedition in 1176 and 1179, ibid., nos 649, 776.

[88]   *Cronica Reinhardsbrunnensis*, MGH SS xxx(1).547.

[89]   See below, p. 57, note 136.

[90]   Thus Counts Christian of Oldenburg (from northern Saxony), Siegfried of Libenau (from Austria) and Ulrich of Kyburg (modern Switzerland) each only witnessed one charter of the emperor.

[91]   Henry of Sayn witnessed a number of Otto IV's charters, notably *Urkundenbuch für Niederrheins*, i, nos 561 (July 1198), 568 (1200); given his family's dependence on the see of Cologne, he doubtless followed the lead of Archbishop Adolf. His brother Bruno was Otto's envoy to the papal Curia in 1198. However, when Adolf changed sides in 1205, King Otto then engineered the election of Bruno as the new archbishop, B.U. Hucker, *Kaiser Otto IV* (MGH Schriften 34: Hanover 1990), pp. 447–8. Henry of Kuick was one of the signatories to the announcement of Otto's election that was sent to Pope Innocent III, *Regestum Innocentii III Papae super Negotio Romani Imperii*, pp. 23–6 no. 10. Charters of Otto witnessed by Simon of Tecklenburg included *Urkundenbuch für Niederrheins*, i, nos 562–3 (July 1198), 566 (January 1200).

was later to be one of the first and most consistent supporters of Barbarossa's grandson Frederick II when he claimed the German throne in 1212.[92]

Second, the detailed chronology provided by the *Historia de Expeditione* and Tageno (in contrast to the *Historia Peregrinorum* which omits dates) allows one not only to ascertain the route that the army took, but to follow its route, progress and rate of march in detail. The army in fact averaged about 20 km a day, even when under attack in hostile territory, which, given the need to carry and to guard baggage, the shortage of supplies in Asia Minor and the difficult terrain traversed, is impressive testimony to its members' discipline and determination. Indeed, in the three days before the emperor's death, and despite its travails at the hands of the Turks, the army marched about 66 km, albeit along a good and level road. Progress was slower only in Bulgaria and northern Macedonia, perhaps because of the terrain but probably also because there, with relatively ample supplies, there was no great need for haste.[93] For much of the journey through the Balkans, the expedition followed the old Roman military road from Belgrade towards Constantinople, still the main trunk route through the medieval Balkans,[94] and indeed it continued to follow the old Roman roads through Asia Minor, although the surfaces of these roads were already in decline under Byzantine rule in the early Middle Ages and may well have deteriorated further through lack of maintenance in those regions now under Turkish control.[95] And in addition, while saying little about the financial preparations for the expedition, the contemporary accounts are well informed about matters of supply and scarcity, and display a close interest in the provision of markets – showing therefore that the intention was that foodstuffs should be purchased whenever possible. (Modern estimates would suggest that an army of 12,000–15,000 men would require between 236,000 and 288,000 kg of foodstuffs every two to three weeks, as a minimum, and the more that could be purchased locally and consumed soon after purchase, the less that would have to be carried, with quality deteriorating and wastage increasing as time went on.[96]) While we lack such detailed information on logistics as is given by earlier Byzantine tactical treatises, the level of day-to-day detail about the march supplied by the *Historia de Expeditione*, Tageno and to a lesser and

---

[92]   *Die Urkunden Friedrichs II. 1212–1217*, ed. Walter Koch (MGH Diplomata Regum et Imperatorum Germaniae xiv[2], Hannover 2007), nos 171–3 (September 1212), 197, 199–201 (all March 1213), 210 (September 1213), 223 (March 1214), 236 (June 1214).

[93]   Eickhoff, *Friedrich Barbarossa im Orient*, pp. 51–3, 156. J.W. Nesbitt, 'Rates of march of Crusading armies in Europe: a study in computation', *Traditio* 19 (1963), 167–82, especially 178–80.

[94]   For this, Dimitri Obolensky, *The Byzantine Commonwealth. Eastern Europe 500–1453* (London 1971), pp. 18–21.

[95]   John Haldon, 'Roads and communications in the Byzantine Empire: wagons, horses and supplies', in *Logistics of Warfare in the Age of the Crusades*, ed. John Pryor (Aldershot 2006), 136–41.

[96]   Based on the figures in Haldon, 'Roads and communications', pp. 148–9.

more derivate extent by the *Historia Peregrinorum* is unmatched by accounts
of the earlier Crusading expeditions that traversed Asia Minor. Finally, although
the *Historia de Expeditione* only provides somewhat haphazard details about
the diplomatic background to the Crusade, the author does provide a very full,
interesting and valuable discussion of the relations between the emperor and the
Byzantines once the expedition was under way, including giving the text of the
eventual treaty between the two emperors in February 1190, an account that can
be read alongside that from the Byzantine point of view in the history of Niketas
Choniates, whose appointment as Governor of Philippopolis at the time of the
Germans' arrival gave him a particular interest in the Crusade.[97] But valuable as
the account of Choniates is in revealing the Byzantine mindset when faced by
the arrival of the German army, the account of the negotiations in the *Historia de
Expeditione* is considerably fuller and more circumstantial.

That the *Historia de Expeditione* omits some of the earlier diplomatic effort
can be attributed to the composite nature of the text, stitched together after the
event from a number of disparate sources. One further significant omission is
also due to this same factor. After describing the drowning of the emperor, the
text gives only a very brief description of the arrival of the army at Antioch, and
the disastrous epidemic there that thinned its ranks, and effectively destroyed the
expedition. Yet it has been suggested from other sources, and in particular from a
brief passage from the Marbach Annals (a source from the Staufen homeland of
Swabia), that on the arrival of the German army Prince Bohemond III of Antioch
became a vassal of Frederick of Swabia, and made his principality subject to the
empire. Furthermore, Duke Frederick left some, or perhaps most, of the army's
war chest behind at Antioch, and installed a German garrison in the citadel
there.[98]

It would, however, be wrong to dwell on such omissions in the texts below, and
in the *Historia de Expeditione* in particular. While this account is a compilation,
and the product of considerable literary art, it is very largely based upon, and
incorporates within it, eyewitness testimony, while the diary of Tageno and the
Epistola de Morte (and the account of the capture of Silves) are clear examples of
such first-hand evidence. As such, they are of inestimable value to modern scholars

---

[97]   *Choniates*, p. 221.

[98]   *Annales Marbacenses*, pp. 61–2: 'The prince of Antioch did homage to the duke
in place of the Roman emperor, confirming on oath and with a written privilege that he
wished always to be subject to the Roman empire in every matter.' Hiestand, 'Antiochia,
Sizilien und das Reich am Ende des 12. Jahrhunderts', pp. 94–101. As Hiestand points
out, the account in the Marbach Annals is supported by various cryptic references in the
contemporary Arabic sources, as well as by Arnold of Lübeck, *Chronica Slavorum*, IV.13,
pp. 138–9, who mentions the garrison, and by the English *Itinerarium Peregrinorum* (pp.
302–3). Hiestand also prints, art. cit. 116–17, the text of an earlier letter of September 1187,
in which Bohemond had offered overlordship over the principality to the King of Sicily in
return for the latter's military assistance.

and students. And reading these accounts may suggest to us the correction of certain modern misconceptions concerning the Crusade of Frederick Barbarossa. Three indeed may briefly be mentioned here. First, while clearly suffering severely as it marched through Turkish Asia Minor, Frederick's army was far from being defeated there. Indeed, in capturing Iconium and securing the submission of Qilij Arslan, the emperor gained a significant military victory, comparable with the triumphs of the First Crusade almost a century earlier and in stark contrast to the failure of Conrad III to traverse Asia Minor in 1147. At the time of the emperor's unexpected death, he still had a powerful army, and had reached friendly territory in which further losses to enemy action were unlikely. Nor was it the death of the emperor that led to the immediate dissolution of his army, which was after all only two to three weeks' march away from Antioch when he died. Although they pass over this episode quite briefly, the contemporary accounts make clear that it was the epidemic that ravaged the army *after* it had arrived at Antioch that shattered the German Crusade. Admittedly, the seeds of this epidemic – what it was cannot be deduced from the contemporary descriptions – may already have been sown, or at least the resistance of the Crusaders undermined by their travails in Asia Minor. The *Historia de Expeditione* described leading men in the army being carried in litters before the death of the emperor, and Frederick of Swabia's arrival at Antioch was delayed by illness.[99] Indeed, according to the Muslim historian Ibn al-Athīr, 'they reached Antioch looking as though they were exhumed from their graves.'[100] And although the early thirteenth-century pilgrim Willibrand of Oldenburg praised the climate of the Tarsus region, the Cilician plain through which the army marched is extremely hot and prone to malaria in summer.[101] However, both Arnold of Lübeck and the English author of the *Itinerarium Peregrinorum* ascribed the disease to the hungry army's over-indulgence in wine and good food once it arrived at Antioch.[102] (This is not, incidentally, as far-fetched as one might think if the disease was some sort of

---

[99] Below, p. 115. *Estoire d'Eracles*, c. 97, in Edbury, *The Conquest of Jerusalem and the Third Crusade*, p. 89; *The Rare and Excellent History of Saladin*, trans. D.S. Richards (Aldershot 2002), p. 117.

[100] *Chronicle of Ibn al-Athīr 1146–1193*, p. 375.

[101] Eickhoff, *Friedrich Barbarossa im Orient*, p. 164. Willibrand of Oldenburg described the region of Tarsus as 'in woods, waters and good air similar to our Germany', *Itinerarium Terrae Sanctae* c. 26, in *Itinera Hierosolymitana Crucesignatorum (saec xii–xiii)*, ed. S. De Sandoli (4 vols, Jerusalem 1978–85), iii.226. But what time of year did he visit it?

[102] *Chronica Slavorum*, IV.13, p. 138: 'The famished people began to indulge themselves immoderately in wine and the other delicacies of the city, and huge loss of life arose among them, so that more people died from [this] great indulgence than from their earlier shortage. Many of the common people died there because of their intemperance, while the nobles and good men perished because of the great heat.' Cf. *Itinerarium Peregrinorum*, I.24, p. 302 = Nicholson, *Chronicle of the Third Crusade*, p. 67.

gastric infection. One should remember that, 23 years earlier, a German army in Rome during the hot summer months had been similarly ravaged, and with equally catastrophic results, by an outbreak of bacterial dysentery.[103]) While a few of the leading men of the expedition may have returned to the west quite speedily – both the imperial marshal Heinrich of Kalden and Count Gebhard of Dollnstein were, for example, with Henry VI in Italy by March 1191, and Count Rupert of Nassau was back in Germany by June of that year (he died soon afterwards),[104] while Bishop Rudolf of Liège had also returned before *his* death of 5 August 1191 – the major losses to the expedition came through disease. Six of the 11 bishops who took part in the Crusade perished either at Antioch or later during the siege of Acre.[105] So too did Tageno and all his fellow clerics from the chapter of Passau who had joined the expedition. A number of casualties can also be identified among the most prominent lay participants.[106] It would therefore appear perverse to ascribe the collapse of the German Crusade to alleged deficiencies in the leadership of Duke Frederick of Swabia, Barbarossa's son and successor as the commander of the Crusade, as some modern historians have done.[107] The duke would appear to have been the victim of forces beyond his control, and he

---

[103]   P. Herde, 'Die Katastrophe vor Rom im August 1167. Eine historisch-epidemioiligische Studie zum vierten Italienzug Friedrichs I. Barbarossa', *Sitzungsberichte der wissenschaftlichen Gesellschaft an der Johann-Wolfgang-Goethe-Universität Frankfurt am Main* 26 (1991), 139–66. Those who died in 1167 included the Archbishop of Cologne, five other bishops and the emperor's cousins Duke Frederick of Swabia (son of Conrad III) and Welf VII; see the list given by the *Historia Welforum Weingartensis*, MGH SS xxi.471.

[104]   Clementi, 'Calendar' no. 2; *Mainzer Urkundenbuch* ii(2).912–14 no. 552. The return of Henry of Kalden may have been politically motivated; certainly he became a key agent of the Emperor Henry VI, and it is quite possible that the latter sought his return to take part in the upcoming invasion of the kingdom of Sicily.

[105]   Gottfried of Würzburg (8 July 1190), Martin of Meissen (17 July 1190), Diepold of Passau (3 or 13 November 1190), Henry of Basel (1191), Arnold of Osnabrück (15 December 1191) and Peter of Toul (for whose death *Gesta Episcoporum Leodensium*, c. 46, MGH SS xxv.113). For Rudolf of Liège, *Le Chronique de Gislebert de Mons*, p. 257 [Gilbert of Mons, *The Chronicle of Hainaut*, p. 141].

[106]   For example, Margave Herman of Baden, Count Florenz III of Holland, Count Liudolf of Hallemund and his brother Willibrand, Counts Poppo of Henneberg, Frederick of Berg, Adalbert of Hildenburg and Adalbert of Grumbach, as well as Landgrave Ludwig III of Thuringia, who travelled to the Holy Land by sea (for these last two, *Chronica S. Petri Erfordensis*, in *Monumenta Erphesfurtensia*, p. 196), while others who appear to have died on the Crusade (though this is not absolutely certain) include Counts Conrad of Falkenstein and Siegfried of Libanau, and Conrad the Burgrave of Nuremberg.

[107]   E.g. Steven Runciman, *A History of the Crusades*, iii *The Kingdom of Acre* (Cambridge 1954), 16; H.E. Mayer, *The Crusades* (2nd ed., Oxford 1988), p. 141; John France, *The Crusades and the Experience of Catholic Christendom 1000–1714* (London 2005), p. 153.

ultimately himself became a casualty of disease at the siege of Acre. Indeed, the contemporary accounts highlight how important and successful Duke Frederick was as a military leader of the expedition: It was he, just as much as his elderly father, who exercised effective tactical leadership during the campaign. He was, so the *Historia de Expeditione* described him, 'an indefatigable guardian of the pilgrims of Christ', and on a number of occasions, as at the storming of Dimotika in Greece and in the assault on Iconium, the Swabian author of the *Historia Peregrinorum*, in particular, showed him rallying and encouraging his men when the going got tough. Similarly, Arnold of Lübeck portrayed him as rallying the army immediately after his father's death, urging them to be steadfast and trust in the help of God.[108] It was his death, in January 1191, rather than that of his father that marked the real end of the Crusade of Frederick Barbarossa. Hence, after recording his premature death, Arnold of Lübeck concluded: 'And so that expedition was ended, so that it seemed to have been almost completely wiped out'; while the Cologne chronicler noted that the surviving Crusaders were 'like sheep lacking a shepherd; they were scattered and divided one from another, and everyone set off on his own way home, with the more sensible ones being first'.[109]

Nevertheless, the achievement of the Crusade had been considerable, and the Muslims had been notably apprehensive at the news of its coming. Saladin had indeed withdrawn substantial forces from the siege of Acre and sent them to northern Syria in anticipation of its arrival.[110] Nor indeed did the death of Frederick of Swabia and the break-up of the imperial expedition mark the end of the German contribution to the Third Crusade. The Duke of Austria and those others who arrived by sea played a significant part in the siege of Acre, and (as the last part of the *Historia de Expeditione* and Otto of Sankt Blasien explain in detail) the duke's quarrel with Richard of England had important ramifications both for England and the *Reich*, not least in that his ransom helped to finance Henry VI's conquest of the kingdom of Sicily in 1194. Most Anglophone histories have tended to reflect the views of the contemporary Anglo-Norman chroniclers, such as William of Newburgh, who, when writing of King Richard's imprisonment, described Henry VI as 'another Saladin'.[111] By contrast, the German sources for this episode are instructive, not least in showing how much Richard's arrogant leadership of the later stages of the Crusade was resented, as well as reflecting the

---

[108]   Below, p. 85, and *Historia Peregrinorum*, pp. 146, 169; Arnold of Lübeck, *Chronica Slavorum*, IV.13, p. 138. The source quoted by Burchard of Urspberg described him as 'most valiant in arms' (*armis strennuissimus*), *Burchardi Praepositi Urspergensis Chronicon*, pp. 61–2.

[109]   *Chronica Slavorum*, IV.13, p. 139; *Chronica Regia Coloniensis*, p. 152 (which gave a, no doubt embroidered, account of Duke Frederick's holy deathbed).

[110]   *The Rare and Excellent History of Saladin*, p. 116. Cf. *Chronicle of Ibn al-Athīr 1146–1193*, p. 376.

[111]   *Historia Rerum Anglicarum*, V.7, in *Chronicles of the Reigns of Stephen, Henry II and Richard I*, ed. R. Howlett (4 vols, Rolls Series, London 1884–90), i.429–30.

widespread suspicion that he had had a hand in the murder of the imperial ally Conrad of Montferrat, a distant relation of the Staufen family.

Finally, there is the matter of Frederick's posthumous reputation. One might expect this to have been high in Germany, given his long and for the most part successful reign, and his death while waging war for Christendom, as well as his high repute during his lifetime, not least among the *minnesanger*.[112] In fact, it was overshadowed by the disastrous conclusion to the expedition, and subsequently by the internal problems that developed with the *Reich* after the premature death of Henry VI in 1197. As we have seen, the contemporary historians of the next generation said relatively little about his Crusade. Some of the subsequent accounts of Frederick's death did emphasise the holy nature of his end; thus according to the Stade annalist, he exclaimed before he expired: 'Blessed Cross of the Son of God, that water [which] receives me has regenerated me, and [what] makes me a Christian will make me a martyr.'[113] But other commentators revealed the doubts and disappointment engendered by the ultimate failure of the German part of the Crusade. Perhaps most damning was another Saxon annalist, from the abbey of Stederburg, although his comments may also reflect the lingering loyalty felt in eastern Saxony to Henry the Lion and the Welf family, and resentment at Barbarossa's interference in the duchy in 1180:

> While Henry [VI] was preparing his journey to Apulia, he heard of the death of the emperor, of whom we can say nothing glorious and nothing worthy of memory, except that he died in exile. For whatever had been his intention at the start of his expedition, his life ended ingloriously, as He who knows the hearts of men made obvious.[114]

A more balanced view of the expedition came from Arnold of Lübeck, despite the sympathy that he displayed in his chronicle towards Henry the Lion. He admitted that the eventual break-up of the expedition had led some to criticise it, 'saying that it had not been well begun, thus it had not finished well'. Nevertheless, he wrote, Christian men had left their homes, families and possessions, and exposed themselves to hard labour and suffering. Many of them 'chose to die in the service of the Lord' (*eligerent in confessione Domini occumbere*) rather than return home. Thus, while the expedition had not achieved its desired end, one should not therefore think 'that they will not receive the desired crown, since this death of holy men is precious in the sight of the Lord'. Yet Arnold had said little about Frederick himself at this point, except that his death had caused universal grief among his army.[115]

---

[112]   For this last, Pacaut, *Frederick Barbarossa*, pp. 205–6.

[113]   *Annales Stadenses*, MGH SS xvi.351.

[114]   *Annales Stederbergenses*, MGH SS xvi.223.

[115]   *Chronica Slavorum*, IV.13, pp. 138–9.

Perhaps most instructive was the view of the Byzantine chronicler Niketas Choniates, whose opinion of Frederick was considerably more flattering than his view of his own ruler Isaac Angelos. Indeed he wrote of Frederick that: 'he was a man who deserved to enjoy a blessed and perpetual memory ... his burning passion for Christ was greater than that of any other Christian monarch of his time.' Scorning his own comfort, said Choniates, he endured the hardships of the journey, for 'following the example of the Apostle Paul, he did not count his life dear to him but pressed forward, even to die for the name of Christ.'[116] The emperor himself would surely have wished for no finer epitaph.

---

[116] *Choniates*, pp. 228–9. There is an excellent discussion of the nuances of Choniates's attitude towards the Latins, as compared with his opinion of Isaac, by Jonathan Harris, *Byzantium and the Crusades* (London 2003), pp. 137–40.

The History of the Expedition of the Emperor Frederick

When I consider the desolation and the miserable captivity through which the land of the Lord and the city of the King of all kings, which was once the Lady of [all] peoples and the ruler of every province, is now made subject to the slavery of barbarian foulness, I judge it worthy of lamentation by every Christian. For when I think how the worship of the Christian religion has collapsed there, where the origin of our salvation is derived and the Catholic faith had its beginning, as I think over the praiseworthy struggles of these men and that 'those who stood against the wall for the house of the Lord'[1] did deeds worthy of memory, I am compelled to weep with the prophet and with Him in whom the truth of all prophecy is explained. For indeed this truth, and the prophet of the truth, challenges us to sorrow as we weep over the various ruins of that same city, and especially since the reason for the lamentation in our time is much more serious than the previous evil that gave rise to lamentation. But, according to the dispensation of human destiny, when we read that Jesus wept over the ruin of this same city and had mercy upon it, we hope and trust that we shall appease this manifestation of His wrath and anger, which we have undoubtedly deserved and it is certain that we have provoked against us, and we shall receive assistance through His pious compassion: 'for though He cause us grief, He who has smitten us will revive us',[2] namely so that Jerusalem will be restored to those of us who survive on earth, and those who die for this same land will receive as reward the vision of eternal peace in that heavenly homeland, whose citizens are they who prove through their triumph in a glorious battle that it is granted [to them] as a habitation. Therefore, among other matters and after other grave and frequent desolations, I propose to describe what took place in the year of our Lord 1187, in the time of the most glorious Frederick, august Emperor of the Romans, when the church beyond the seas started to be shaken by Saladin of Egypt, insofar as I can reveal it from the truthful account of those who were present at this capture, desiring to recount this not as a history but as a lamentable tragedy.

I have indeed judged it suitable to place the letters that those across the sea have written concerning these sad events to those on this side of it at the beginning of this work.[3]

---

[1]   Ezekiel 13:5.

[2]   Lamentations 3:32, and Hosea 6:1–2.

[3]   This letter has been translated by Edbury, *The Conquest of Jerusalem and the Third Crusade*, pp. 160–2. I have used this translation, but not slavishly.

We make known to you, Lord Archimbald, Master of the Hospitallers of Italy, and the brothers all the events that took place in those regions beyond the sea. You should therefore know that the King of Jerusalem was at Saffuriyah around the feast of the apostles Peter and Paul[4] with a great army of at least 30,000 men. He had been fully reconciled with the Count of Tripoli, and the count was present with him and his army. And behold Saladin, the pagan king, marched on Tiberias with 80,000 horsemen, and he captured Tiberias. After this had happened, the King of Jerusalem was informed, and he moved from Saffuriyah and marched with his men against Saladin. The latter attacked him at Meskenah on the Friday after the feast of the apostles Peter and Paul.[5] Battle was joined, and they fought fiercely throughout the day, until night put an end to the struggle. With the coming of night the King of Jerusalem pitched his tents near Lubiyah, and the next day, which was a Saturday, he set off with his army [once again]. At around the third hour the Master of the Temple began the battle with all his brothers, but they did not receive help, and God allowed them to lose the majority of their men. After that the king with his army forced his way with great difficulty to a point about a league from Nimrin, and then the Count of Tripoli came to the king and had him pitch his tents next to a mountain that is like a castle, but they were only able to erect three tents. As they did this, the Turks saw them throwing up their defences and lit fires around the king's army, and these were so hot that the horses were roasting, and they were unable either to eat or drink. Then Baldwin of Fatinor, Bachaberbochus of Tiberius and Leisius, along with three other companions, deserted the army and went to Saladin, and, what is sad to say, they renounced their faith. They surrendered themselves, and they told him about the situation of the army of the King of Jerusalem and its dire straits. Thereupon Saladin sent against us Taqi-al-Din with 20,000 chosen knights, who fell upon the Christian army. Ferocious fighting continued from Nones until Vespers, and on account of our sins many of our men were killed, and the Christian people were defeated. The king and the Holy Cross were captured, as were the count *Gabula*,[6] Milo of Colaverdo,[7] Humphrey the younger,[8] Prince Rainald, who was captured and put to death, Walter of Arsur, Hugh of Gibelet, the lord of Botrun and the lord of Maraclea. A thousand other of our better men were captured or killed, so that among the knights and foot soldiers no more than 2,000 escaped. The Count of Tripoli, lord Balian and Rainald, lord of Sidon, escaped.

---

[4]   29 June.

[5]   3 July.

[6]   The name is garbled: this was probably Joscelin of Courtenay, the royal seneschal and titular Count of Edessa.

[7]   A royal vassal known from charters of 1181–3, who from 1189 onwards lived in the principality of Antioch, Edbury, *Conquest of Jerusalem*, p. 161 note 15.

[8]   Humphrey IV of Toron.

After this Saladin gathered his army once again, and on Sunday he came to Saffuriyah and captured it, along with Nazareth and Mount Tabor. On Monday he came to Acco, which is called Acre, and the people of Acre surrendered themselves [to him]. Similarly the people of Haifa, Caesarea, Jaffa, Nablus, Ramla, St George,[9] Ibelin, Belfort, Mirabel, Toron, *Gwalêr*,[10] Gaza and Daron all surrendered. After this, just as our galley was sailing from Tyre, they sent Balian[11] to Saladin, that he might go to Jerusalem and they would surrender the city. And we fled on the galley to Lattakia, and we heard that Tyre was to be surrendered. However, these cities are still safe, and they desperately need the assistance of the western Church: namely Jerusalem, Tyre, Ascalon, Marqab, Antioch, *Lassar*,[12] Sahyun and Tripoli. But so great is the multitude of Saracens and Turks that from Tyre, which they are besieging, as far as Jerusalem they cover the surface of the earth like countless ants. And unless help is brought quickly to these remaining cities listed above and the very few eastern Christians who are left, they too will be left to the plundering of the raging gentiles, who are thirsting for Christian blood.

Another letter was sent to Leopold, the illustrious Duke of Austria.[13]

Hermenger, through the patience of Christ the servant of the poor and humble provisor of the brothers of the holy Hospital of Jerusalem, with the whole convent of brothers, [sends] greeting to the most illustrious lord and his benefactor Leopold, the distinguished Duke of Austria, with sincere devotion and the gift of appropriate prayers. We believe, most illustrious duke, that the wretched fall of the land of Jerusalem is well known to your exalted lordship. As a deserved consequence of its sins, the Lord has become ashamed of His land and has laid a heavy hand on His patrimony. Justly and rationally expending His wrath and fury on our unrestrained faults, He allows the cause of the Christians beyond the sea to grow daily worse. For in this present summer the wicked Saladin has utterly destroyed the town of Tortosa, apart from the Templars' citadel,[14] and after burning down the town of Valania has entered the land of Antioch. He has seized all that region right up to the gates of Antioch itself, including the most

---

[9]   Lydda.

[10]   Not identified.

[11]   The Latin text has Sabanos, but this was clearly Balian of Ibelin, cf. Edbury, *Conquest of Jerusalem*, p. 49.

[12]   Edbury, *Conquest of Jerusalem*, p. 162 note 19, suggests that this may refer to Gibelcar in the county of Tripoli.

[13]   Leopold V of Babenberg, Duke of Austria 1177–94 (born 1157).

[14]   The citadel of Tortosa and a substantial part of the lordship had been given to the Order of the Temple in 1157, Jonathan Riley-Smith, 'The Templars and the Castle of Tortosa in Syria', *English Historical Review* 84 (1969), 278–288.

celebrated towns of Gibelet and Laodicia,[15] and the very powerful castles of Saone, Gorda, Cavea and Rochefort. He has besieged and captured Tarpasac and Gaston on the far side of Antioch, and almost the whole principality apart from our mighty castle of Margab has been laid waste and lost. What is even worse is that the prince and the people of Antioch have made an agreement with Saladin, that if they do not receive help within seven months from the start of this October they will surrender and shamefully hand over Antioch [itself], which was gained through the blood of faithful Christians, without even one stone being thrown. You should also know that in the land of Jerusalem the most powerful castles of Kerak and Montreal [which are] in Arabia beyond the River Jordan and near the Dead Sea have surrendered owing to starvation. We are most fearful concerning Saphet, which belongs to the Temple, and we have heard nothing about our castle of Belvoir, although [we do know that] they have been under close siege for some time and are forced to endure dreadful hardships.[16]

I have put these letters here so that the attentive reader can realise what mighty grief swayed the hearts of all Christians throughout the world to avenge the injury done to the Cross and to Christ.

Thus 'the land of promise' and the 'inheritance of the Lord',[17] the Holy Land where the feet of the Lord trod, was with the city of Jerusalem miserably given over to destruction. Some of its inhabitants were slain, while others were led off with the king into captivity, while thanks to our sins the Holy Cross was carried away by its enemy, Saladin. Dreadful sadness and faint-heartedness indeed afflicted all the followers of Christ throughout the world. Therefore God roused the spirit of Frederick, the most serene Emperor of the Romans, and directed his thinking towards rescuing the land of redemption from the hands of the Saracens who were afflicting the Christians and punishing their unbridled audacity. Indeed, neither the aches and pains of old age nor the efforts of the lengthy campaigns which he had waged for many years against rebels to restore the well-being of the Roman Empire and on which he had won most notable victories, not even an abundance of wealth and comforts nor pressing affairs of state could prevent him from boldly undertaking the lengthy and difficult road of holy pilgrimage with all the forces of the empire. He spared neither himself, nor his long-stockpiled wealth, nor his

---

[15]   Now Jabala and Latakiah.

[16]   This letter would appear to date from August or September 1188, soon after Saladin's invasion of the principality of Antioch and the county of Tripoli, for which see especially M.C. Lyons and D.E.P. Jackson, *Saladin, the Politics of the Holy War* (Cambridge 1982), pp. 286–91. However, if this was so, the reference to the surrender of Kerak and Montreal was premature: the former surrendered in November 1188, the latter in April/May 1189. These may have been presumed already to be lost, or this conclusion may stem from an editorial emendation by the compiler. Saphet (Safed) surrendered to the Muslims on 6 December 1188, *The Rare and Excellent History of Saladin*, pp. 88–9.

[17]   Hebrews 11:9, I Samuel 26:19.

much-loved sons. This glorious elderly man inspired the young by his example to wage war for Christ, considering this to be a good 'fulfilment of his courageous endeavours',[18] if by driving out the enemies of the Christian faith he might restore peace to the eastern Church and restore the holy places that they had profaned to the service of God.

Meanwhile Pope Gregory of holy memory, who had previously been called Albert and under his predecessor held the office and rank of chancellor in the Roman Church, was appalled by the ruin of the church of Jerusalem.[19] For, as it is written, 'he that increaseth knowledge increaseth sorrow',[20] and he feared that the wrath of Almighty God posed an immediate threat to the entire Church, that He might, as is read in Ezekiel, 'begin at my sanctuary',[21] that is He might first wreak destruction upon the land of our salvation in retribution for the sins of the Christian people, and thereafter extend this havoc more widely through the entire Church, if we did not humble ourselves with the worthy fruits of penitence. Hence he sent out apostolic letters to all the churches of these lands with timely advice and encouragement to all the sons of the holy Catholic Church, their mother, in which he roused them to free the land of Jerusalem and the Holy Sepulchre of the Lord from the hand of the barbarians. He promised everyone pardon for their sins and the certainty of eternal blessedness through entry to the kingdom of Heaven for those who faithfully undertook the journey of salvation overseas against the common enemies of the Church.

We have thus good reason to include below his letter of exhortation sent to all the faithful.[22]

On hearing with what severe and terrible judgement the Divine hand has smitten the land of Jerusalem, we and our brothers have been confounded by such great horror and struck by such great sorrow that we could not easily decide what we ought to say or do. For this the Psalmist laments, when he says: 'O God, the heathen are come into thine inheritance.'[23] Taking advantage of the dissension that the malice of men has recently, at the instigation of the devil, created in the land of the Lord, Saladin arrived in those regions with a multitude of armed men. The king went to meet him, accompanied by the bishops, Templars, Hospitallers, and the barons, knights and people of the land, along with the Lord's Cross,

---

[18]   Ecclesiasticus 50:11 (Vulgate), and cf. ibid., 39:34.

[19]   Albert of Morra, a native of Benevento and a Praemonstratensian canon, was elected Pope on 21 October 1187. He had formerly been cardinal priest of S. Lorenzo in Lucina and papal chancellor.

[20]   Ecclesiastes 1:18.

[21]   Ezekiel 9:6.

[22]   The bull *Audita Tremendi*, of 29 October 1187. There is another translation of this text in Louise and Jonathan Riley-Smith, *The Crusades. Idea and Reality 1095–1274* (London 1981), pp. 64–7, with which this version has been checked.

[23]   Psalm 78:1 (Vulgate), 79:1 (AV).

which, as a reminder and testimony to the Passion of Christ who hung upon it and on it redeemed the human race, was customarily a certain protection and the defence that was wanted against the attacks of the pagans. The enemy attacked them and our side was defeated. The Cross of the Lord was captured, the bishops were slain and the king made prisoner. Almost the whole army was either put to the sword or fell into enemy hands, so that only a very few are believed to have escaped through flight. Moreover, the bishops, Templars and Hospitallers were beheaded as Saladin looked on. We do not believe that a letter can describe how, after defeating our army, the enemy have subsequently invaded and seized everything, so that very few places are said to remain that have not fallen into their power, [at least] until someone comes to us from that region who can explain these events more fully and truthfully. But although we shall have to say with the prophet: 'who will give water to my head and a fountain of tears to my eyes, that I might weep day and night for the slain of my people',[24] we ought not however to be so downhearted that we sink into doubt and believe that God is so angry with His people that He will allow Himself to be enraged by what has been done by a host of common sinners, that He will not be speedily placated through penitence and raise us up, and that after weeping and tears He will not bring rejoicing. For what person of sound mind does not weep, given such great reason for weeping, if not in body at least in his heart? He would seem to have forgotten not only the Christian faith, which teaches that one ought to mourn with everyone else who mourns, but also his very humanity, since every sensible man ought to bear in mind those matters about which we keep silence, from the very magnitude of the danger and the barbaric ferocity of those who thirst after the blood of Christians and devote their every effort to profane the Holy Places and drive the worship of God from the land. First the prophets laboured with all their might, and after them the Apostles and their followers, to establish the worship of God in that land, and then that it would flow from there out to every region of the world. And what is assuredly the greatest and most inexplicable fact; God through whom all things are created wished to be made flesh. Through His ineffable wisdom and incomprehensible mercy, he wished here to bring about our salvation through the infirmity of the flesh, namely through hunger, thirst, the Cross, death and resurrection, in accordance with the saying that 'he works salvation in the midst of the earth'.[25] He deigned to work through His own person, something of which the tongue cannot speak nor can the mind of man contemplate. That land has now endured what one reads it suffered under the people of old, which should be a cause of mourning to us and to all Christian people.

We ought not to believe, however, that these things have taken place through the injustice of the judge, but rather they have been brought about through the

---

[24]   Jeremiah 9:1.

[25]   Psalm 73:12 (Vulgate), 74:12 (AV).

iniquity of a sinful people, since we read that when people turned to the Lord 'one chased a thousand and two put ten thousand to flight',[26] and thus when the people were at peace the army of Sennacherib was consumed by an angelic hand.[27] But 'that land eateth up the inhabitants thereof',[28] nor could it remain peaceful for long, nor could it restrain those who transgressed against the Divine law. These events have provided lessons and examples for those who were making their way to the heavenly Jerusalem, that they cannot arrive there except by the performance of good works and through many temptations. These things could indeed have been feared long ago, when Edessa and other land passed into the power of the pagans,[29] and it would have been prudent indeed if the people who were left had returned to penitence and pleased the Lord whom they had offended through their backsliding by their conversion. For His anger does not come suddenly, as He postpones punishment and allows time for repentance. Finally, however, He who while merciful does not omit judgement exacts His revenge in the punishment of those who transgress and as a warning for those who are to be saved. Moreover, with regard to the dreadful situation of that land, we ought to be mindful not only of the sins of its inhabitants but of our own and those of the entire Christian people, and be fearful lest what is left of that land should perish and the power of the infidel should also rage in other regions, since from every part of the world we hear of quarrels and scandalous disputes between kings and princes, cities and other cities. We can weep with the prophet and say: 'there is no truth, nor knowledge of God in the land. By lying, and killing, and stealing and committing adultery they break out, and blood toucheth blood.'[30] Hence it is incumbent on all of us to reflect upon our sins, and to decide to correct them through voluntary chastisement, that we may turn to the Lord our God through penitence and good works. We should first correct in ourselves what we have done wrong, and then direct our attention to the pollution and evil of the enemy. We should in no way hesitate to do for God what they are not afraid to attempt against the Lord.

Consider, therefore, my sons, how you came into this world and how you are going to leave it, how all things are transitory, and how you too have a transitory existence. Welcome with open arms the opportunity for repentance and doing good, insofar as it pertains to you, and give yourselves over not to destruction but to the service of Him, from whom you have received your life and all that you have, since you cannot exist by yourselves nor have anything from yourselves, you who cannot create [even] one single gnat on the earth.

---

[26]   Deuteronomy 32:30.

[27]   II Chronicles 33:21.

[28]   Numbers 13:32.

[29]   The city of Edessa was captured by Zenghi, Sultan of Mosul and Aleppo, on Christmas Day 1144; the rest of the county was conquered by him and his son Nur-ed-Din over the next six or so years.

[30]   Hosea 4:1–2.

We do not say – leave what you have, but rather send it on ahead of you to that heavenly storehouse, and deposit it therein, 'where neither moth nor rust doth corrupt, and where thieves do not break through nor steal',[31] striving for the recovery of that land in which for our salvation truth arose from the earth, and where He did not disdain to suffer for us on the gallows of the Cross. And do not direct your way there for money or earthly glory, but in accordance with the will of God, who taught by his own action that one ought to lay down one's life for one's brothers, and commend your wealth to him, which in the end, whether you like it or not, you will leave to heirs whom you do not know. Nor is it anything new for this land to be struck by Divine judgement, but neither is it unusual for it after being whipped and chastised to seek mercy. The Lord could indeed rescue it through His will alone, but it is not for us to say to Him, 'Why have you done this?' For perhaps He wishes to bring this to the notice of others, and to discover whether there is anyone who has knowledge of Him, or who seeks after the Lord and who will joyfully embrace the opportunity of penitence offered to him, and who by laying down his life for his brothers may [indeed] perish momentarily but gain everlasting life. Hear how the Maccabees burned with zeal for the Divine law and exposed themselves to extreme danger to free their brothers. They taught that one should lay down not only riches but your persons for the salvation of your brothers, encouraging each other and saying: 'Gird yourselves and be valiant men, for how much better is it to die in battle than to see the evils of our people and of holy things.'[32] And what they did, subject only to the law [of Moses], you should do without a trace of fear, led to the light of the truth by the Incarnation of our Lord Jesus Christ and profiting by the examples of many saints. Do not be afraid to surrender earthly things that are few and of brief duration, in exchange for those goods which are promised and reserved for you, which 'eye hath not seen, nor ear heard, neither have they entered into the heart of man',[33] concerning which the apostle says, 'for the sufferings of this present time are not worthy to be compared with the glory that shall be revealed in us'.[34] To those indeed who with contrite heart and humble spirit undertake the labour of this journey and who shall die with true faith and in penitence for their sins, we promise plenary indulgence for their wrongdoing and eternal life. They should know that, whether they survive or die, they will receive relaxation of the reparation imposed for all their sins for which they have made true confession, through the mercy of Almighty God and the authority of saints Peter and Paul, and our own authority. From the time when they receive the Cross, their property and families shall stand under the protection of the Holy Roman Church, and that of the archbishops, bishops and other prelates of the Church of God. They shall suffer no legal claims to that property which they held in peace before their

---

[31] Matthew 6:20.
[32] I Maccabees 58:59.
[33] I Corinthians 2:9.
[34] Romans 8:18.

taking of the Cross, until there is absolutely certain knowledge of their return or of their death; all their property shall in the meantime remain undiminished and unchallenged. They shall not be forced to pay usurious interest, even if they should be obligated to someone; rather they shall remain absolved from it and unmolested. They are not, however, to set out in rich clothes, nor with dogs or birds or other things that seem rather to serve for enjoyment and luxury than to be necessities. They should instead go with limited baggage and modest dress, in which they appear rather to do penance than strive after foolish pomp.

The pope sent from his side as his agent in this holy business, and as the preacher and recruiter for expedition pleasing to Christ, a wise, discreet and religious man, Henry, Cardinal Bishop of Albano, who had once been Abbot of Clairvaux.[35] Even though he was French, and ignorant of the German language, he explained his sweet doctrine through an interpreter, and prepared the minds of many valiant knights in Germany for that journey.

I add below the letter that he sent to all the leading men of Germany containing this beneficial counsel.[36]

To his dearest brothers in Christ and friends, by the grace of God the venerable archbishops, bishops, abbots, provosts and other prelates of the Church, and to the noblemen beloved in the Lord, the dukes, counts, margraves and all the other princes spread through the kingdom of the Germans to whom this letter shall come, Henry by this same grace Bishop of Albano and legate of the Apostolic See [sends] greeting in the Lord. Because 'the voice of the turtle',[37] a voice of groaning, a voice of sadness, has recently spread news of lamentable sorrow, who among Christian people has not groaned at such a disaster? Who does not mourn that the Holy Land, which the feet of the Lord dedicated for our redemption, is exposed to the filthiness of pagans? Who does not deplore the capture and trampling underfoot of the life-giving Cross, and the profanation of the sanctuaries of the Lord by the unbelievers [*ethnici*]? Alas, alas, when

---

[35]   Henri de Marcy, Cistercian abbot of Hautcombe in Savoy 1160–76 and of Clairvaux 1176–9; Alexander III appointed him as Cardinal Bishop of Albano at the Third Lateran Council in March 1179. Much of his career, both as abbot and cardinal, had been spent in the campaign against heresy in Languedoc. He died on 1 January 1189, and was buried at Clairvaux next to the tomb of St Bernard. See Yves Congar, 'Henri de Marcy, abbé de Clairvaux, cardinal-évêque d'Albano et légat pontifical', *Analecta Monastica* v (*Studia Anselmiana*, fasc. 43, Rome 1958), 1–90.

[36]   As Congar, 'Henri de Marcy', pp. 85–6, points out, this letter has unmistakable overtones of, and some quotation from, St Bernard's view of the Crusade, both in his letter to the people of England summoning them to the Second Crusade (also sent to the Franconians and the Bavarians), *The Letters of St Bernard of Clairvaux*, trans. Bruno Scott James (London 1953), pp. 460–3 no. 391, and in his *De Laude Novae Militiae*, chaps 1–2.

[37]   Song of Songs 2:12.

something similar was heard, when that Cross received the fixing of the nails, 'the earth did quake, the sun was terrified, and the rocks rent; and the graves were opened'.[38] Whose stony breast is not softened after hearing of this, when He was mocked with thorns, crucified, and mocked with insults once more? O admirable Cross, the medicine for our wounds, the restorer of our health, sweet wood, the symbol of life, the banner of Christian knighthood! We shall confess that it was necessary, because we shall suffer less through all its merits, although we might fear that this be more. Nevertheless, since mercy and truth comprise the whole way of the Lord, we ought not to throw [them] far aside, since it should always be before our eyes that He who has punished the Christian people in judgement for their sins, and who has averted His eyes from their land as a result of their lusts, has [also] decreed redemption for us through His mercy. For who would allow the wood of the Cross to be carried away by unbelievers, unless it was for Him to be crucified once again by these people? Behold, we see once again the mystery of our redemption, when for us he did not now spare either his name or the Cross: 'He that spared not his own son, but delivered him up for us all'.[39] For the hand of the Lord is not shortened,[40] nor is His arm so weak that He is unable to redeem, but the inscrutable sublimity of the wisdom of God performs his work of mercy, so that He rouses the sluggish devotion of the world, and through our service and that of others whom He has deigned to choose for this He shall for our benefit, and for His, triumph gloriously over the hostility of barbarian people. 'Now is the acceptable time, behold, now is the day of salvation',[41] in which would that the knights of Christ, 'casting off the works of darkness' and assuming 'the arms of light, the breastplate of faith and the helmet of salvation', shall not hesitate to avenge the injury inflicted upon the Cross.[42] Evil (*Malitia*) was not knighthood (*militia*), because those who were once intent upon the slaughter of Christians, plunder and horrible tortures have deserved the eternal fire and to suffer from worms everlastingly. Happy is knighthood to those who seek to conquer for glory rather than 'for sake of gain'.[43] Today He who loves souls and does not spare injury Himself invites you for this purpose, that He has placed this duty on those [who are] faithful to Him, forcing them to [undertake] this knighthood. He is the one who places the sign of life on those who lament such great evils, to escape this intolerable harm; and although the aggressors, having already attacked [us], hold many weapons of destruction on account of our sins, they will injure only those who refuse the sign of life that has been granted by Him in Heaven. Thus it is that a solemn court has been arranged at

---

[38]   Matthew 27:51–2.

[39]   Romans 8:32.

[40]   Cf. Isaiah 50:2; 'Is my hand shortened at all, that it cannot redeem'; quoted by St Bernard, *Letters*, p. 461.

[41]   II Corinthians 6:2, also quoted by St Bernard, *Letters*, p. 461.

[42]   Romans 13:2; I Thessalonians 5:8.

[43]   Philippians 1:21; the AV reads 'all seek their own'.

Mainz, on the Sunday when 'Rejoice Jerusalem, they will make a festival for the Lord' is sung,[44] by the most serene lord Frederick, Emperor of the Romans and always Augustus, and by us who labour in accordance with the instructions of the Apostolic See to the same end, insofar as, with the Lord's help, our powers permit – there all those who love Him will meet together. Since therefore that same court has been entirely dedicated to our Lord and Saviour, so the imperial majesty summons you by his authority, [while] we summon your whole community to that same court on behalf of God and through that authority we exercise as legate, and we strictly enjoin and instruct you lest anyone among you refuse to attend the aforesaid council of Christianity except in case of legitimate and undoubted necessity. We also instruct you the venerable bishops to take care to summon the abbots and those other prelates subject to you, [working] together with the bearer of this present missive, who will perhaps be unable to reach everyone. Finally, we must enjoin you all to take care to attend the court of Jesus Christ with appropriate gravity and modesty, putting aside all idleness, curiosity and temporal glory, with everyone however inflamed by the fire of charity and obedience for the exaltation of the Christian name, so that dress and behaviour will proclaim the faith that we speak with our tongue.

And indeed the trumpet of the preaching of the overseas expedition first resounded in the city of Argentina, otherwise known as Strassburg, in a solemn court of the lord emperor, to which Archbishop Philip of Cologne had been summoned to render satisfaction concerning various issues.[45] It was sounded by a certain legate of the Apostolic See and the Bishop of Strassburg, who roused the minds of many men of distinction to undertake the journey of Christ.[46] These men enthusiastically took the sign of the Cross there, and they gloriously set an example for many others who piously imitated them thereafter. Gottfried, the venerable Bishop of Würzburg, most energetically encouraged and cooperated towards this same end at this time; he was a man of most noble birth, who was at this time most highly

---

[44]   Psalm 121:1–2. These are the opening words of the Mass on the fourth Sunday in Lent.

[45]   Philip of Heinsburg, Archbishop of Cologne 1167–91, who had been in dispute with Frederick I [see above, p. 14], and against whom Frederick had complained to the princes at a court held at Worms in August 1187, *Chronica Regia Coloniensis*, p. 136. The Strassburg council took place in December 1187. The witness list of the one surviving privilege that was probably granted during this council included the bishops of Strassburg, Speyer and Worms, Duke Frederick of Swabia, Duke Welf (VI), the son of the Duke of Lotharingia, and the count of Dagsburg (in the Moselle region), *Dipl. Fred. I*, no. 967.

[46]   Henry of Hasenburg, Bishop of Strassburg 1181–90, was described by the *Historia Peregrinorum*, p. 123, as 'experienced and prudent in both Divine and secular matters'. He died on 25 March 1190. According to the Marbach Annals, this legate was not Henry of Albano but his colleague the Cardinal Bishop of Palestrina, and he sent two envoys to the council rather than appearing in person, *Annales Marbacenses*, pp. 58, 61 (for his death). Congar, 'Henri de Marcy', pp. 45–6.

regarded for his knowledge of letters and his eloquent speech, and he was learned in both laws.[47] But while he inclined the minds of many to some extent towards the way of the Lord, he suddenly changed his mind, and decided to undertake the journey by sea, as being easier, even if longer, than the difficult expedition by land. This was caused by the malice of him 'who frequently transforms himself into an angel of light',[48] who with his accustomed envy was trying to deprive the army of the life-giving Cross of the services of this distinguished man. Through the shilly-shallying of this great man, the brave hearts of many warriors, in which desire had been kindled to undertake this journey, would have shamefully cooled, had not the wise forethought and the imperial authority of the most illustrious Emperor Frederick recalled both the bishop and various others from their uncertainty of purpose. Furthermore Apostolic authority and a stern warning by the supreme pontiff Clement, formerly Bishop of Palestrina, who had succeeded Pope Gregory and was determined to further this expedition in every way, was added to the urgings of the emperor.[49] For indeed throughout Germany the most chosen knights of Christ fixed the sign of the Lord's Cross on themselves and prepared for the campaign against the ancient enemy and his members, who 'had come into the inheritance of the Lord and had defiled his holy temple'.[50] Moreover the enthusiasm of the King of France and the King of England was no less. They took the Cross along with a great force of troops from each kingdom and vowed to undertake the journey, a vow that they did not however in fact fulfil. To encourage the most virtuous warfare by the expedition of those who had sworn, a solemn court at Mainz was called by the lord emperor, on the advice of the Cardinal Bishop of Albano, legate of the Apostolic See, and he was pleased to call it the 'court of Christ'.

Thus in the year from the Incarnation of the Lord 1188, sixth in the indiction, in the middle of Lent and on the Sunday *Laetare Jerusalem*, which then fell on 27 March,[51] this 'court of Christ' was celebrated in the metropolitan seat of Mainz, where princes, bishops, dukes, margraves, counts and most distinguished noblemen were gathered, along with a great flood of knights, and there the lord

---

[47]   Gottfried of Helfenstein, Bishop of Würzburg 1186–90, and previously imperial chancellor; the 'two laws' were civil and canon law. For him, see especially Peter Herde, 'Das staufische Zeitalter', in *Unterfränkische Geschichte* i *Von der germanischen Landnahme bis zum hohen Mittelalter*, ed. Peter Kolb and Ernst-Günter Krenig (Würzburg 1989), 348–50.

[48]   That is Satan, II Corinthians, 11:14.

[49]   Gregory VIII had died after a pontificate of 57 days on 17 December 1187: his successor was Paolo Scolari, Cardinal Bishop of Palestrina, as Clement III (1187–91).

[50]   Psalm 78:1 (Vulgate), 79:1 (AV).

[51]   The anthem Laetare Jerusalem was often expressly cited in a Crusading context, cf. J. Phillips, *The Second Crusade. Extending the Frontiers of Christendom* (New Haven 2007), p. 262. But the day was also significant as the anniversary of Frederick I's coronation as king of Germany in 1152, *Chronica Regia Coloniensis*, p. 89.

emperor received the sign of the Cross of Christ, and declared that he would in a spirit of constancy make preparations for the celebrated journey of Christ, while many present were in floods of tears.[52] Thus he placed himself as a distinguished head and a glorious standard-bearer to the faithful members of those bearing the sign. Then, following his example, the most distinguished princes, bishops, dukes, margraves, counts, and the brave and honourable knights, as well as many religious priests, in the same way signed themselves with the Holy Cross. We shall name them in the account that follows. In addition there was from the start a host of skilled knights, enough to make a great army that would strike fear into the enemies of Christ, although some people afterwards went back home – these we shall also identify by name. Almost nobody in the whole of Germany who had any sort of reputation for manhood was then to be seen without the life-giving sign of the Cross, and who would not be associated with the company of those who wore the sign of Christ. A glorious desire now burned bright among the most valiant of warriors for battle against those who had invaded the holy city and the most Holy Sepulchre of the Lord. That whole vast multitude of men seemed to think of nothing except 'to live is Christ, and to die is gain'.[53]

In that same year envoys of Isaac, the Emperor of Constantinople, arrived at an imperial court celebrated with the princes at Nuremberg, namely his chancellor John and some other leading men among the Greeks,[54] along with envoys from the Sultan of Iconium, the Prince of the Turks.[55] These envoys addressed the lord emperor on behalf of their masters with pompous salutations. For rumour of the great expedition to Jerusalem had filled both the whole of Illyria and many parts of the east with no little fear of the knights who had taken the sign of Christ. And indeed the Emperor of Constantinople informed our lord Emperor of the Romans that since he had his suspicions, which derived from the general opinion of his people, that the expedition to Jerusalem would [in fact] be a hostile invasion of

---

[52] According to the *Annales Magdeburgenses*, MGH SS xvi.195, some 4,000 'chosen men' (*viri electi*) attended this court, which set a date and place for departure, St George's Day, 23 April 1189, from Regensburg, which timetable was indeed adhered to (this is confirmed by the *History of the Pilgrims*, below p. 144). The *Cronica Reinhardsbrunnensis*, MGH SS xxx.543, said that in all 13,000 men were present at this court, while the contemporary Jewish writer Rabbi Moses ben Eleazar claimed that 10,000 men took the Cross there, Chazan, 'Emperor Frederick I, the Third Crusade and the Jews', p. 88. For the diet at Mainz, see also *Chronica Regia Coloniensis*, pp. 138–9; *Dipl. Fred. I*, no. 968.

[53] I Philippians 1:21.

[54] John Dukas Kamateros, the Logothete of the Drome (effectively the Byzantine foreign minister), led the embassy from Isaac Angelos, Emperor of Constantinople 1185–95. See C.M. Brand, *Byzantium Confronts the West 1180–1204* (Cambridge MA., 1968), p. 177.

[55] Qilij Arslan II, Sultan of Iconium (Konya) 1155–92. This would appear to have been at the very end of December 1188 or early in January 1189. The emperor had spent Christmas at Eger, some 70 km north of Nuremberg, but his land peace (see below, pp. 209–12) was issued at Nuremberg on December 29.

his kingdom, both by the emperor and the King of France, then if he was not given satisfactory assurances concerning this suspicion he would not allow us entry through the Bulgarian gates, and would resist us in every possible way. The invincible emperor was a true lover of peace, and therefore out of a clear conscience he absolved himself and all his men from this suspicion through an oath taken by three of the most distinguished princes, namely the Bishop of Würzburg, the Duke of Swabia and the Duke of Austria.[56] This action greatly pleased the Greek chancellor and his companions, and on behalf of his own lord king and of all the princes of Greece he swore on the Gospels true and firm friendship to the lord emperor and the whole army of Christ, and that escort on a good road, the best possible market preparations and free passage across the sea would be provided.[57] But their tongues were deceitful and 'the poison of the snake was on their lips',[58] since none of the things that they had sworn was afterwards fulfilled. By contrast, on the order of the lord emperor the three princes once again swore that the passage of our men would be quiet and peaceful, and in accordance with the pact sworn by the Greeks. Therefore, reassured by the oath of the Greeks, the pious emperor sent distinguished and assiduous envoys, namely the Bishop of Münster, Count Rupert of Nassau, his relation Count Walram, Henry the younger Count of Diez, and Markward his chamberlain,[59] to represent him and before the army of the Holy Cross should set out from its various homes, so that he might find those things that had been promised on oath by the Greeks might actually be fulfilled by them and made ready for the army. But neither the wise emperor nor the simple and faithful envoys were aware that 'they were sent forth as sheep in the midst of wolves'.[60]

In the year from the Incarnation of the Lord 1189, seventh in the indiction, in the thirty-fifth year of his rule as emperor and his thirty-ninth as king, after making

---

[56]   Duke Frederick of Swabia, the emperor's second surviving son (1167–91), and his first cousin Duke Leopold V of Austria (1157–94). Duke Frederick, the third son of the emperor, was born in February 1167, and had been baptised Conrad, but was renamed after the death of his eldest brother Frederick in mid-1169, Erwin Assmann, 'Friedrich Barbarossas Kinder', *Deutsches Archiv für Erforschung des Mittelalters* 33 (1977), 444–5.

[57]   The sea passage in question was across the Bosphorus.

[58]   Psalm 13:3.

[59]   Herman of Katzenellenbogen, Bishop of Münster 1174–1203; Rupert (III), Count of Nassau (d. 1191), who was a close associate of Frederick, having taken part in his Roman expedition of 1167 and the battle of Legnano in 1176; Henry (III), Count of Diez (d. 1234), and Markward of Neuenburg the chamberlain. This last was an imperial *ministerialis* from Neuenburg on the River Aisch, c. 40 km west of Nuremberg and 50 km southeast of Würzburg. The Cologne chronicle claimed that they had an escort of 500 knights, *Chronica Regia Coloniensis*, p. 145. Henry (II) of Diez the elder had been sent in May 1188 as envoy to Saladin, to convey the message that he would be attacked unless he relinquished Jerusalem and restored the True Cross (see below, pp. 144–5).

[60]   Matthew 10:16.

all the necessary preparations for an overseas expedition and entrusting the affairs of the empire to his son Henry, the illustrious King of the Romans, Frederick, the most victorious Emperor of the Romans, set off from Regensburg with the army of those wearing the sign of the Cross.[61] He sailed by ship along the River Danube as far as Vienna, although he had sent the greater part of his army before him by the land route. During his journey by ship, he rightly ordered the destruction by fire of a village called Mauthausen, sited on the bank of the Danube, since the inhabitants of that place had with overweening pride levied a new toll, for which they had no justification, on the pilgrims crossing the river, wearing the sign of Christ.

From the city of Vienna he journeyed into the land of Hungary, which is called 'beyond the gates'.[62] On 25 May he and the army of the Lord entered the plain that is called in the vernacular Virvelt. They pitched camp and remained for four days outside the city of Pressburg, while the entire army of pilgrims was mustered there.[63] But in the meanwhile the lord emperor was not taking his ease, for now he was making plans for the pilgrims' journey, then discussing the disputes between various litigants, two of whom indeed fought a judicial duel with each other, but before one or the other was killed he exercised his power of mercy, and with pious kindness ended the dispute and made peace between them.

He and the army celebrated the holy day of Pentecost there.[64] There were present with him in this company various princes who had previously taken the Cross, namely the bishops of Bamberg and Freising and the Duke of Austria, and many counts and barons.[65] There too he met the envoys of Bela, the glorious King of Hungary, to whom he gave a magnificent reception and entertainment, and he took these dukes and counts with him on his journey.[66]

During the aforesaid stay in this vast plain, these were numbered among the leaders and more notable men in the army of Christ: Frederick, Emperor and

---

[61]   Frederick was at Regensburg on 10 May 1189, *Dipl. Fred. I*, no. 1002, having previously been at Donauwörth between 29 April and 3 May, ibid., nos 997–9.

[62]   According to Arnold of Lübeck, *Chronica Slavorum*, IV.8, p. 129, the emperor forced 500 men, 'fornicators and thieves and other useless men', to return home from Vienna. He issued a privilege in favour of the bishopric of Freising at Vienna on 18 May, *Dipl. Fred. I*, no. 1002.

[63]   He issued a charter in favour of Count Engelbert of Berg at the Virvelt on 27 May, *Dipl. Fred. I*, no. 1006.

[64]   28 May 1189.

[65]   Otto [II] of Andechs, Bishop of Bamberg 1177–96; he was the younger son of Count Berthold III of Andechs (d. 1151) and the uncle of Duke Berthold of Merania, who played such a prominent part in the expedition [see below note 77]. Despite his vow, he did not in fact go on the Crusade [see introduction, p. 22]. His nephew Otto of Berg was Bishop of Freising 1184–1220; he was a son of Count Diepold II of Berg and of Gisela, a daughter of Berthold III of Andechs. The counts of Berg (in Bavaria) were relatives of the Staufen, descended from a daughter of Barbarossa's grandfather Duke Frederick of Swabia (d. 1105).

[66]   Bela III, King of Hungary 1173–96.

Augustus of the Romans, and his son Duke Frederick of Swabia; Bishop Rudolf of Liège, brother of the Duke of Zähringen;[67] [Bishops] Gottfried of Würzburg, Diepold of Passau,[68] Conrad of Regensburg,[69] Henry of Basel,[70] Martin of Meissen,[71] Arnold of Osnabrück,[72] and two others who arrived later, Archbishop Haimo of Tarentaise[73] and Bishop Henry of Leuci, that is of Toul,[74] as well as the Bishop of Raab from Hungary.[75] There was furthermore Herman of Münster, who was however not then present there, since he had earlier set off with some companions on an embassy of the lord emperor to the King of Constantinople, and also the

---

[67]   Rudolf, Bishop of Liège 1167–91, was the younger brother of Duke Berthold IV of Zähringen, who had died in 1186. Gilbert of Mons described him as 'an austere man, who would not agree to any counsel when he could do so, but was always intent on doing his own will', *Le Chronique de Gislebert de Mons*, p. 205 [*The Chronicle of Hainaut*, p. 112]. Giles of Orval (writing c. 1247–51) considered him to be 'a man of great cleverness, wise and experienced in secular matters', but painted a generally unsympathetic picture of him as bishop, accusing him of avarice and complaining about his persecution of Lambert, the founder of the Beguin movement, *Gesta Episcoporum Leodensium*, cc. 37–46, MGH SS xxv.108–13 (quote pp. 108–9).

[68]   Diepold of Berg, Bishop of Passau 1172–90, was the brother of the Bishop of Freising.

[69]   Conrad [III] of Laichling, Bishop of Regensburg 1187–1204.

[70]   Henry of Horburg, Bishop of Basel 1180–91. He was a relative of Bishop Henry of Strassburg, with whom he had close and friendly relations, *Regesten der Bischöfe von Strassburg* i *Bis zu Jahre 1202*, ed. Paul Wentzcke (Innsbruck 1908), 360 no. 649.

[71]   Bishop 1170–90. He took the Cross at Mainz in 1188 and died on the Crusade, *Monumenta Erphesfurtensia*, pp. 195–6.

[72]   Arnold of Altena, Bishop of Osnabrück 1173–91; son of Count Adolf IV of Altena and Berg (d. 1161/5). (This Berg was near Solingen in the Ruhrgebiet.) For his role in Italy in 1176–7, see introduction, p. 22.

[73]   Haimo of Briancon, Archbishop of Tarentaise in imperial Burgundy 1171–1211. A former Carthusian, he had supported Alexander III in his dispute with the emperor up to 1177, but relations with Frederick had been restored by May 1186, when at Pavia the emperor confirmed the property of his see and invested him with the *regalia* pertaining to it, *Dipl. Fred. I*, no. 938. Subsequently, in 1198, he crowned Philip of Swabia as King of Germany. Bernd Schütte, *König Philip von Schwaben. Itinerar, Urkundenvergabe, Hof* (MGH Schriften 51, Hanover 2000), pp. 420–1.

[74]   Actually Peter de Brizey, Bishop of Toul (in Alsace) 1165–c.1192, who appears in a number of Barbarossa's charters, and to whom the emperor had granted the right to have a mint in September 1178, *Dipl. Fred. I*, no. 763. He had been present at the Mainz diet of 1184, and had acted as the representative of the Count of Champagne at the imperial court when the latter was lobbying the emperor during the dispute over the succession to Namur. Gilbert of Mons considered him 'a most outstanding and energetic man', *Le Chronique de Gislebert de Mons*, pp. 158, 229 [*The Chronicle of Hainaut*, pp. 88, 124–5]. He died on the Crusade.

[75]   *Episcopus Iavarensis*, probably Bishop Ugrinus of Raab 1174–1203: while the name of the see might refer to Zara, the prelate there was an archbishop.

venerable Abbot Isenrich of Admont.[76] In addition there were present Berthold, Duke of Dalmatia, who was also Margrave of Istria;[77] Berthold, Margrave of Vohburg;[78] Herman, Margrave of Baden;[79] Florenz, the elder Count of Holland, his son, and his brother Count Otto of Bentheim,[80] Count Henry of Sayn,[81] Count Henry

---

[76]   Isenrich, Abbot of Biberg 1169–78, and of Admont 1178–89: the latter was a monastery in Styria founded by the noted reformer Gebhard, Archbishop of Salzburg 1060–88. Isenrich died while the army was in Bulgaria.

[77]   Berthold V of Andechs, Duke of Merania 1188–1204. The counts of Andechs were a Bavarian family; his father Berthold IV had been appointed Margrave of Istria in 1173, and Duke of Merania (more or less modern Slovenia) in 1180 after the death without heirs of the previous duke, who was a distant relative of the Wittelsbach family, B. Arnold, *Princes and Territories in Medieval Germany* (Cambridge 1991), p. 103. His grandfather, Berthold III, had taken part in the Second Crusade, Phillips, *The Second Crusade*, p. 102.

[78]   Berthold III of Vohburg, Margrave of the Bavarian Nordgau; he was married to Elizabeth, sister of Duke Ludwig of Bavaria, who took over his lands when Berthold died without a direct heir in 1204, Arnold, *Princes and Territories*, p. 242. His father Berthold II (d. 1182) was a regular witness of Barbarossa's charters; he was not. Berthold II's half-sister Adela had been Barbarossa's first wife, although this marriage was annulled c. 1153, Munz, *Frederick Barbarossa*, pp. 66–7.

[79]   Herman IV, Margrave of Baden and Verona (d. 1190), whose father had taken part in the Second Crusade. He died on the Crusade, *Annales Marbacenses*, p. 62. The margraves of Baden were a branch of the Zähringer family, descended from a younger son of Berthold I, Duke of Carinthia (d. 1078).

[80]   Count Florenz III, who died at Antioch in August 1190, and his younger son William (d. 1223). The count's elder son Dietrich (d. 1203) remained at home. Bentheim is near Osnabrück. The brothers Florenz and Otto occasionally witnessed Barbarossa's charters in Germany, *Dipl. Fred. I*, nos. 826–7 (May 1182), 963 (August 1187), but Florenz had played a significant part in his fifth Italian expedition, from March 1176 until the Venice conference of August 1177. Count Otto survived the Crusade, *Reg. Henry VI*, nos 476 (October 1195), 500 (March 1196).

[81]   Sayn is just north of Koblenz. Count Henry was an occasional witness of Barbarossa's charters, *Dipl. Fred. I*, nos 858, 861 (both June 1184), 963 (August 1187, text doubtful). His father Count Eberhard had taken part in the emperor's fifth Italian expedition. The counts of Sayn were the hereditary advocates of the archbishopric of Cologne, and regularly witnessed the charters of the archbishops, including one in July 1187 when Archbishop Philip was in dispute with the emperor, *Urkundenbuch für Niederrheins*, i.353–4 no. 503. Count Henry survived the Crusade, and after 1198 followed Archbishop Adolf of Cologne in supporting Otto IV.

of Spanheim and his brother Simon,[82] Count Henry of Kuick,[83] Count Dietrich of Wied,[84] Count Engelbert of Berg, who during the journey left this mortal world at Kubin on the Hungarian border,[85] Count Henry of Saarbrücken,[86] Count Frederick of Abenberg[87] and Count Poppo of Henneberg.[88] From Swabia there were Count Conrad of Öttingen,[89] Count Ulrich of Kyburg and his brother Count Adalbert

---

[82]   Count Simon, who had taken part in the 1184–6 Italian expedition, died at Adrianople during the early months of 1190. Spanheim is near Bad Kreuznach in the Palatinate. Immediately before his departure Simon had witnessed a charter of Archbishop Conrad of Mainz, on 15 March 1189, *Mainzer Urkundenbuch* ii(2).845–7 no. 514. Count Henry survived the Crusade and was back in Germany by August 1192, ibid., 938–40 no. 569 [= *Reg. Henry VI*, no. 244]. There were two other brothers, Albert and Ludwig. Albert took part in Henry VI's south Italian expeditions in 1194–5 and 1197, cf. *Mainzer Urkundenbuch* ii(2), no. 640 (May/June 1196).

[83]   Kuick or Cuyk, in north Brabant. He took part in the siege of Alessandria in 1174, and witnessed the Gelnhausen charter of April 1180, *Dipl. Fred. I*, nos 634, 795. He survived the Crusade and witnessed the settlement by Henry VI of a dispute about tolls involving the Bishop of Utrecht at Koblenz in June 1193, *Reg. Henry VI*, pp. 122–3 no. 302.

[84]   From the Rhineland; he was the nephew of Arnold II, Archbishop of Cologne 1152–6, and his son, also called Dietrich, was Archbishop of Trier 1212–42. The family died out soon after this last date.

[85]   From Altenberg, northeast of Cologne. See introduction, p. 23. His elder son, Count Adolf, died at Damietta on the Fifth Crusade; his younger son was Engelbert, Archbishop of Cologne 1216–26. For this family, *Urkundenbuch für Niederrheins*, ii, introduction, pp. xxvii-xxx.

[86]   Henry was Count of Saarbrücken 1180–1225. His family was closely connected with the Staufen; his father Count Simon had fought at Legnano, and died some time after June 1187, *Dipl. Fred I*, no. 959.

[87]   From Abenberg, 30 km southwest of Nuremberg, this family were hereditary advocates of Bamberg cathedral. His father, also called Frederick, had perished when a building collapsed while the emperor was holding a court at Erfurt in 1184, *Cronica Reinhardsbrunnensis*, MGH SS xxx(1).543. The count witnessed occasional imperial charters, but usually only when Frederick was in Bavaria, *Dipl. Fred. I*, nos 830–1, 1003. He survived the Crusade, witnessing a privilege of Henry VI at Würzburg in June 1192, *Reg. Henry VI*, no. 225, and died c. 1198/9, without leaving a male heir, Schütte, *König Philip von Schwaben*, p. 235.

[88]   Poppo (VI), Count of Henneberg, in Eastern Franconia, 1159–90, who died on the Crusade, *Monumenta Erphesfurtensia*, p. 196, had taken part in several of Frederick Barbarossa's Italian expeditions, and was married to a daughter of Duke Berthold IV of Merania. His family had a long-standing territorial rivalry with the bishops of Würzburg, Arnold, *Princes and Territories*, pp. 256–7.

[89]   Conrad, Count of Öttingen (15 km northeast of Nördlingen in eastern Swabia), 1189–96.

of Dillingen,[90] Count Berthold of Neuenburg[91] and Count Henry of Vöhringen.[92] From Bavaria there were Count Gebhardt of Dollnstein,[93] Count Siegfried of Liebenau,[94] Count Conrad of Nuremberg[95] and Count Cono of Falkenstein.[96] From

---

[90]   Kyburg, near Zürich (Switzerland) and Dillingen on the Danube, 30 km northwest of Augsburg. The brothers Count Ulrich III (d. 1227) and Adalbert III (d. 1214) were sons of Count Herman III of Kyburg and Dillingen (d. 1180). Count Ulrich witnessed Frederick's privilege to the monastery of Salem in June 1183, *Dipl. Fred. I*, no. 847. He was married to a sister of Duke Berthold V of Zähringen. One of their ancestors had taken part in the First Crusade, Albert of Aachen, *Historia Ierosolimitana*, ed. Susan B. Edgington (Oxford 2007), pp. 60–1.

[91]   Probably Neuenburg near Hagenau, in Alsace. He witnessed charters of Bishop Henry of Strassburg in 1187 and 1188, *Regesten der Bischöfe von Strassburg* i.356–7 nos 636, 641.

[92]   Near Biberach, not far from the border with the duchy of Bavaria. Count Henry and his brother Markward witnessed a charter of Barbarossa at Konstanz in May 1179, *Dipl. Fred. I*, no. 779, and Henry was also a witness, along with Barbarossa's sons Henry and Frederick, to an exchange of property involving Duke Welf VI at Ulm in May 1181, *Württembergisches Urkundenbuch*, ii (Stuttgart 1858), 212–13 no. 425. Count Markward subsequently took part in the invasion of the kingdom of Sicily in 1194, Clementi, 'Calendar', no. 118, and was a supporter of Philip of Swabia after 1198, Schütte, *König Philip von Schwaben*, p. 481.

[93]   On the River Almühl west of Eichstätt: he witnessed a privilege of Barbarossa for the abbey of Weingarten in September 1187, *Dipl. Fred. I*, no. 964, and survived the Crusade, subsequently witnessing a number of the charters of Henry VI and Philip of Swabia, Clementi, 'Calendar', no. 2 (March 1191), *Reg. Henry VI*, nos 224–5, 227, 285; Schütte, *König Philip von Schwaben*, p. 464. The last of the latter was in April 1203. Gebhardt's brother Hartwig was Bishop of Eichstätt 1196–1223.

[94]   Siegried IV, Count of Libenau (near Freistadt, modern Austria) 1163–90/1. He witnessed a single charter of the emperor, at Eger in May 1183, *Dipl. Fred. I*, no. 845. The counts of Libenau were cousins of the Spanheimer, dukes of Carinthia.

[95]   Conrad of Dornberg was Burgrave of Nuremberg; his brother Frederick also took part in the Crusade. Conrad had taken part in the Italian expeditions of 1167 and 1184/6, *Dipl. Fred. I*, nos 526, 536, 867, 869–70, 875, 883–5, 887–8, 890, 896, 900, 919. Conrad appears to have died on the Crusade: subsequently his son-in-law Frederick, Count of Zollern (d. c. 1200), was recorded as burgrave, Schütte, *König Philip von Schwaben*, p. 454.

[96]   Conrad (Cono/Kuno), son of Count Sigiboto IV of Falkenstein (who died in 1198). He probably died while on the Crusade; certainly he was dead by 1193. For his family, whose lordship lay in the valley of the lower Inn, near the Chiemsee, see J.B. Freed, *The Counts of Falkenstein. Noble Self-Consciousness in Twelfth-Century Germany* (Transactions of the American Philosophical Society 74(6), Philadelphia 1984).

Saxony there were Count Adolf of Schaumburg,[97] Count Christian of Oldenburg,[98] Count Liudolf of Hallemund and his brother Willibrand,[99] Count Burchard of Wöltingerode,[100] also Count Rupert of Nassau and his kinsman Count Walram,[101] and Count Henry the younger of Diez,[102] who was employed along with the Bishop of Münster on the emperor's legation to Greece. Furthermore, the Count of Salm and the brother of the Count of Vianden,[103] who had followed the army, caught up with it at Branitschevo, and along with them were various citizens of Metz. Also Gaubert of Aspremont and his associates arrived along with the Bishop of Toul on the Bulgarian frontier. There were also these men from among the higher

---

[97]   Adolf III, Count of Schaumberg and Holstein (d. 1225), one of the most prominent figures in northeast Saxony, was a determined enemy of the former duke, Henry the Lion. Arnold of Lübeck recorded that he returned from the Holy Land because his lands were under attack by Henry. Adolf also took part in the Crusade of 1196–7, Arnold, *Chronica Slavorum*, V.7, 25, pp. 153, 197.

[98]   Christian II of Oldenburg, who was later murdered by his brother Moritz in 1192, *Annales Stadenses*, MGH SS xvi.352. He witnessed Barbarossa's confirmation of the rights of the citizens of Bremen at Gelnhausen in November 1186, *Dipl. Fred. I*, no. 955.

[99]   Hallemund, near Hanover. They had been among the vassals of Henry the Lion, who had abandoned him in 1180, Arnold of Lübeck, *Chronica Slavorum*, II.13, p. 51. The 'two brothers of Hallemund' (not identified by name) witnessed a diploma of Frederick I issued at Erfurt in November 1181, *Dipl. Fred. I*, no. 814; and Liudolf witnessed a charter in April 1183 in which the Bishop of Hildesheim distributed property confiscated from Duke Henry to two of his vassals, *Urkundenbuch des Hochstifts Hildesheim und seiner Bischöfe i bis 1221*, ed. Karl Janicke (Leipzig 1896), 410 no. 422. Both brothers appear to have died on the Crusade, *Annales Stederburgenses*, MGH SS xvi.222.

[100]   c. 10 km northeast of Goslar, in eastern Saxony. He was one of three brothers; his elder brother Count Liudolf witnessed a charter of Henry the Lion in June 1191 (*Urkunden HL*, 185–6 no. 128). Burchard may have been quite elderly, since he appeared in *Urkunden HL*, nos 27 (June 1154), 32 (c. 1156), 45 (1160), assuming this is the same man. He also witnessed a number of charters of the Bishop of Hildesheim in the 1170s, *Urkundenbuch Hildesheim*, i, nos 368, 372, 375, 386. Burchard witnessed *Dipl. Fred. I*, no. 814 (Erfurt, November 1181), along with his brother Count Hogerus, and was at Goslar in late July 1188, at the meeting between the emperor and Henry the Lion, *Dipl. Fred. I*, no. 974. This was one of several of Frederick's charters in which he appeared during the emperor's visit to Saxony in the late summer of 1188; see also *Dipl. Fred. I*, nos 978–80, 984.

[101]   Nassau, on the River Lahn, 15 km east of Koblenz. For Count Rupert III (d. 1191), see introduction, p. 23. He was active as far back as 1161, *Dipl. Fred. I*, no. 338. Walram (d. 1198) was the younger son of Count Rupert I of Nassau (d. 1154), and uncle to Rupert III. He was the ancestor of the later counts of Nassau. Count Rupert's only known son, Herman, was a churchman, a canon of Mainz.

[102]   Diez, on the River Lahn in Hesse, 30 km east of Koblenz.

[103]   Salm and Vianden are both in modern Luxemburg; the latter was presumably a younger brother of Frederick II, Count of Vianden 1187–1220. The two families were related by marriage. The *Historia Peregrinorum*, p. 132, names the Count of Salm as Henry.

nobility: from Saxony the prefect of Magdeburg,[104] Widukind of Schwalenburg[105] and Liutger of Wohldenbruch;[106] from Austria Frederick, advocate of Berg,[107] and Otto of Ramsberg;[108] and from Carinthia and the March [of Styria] Liutold of Walstein[109] and Adalbert of Wisselberg. From Bavaria there were Diepold of

---

[104] Burchard IV, Burgrave of Magdeburg, who died on the Crusade, *Cronica Reinhardsbrunnensis*, MGH SS xxx(1).545. He had been with the emperor in Italy in 1176 and again in 1178, *Dipl. Fred. I*, nos 649, 726, 729–30, 732.

[105] He was one of the family who became known from about this period onwards as the counts of Waldeck, from the castle that was the centre of their main complex of lands, Arnold, *Princes and Territories*, pp. 235–6. Schwalenberg is west of the River Werra, 10 km northwest of Korvey. This man was probably Widukind III of Schwalenburg. His father, Widukind II (d. 1188/9) and uncle Volkwin (d. 1177/8) had been occasional witnesses of the charters of Henry the Lion, *Urkunden HL*, nos 34 (1156), 66 (1163), 73 (1166). Widukind III survived the Crusade; he and his brother Herman formally abandoned their claims to the advocacy of the bishopric of Paderborn in December 1193, *Reg. Henry VI*, no. 327.

[106] Chroust, *Quellen*, p. 21 note 6, identifies the *Waldenberhc* of the Latin as Woldenberg, but it is more probably Wohldenbruch, near Hildesheim. Liutger survived the Crusade, witnessing the imperial confirmation of an agreement between the Archbishop of Bremen and the Count of Holstein at Gelnhausen in October 1195, *Reg. Henry VI*, no. 477.

[107] Frederick of Berg was advocate of the see of Passau and of the monastery of Melk. He first appeared as a witness to a charter of Duke Henry of Austria for the monastery of Admont in 1171, *Urkundenbuch zur Geschichte der Babenberger in Österreich*, iv *Ergänzende Quellen 976–1194*, ed. Heinrich Fichtenau and Heide Dienst (Vienna and Munich 1997), p. 174 no. 838. He died at Antioch on 15 July 1190, *Necrologia Mellicensis*, in *MGH Necrologia Germania* v *Diocesis Pataviensis pars altera: Austria Inferior*, ed. Adalbert R. Fuchs (Berlin 1913), 555; and Duke Leopold of Austria subsequently took over his lands, Lechner, *Die Babenberger*, p. 183. A charter of his was recorded in *Die Traditionsbücher des Benediktinerstiftes Göttweig*, ed. Adalbert Fuchs (Fontes Rerum Austriacum, 2 Abteilung Diplomataria et Acta 69, Vienna 1931), 530–1 no. 396 (1182–9).

[108] From Lower Austria, he was the son of Hademar of Kuffern, to whose donations to the abbey of Gottweig he consented, *Traditionsbuch Gottweig*, 527 no. 392, 539 no. 403. Duke Leopold had earlier restored a property he had seized from the monastery of Raitenhaslach (1183–8), *Urkundenbuch zur Geschichte der Babenberger*, iv.194 no. 872. He survived the Crusade, subsequently witnessing a charter of Bishop Wolfger of Passau for the monastery of Sankt Polten (1192, after March), *Regesten der Bischöfe von Passau*, i.296 no. 974, and two charters of Henry VI for the bishopric of Passau, *Reg. Henry VI*, no. 285 (Speyer, 28 March 1193), no. 514 (Mainz, 31 May 1196). His sister married Henry of Murstätten, *vir nobilis*, *Traditionsbuch Gottweig*, 518–19 no. 385.

[109] His name appears in the witness list of a probably forged charter of Bishop Otto II of Bamberg for the monastery of Gleink, dated August 1183, *Urkundenbuch des Landes ob der Enns*, ed. Erich Trinks ii (Vienna 1856), 385 no. 263.

Leuchtenberg,[110] Henry of Grunenbach,[111] Hadubrand of Arnsberg,[112] Poto of Massing,[113] Conrad of Harbach,[114] Adalbert of Bruckberg,[115] Arnold of Hornberg[116] and Beringer of Gamburg.[117] From Swabia and Alsace there were Conrad of Swarzinberg, Herman of Hirzeke, Berthold of Künigsberg[118] and Henry of Isenburg. From Franconia there

---

[110]   Leuchtenberg, near Weiden, 70 km north of Regensburg. This man may have been the Diepold of Leuchtenberg who witnessed *Dipl. Fred. I*, no. 512 (April/May 1166); if so, he must have been quite elderly by the time of the Crusade. More probably he was the latter's son and homonym (died c. 1209), who was given the title of Landgrave of Leuchtenberg by Henry VI in 1196, and was a supporter of Philip of Swabia after 1198, Schütte, *König Philip von Schwaben*, p. 436.

[111]   Grunenbach, near Wangen, east of Lake Konstanz.

[112]   Arnsberg is c. 20 km north of Ingolstadt.

[113]   Massing is near Eggenfelden, 60 km east of Freising and 55 km west of Passau. Poto had witnessed charters of Archbishop Conrad of Mainz in the autumn of 1183, *Mainzer Urkundenbuch* ii(2).745 no. 458, and of Bishop Diepold of Passau to the monastery of Formbach in August 1188, *Urkundenbuch des Landes ob der Enns*, 413 no. 281 [= *Regesten von Passau*, i.281–2 no. 923]. The History recorded that Poto died on 16 March 1190 [see below, p.95].

[114]   There are two possible identifications for Harbach: either near Osterhofen, c. 30 km northwest of Passau, or near Dorfen, c. 35 km east of Munich.

[115]   Probably from Bruckberg near Landshut, c. 50 km northeast of Munich.

[116]   He survived the Crusade, and took part in all three of Henry VI's Italian expeditions, *Reg. Henry VI*, nos 171–2 (October 1191); Clementi, 'Calendar', nos 72, 79 (both April 1195), 115, 117–18, 120, 124, 130 (June–September 1197). For him, see too, below, pp. 83–4.

[117]   Probably from Gamburg on the River Tauber, near Tauberbischofsheim. He survived the Crusade, and later took part in Henry VI's conquest of the kingdom of Sicily, Clementi, 'Calendar', p. 160 no. 72.

[118]   Künigsberg is now Haute Kounigsberg (Alsace). He was one of the most active agents of the Staufen, and was recorded as *legatus Italiae* in *Dipl. Fred. I*, nos 896, 898–9 (February/March 1185), 916–17, 919 (August/September 1185); this office probably referred to Romagna and central Italy, Karl Bosl, *Der Reichsministerialität der Salier und Staufer* (MGH Schriften 10, Stuttgart 1951), pp. 209–210 (Berthold was, however, almost certainly a free noble, not a *ministerialis*). He later commanded Henry VI's army which invaded Apulia in 1192, Clementi, 'Calendar', no. 17 (March 1192), and was killed by a missile while besieging Monteroduni in Apulia in 1193, *Annales Casinenses*, MGH SS xix.317; Richard of S. Germano, *Chronicon*, ed. C.A. Garufi (Rerum Italicarum Scriptores, Bologna 1938), p. 16; Otto of St Blasien, *Chronica*, , p. 59 [below, p. 185].

were Adalbert of Hildenburg,[119] Adalbert of Grumbach,[120] Adalbert of Hohenlohe, Eberhard and Reinold of Reifenberg[121] and Heinrich of Hagen. Who would be able to list individually the fearsome and well-disciplined force of *ministeriales* and other chosen knights?

There were indeed, for shame, those among the princes of the Christian knighthood signed with the Cross who, on various excuses of local conflicts and through the incitements of the ancient enemy, turned back, and, as violators of their vow and 'having no root',[122] abandoned the way of Christ in time of temptation: King Philip of France, King Henry of England, the Count of Flanders,[123] Duke Otto of Bohemia,[124] the Duke of Leuven,[125] the Duke of Limburg,[126] the Bishop of

---

[119] Hildenburg in the modern district of Rhön-Grabfeld, north of Schweinfurt: Adalbert had taken part in the siege of Alessandria in 1174, *Dipl. Fred. I*, no. 633, Frederick's campaign in Saxony in 1180, ibid., nos 800–1, his last Italian expedition, ibid., nos 867, 883, had witnessed his privilege to Salem in September 1187, had been with him during his visit to Saxony in 1188, ibid., 966, 972–5, 978–9, and had witnessed a diploma issued at Regensburg just before the expedition's departure, ibid., no. 1003. He died at Acre in 1191, *Cronica Reinhardsbrunnensis*, MGH SS xxx(1).547.

[120] Grumbach is near Würzburg. Adalbert had also been with Frederick during his visits to Saxony in 1180 and 1188, *Dipl. Fred. I*, nos 800–1, 972–5, 978–9, and died on the Crusade, *Monumenta Erphesfurtensia*, p. 196. His father, Markward of Grumbach, had been a regular witness of Frederick's diplomata from the early years of the reign, and an extremely unpopular *podestà* of Milan in 1164–6, Munz, *Frederick Barbarossa*, pp. 273–5. He was described among the leading men of Frederick's army by Acerbio Morena in 1163, *Geschichtswerk des Otto Morena und seiner Fortsetzer*, p. 170. Markward also founded the Cistercian nunnery of Ichterhausen in Thuringia, *Dipl.Fred. I*, no. 785 (July 1179).

[121] Now part of Weilersbach, near Forcheim in eastern Franconia, c. 30 km north of Nuremberg. These two (brothers?) were with the emperor in Italy in May 1177 and witnessed a charter of his at Nuremberg in March 1183, *Dipl. Fred. I*, nos 672, 840.

[122] Matthew 13:6, 21.

[123] The two kings and Count Philip of Flanders had all received the Cross at Gisors in January 1188. All three subsequently did take part in the Crusade, and Count Philip died at Acre in 1191.

[124] Ottokar, duke and subsequently (from 1198) King of Bohemia (d. 1230). His taking of the Cross was also specifically noted by the *Annales Stadenses*, MGH SS xvi.351.

[125] Duke Gottfried of Brabant, who died in August 1190. He and his son Henry were at war with the Count of Hainaut during the summer of 1189, *Le Chronique de Gislebert de Mons*, p. 241–2 [Gilbert of Mons, *The Chronicle of Hainaut*, pp. 131–2]; *Chronica Regia Coloniensis*, p. 143.

[126] Henry III, Duke of Limburg (d. 1221). Gilbert of Mons commented that after taking the Cross, he and his sons 'tossed this aside quickly and caused many evils and wars throughout the empire', *Le Chronique de Gislebert de Mons*, p. 207 [*The Chronicle of Hainaut*, p. 113].

Speyer,[127] the Bishop of Cambrai,[128] the Count of Looz,[129] the Count of Jülich,[130] the Count of Lohra,[131] the Count of Duras,[132] the Count of Hochstaden[133] and the Count of Pfirt.[134] These people in some way detracted from the efforts of our men

---

[127]   Otto of Henneberg, Bishop of Speyer 1188–1200, was the uncle of Count Poppo of Henneberg [above note 88].

[128]   Roger de Waurin, Bishop of Cambrai 1179–91, who later came to the Holy Land and died before Acre, *Le Chronique de Gislebert de Mons*, pp. 122, 256, 274 [Gilbert of Mons, *The Chronicle of Hainaut*, pp. 70, 140, 150].

[129]   Count Gerard of Looz or Lon (near Borgloon in Lower Lotharingia, modern Belgium), whose sister was married to Duke Gottfried of Brabant. Despite this, he had taken the side of the Count of Hainaut during the conflict of 1189. Count Gerard, as well as Duke Ottokar, witnessed a charter of Henry VI in favour of the archbishopric of Cologne, issued at Frankfurt on 25 March 1190, *Reg. Henry VI*, p. 43 no. 74. Gerard had taken part in the 1184–6 Italian expedition, *Dipl. Fred. I*, nos 866–7 (September 1184), 869–70, 875–6 (October 1184), 879, 883–4, 886 (November 1184), 890–2 (January 1185), 151 (February 1185), 899–900 (March 1185), 903 and 905 (May 1185).

[130]   William (II), Count of Jülich, in the Rhineland, 1176–1207. He was later a supporter of Otto IV, and married a daughter of Duke Henry III of Limburg.

[131]   Near Erfurt, in Saxony, this was almost certainly Count Ludwig, who with his brother Berengar witnessed several of Barbarossa's diplomata in 1188, *Urkunden Friedrichs I*, nos 972–3, 978–9; cf. *Mainzer Urkundenbuch* ii(2), nos 463, 465 (both July 1184), *Reg. Henry VI*, no. 257 (October 1192), *Mainzer Urkundenbuch* ii(2), nos 578–9 (August 1193), 592 (February 1194).

[132]   Count Cono of Duras, near Limburg in Lower Lotharingia (modern Belgium). He was, according to Gilbert of Mons, 'small in body, smaller in mind and knowledge', and in 1189 was in conflict with his lord the Duke of Limburg. Since he and his brothers were childless much of their property eventually passed to either the duke or Count Gerard of Looz, *Le Chronique de Gislebert de Mons*, p. 239 [*The Chronicle of Hainaut*, pp. 130–1].

[133]   Count Dietrich of Hochstaden, attested from 1174, when he witnessed a diploma of Frederick I for the monastery of Siegburg, *Dipl. Fred. I*, no. 618. He regularly witnessed the charters of the Archbishop of Cologne, and also witnessed Henry VI's charter to Cologne in March 1190, *Reg. Henry VI*, no. 74; according to Gilbert of Mons he did eventually set out, two years after he took the Cross, but never got further than Apulia and eventually returned home, *Le Chronique de Gislebert de Mons*, p. 207 [*The Chronicle of Hainaut*, p. 113]. Presumably this refers to Henry VI's south Italian expedition of 1191, in which Count Dietrich is known to have taken part, Clementi, 'Calendar', nos 4–5, 7, 9, 13 (all May–June 1191). His son Count Lothar was a supporter of Philip of Swabia in the civil war after 1198, Schütte, *König Philip von Schwaben*, pp. 519–20. The counts of Hochstaden held a very small county in the Rhineland, which eventually, in 1246, came into the possession of the archbishopric of Cologne, *Chronica Regia Coloniensis*, p. 289; Arnold, *Princes and Territories*, p. 226.

[134]   Count Ludwig of Pfirt (near Altkirch in southern Alsace, now in France). He had witnessed a charter of Henry VI to the Bishop of Basel in July 1185, *Reg. Henry VI*, no. 4, and made a donation to the monastery of Pairis in March 1187, *Regesten der Bischöfe von Strassburg* i.354 no. 631.

who had undertaken the Cross, who were most constant of mind and ready to undergo whatever dangers there might be, who remembered the word of God in the good and the stoutest of hearts and offered as a gift to the Lord a condign fruit, that is with their own body. The Archbishop of Bremen,[135] the Landgrave of Thuringia,[136] the Count of Geldern and the Count of Tecklenburg chose to travel by sea.[137] It was noteworthy both in them and in many others from our country, whom it would be shame to name, that they preferred to avoid the effort of this praiseworthy expedition by undertaking a long voyage but from which they would have less to fear from the enmity of the pagans, while in one of the cities still left to the Christians they cravenly awaited the arrival of our men. However, we did hear of extraordinary courage that the landgrave later displayed in the land of Jerusalem. Moreover, I do not think that I should omit mention of the resolve of the Archbishop of Tarantaise, the Bishop of Toul and their companions, for as they, accompanied by a large number of knights from Burgundy and Lotharingia, followed somewhat later after the army of Christ, they were upset by various false rumours that our men had been hard hit by attacks from the Hungarians and that they were suffering from hunger and in dire straits. Then, indeed, almost all the companions of the Archbishop of Tarentaise fled in terror back towards the sea. Nevertheless the archbishop himself carried on undaunted towards the army, as did the Bishop of Toul, and after almost six weeks of rapid and steadfast travelling both saw with their own eyes that what they had been told was false.

While they were staying at the place mentioned above, the lord emperor acted on the advice of all the princes and promulgated some admirable, necessary and sensible regulations, and he had an oath sworn in every tent to observe these, appointing judges who would impose an appropriate punishment on transgressors. We have inserted these regulations into this work for the notice and edification of posterity.

---

[135]   Hartwig of Utlede, Archbishop of Bremen 1184–1207. He eventually went to the Holy Land by sea in 1197, *Annales Stadenses*, MGH SS xvi.353.

[136]   Ludwig III 'the Pious', Landgrave of Thuringia 1172–90 and Count Palatine of Saxony from 1180, was the son of Barbarossa's half-sister Judith. He had taken part in the fifth Italian expedition, *Dipl. Fred. I*, nos 649 (summer 1176), 653 (July 1176); the campaign against Henry the Lion in 1180, ibid., no. 795, *Annales Magdeburgenses*, MGH SS xvi.194; and the last Italian expedition of 1184–5, *Dipl. Fred. I*, nos 867–70, 877 (all 1184, September–October), 879, 881–5, 887 (November 1184), 923 (November 1185).

[137]   Otto, Count of Geldern 1182–1207, who was married to a sister of Duke Ludwig of Bavaria, and Simon, Count of Tecklenburg, near Osnabrück in Westphalia (d. 1202). Count Simon had recently been in dispute with the Bishop of Osnabrück concerning rights of advocacy over churches in this diocese, *Germania Sacra*, ix(3), ed. Theodor Schieffer (Göttingen 2002), 128 nos 62–3. He was a supporter of Otto IV after 1198, *Urkundenbuch für Niederrheins*, i, nos 562–3, 566.

> In the name of the Father, Son and Holy Spirit, this is the ordination to keep the
> peace according to the form and tenor of these regulations, arising from the will
> of the lord emperor … [*the rest of the text of these regulations has been omitted
> in the surviving manuscripts*].[138]

It was to discern 'the years of the right hand of the most High'[139] that at any time
in such a multitude of sinners and of the proud, both knights and servants, in
such an extraordinary and unusual way sworn peace, concord and the utmost
tranquillity prevailed in this army of Christ and the Holy Cross, to such an extent
that on numerous occasions purses full of money dropped by someone or lost
through carelessness were produced and made public by those who found them,
and they were restored without delay to those who had made public a true report
of the number of lost pence or the weight of silver. The same thing happened
with horses and other lost property. Some indeed of the pilgrims who wounded
others immediately had their hands cut off in accordance with the punishments
prescribed, while several men accused of breaching the market regulations were
ordered to be beheaded.

Both the lord emperor and the whole army were joyfully received by the
illustrious King Bela of Hungary, when they met each other and had a discussion
near Strigonia, or as it is also called Gran, the leading city of Hungary,[140] on the
octave of Pentecost, that is 4 June, and there was great celebration among all the
people and from each different group. Queen Margaret of Hungary, the sister of
the King of France, gave the emperor a double-[skinned] tent of great beauty and
size, the interior of which had four rooms, admirably lined in red linen, the breadth
of the exterior was such that, as I said, it covered four rooms. Moreover the king
provided him and his men with laden ships and wagons filled with loaves of bread,
wine, and barley as fodder for the horses, as well as oxen and sheep sufficient
for many days, along with three camels. Moreover, he entertained the emperor
for two days on a broad island on the Danube with hospitality and hunting, and
he lodged the army in the most fertile grassy plain in his whole country. He also
allocated two houses in the city of Gran, from one of which flour and from the
other oats were distributed to the poor pilgrims. He ordered that the lord emperor
be received with solemn procession and great splendour in episcopal cities and
other towns. But whether he did this with the eye of simplicity or otherwise, that
is from love or fear, was not clear at this time, since afterwards, during our dispute
with the Greeks, the king rendered himself somewhat suspect. The Hungarians
took considerable advantage of our men in one matter, the changing of money or
silver, inasmuch as for two pennies of Cologne they gave as many as five of their
own pennies, and four Hungarian pennies for two pennies of Freising, and for a

---

[138]   According to the *Chronica Regia Coloniensis*, p. 144, this *lex malefactorum* was
promulgated on 28 May.
[139]   Psalm 76:11 (Vulgate), 77:10 (AV).
[140]   Modern Esztergom.

penny of Regensburg or Krems they gave one Hungarian penny, which was barely worth one of Verona.[141]

The entire army was put to great labour in crossing the River Drau, called in the vernacular the Trâ, where some men and horses were swept under by the river's current, while everybody else looked on. We celebrated the nativity of St John the Baptist at a village called St George, at one mile's distance from Francavilla, in the march that lies between Hungary and the frontier of Greece.[142] We then passed Sirmium on the vigil of the apostles Peter and Paul.[143] This was once a famous city, but now it seems to be in ruins and is a quite miserable place. We crossed the River Sava or Saue where it flows into the Danube, more easily than the Drau, and soon we were in the land under the jurisdiction of the Greeks, at the end of the fifth week after we had entered Hungarian territory at Pressburg. We celebrated the feast of the most blessed apostles there on the bank of the Sava, in a semi-destroyed Greek town, called in German Wizzenburch, and in Greek Belgrade, sited opposite the town of Kubin. It was extremely peaceful there, and a milder climate than usual smiled upon us, so that the midges, gnats, flies and serpents which had much annoyed us as we travelled on horseback through the summer heat in Hungary did not harm either us or our animals, something that we had rarely experienced as we journeyed through Hungary.

We crossed the river on 1 July.[144] On the 2nd, we came through the forest to Branchevo, where we sent back all the ships, and started to load our carts and wagons. With imperial generosity the glorious emperor gave all these ships,[145] constructed by the carpenters with extraordinary skill for the pilgrims of Christ, to the king of Hungary, recompensing his gifts with greater ones. Count Frederick of Abenberg, a young man of quality, was girded with the sword there.[146] There too those counts whom we mentioned above and the citizens of Metz, along with the Archbishop of Tarantaise, joined our army. During that stay Count Engelbert of Berg ended his days at Kubin. There also the King of Hungary honoured the lord emperor through his envoys bearing most welcome presents. The Duke of Branchevo received the emperor well, so far as the eye could see, but 'the result

---

[141] The *denarius* of Cologne was the most widely distributed coin in twelfth-century Germany, and almost two-fifths of the so-called Barbarossa Hoard of coins abandoned on the Crusade were pennies from Cologne, Murray, 'Finance and logistics', pp. 359, 363. The Freising mint had been granted to the bishop by Conrad III in 1140, *Die Urkunden Konrads III. und seiner Sohnes Heinrich* , ed. F. Hausmann (MGH Diplomata Regum et Imperatorum Germaniae ix, Vienna 1969), pp. 77–8 no. 46.

[142] 24 June: St George, now Tschalma. Francavilla was also called Mangyelos.

[143] 28 June: modern Mitrovica.

[144] The Sava was the frontier between the kingdom of Hungary and Byzantine territory, *Historia Peregrinorum*, p. 131.

[145] Following the reading *omnes* of the Strahov manuscript rather than the *omnium* of the Graz one.

[146] *gladio est accinctus*: that is, he was knighted.

proves the deeds',[147] as was made clear by what followed, for he showed the emperor and the whole army that he was deceitful and most wicked, just like the other Greeks. For he led us away from the public road of Bulgaria, or as they say the beaten track, into other places; and furthermore the road by which he took us was rocky and not a main one. He held us up on the instructions of his lord the Emperor of Greece. However, our fellow pilgrims, the Hungarians who had taken the Cross, knew these roads, and travelled two or three days ahead of the army, and with some difficulty they found a road for us, the Greeks being unable to resist. Thus, from the treacherous Greeks 'false witnesses have risen up against me'.[148] But neither was this malevolence sufficient for them, for in that most lengthy forest of Bulgaria, which we started to traverse when we left Branchevo on 11 July, the Greeklings [*Greculi*], Bulgars, Serbians and the semi-barbarous Vlachs lay in ambush, springing forth from their secret lairs to wound those who were last into camp and the servants who went out to collect edible plants or fodder for the horses with poisoned arrows.[149] A few of these were captured, and they then confessed that they had been forced to do these things on the order of their lord the Duke of Branchevo, and above all on the instructions of the Emperor of the Greeks; even so they soon paid the due penalty by very properly being hanged. Nevertheless the whole army of pilgrims laboured greatly in that forest; foragers were murdered wholesale during the daytime, while robbers sent by the Greeks sallied forth, endlessly stealing horses and plundering any carts travelling without an armed escort. The way was extraordinarily difficult, and there was a heavy death toll among those on foot and those of the poor who had rashly eaten up their supplies of food. But even beset by these perils, all of our brave men marched on ever more courageously as a tight-knit force.

Still in the forests of Bulgaria, we were drawing near to the more or less deserted town of Rabnel,[150] when once again an envoy from the King of Hungary to the emperor overtook us. He had news that a short time before the Emperor of Constantinople, the king's son-in-law, had set out from Greece 'beyond the sea', that is the Arm of St George, owing to a military emergency, and after a long march was besieging Philadelphia, where he still was.[151] It was therefore less surprising

---

[147]   Ovid, *Heroides*, 2.85.

[148]   Psalm 26:12 (Vulgate), 27:12 (AV).

[149]   The *Historia Peregrinorum*, p. 133, said that a group of Crusaders returned to burn down Branchevo as a reprisal for the attacks on the army.

[150]   Chroust, *Quellen*, p. 28n, suggested that this was Dubrovica, near the junction between the River Morawa and the Danube. Eickhoff, *Friedrich Barbarossa im Orient*, p. 59, prefers modern Cuprija.

[151]   Philadelphia (in Asia Minor) was held by the rebel Theodore Mangaphas, with whom Isaac eventually reached an agreement, allowing him to remain as governor of that city in return for abandoning his rebellion and any claim to the throne, Brand, *Byzantium Confronts the West*, p. 85. Isaac had married King Bela's young daughter Margaret soon after his accession to the throne [see below, note 207].

that we had still not been greeted or welcomed by any messengers from him. In addition, he revealed that a force of pilgrim knights signed [with the Cross] from Germany had recently entered his kingdom, and wished to join our army.

Meanwhile a messenger from the chancellor of this same emperor of Constantinople arrived with a letter, in an attempt to trick the Emperor of the Romans. The gist of this letter was as follows: that his lord the emperor was indeed quite amazed that our emperor had not previously notified him by accredited envoys of his arrival and that of his army, so that he might have provided him and his army more properly with a hospitable welcome from his own men and prepared a good market for it. However, now that he had been informed of its entry into his kingdom, he had sent some men to meet them who had arrived in secret in the town of Sofia. To this the wise emperor responded briefly, answering word for word: he had already sent on in advance distinguished envoys, namely the Bishop of Münster, the Count of Nassau and his chamberlain, and thus he [*the Byzantine Emperor*] was offering him this opportunity to no purpose. Nevertheless, a letter from these respected envoys had reached the lord emperor, informing him that they had made slow progress but had arrived near Constantinople unharmed; they would remain there during the absence of the Greek emperor, of which they informed him.

At this time messengers from the 'Great Count' of Serbia and Rashka and his brother, an equally powerful count, arrived, announcing the arrival of the counts their lords to meet the most serene emperor, and promising him all sorts of services and obedience. When therefore the army arrived at Nish, once a fortified city but which had been partly destroyed by the often-mentioned King Bela of Hungary during the time of the tyrant of Greece Andronikos,[152] it remained there for three or more days because of the market. This same 'Great Count', called Neaman, and his brother, called Casimir, met the lord emperor there with great ceremony, and they were honourably welcomed by him and by the princes of the army on 27 July.[153] Indeed, as a sign of their devotion they gave the lord emperor splendid and copious amounts of wine, barley, flour, sheep and oxen, and among the other gifts that they gave were six of what they call 'sea cows' or seals, a tame boar and three live deer, which were equally tame. They also honoured the princes who were closest to the emperor in a similar fashion with generous gifts of wine, oxen

---

[152]   The emperor Andronikos Komnenos (1182–5). There was a bridge across the River Morava at Nish, Eickhoff, *Friedrich Barbarossa im Orient*, p. 64.

[153]   Stephen Nemanja was Grand Zupan of Serbia from 1159 onwards, the founder of the medieval Serbian kingdom and ancestor of a dynasty that lasted until 1371. He renounced Byzantine overlordship after 1180 and expanded his principality towards the coast, annexing Kotor. In an attempt to conciliate him, Isaac Angelos gave his niece Eudocia as a wife for his eldest son, c. 1185/7. He abdicated in 1196 and became a monk on Mount Athos, where he founded the monastery of Chilandar and died in 1200. See especially Obolensky, *The Byzantine Commonwealth*, pp. 221–3; and for the marriage of Eudocia, Brand, *Byzantium Confronts the West*, p. 80.

and sheep. Furthermore, they earnestly offered armed assistance from themselves and all their men to the present expedition, and in particular against the Emperor of the Greeks, if it were to happen that he should fight against the army of Christ, something which they now considered he was doing, because of the bandits sent forth by his officers, who were harassing our men at this time (as we have noted earlier), which was causing loss both in people and goods. Moreover these same counts, along with their third brother Miroslav, had occupied the city of Nish with sword and bow, and they claimed all the land around it as far as Stralitz, which they had taken from the Greeks and made subject to their own rule,[154] and they also intended to extend their lordship and power further in every direction. They offered to receive the lands they had conquered through their warlike valour from the hand of the Emperor of the Romans, and to render him homage and fealty, to the everlasting glory of the Roman Empire. They did not indeed offer this because they were in any way forced by fear, but they were moved only by love of him and of the German kingdom. But the lord emperor was mindful that, 'he that walks uprightly walks surely',[155] and he was unwilling to change or abandon the planned journey to the Holy Sepulchre of the Lord through becoming involved in any other conflict; thus he responded graciously to these counts, rendering thanks for their offer, [but saying that] he had undertaken the arduous pilgrimage against the oppressors of the land of Jerusalem for love of Christ, and he had no wish to plot any harm against another Christian ruler through pride or ambition, nor indeed against the King of Greece, provided that the latter provided for the army trustworthy guides and good markets, as he had so often promised. He and his men would, however, take up arms to force their way through, sword in hand, against false Christians who ambushed the pilgrims of Christ, just as though they were pagans.

They also drew the attention of the emperor to another matter that had previously been under consideration, requesting that it be brought to a decision by imperial authority while they were there. This was that the daughter of the illustrious Berthold, Duke of Dalmatia, also called Croatia or Merania, also Margrave of Istria, might be given in marriage to the son of their brother Count Miroslav, Prince of Zachlumia and Rashka, which are the provinces next to Dalmatia. This petition was pleasing to the emperor and the council of princes, who chose to put it into effect, and so Berthold swore that his daughter would in accordance with the agreement be given to the young man Tohu in the Istria region at the next feast of St George,[156] in return for which this same Tohu and his heirs by the daughter of Duke Berthold would on his father's death succeed to his full power before any of his brothers. These counts also confirmed this agreement by giving their right hands.

---

[154]   Stralitz may refer to Sardica, but more probably to Sofia.

[155]   Proverbs 10:9.

[156]   24 April 1190: the prince's name may have been Timoslav.

The reason why these counts had at this time so boldly invaded part of the Greek kingdom was this. On the death of the Emperor Manuel of Constantinople, his son Alexios held the sceptre of rule, but being still quite young he ruled through guardians. A little while earlier his father had also arranged his betrothal to a sister of King Philip of France. However, there arose a certain wicked relation of his called Andronikos, an evil tyrant who had earlier been exiled from the kingdom by Manuel, and with the help of the Turks and other peoples this man invaded the empire of Constantinople. He murdered the boy king and his guardians, poisoned Maria, the sister of King Alexios, and her husband, the son of Margrave Rainier of Montferrat, and exercised his tyranny in Greece for almost six years.[157] Under his rule the empire of Greece was undoubtedly damaged in many ways; for the King of Hungary and the other kings and princes on its borders seized its land for themselves, while the army of the King of Apulia ravaged the coastal cities of Greece. Andronikos was also so moved by cruelty and envy that he sought out almost all the princes of his kingdom with the intention of killing them. It happened that he cunningly summoned a certain Isaac, a poor but noble prince, the eldest son of another Andronikos, planning to murder him. But Isaac was forewarned, and rushed upon him along with the other princes and knights with whom he had conspired. Andronikos was beaten to a pulp, placed on a camel, and led in shame around the city, with the whole populace showering him with stones and filth, and then brought to the sea gate where he was beheaded. Thus this wretched man was 'fallen into the ditch which he made'.[158] His killer, Isaac Angelos, seized the empire and ruled in his place, and to strengthen his throne he received in marriage the daughter of King Bela of Hungary, who had previously been betrothed to Duke Ottokar of Styria.[159] He overcame the army of the King of Apulia through the treachery of some of its members whom he corrupted with bribes, and all but destroyed it.[160] However, the forces of the kingdom of the Greeks grew weaker day by day, for as Scripture truthfully testifies: 'every kingdom divided against itself is brought to desolation'.[161] The kingdom was split into four, and at the time when we were crossing it was very weak and under threat. For in Cyprus a certain man of the royal blood named Isaac had usurped the royal dignity for himself; beyond the Hellespont, that stretch of sea popularly called the Arm of St George, a

---

[157]   Rainier was actually her husband; his father was Margrave William III of Montferrat. Andronikos was emperor for only three years, 1182–5.

[158]   Psalm 7:15.

[159]   Ottokar IV, Margrave and subsequently (from 1180) Duke of Styria (who died childless in 1192). His lands passed by previous agreement to Duke Leopold of Austria [see below, p. 123, note 376].

[160]   The forces of King William II of Sicily captured Thessalonica in 1185 but were eventually defeated.

[161]   Luke 11:17.

certain Theodore was in rebellion in the region of Philadelphia;[162] while Kalopeter the Vlach and his brother Asen with the Vlachs subject to them were exercising tyrannical rule over much of Bulgaria, and especially in the region where the Danube flows into the sea.[163]

During this disturbance in the Greek kingdom, and at the time when the army of the Cross was traversing Bulgaria, the aforesaid counts of Serbia and Rashka took the opportunity to make part of Bulgaria subject to their rule, and they concluded an agreement with Kalopeter against the Emperor of Constantinople. Kalopeter indeed greeted the lord emperor [*Barbarossa*] courteously, both by letter and through messengers, offering his majesty due respect and a promise of faithful assistance against his enemies.

At this time too a certain prince of Greece, Alexios by name, the uncle of the Emperor of Constantinople, was sent as an envoy and deceitfully greeted the lord emperor at Nish on behalf of his emperor, promising guidance and market throughout the whole of Greece, provided however that the entry of him and his army was peaceful: [he said that] the Duke of Branchevo had greatly erred, because he had not guided the emperor faithfully and had not given him in any way the service that his lord had instructed him to do. He also informed the emperor that he himself was marching with an army of warriors against the counts of Serbia, the invaders of the realm of Greece, to keep watch on the frontiers of that land from Sofia, but that the emperor should have no suspicions against him, nor against the Greeks, on that account. But, just like all that the chancellor of the emperor of the men of Constantinople said, while he spoke with his mouth he was lying in his heart.

Meanwhile, as the knighthood of Christ rested at Nish for four days, the lord emperor, the follower of peace and truth, saw that the servants and boys of the army were using the excuse of gathering fodder to plunder the district, and were gradually becoming more unruly and breaking the holy laws that should have been observed to preserve the peace in the land of the Greeks. He took the advice of the princes, and had the Bishop of Würzburg, a sensible and eloquent man, summon others among the knights, and sternly rebuked them all for the breach of the peace and the sworn oath involved in the robberies committed by everyone's boys while collecting corn, honey and vegetables. The bishop then addressed them, and among other things he began with this quotation: 'the people were accursed; neither will I be with you any more unless you repent.' He cited this, and told them of the curse of Achan, for his theft from Jericho, when through the sin of one person a whole

---

[162]   Theodore Mangaphas, for whose revolt in Asia Minor, which was aided by the Sultan of Iconium Qilij Arslan, *Choniates*, pp. 219–20 [above, note 151].

[163]   The Vlachs of eastern Bulgaria had revolted against Isaac Angelos in the summer of 1186. See R.L. Wolff, 'The Second Bulgarian Empire. Its Origin and History to 1204', *Speculum* 24 (1949), 167–206, especially 180–4. The 'tyrannical' nature of their rule can only have been, in the author's opinion, because they were not entitled to exercise it; their revolt had been in reaction to Byzantine exploitation.

people were ruined, whence it is read that the Lord said: 'There is an accursed thing in the midst of thee; O Israel, thou canst not stand before thine enemies.'[164] Through this sermon, which was inspired by the Lord, the disorder that was rife among the servants, which the bishop had condemned, was very much reduced by the action of those knights who had been singled out for rebuke.

The emperor then sensibly and far-sightedly divided the army in future into squadrons and divisions, to ensure that when the enemy arrived they should not find the army of Christ unprepared and in disorder. He appointed as the advance guard the division of his son Frederick, the illustrious Duke of Swabia, and with him were the troops of Bishop Conrad of Regensburg, Margrave Berthold of Vohburg and Margrave Herman of Baden, and those of the five counts from Swabia and the four counts from Bavaria. It was agreed that the standard-bearer of this division should be Count Berthold of Neuenburg. The second division was that of the Bohemians and Hungarians, with each of these peoples having their own standard-bearer. The third division was led by Berthold, the distinguished Duke of Dalmatia,[165] and comprised the troops of six bishops, namely of the venerable Gottfried, Bishop of Würzburg, who was also Duke of eastern Franconia,[166] and of Rudolf of Liège, Diepold of Passau, Herman of Münster, Henry of Basel and Arnold of Osnabrück. This same Duke of Merania was designated as [one] standard-bearer of this division; the other was Count Poppo of Henneberg, who bore the banner of the Bishop of Würzburg. The emperor took the fourth division as his own imperial guard, and in this were the Archbishop of Tarentaise and the Bishop of Meissen, the Count of Holland and his brother, along with another 16 counts, that is the rest of main force of the army. Count Rupert of Nassau was chosen as the standard-bearer of this division; he was a man of experience and skill in matters of war, although he was then being kept at Constantinople along with the other envoys of the lord emperor. Afterwards, at Philippopolis, a fifth division was organised, comprising the infantry and the stronger among the servants of the army.

After making these arrangements, the camp of God moved from Nish and, bidding farewell to our friends the 'Great Counts' of Serbia, we marched onwards through difficult and uneven roads through the forests, and we encountered renewed battles as the enemy Greeks and Vlachs set ambushes and attacked us more strongly.[167] It was reckoned that this was at the behest of Isaac, the Emperor

---

[164]   Joshua, Chapter 7; the quotations are from 7:12–13. The *Historia Peregrinorum*, p. 138, suggested that the bishop preached this sermon during a halt while the army was on the journey between Nish and Sofia. The *Estoire d'Eracles*, c. 92, noted that Bishop Gottfried 'often inspired the Christians by his holy preaching and pious exhortations', Edbury, *Conquest of Jerusalem*, pp. 86–7.

[165]   That is Duke Berthold of Merania.

[166]   The ducal status of the bishop had been confirmed by Frederick in July 1168, *Dipl. Fred I*, iii. 5–7 no. 546.

[167]   From Nish the road left the valley of the Morava and went southeast along the River Nisava; then it climbed over the watershed between the Nisava and Maritsa rivers,

of the Greeks, and we sustained no little loss, both in goods stolen and in the murder of the foragers. Once again some of these bandits hid in the dense thickets alongside the main road, and time and again they unexpectedly shot poisoned arrows at our men as they went along unprotected and unprepared, until wiser counsel prevailed and our columns were guarded by crossbowmen and knights. Those who were captured while committing these nefarious acts duly paid the penalty by deservedly being hanged. It happened, indeed, that the Bishop of Passau and his relative the Duke of Merania were accompanying the baggage train with an armed escort because of this danger when bandits suddenly sprang out from ambush; they immediately manfully set about them with great effect, slaying more than 40 of them, while 24 prisoners were brought back to the camp tied to the tails of horses.[168] We saw them hanging from one gibbet by their feet, as wolves are hung. Frederick the advocate of Berg was most valiant in punishing the bandits in the following way. He saw one of them clinging to the top of a tree, ready to shoot arrows at our men. He [in turn] was shot from the tree by an arrow, and then as an appropriate punishment Frederick had him hanged securely from that same tree to which he had previously been less firmly attached; he then condemned six others to a similar shameful death by hanging, to the terror of the other bandits. The illustrious Duke of Swabia with his columns of Swabians and Bavarians was marching ahead of his father the emperor, in accordance with the ancient legal custom that the Swabians (or Alemanni) and the Bavarians (or Norici) ought always in any open conflict to form the first line of battle to receive the assaults of the enemy. He also captured a great many Bulgarian bandits, and put them to death ignominiously by hanging. Moreover, when they sprang upon the Count of Sayn, who was with his men marching in front of the emperor because of the extraordinary difficulty of the roads, he similarly put up a resolute fight and routed

---

Obolensky, *The Byzantine Commonwealth*, p. 19.

[168]   'Certain men who were marching without proper care fell into the hands of the enemy, by whom they were plundered, two knights were killed, and many others who were leading carts were mortally wounded. Then it happened that when Berthold, the distinguished Duke of Merania, wished to travel on this same road, lo a great force of the enemy sprang from the mountains and attacked from both sides, while the great noise [they made] echoed around the forest and between the mountains. Fiercely attacked by these men on every side, it seemed as if the small force of our men would be unable to resist their multitude, when the duke snatched up his own banner and called out to his men, who were contemplating flight, rallying them. And like a wild boar grinding its teeth which plunges into the middle of the dogs that are harassing it, so this valiant man gallantly plunged into the midst of his enemies and opened the way with his sword. They were forced to retreat. Following the duke's example, our men recovered their courage and manfully attacked their enemies, inflicting many wounds, cutting them to pieces, and knocking them down from the trees in which they had hoped in vain to hide, to receive the death that was waiting for them, and to deter others they hanged 30 of them from one gallows. As a result the wickedness of these people ceased for a little while, while the army of the pilgrims that followed passed through [this place],' *Historia Peregrinorum*, pp. 136–7.

them, so that 12 of them fell in but a moment. There was a knight who was quite ill and being carried in a litter, but as the bandits rushed out his will-power restored his strength, for as the text says, 'the righteous are as bold as a lion'.[169] He leaped from his bed, and fighting bravely he struck one of them in the mouth with his sword, and put the rest to flight; however, as soon as they had scattered in flight his illness returned and he lay down once more in his bed.

Skirmishes of this sort continued for days. The Greek enemies who attacked us were routed in close-quarter fighting by the swords of our men and from afar by the crossbows, and suffered ghastly losses. Nevertheless, the remaining evildoers followed us all the way through the forests of Bulgaria, attacking us from the flanks along the mountain slopes and harassing us with night-time raids, even though they suffered appallingly from all the different missiles launched by our army. While we were on that road the venerable in Christ Abbot of Admont, Isenrich, a man worthy of admiration for the good character, charitable activities and religious life for which he had been distinguished from an early age, migrated to the Lord on 10 August, that is the feast of St Lawrence the Martyr, after making a full confession and while the Divine praises were being sung; he was honourably interred the next day beside the road in a common grave along with [other] pilgrims by Martin, the reverend Bishop of Meissen. We can, not unworthily, say about him what is in the Book of Wisdom: 'he is taken lest evil should change his understanding, or lest deceit should lead his soul astray'.[170] Thus the Lord took him from the midst of iniquity, before the abuse of plundering spread among all in the army of Christ, both through need and through the avaricious greed of certain people, and before, after a little while had elapsed, 'the love of many waxed cold'.[171]

On the fourteenth day after we had left Nish, that is on 13 August, we came to the town of Sofia, which we found empty and lacking through poverty in all human comfort, and it was then that the perjury and open deceit of the Greek emperor and his men began to become clear. Indeed, the foresworn emperor had ordered the market and exchange, promised under oath, to be taken from us, under threat of punishment, and furthermore there was absolutely no sign of the meeting that his chancellor John and the *sebastos* Alexios, a relation of this same Greek emperor, had previously promised to the lord emperor of the Romans. We found no market; except that with all their strength and in every way, 'they have digged a pit for our soul'.[172] On the emperor's orders they had blocked the road junctions with trees that had been cut down and covered with an extraordinary quantity of rocks, and they had fortified the ancient passes of St Basil by renewing the towers and bastions in defiance of the pilgrims of Christ. Our men were, however, aided

---

[169]   Proverbs 28:1.

[170]   Sapientia 4:11. The date of his death is confirmed by the necrology of St Rupert, Salzburg, *Necrologia Germania* (MGH) ii *Dioecesis Salisburgensis*, ed. S. Herzberg-Fränkel (Berlin 1904), 157.

[171]   Matthew 12:24.

[172]   Jeremiah 18:20.

by Divine protection. Placing fire from the machines of the Greeks on the stones and their wooden supports, they reduced them 'to dust and ashes'.[173]

Moving on from Sofia, we camped on the following day, where we were greatly cheered by the arrival of a new group of our pilgrims, who had followed in our tracks with great effort through Hungary and Bulgaria, and now caught up with us. These were Bishop Henry of Toul,[174] and the nobleman Gaubert of Aspremont, along with a noble force of other chosen knights, whom both the emperor and the whole army of the life-giving Cross received with great joy. Marching onwards in full force, we came at length to the last and most narrow passes of Bulgaria, which had been blocked with treacherous devices by the Greeks, as before. There the lord emperor heard that an army of the Greeks was keeping our entry into the plains of Greece under observation.[175] He left part of the army in camp, and accompanied by the squadrons of armoured knights, he broke through the passes after a brief but triumphant fight, intending sensibly to cut through the obstacles that had been placed in various places by the Greeks. The latter turned tail and fled, running away from the imperial majesty and the champions of Christ; anyway they never dared to await the charge of our men.[176]

The emperor came back that same day and efficiently arranged the passage of our men through the passes. So, on 20 August, after burning the machines of the Greeks, we left these many gloomy passes. We had spent six weeks in Bulgaria

---

[173]   Job 30:18. The 'fire from the machines' would seem to be a reference to 'Greek fire', a naptha-based compound that was the napalm of the Middle Ages. Unless this attack was made by an advanced force, the placing of this passage here may be misleading, for the 'passes of St Basil' were the so-called Trajan's Gates, now Vasilitza, the last of the passes to be crossed, Eickhoff, *Friedrich Barbarossa im Orient*, p. 67 (see below).

[174]   *Recte* Peter [see above note 74]. The *Historia Peregrinorum*, p. 139, cites his name correctly at this point.

[175]   *Choniates*, p. 221, said that this force was commanded by the Domestic Alexios Gidos and the Protostrator Manuel Kamyzes. These passes were the Vakerel, at 840 m the highest point on the journey, and the Succi, more usually known as Trajan's Gates, which was the last pass on the route. The road then descended to follow the River Maritsa eastwards, Obolensky, *Byzantine Commonwealth*, pp. 19–20.

[176]   The *Historia Peregrinorum*, p. 139, the account of which is clearer at this point than that of the *Historia de Expeditione*, said that this force, comprising 500 knights 'from among the most outstanding of his army, whose horses also had iron surcoats', was commanded by the Duke of Swabia, and this is supported also by the *Gesta Federici I Imperatoris in Expeditione Sacra*, p. 80. The *HP* added: 'As soon as the Greeks saw those who had been sent in advance to the Gates of St Basil, immediately fear and confusion of mind fell upon them and they withdrew as fast they could, spreading the news throughout the whole army of the Greeks that the indomitable and iron-clad army of the Germans had arrived on iron-clad horses, and it was safer to hasten in flight than to await their terrible attack. On hearing this, the army was greatly afraid and immediately turned and told the citizens of Philippopolis to flee, announcing the arrival of the German people, whose valour no human force could resist in battle.'

from Branchevo onwards, and seven and a half weeks had passed from the feast of the apostles Peter and Paul, when we had crossed the Sava. We now found a level plain full of vines and all sorts of good things, called Circuviz, which came like help to the tired, for there through Divine grace the thirsty army found water and all its wants were relieved. Arriving at the city of Philippopolis on 24 August, which was the feast day of St Bartholomew the Apostle, we found that this town, strongly fortified both by natural position and the work of the engineer, had been left deserted and empty by the Greeks through fear of our men. We pitched camp there.[177] The next day a letter arrived from Isaac, the Greek emperor, full of pride and arrogance, flatly refusing to allow us transit.[178] The lord emperor received this with his customary mildness, opposing his complete humility to the unbridled pride of that man. Clear news then arrived for the first time of the imprisonment of his venerable envoys, namely the Bishop of Münster and his companions.[179] The Emperor Isaac had, with hitherto unheard-of wickedness, thrown them into prison, stripped them of their goods and inflicted all sorts of insults upon them, to the shame of the army of the Holy Cross and of the whole of Christendom, even though they had been sent to him for the sake of peace and friendship, and in defiance of the law and custom of all nations, not only those fighting for the Christian religion but even of barbarian ones. He did this because he wanted to gain the favour of his friend and confederate the Saracen Saladin, the enemy of the Cross and of all Christians.[180] The whole army was infuriated about this, and thereafter they freely plundered the property of the Greeks, and destroyed what they did not plunder.

On 26 August we entered Philippopolis with the utmost enthusiasm, and we found in it much that was useful to the army, as though it had been put there by God for our benefit.[181] And since transit by sea had been denied to us by the Greek emperor, we decided to remain there for the time being, as though it was our own home, gathering the vintage and pressing it, and the crops from the [grain] pits

---

[177]   Now Plovdiv (Bulgaria). To begin with the army camped outside the walls, *Historia Peregrinorum*, p. 140, which noted the fertility of this region.

[178]   The letter was brought by James the Pisan, 'who had first sought safe conduct', *Historia Peregrinorum*, p. 140. The author of the *Historia de Expeditione* returned to the subject somewhat later in his account; see below, p. 75 and note 196.

[179]   The letter written by Bishop Diepold of Passau to the Duke of Austria on 11 November 1189 also mentioned the imprisonment of the envoys, *Chronicon Magni Presbiteri*, MGH SS xvii.510 [translated below, p.150].

[180]   Cf. the very similar sentiments expressed by the 'Itinerary of the Pilgrims', trans. Nicholson, *Chronicle of the Third Crusade*, p. 58.

[181]   Nesbitt, 'Rates of march', 180, suggests that the delay before entering Philippopolis was explicable if the army was because of its size actually strung out over three days' march, and the author of the report on which this section was based was travelling in the rearguard. However, the *Historia Peregrinorum*, p. 140, said that the emperor ordered them to stay outside the walls 'for some days'.

that had been dug, and everyone took back what he needed to the lodging he had been assigned. Indeed, we passed almost eleven weeks in that city; 'since the land was silent in our sight', and the Lord had made them afraid, 'there was neither adversary nor evil occurrent'.[182]

The emperor endured frequent and treacherous plots by the Greeks, who had from the start sought to obstruct him and turn him back – he was, however, unperturbed, and valiant in the face of danger he continued his endeavour with determination. He would have occupied the whole of Macedonia, had not the cause of the Cross, which he had undertaken to conduct, restrained him. He sent an envoy with a letter to his son Henry, the glorious King of the Romans, complaining about this treachery, a copy of which we have also included below.

> Frederick, by the grace of God Roman Emperor and always Augustus, to his beloved son Henry, august King of the Romans, greeting and sincere and fatherly affection. Our imperial goodness has rejoiced in mind and spirit at the receipt of a letter from your excellency, the content of which overjoyed us, and we are happy and greatly reassured to hear of your convalescence. Furthermore, since your royal serenity wishes to learn of how we are personally and of the progress of the glorious army of the life-giving Cross, we shall deal with this first. As soon as we reached the frontiers of the empire of our brother the Emperor of Constantinople, we suffered no small loss through robbery of our goods and the murder of our men, which it was reckoned was undoubtedly done at that emperor's behest. For some of these bandits hid in the dense thickets alongside the main road, and time and again they unexpectedly shot poisoned arrows at our men as they marched by unprotected and unprepared, until wiser counsel prevailed and our columns were guarded on all sides by crossbowmen and knights. Those who were captured while committing these nefarious acts duly paid the penalty by deservedly being hanged; indeed on one day thirty-two of them were hanged on one gallows as wolves are, and thus they shamefully ended their lives. Nevertheless, the remaining evildoers followed us all the way through the forests of Bulgaria, attacking us from the flanks along the mountain slopes and harassing us with night-time raids, even though they suffered miserably from all the many different missiles launched in response by our army. Then the aforesaid Emperor of Constantinople not only did not hesitate to break all the promises which had been publicly sworn in his name and on his behalf by his chancellor at Nuremberg, but he also deprived us of exchange and market, under threat of punishment. He ordered the road junctions to be blocked with trees that had been cut down and covered with huge rocks, and he instructed that certain ancient fortifications in the passes, ruined through age, which served as a protection and defence for all of Bulgaria, should be strengthened by renewing the towers and bastions, against the honour of God and of the holy and life-giving Cross, to our detriment and that of the whole of Christianity. Our men were, however, aided by Divine protection. Placing fire

---

[182] I Maccabees 1:3; I Kings 5:4.

from the machines of the Greeks on the stones and their wooden supports, they reduced them 'to dust and ashes'. Therefore, after through the grace of God victoriously crossing all the passes, we came into the plain of Circuviz, filled with all sorts of good things, and so we spent six weeks in this most laborious crossing of Bulgaria. Then we came to the city of Philippopolis, a very wealthy town, strongly fortified both by natural position and the work of the engineer, left utterly deserted and seemingly abandoned, which we occupied. And behold, the next day we received a letter from the Emperor of Constantinople, written with great pride, which resounded with threats, blandishments and complaints in equal measure. Then also we received clear and detailed news for the first time of the imprisonment of our envoys, the Bishop of Münster, Count Rupert and Markward the chamberlain. While we were still stationed in Hungary, he ordered them to be arrested, which was an insult to the Creator and a scandalous denigration of the Cross for which they were fighting, and with little regard for his reputation and against the law of all nations regarding envoys he shamefully ordered them to be thrown naked into prison. On hearing this, the whole army of the Cross was infuriated, and thereafter unceasingly occupied and plundered towns, castles and villages, until the Emperor of Constantinople told us by letter that he was prepared to return these envoys of our majesty to us with great honour. Finally, after many embassies and deceitful claims by whining envoys, with which he has now been trying our patience for a long time, we have halted our march during the winter's cold. Our envoys have been sent back to our majesty, like goods well used, but he has kept more than two thousand marks of their money. He has made cunning offers to us, promising once again safe transit, an abundance of ships, good markets and the customary exchange. But since, as the popular saying goes, 'he who has been burned fears the fire', we have decided to winter at Philippopolis, having no trust any more in the oaths and pretences of the Greeks. Our son the Duke of Swabia, your highness's brother, will be staying with a substantial part of the army at another town, named Berrhoë, some ten miles from our quarters, until the warmth of spring replaces the inclemency of the winter season.

Since, therefore, our crossing of the Arm of St George will be impossible until we obtain hostages from the Emperor of Constantinople, [who must be] without exception men of great distinction and importance, and we make the whole of Romania subject to our empire, we urgently request your prudent and noble royal person to send suitable envoys from your serene majesty to Genoa, Venice, Ancona, Pisa and other places to obtain a squadron of galleys and other vessels, to meet us at Constantinople around the middle of March, so that they may attack the city by sea while we do so by land. Furthermore, we urge [your] royal discretion to have the money that is owed to us in various places collected at once, with the assistance of the chancellor, and of H[enry?], Werner of Boland and Richolf our notary,[183] and you have it deposited in the house of Bernardo the Venetian, our

---

[183]   The chancellor was presumably still John, Archbishop of Trier 1189–1212, though the last record of him as such was on 12 May 1189. H. was probably the protonotary Henry,

agent, and then with the advice of the wise it is to be transported to Tyre. For you know that this will be very necessary to us because of the unexpected delay we are about to make, and especially since we have not received the money from Ancona and also various other places, namely Metz and Bremen, and from the Count of *Honau*.[184] We do indeed have a host of chosen knights in the army of the life-giving Cross, however what we really need is the assistance of prayers to the Almighty, for 'there is no king saved by much strength',[185] but rather through the grace of the Eternal King, which surpasses the merits of individuals. Therefore may we ask your royal kindness that you make every effort to ensure that the men of religion of our empire unceasingly pour out prayers to God on our behalf. We also remind your discretion and encourage you in Christ to exercise your royal hand in judgement and act with burning zeal against evildoers [as is worthy] of your royal dignity. By doing this you will acquire the grace of God and the favour of the people. Do not forget to write to the Pope, asking him that he send out men of religion through the various provinces, who are to encourage the people of God against the enemies of the Cross, and especially against the Greeks, since the Patriarch of Constantinople preached publicly in the church of St Sophia, in the presence of our envoys, the Bishop of Münster and his colleagues, that if any Greek should kill a hundred pilgrims, and even if he was guilty of the murder of ten Greeks, he would be granted indulgence by the Lord. You are to have the island castle of Suibert and [the fortifications at] Nymwegen completed and carefully guarded, since we judge these to most important. We have lost more than a hundred pilgrims, who through their deaths have journeyed to the Lord. We have [also] sustained a huge loss in horses. Many pilgrims from our empire, especially from Provence and Soest, who travelled to Constantinople to meet us, are being held prisoner there. We have now remained for twelve weeks at Philippopolis.[186] Every town and castle between Philippopolis and Constantinople has been found uninhabited.[187]

---

subsequently Bishop of Worms 1192–6. Werner (II) of Boland was an imperial *ministerialis* from the Rhineland, probably the wealthiest *ministerialis* in Germany at this period, who at one time or other held benefices from no fewer than 44 different lords: for him Bosl, *Reichsministerialät*, pp. 260–74. Master Richolf 'our notary' witnessed a privilege of the emperor for the Archbishop of Tarantaise at Pavia in May 1186, *Dipl. Fred. I*, no. 938.

[184]   Probably Baldwin V, Count of Hennegau, although Chroust, p. 42 note 5, suggests as an alternative, perhaps a royal official from Hagenau.

[185]   Psalm 32:16 (Vulgate), 33:16 (AV).

[186]   If taken literally this would suggest that this letter was written on 18 November 1189, which was indeed the day before Frederick sent back an envoy with the departing Hungarian contingent. See below.

[187]   The Latin text of this letter is also given by *Dipl. Fred. I*, iv.302–5 no. 1009. At the same time, Frederick sent a much shorter letter to Duke Leopold of Austria, ibid., pp. 306–7 no. 1010.

During this period, Frederick, the illustrious Duke of Swabia, heard that an army of Greeks had taken station about three miles away from our men, not indeed to seek open battle with us but staying hidden to observe our army. He mustered a force of picked knights, who got ready while it was still dark, and at dawn he ordered them to attack the enemy, sword in hand. He would indeed have succeeded in this as he intended if they had not been forewarned of this deadly danger and escaped as best they could through a wild flight. As they fled from their camp our men burst forth and attacked them from the flank, inflicting savage wounds, from which more than fifty of them fell, including a standard-bearer. The rest escaped death by flight.[188] After this victory it was then decided by the emperor and the princes that this same glorious duke, together with his relative Duke Berthold of Merania, would be sent with the bulk of the army to storm a very wealthy city called Berrhoë, which was held by some pagans and Turks who were mercenaries [*tributarii*] of the Emperor of Constantinople. As he was approaching the city gate one Tuesday,[189] and was drawing up his knights in squadrons either to fight the enemy in the open or for an attack on the city itself, lo they saw the enemy in arms outside the gates, observing our men. They seemed as if they were about to do something significant, and to offer the battle that was desired to our men, but this was far from the case, for as soon as they heard the noise of the sergeants and squires [*pueri militiari*] rushing noisily upon them they shamefully turned tail, and sought safety by fleeing through the opposite gate of the city and climbing up into the mountains. Our men took possession of the city, and they found there a great abundance of wheat, barley, flour, wine, oxen and sheep, and they also collected a quantity of all sorts of clothing, until they were almost tired of doing so. They remained there for four days, and then returned to [the rest of] our men laden with booty.[190]

---

[188] The *Historia Peregrinorum*, p. 141, suggested that this Greek force was hoping to ambush foragers from the Crusader army, and added that the 50 dead (which number it confirms) were Alan mercenaries rather than Greeks. This 'Greek' army was commanded by Manuel Kamytzes, Brand, *Byzantium Confronts the West*, pp. 180–1.

[189] This would seem to have been either 30 August or 6 September 1189. Berrhoë is now Stara Zagora, Eickhoff, *Friedrich Barbarossa im Orient*, p. 69.

[190] 'A few days went by and news arrived that another army of the Greeks had recently mustered at the city of Berrhoë. The aforesaid duke and his relation the Duke of Merania planned similarly to launch an attack on this with a strong force. When the Greeks heard of the arrival of our men, they drew up their squadrons and left the city as if threatening to perform some great deed. But as soon as they saw the columns of our men with their arms glittering threateningly, they immediately abandoned the city like stupid sheep attacked by wolves and fled to the mountains. Our men entered the city, and then returned victoriously to Philippopolis, with their horses and carts laden with booty and spoils.' *Historia Peregrinorum*, p. 141.

Nevertheless the marshal of the emperor, Henry of Kalden, a man who was valiant in battle but impatient in idleness,[191] forced the inhabitants of a castle called Scribention, which was famous for the strength of its defences, to surrender unexpectedly, made this subject to the lordship of his imperial majesty, and established a garrison there. Above this place a monastic cloister had been established, the abbot of which was a man born in Ireland, whom Henry brought to the emperor. The latter thereafter treated him in a friendly fashion and was at pains to show him unexpected honour. The marshal, accompanied by the Bishop of Passau and the Duke of Merania, then took his lord's military household and launched an attack on a town called Brandovei.[192] The inhabitants made a fierce attack on our men, and fought bravely for some time, but finally they turned tail in the usual manner and took refuge in the town, throwing stones and firing arrows at our men from the walls. Our men besieged the town and sent a messenger to the lord duke asking him to bring reinforcements. But before he arrived, the inhabitants became disheartened and surrendered. They were granted their lives, handed over the town and its wealth to our men, and abandoned it. The fortified town of Perna similarly surrendered to our men.[193] So, in short, the army of Christ and the Holy Cross gained the three towns mentioned above and some ten castles, along with the entire surrounding region. Hence the Armenians and some of the Bulgarians who dwelt in part of that land in return for tribute went to the lord emperor and the leaders of the army. They most humbly sought, and indeed urgently begged, that they and their villages might be granted peace, taking an oath of fealty and subjection, and on condition that they would provide a market at Philippopolis to sell goods to the army for the entire length of its stay there. This they faithfully did.[194]

---

[191]   He was an imperial *ministerialis*, son of Henry of Pappenheim, who had been Frederick I's marshal in the early part of his reign. He was one of the Staufen dynasty's most loyal servants, who subsequently played an important part in the conquest of the kingdom of Sicily by Henry VI, and then in 1209 avenged the murder of Philip of Swabia. He took part in Otto IV's Italian expedition of 1210–11, before returning to his family's traditional allegiance to the Staufen. He died probably on 8 March 1214. See Hucker, *Kaiser Otto IV*, pp. 394–5.

[192]   Modern Woden/Vodena.

[193]   Modern Petritch, south of Plovdiv, Eickhoff, *Friedrich Barbarossa im Orient*, p. 70.

[194]   *Choniates*, p. 222, noted that the Armenians of Philippopolis welcomed the Germans, something he ascribed to the fact that 'they agree with each other in most of their heresies'. The Armenian Archbishop of Philippopolis had earlier been involved in the negotiations between the papacy and the Armenian Church, for which Introduction note 61, above, and Dédéyan, 'Le Revirement politico-religieux', p. 190. The *Chronica Regia Coloniensis*, p. 146, added that after this agreement some young men of the army robbed the Armenians who were bringing supplies to the army. The emperor ordered them to be beheaded, and despite pleas to him for mercy insisted that this sentence be carried out. Seeing this, the Armenians brought in more and more supplies.

Meanwhile the most serene emperor, as 'a faithful and wise steward of the Lord's household',[195] took steps for the welfare of the army of the Holy Cross. He appointed pentarchs, or masters for each fifty knights, so that all the knights were divided up into groups of fifty, commanded by their own masters both in matters of warfare and for the settlement of disputes, although he reserved the rights of the imperial marshal. He also chose sixty of the best and wisest men from the army, by whose advice and direction all the affairs of the army might be ordered. However, somewhat later wiser counsel prevailed, and with good reason a smaller number of masters were appointed, and the previous sixty were reduced to sixteen.

While this was taking place, the often-mentioned emperor was also concerned by the captivity of the illustrious men whom he had sent as his envoys. He ignored for the time being the vainglorious and quite unworthy embassy sent from the Greek emperor to him as Roman emperor and its shameful cunning,[196] while he now sent two prudent envoys to Constantinople, Werner a canon of St Victor of Mainz and a knight, Gottfried, after first securing a sworn undertaking from some of the Greek princes that they would be allowed a safe journey.[197] These envoys were to reassure the Greek emperor concerning the problems that the latter had raised with our emperor of the Romans, namely that he had never given Bulgaria or any other land under Greek jurisdiction as a benefice to the Great Count of Serbia, the enemy of Greece who had met with us at Nish, nor had he ever conspired with any king or prince against the kingdom of Greece. For that cunning man had used these difficulties and quibbles against us as excuses to explain away his sins and to conceal his wickedness and the treacherous imprisonment of the innocent envoys of the emperor and the army of Christ. The aforesaid envoys, however, received instructions to remind Isaac, the Emperor of the Greeks, of the oath sworn on his behalf to the Emperor of the Romans and the army of Christ by his chancellor at Nuremberg, to provide safe passage by road and a sea crossing for this same glorious army, and how right from the start he had violated this in every way, and that the imprisonment of his envoys was a crime unheard of for many centuries,

---

[195]   Luke 12:42.

[196]   This was still the same embassy that included James of Pisa, discussed by the *Historia Peregrinorum*, p. 140. The salutation of the emperor's letter quoted in that text would certainly justify, in German eyes, the adjective 'vainglorious', addressed as it was from the 'Emperor appointed by God, the most holy, the most excellent, the most powerful [and] sublime ruler of the Romans, heir to all the world and to the great Constantine', while calling Frederick simply 'great prince of Germany'. The account then summarised the letter, claiming that Isaac did offer free passage and provision of markets, but only if Frederick handed over his son the Duke of Swabia and six bishops or other leading men as hostages, in addition to the envoys who had already been detained. See below pp. 78–9, where the episode was discussed once again.

[197]   Gottfried, subsequently identified as Gottfried of Wiesenbach [below, p. 92], had earlier been sent on an embassy to the Sultan Qilij Arslan, *History of the Pilgrims* [below, p. 146]. Werner was probably the Werner, *scholasticus* of St Victor, Mainz, who had witnessed a charter of Archbishop Conrad in March 1189, *Mainzer Urkundenbuch* ii(2).847 no. 514.

and that with regard to all these matters he ought to consider both his reputation and honour, and the safety and stability of his kingdom. These two subordinate envoys were similarly detained for such a long time that we began to despair of their return, but eventually, after many subterfuges and deceitful stories on the part of the Greeks, both in letters and through their envoys, we recovered through [the assistance of] Divine power the envoys whose return we had long sought, namely the Bishop of Münster, Count Rupert of Nassau and his relative Count Walram, Count Henry the younger of Diez, and Markward the emperor's chamberlain, who with the other picked knights were freed from their chains, and returned with the two subordinate envoys. They were welcomed with great rejoicing by the whole army and a ceremonial greeting by everyone at Philippopolis on 28 October, which is the feast of saints Simon and Jude. O how many tears of joy were shed by the multitude when many raised their voices and whole-heartedly repeated over and over that passage from the Gospel, 'It was meet that we should be glad, for this thy brother was dead, and is alive again; and was lost, and is found'?[198] Indeed, the emperor himself could not restrain his tears, as he welcomed these valuable and much-wanted men whom he had snatched when hope seemed lost from the jaws of death and the throats of the wolves. A number of leading men among the Greeks arrived with them, namely the chancellor and four other noblemen, whom the Greeks customarily call *sebastos*, sent by their lord, who deceitfully promised, as though these were things that had actually been done, the sea crossing over the Hellespont, the market that had already been promised for a long time and that fair exchange for the army had just been arranged.[199] For the crafty Greek emperor had postponed the crossing of the pilgrims of Christ until the harsh winter season; furthermore in this crossing he had prepared for us, innocent and unprepared as we were, a triple ambush through his Turks and Cumans,[200] so that our army would become divided into two parts, on either side of the Arm of St George, ostensibly through a shortage of ships. It would then be attacked, while those who were at sea would be surrounded by the galleys of these same enemies and given over to death.

This sea, the Proponticum, which is called by the local inhabitants the Arm of St George, lies between Seston and Abydon, and from the famous story of Phrixus and Helle is called the Hellespont, and is called the Proponticum because it lies before the Pontic Sea. The historians claim that the current is driven by two great rivers, the Tanais and the Danube; it flows finally and more weakly into the

---

[198]   Luke 15:32.

[199]   The leader of this embassy was once again John Dukas Kamateros, the Logothete of the Drome.

[200]   The Cumans were a nomadic people who had taken over the region in south Russia between the Dnieper and the Don during the later eleventh century, and had penetrated into Bulgaria after their defeat of the Pechenegs, in alliance with the Byzantines, in 1091, Obolensky, *The Byzantine Commonwealth*, pp. 214, 229.

Adriatic or Tirrenian Sea near ancient Troy.[201] In this crossing the snares of his treachery were set in motion against us.

However, since 'in vain the net is spread in the sight of any bird',[202] and, as the popular saying goes, he who has been burned fears the fire, the tricks of the Greeks, which had been revealed by many instances, and both by our often-mentioned envoys and by those Armenians who were more loyal to our most victorious emperor, were not unknown us, and the emperor was careful not to put any trust in their treacherous tales unless their truthfulness was corroborated by the giving of agreed and most carefully chosen hostages.

The day after the triumphal return of the sought-after envoys, that is on 29 October, these same envoys recounted to the assembled princes, clergy and knights the miserable tragedy of their shameful captivity, robbery, hunger, mockery and many other insults, and how the Greek emperor had added to their grief by giving the best of the horses that the embassy had as a gift to the envoys of Saladin the Saracen; the latter then mounted them, and riding round and round they made gestures over their necks by way of insult. The envoys then described how at this same time when that pseudo-Apostle the Patriarch of Constantinople preached to the people on feast days he called the pilgrims of Christ 'dogs', and how he was accustomed also to preach that if any Greek should kill a hundred pilgrims, even one who was guilty of the murder of ten [other] men, he would be free and absolved, both from the guilt of his former murders and from all his other sins.[203] After this sad tale had been told, the envoys of the Greeks were then admitted, among whom was the chancellor. After making the customary greeting, he produced a letter full of lies and deceit, in which indeed he [*the Greek emperor*] expressly promised to the army of Christ the setting-up of a fair and [to arrange] a crossing over the Hellespont between the towns of Abydos and Systos, 'but there is no faithfulness in their mouth, and the Lord will abhor the bloody and deceitful man'.[204]

---

[201]   This passage was taken from the *Gesta Friderici I Imperatoris*, I.47 [*The Deeds of Frederick Barbarossa by Otto of Freising and his Continuator Rahewin*, trans. C.C. Mierow (New York 1953), p. 80]. The Tanais is the River Don. The 'Adriatic or Tirrenian' should of course more properly be the Aegean. Phrixus and Helle were the cousins of Jason, in the legend of the Argonauts. Helle drowned in the Bosphorus (Hellespont) as she and her brother fled from their father Athamas, whose mind had been poisoned against them by their stepmother Ino.

[202]   Proverbs 1:17.

[203]   John Dositheus, patriarch from c. May 1189 (after an abortive attempt by Isaac II to install him a year or so earlier had been frustrated by clerical opposition), who abdicated his see in September 1191. For his career, *Choniates*, pp. 222–4; Brand, *Byzantium Confronts the West*, pp. 100–1; Michael Angold, *Church and Society in Byzantium under the Comneni 1081–1261* (Cambridge 1995), pp. 122–4. A very similar account of the envoys' denunciation of 'the treachery of the Greeks' is given by the *Historia Peregrinorum*, p. 143.

[204]   Psalm 5:6, 9. The crossing proposed was at the narrowest point of the Hellespont, Abydos on the southern shore being near modern Cannakale.

To begin with, the greeting clause of this letter caused no little offence to the ears of all who were listening, for in his customary fashion this same little Greek mendaciously called himself the Emperor of the Romans, while he referred to our most serene and august lord not as Emperor of the Romans but only as 'King of the Germans'. Once this letter had been read and translated, the lord emperor, filled with Divine grace, was unwilling any longer to suffer in silence the rash pride of this foolish king and the borrowed title of the false emperor of the *Romeón*. He came out with these words among others. 'To all those who are of sound mind,' he said, 'there is only one Roman emperor, the sole ruler or *monarchos*, just as there is one universal father, namely the Pontiff of the Romans. I have held the sceptre of the Roman empire in peace for more than thirty years, with no contradiction from any king or prince, and I have been anointed and raised up by the imperial blessing by the supreme pontiff in the city of Rome, while my predecessors who have ruled as Roman emperors for more than four hundred years have gloriously transmitted their rule to me. This rule has been translated from the city of Constantinople back to Rome, the original seat of the empire, the capital of the world,[205] to the acclamation of the Romans and the princes of the empire, and by the authority of the supreme pontiff and the holy Catholic Church, because of the tardy and ineffective assistance offered to the Church by the Emperor of Constantinople against tyrants. I am, therefore, amazed that my brother, your Emperor of Constantinople, usurps for himself an inappropriate and unwarranted title and glories in an honour that does not belong to him and is utterly foolish, when he should clearly know that I, Frederick, am in name, word and reality Emperor of the Romans and always Augustus. Furthermore, he greets me in writing in the fellowship of fraternal love, when he has excluded himself from fraternal trust, indeed also from the holy Christian religion, by his arrest and imprisonment of my faithful envoys, noblemen and pilgrims of Christ who were wearing the sign of the Holy Cross, and who were entirely blameless; he has [also] stolen their property, he has made them suffer hunger, and he has inflicted many insults upon them. Unless therefore he restores what has been taken to my envoys and makes suitable satisfaction for the injury done to them without cause, unless he greets me in his letters with proper respect and the name of Roman emperor, and unless he pledges his faith to us with most distinguished hostages for the proper fair and market, and for safe transit over the sea that is called the Arm of St George, he should in no way dare to send envoys or letters to us again. However, he should know that with Divine help we will undoubtedly carve our way to the sea, sword in hand. Nor,' he said, 'shall I conceal this, that in his previous embassy this same lord of yours demanded with foolish pride his grace of me, while as all

---

[205]   This linking of German imperial rule with Rome as the *caput orbis* had first appeared under Otto III and this imperial rhetoric had been further developed under the early Salians, T. Struve, 'Renovatio imperii', in *Europa in Construzione. La Forza delle identità, la ricerca di unità (secoli IX-XIII)*, ed. G. Cracco, J. Le Goff, H. Keller and G. Ortalli (Bologna 2006), p. 89.

the world knows I do not require grace of any man, but only the grace of God Almighty and the prayers to God of men of goodness.'

The envoys replied that they were unable to respond to these reproaches, and after they had tried to deceive the emperor with all sorts of evasions and unlikely promises, to absolutely no effect, they returned in confusion to their homeland, using the imperial speech recorded above as an excuse.[206] The lord emperor of Constantinople did indeed to some extent heed the emperor in the wording of his reply, for while in his first letter this same Greek emperor had dared to address our lord, the august Emperor of the Romans, as the King of Germany, in his second one he called him 'the most high-born Emperor of Germany', and then in his third and subsequent letters he wrote of him as 'the most noble Emperor of ancient Rome', so that the greeting clause of his letter was translated as follows: 'Isaac Angelos, the follower of Christ, crowned by God, the sublime, powerful and exalted heir to the crown of Constantine the Great and Governor of the *Romaioi*, to the most noble Emperor of ancient Rome and King of the Germans, the beloved brother of his empire, greeting, fraternal affection and love, etc.'.

Meanwhile, once this meeting had been concluded, we were making preparations to move on from Philippopolis, when an envoy of the King of Hungary arrived with a letter, concerning which every wise man could quietly pay heed, since [in it] this same king appeared indeed less faithful to the lord emperor and to the whole army of Christ, but he was an indefatigable protector or helper to his son-in-law the Greek emperor, to the detriment of all our men. He was also less mindful that he had [another] most noble son-in-law in the army of Christ, namely the illustrious Duke of Swabia, a man distinguished by the virtues of courage and probity.[207] In the letter that he sent the king asked that, since it appeared that we were making no progress, permission to return to their homes should not be denied to any of the Hungarians who had taken the Cross of Christ and were with us. This

---

[206]   The *Historia Peregrinorum*, p. 144, added that: 'After listening to this [Frederick's speech], the chancellor and the rest of the Greeks, thinking that they were now threatened by the torment of prison, were greatly afraid, and they saw that their most recent mistake was worse than the previous one. The emperor realised their fear, and noting their pallor he continued, in addition to his previous words. "It is obvious that all this is not your fault, insofar as your lord has acted against his proper dignity, but however this has happened, it is not going to cause you any harm, since it is not the custom of the Roman Empire to harm any envoys or cause them injury, and we are not going to follow your example in this. I trust, however, that my brother, your lord, will do one thing before I leave the borders of his kingdom; he will restore in full whatever is acknowledged to have been taken from the property and valuables of my ambassadors." After the emperor had spoken, the Greeks said that they had not come instructed or empowered to respond to such things. So the peace negotiations remained inconclusive and they returned to Constantinople, announcing nothing apart from news of dispute and the threat of wars.'

[207]   This is the only mention of the (presumably) betrothal of Duke Frederick to a daughter of the King of Hungary. Isaac Angelos had married his daughter Margaret (then aged about ten) in 1185, Wolff, 'The Second Bulgarian Empire', p. 182.

implied that the army of Christ and the Holy Cross would be rendered weaker by their withdrawal, although after their departure we did not notice any diminution. The lord emperor postponed his reply to this message for a while, since he was busy in arranging for our departure from Philippopolis, and was trying to decide what to do about that town, for if everyone set off together it would be left entirely empty – it might then be occupied once again and garrisoned by our enemies – this would be the work of Satan and would do us harm. Therefore five bishops from the army were selected to guard the city, along with all their men; these were the bishops of Liège, Passau, Münster and Toul, and the Archbishop of Tarentaise, along with other distinguished knights and some picked troops. The bulk of the army's baggage and of its money was also left here.

Once these matters had been arranged, we left Philippopolis on 5 November, and set off on the journey towards Adrianople, in the vicinity of which an army of Greeks once again stood mustered, and on the third day we came to the town of Blisimos. There we stayed for seven days, during which time the lord emperor returned with a few men to Philippopolis and held more secret discussions with the princes whom he had left to guard the city. We then went forward, unwillingly, but when we were not very far from Adrianople the Hungarian contingent agreed to demand to go back, and return thence to 'the flesh pots of Egypt'.[208] Alas! The pious emperor gave them permission to return to their homeland and their lord king, as they wished. Three Hungarian counts or barons and their companions remained with us; all the others, including six counts and the Bishop of Raab returned home on 19 November. The emperor despatched two envoys with them, one to his illustrious son the King of the Romans and the princes of the empire, who was to inform them of his situation and of that of his army; the other he sent to the King of Hungary, explaining to him in detail the tricks and lies of his son-in-law the Emperor of Constantinople, and on the other hand the innocence of both him and all his brothers the pilgrims of Christ.[209] The envoys had an easy journey and around Christmas time they met the King of Hungary at a town of his, called in the German language Czilnburg.

The army of the most Holy Cross pursued the Greek forces wherever they went, and sometimes passed through their deserted camps, but they never brought them to battle. We reached Adrianople, arriving there on 22 November, which just like other places we found to be empty.[210] Entering it joyfully, we made our quarters there and spent the winter season in that city. Meanwhile the venerable Bishop Conrad

---

[208]   Exodus 16:3.

[209]   This was the cleric Eberhard, whose embassy was discussed later in the account. The letter to Henry VI was that copied into the account above.

[210]   Adrianople, which had been the principal Byzantine city in Thrace, is now Edirne (Turkey). 'The city of Adrianople received its name from its founder. It is an admirable and famous city, both from the suitability of its site and from the fertility of the nearby regions. Although it is defended on the western and southern sides by the waters of two rivers flowing through, it lies further strengthened by walls and towers on the outside, while inside

of Regensburg, guided by a pilgrim who was a citizen of Regensburg, but knew this province and the Greek language, occupied the city of Probaton,[211] from which the Greeks had [also] fled, with his troops, although he soon discovered abundant supplies for himself and his companions there. After that the emperor's son, the distinguished Duke of Swabia, valiantly attacked Dimotika, an exceedingly strong city, garrisoned by Cumans and Greeks who were braver and more ardent [than usual]. Although its inhabitants resisted most strongly, confident in the strength of the defences as well as their own efforts, our men set about their task no less fiercely. The first to mount the wall, by a most difficult climb, was a certain knight from Worms called Hugh, who [then] charged steadfastly with his banner into the enemy. The duke's standard-bearer and [his] marshal Dietmar,[212] with some other knights, manfully broke through the city gate and followed him into the town. They stormed this place on 24 November. Although many were wounded by javelins and other missiles, only three of our knights were killed here; however, all those who were found in the town, apart from women and small children, were put to the sword – their number was reckoned to be more than 1,500. During the sack of this city one of our knights recognised three of his horses that had been stolen from him by bandits in Bulgaria.

We have truthfully recounted to our readers the noteworthy deeds performed by our men in battle, in accordance with the just judgement of God. There occurred here another memorable event, which ought not to be passed over in silence. A huge vat was discovered, which in accordance with the local custom was full of wine that had been most wickedly adulterated with poison. Unaware of this, all those of our men who were there drank from it, but through Divine clemency they remained unharmed, and they enthusiastically invited their companions to drink. However, when they observed that some of the Greek common folk were laughing mockingly, as if a nasty fate was threatening our men, the latter began to suspect poison. They realised that this was in fact the case when they poured a beaker of this wine for a prisoner, who was one of the men laughing. When he refused this drink with horror, they forced him with many threats to drink it. Extraordinary to say, as soon as this noxious wine penetrated his innards, this wretched man was overcome by the strong poison and fell to the ground with eyes staring, where he remained half dead, although some of our men had already drunk so much of the

---

the height of its palatial buildings appears to tower over these.' *Historia Peregrinorum*, p. 146.

[211] Now Provadi.

[212] As Chroust notes, *Quellen*, p. 54, it is ambiguous here whether Dietmar the marshal was also now the standard-bearer (earlier we have been told that this was Count Berthold of Neuenburg). The *Historia Peregrinorum,* p. 146, only mentions the standard-bearer (*signifer*) of the duke; but the use of *itemque* here would seem to suggest that the author thought that these were two distinct people. The *Historia Peregrinorum* stressed the leadership of the duke at Dimotika: 'although it seemed impregnable, he was, however, confident of the daring of his men, and he urged them all on to make the assault'.

same wine that they were intoxicated. A similar thing happened when the steward and the butler of the emperor and their companions had occupied the castle of Nikiz.[213] It was known that this place and the whole of the region around it had been charged by the Emperor of Constantinople with the making of poison or venom.[214] Our men were warned by their guides and Greek interpreters to avoid at all costs the wine of this land because of the known danger of poison, and a public edict was promulgated about this. Nevertheless the boys of the knights and clerics, displaying their accustomed constancy, or indeed relying on the mercy of God, boldly and confidently drank the wine and afterwards gave it to their lords; neither party, however, came to any harm from their indulgence in this lethal draught. But when to find out the truth they forcibly administered it to one of the Greeks, he immediately went pale, was sick, his eyes spun round furiously, and he was left by them close to death. Unless one had a heart of stone, one would be astonished by such an event! Thus in the ten plagues of Egypt, the waters of Egypt appeared to the Egyptians to be stinking of blood, but to the Hebrews they were however clear waters that were safe to drink.[215] Now indeed it was no less of a miracle that the wine of the Greeks that was adulterated with poison to kill our men should be fatal to Greeks, but a cup of salvation to our men. Our people now realised that from their entry into Bulgaria onwards poison had often been employed against them, but through the mercy of God this had been changed into a safe antidote for us.

Meanwhile, being placed as we were in the midst of enemies for several weeks, we had not received any reliable information as to the situation of our fellow pilgrims who had remained at Philippopolis. The emperor took counsel and selected Duke Berthold of Dalmatia, the Count of Holland and Frederick, Advocate of Berg, and other excellent knights, accompanied by a force of 1,200 armed men, and dispatched them to Philippopolis on 7 December, with carts and pack animals to carry our baggage; they were to escort all those of our companions who had been left there safely to Adrianople, bringing with them all our baggage.[216]

---

[213]   Identified as Nikè or Nikitza, in the Maritza valley, c. 25 km southeast of Adrianople, by Franck Collard, '*Timeas Danaos et dona ferentes*. Remarques à propos d'un épisode méconnu de la troisième croisade', in *Chemins d'Outre-Mer. Études sur la Méditerranée médiévale offertes à Michel Balard* (2 vols, Paris 2004), i.139–47, at p.144. As Collard points out, this accusation was part of a general western tendency to ascribe underhand methods of warfare to the Greeks, and may well also have misunderstood the taste of resinated wine. The steward and butler were Markward of Anweiler (d. 1202) and Conrad of Waldhausen, both imperial *ministeriales*. Conrad witnessed a number of Frederick's diplomata, *Dipl. Fred. I*, nos 855 (March 1184), 982 (September 1188) and 990 (February 1189). For Markward, see below, note 229.

[214]   The *Historia Peregrinorum*, p. 146, called this 'an annual tribute of poison'. But might it in fact have referred to a levy on crops grown for pharmaceutical purposes? Collard, art. cit., p. 145.

[215]   Exodus 7:17–25.

[216]   The *Historia Peregrinorum*, p. 149, said 'with three hundred chosen knights'.

Once the army had been reunited, plans would be made to continue the journey of the pilgrims of the life-giving Cross. They were also to hold amicable discussions with the Great Count of Serbia at the passes on the frontier of Bulgaria, asking him to send a force to help our men against Constantinople, if he could be persuaded to join the conflict.

Before those of our number who had been sent had reached Philippopolis, the military following of the Bishop of Passau had encountered some Greek troops at Batkun, and was returning victorious after killing a large number of them. But they had become careless, and when the Greeks sprang from ambush they surrounded our men, and while four of the enemy knights fell, fourteen of our men were slain. However, as soon as the Duke of Dalmatia and his companions arrived they sought out the Greek cohorts to exact revenge for the blood of their brothers. The Greeks had mustered once again at Batkun and were about to set off from there towards Philippopolis, intending to destroy our companions stationed there. When our troops spotted them, they boldly rushed upon them, and in the [ensuing] battle they slaughtered more than three hundred of them.

Making armed forays into the region of Graditz, they discovered pictures in the churches and other buildings showing the Greeks sitting on the necks of the pilgrims and binding them in the manner of enemies. Our men were enraged by this, and they burned both the churches and the other buildings, and put many people to the sword. They also ravaged this land, collecting a great deal of booty. Moreover Frederick, Advocate of Berg, went on further, accompanied by a band of particularly warlike knights. They climbed up some mountains held by the enemy, who showered them with stones and javelins, but they defeated them, and Frederick, undaunted, invaded a wealthy region called Vlachia, which is not far from Thessalonica, in which he killed a number of rebels and found such an abundance of supplies that they were unable to carry all of them off. The Bishop of Passau and the Duke of Dalmatia followed with a strong force and after seizing the land they loaded their men with the spoils taken from the enemy.

As they marched further, they encountered a certain zupan, or satrap of Bulgaria, who returned to the duke a knight who had been captured by bandits in Bulgaria, and he sought peace for himself and his lands from the duke and the advocate. Meanwhile, Arnold of Hornberg, a man of noble descent but even nobler through the steadfastness of his mind, had been sent by the Count of Holland to attack some Greek and Cuman troops, along with sixteen distinguished companions in arms, among whom were … of Liège, the brother of the Count of Cleves,[217] a man of wonderful resolution. As they were about to attack, they were suddenly surrounded by more than three hundred enemy cavalry. They could see

---

[217]   Probably Arnold (d. 1200), the younger brother of Count Dietrich III, Count of Cleves 1172–1200/2, for whom *Urkundenbuch für Niederrheins*, i.358–9 no. 510, 360–1 no. 514 (both 1188). This family were traditional supporters of the Staufen. See Thomas R. Kraus, 'Studien zur Frühgeschichte der Grafen von Kleve und der Entstehung der klevischen Landesherrschaft', *Rheinische Vierteljahrblätter* 46 (1982), 1–47, especially 4–5, 20.

no possibility of flight, but Arnold encouraged them to prefer a glorious death in battle to an ignominious flight, and calling on the sign of the Cross, these seventeen, wonderful to say, fought fiercely with almost three hundred enemies. They killed three of their leaders, knocked three others to the ground and wounded many of them, capturing six horses. All the rest turned and fled, for 'the right hand of the Lord doeth valiantly'.[218] These deeds were performed near Philippopolis.

Although the most serene emperor had for a long time enjoyed the upper hand in the conflict against the Greek emperor, he remained, however, mindful amid all this of the original intention to fight against the invaders of the holy city of Jerusalem, and he greatly regretted the unprofitable prolongation of our exile in Greece, especially since he inwardly detested the shedding of the Christian blood, which had to be spilt in these dangerous encounters, whether he wished it or not. He urged the Emperor of Constantinople both by letter and through envoys that, since the latter had acted wrongly towards his first set of envoys, he should in future provide guarantees concerning the peace and security of the envoys who would negotiate peace between them both. If however he was willing to do this, then, once concord had been restored between the two emperors and a guarantee had been given through selected hostages of the crossing and a market, the army of Christ would immediately and peacefully leave his land and would proceed in full force on to the liberation of the Promised Land. The Greek emperor freely and enthusiastically agreed to this, and especially since he saw that his own land and towns were unable to resist our men and were being destroyed. Thus envoys from both sides went back and forth in succession, and finally on the day before Christmas two [came who] said that they would be prepared to restore peace and concord, and to provide the carefully selected hostages, without [further] opposition or delay. But after they had pledged their faith with these words and the conditions of peace and friendship had been mutually agreed in writing, behold the envoys, with their customary excuses and untrustworthiness, raised objections to the terms that had been sworn, refusing to agree to those clauses in the agreement that seemed the most essential. As a result both the emperor and the princes were rightly annoyed, and since the peace terms had been broken the envoys of the Greek emperor were sent back home with a declaration of war. Consequently our men became more and more angry with the Greeks.[219]

While all this was going on, Kalopeter, the lord of the Vlachs and the greater part of the Bulgarians in the region of Thrace, who [called himself] emperor, [sent an envoy and] earnestly entreated that the imperial crown of the kingdom of the Greeks might be given to him. He made a firm offer that he would in early spring send forty thousand Vlachs and Cumans armed with bows and arrows to him [*Frederick*] [to fight] against Constantinople. The lord emperor received this

---

[218]   Psalm 117:16 (Vulgate), 118:16 (AV).

[219]   This account was closely followed by the *Historia Peregrinorum*, p. 148, which however added: 'The city of Constantinople thus trembled, thinking that its imminent destruction and the extermination of its people now threatened.'

envoy kindly, but sent him away for the time being, writing in friendly terms to Kalopeter.[220]

During this time the distinguished Duke of Swabia was of particular assistance to the army, for he was an indefatigable guardian of the pilgrims of Christ while foragers were being sent out and supplies brought in; for this reason he was described by some, in a pious and simple joke, as the *economus* or steward of the army. For having set out from Adrianople with the boys of the army, accompanied by barely three hundred knights, he ranged manfully through Macedonia, occupying the town of Culos and two others, the names of which have vanished from memory, from which the Greeks had fled, and then he went further and boldly marched to the sea, where he stormed a rich city called Menas, once famous because Menelaus and the adulterous Helen lived there. This place is surrounded by the sea on every side but one.[221] The citizens fled from it by ship, and the duke then carried away a rich booty. He soon abandoned all those towns that he took, since in Greece 'have we no continuing city',[222] but we longed to go to that city of the Lord, Jerusalem, which prefigures the heavenly Jerusalem.

The Duke of Swabia returned to Adrianople, but not long afterwards he undertook a third armed sortie, leading his troops towards a certain dense forest, that was further protected by the mountainous nature of the place, from which some of our pilgrim companions had shamefully fled, because of the arrows fired from the dark recesses of the forest, and their goods had been plundered. Attacking those who dwelt in most of these places both with arrows and with the sword, he recovered the arms that had been taken from our men there and brought back no little booty with him. In that battle and in others Count Conrad of Dornberg displayed himself to be a brave and steadfast knight.[223] Afterwards the inhabitants of these mountains and forests sent envoys to the emperor begging that they and their people might in future be left in peace, promising that they would provide a market for goods to be bought and advice and assistance to the army with an alliance against those who were ambushing us. As a sign of their good faith they restored eighteen horses that had been stolen from us to the lord emperor. The lord emperor decided to grant their request because of the promise of a market for supplies, and he sent a certain Greek abbot from Adrianople to them along with one of the imperial huntsmen to conclude a secure agreement about the market. However, their party was promptly captured by enemies who fell upon them in the

---

[220]   There are some words missing from the text in the first sentence of this paragraph, but these can be supplied from the *Historia Peregrinorum*, p. 149, which adds that Barbarossa's principal concern was, however, to continue with his journey and bring help to the Holy Land. See Wolff, 'The Second Bulgarian Empire', p. 185. This passage is also important evidence for the composite nature of the new Bulgarian kingdom, for which see Wolff, art. cit., pp. 174–9, 198–201 (on the Cumans).

[221]   Enez, at the mouth of the River Maritza.

[222]   Hebrews 13:14.

[223]   The Burgrave of Nuremberg [above note 95]

middle of the first night [of their journey], and they were all cut to pieces and thus cruelly put to death. The inhabitants of these forests captured the standard-bearer of these enemies and they hanged him from a gallows. They set ambushes for the rest of the bandits, wishing to hand them over to our men so that they and their people would be absolved from suspicion of causing the death of the imperial envoys.

Because the market for purchasing goods had been taken away and our sea crossing had been prevented, the anger of our men against the Greeks grew hot at this time. The whole army was, however, overflowing with booty taken from these Greek enemies,[224] and since luxuries were available in abundance and many of the army remained idle for a long time this served to encourage bad behaviour among them; for, as the poet says, 'the appetite for riches will expand in direct proportion to your actual wealth'.[225] The plundering now led avarice to rule in many hearts and murders became widespread. Under the excuse of bringing back supplies, almost universal indiscipline prevailed and far more than was needed was dishonestly brought back as plunder. From an overwhelming desire of gain charity and their former love of justice cooled among many of our men, both at Adrianople and at Philippopolis, and whereas good faith and concord had formerly flourished in the army of Christ, they now disappeared among many as avarice and its daughter envy flourished, while some of the common people also shamefully wallowed in filthy drunkenness. There were, however, some who were led by the spirit of God and 'the zeal of the house of the Lord',[226] and, like another Phineas,[227] whenever they found people fornicating, they inflicted upon them a punishment that fit their crime, since they stripped them naked in public, both men and women, and led them with their hands bound behind their backs all around the city by a rope tied to their genitals, which struck terror into others and encouraged them to reform. Finally, on some occasions, they submerged them in the fast-flowing river in the cold of the winter, and left them there amid the derision and laughter they deserved.

---

[224]   Cf. the *Historia Peregrinorum*, p. 142, a passage earlier in that account, but which seems to refer to the current situation since it goes on to denounce the corrupting effect of affluence. 'A host of carts were now going out for plunder and returning laden with spoils and food stuffs, plundering all the land [round about]. There were so many sheep and oxen, and beasts of the field, in the army that an ox was sold for five pence and a ram for two or three.'

[225]   Juvenal, *Satire* xiv.139, the translation is that of Peter Green, *Juvenal. The Sixteen Satires* (Harmondsworth 1974), p. 268.

[226]   Psalm 68:10 (Vulgate), 69:9 (AV); cf. John 2:17.

[227]   Numbers 25:7–11. The *Historia Peregrinorum*, p. 148, compared Barbarossa himself to Phineas: 'having zeal for the law, he poured out his wrath on many of the transgressors. For some, on account of [their] more serious crimes, were deprived of their heads, while others caught in fornication were stripped, along with their mistresses, to be chastised with whips, shamefully exposed and made subject to mockery.'

After this and after many prevarications and excuses in his letters, the Emperor of Constantinople was brought to belated penitence by the devastation of his lands and the ruin of his cities. He sent back his two former envoys, the *pansebastos* and *acolithos* the lord Eumathios Philokales and a certain James the Pisan, to the glorious emperor and the army of Christ, and sought peace, promising a market for the purchase of goods and a fleet of ships for the crossing of the Hellespont, and he confirmed that he would provide the most noble of hostages to prove his good faith and that his promise would be carried out. These envoys appeared before the imperial majesty on Septuagesima Sunday, that is, the feast of the blessed virgin Agnes.[228] The Duke of Dalmatia arrived that same day from Philippopolis and presented to the lord emperor an embassy from the Great Count of Serbia, to hold discussions with whom he himself had been appointed as envoy from the lord emperor [to go] to the passes at the frontier of Bulgaria. Since indeed there was no earlier opportunity [for this], on the day after the embassy was received, he set off for Bulgaria. The embassy from the Greeks was kindly welcomed by the emperor, but he still did not trust what they said. They were sent back home from his serene presence with his own envoys, the nobleman Berthold of Künigsberg, Count of Tuscany, the steward Markward of Anweiler[229] and the chamberlain Markward of Neuenberg, who carefully investigated the truth of the promises, and after they were certain that these were made in good faith, they arranged the terms of a plenary peace agreement.

At this time the cleric and imperial envoy Eberhard arrived from Hungary, who had [earlier] been sent to King Bela. He was carrying warning letters from that king to his son-in-law the Emperor of Constantinople concerning the very injurious and contrary resistance of his whole kingdom. He was indeed quite perturbed and frightened by the victorious progress of the pilgrims of the Cross and the devastation of the kingdom of Greece. For after he had in the meanwhile been informed of the destruction of the city of Dimotika, his face had changed towards that messenger, and 'it was not towards him as the day before',[230] nor thereafter were his expenses given to him as they had been from the household of the king. Furthermore this same envoy brought back a great deal of favourable news from our land and from the princes of the empire of the Germans. He also brought news of the death of two kings, that is Henry of England and William of Apulia, and of how the illustrious King of the Romans, Henry, the son of the most serene Emperor Frederick, was presently claiming the kingdom of Apulia for his

---

[228]　21 January 1190.

[229]　An imperial *ministerialis*, steward to the young King Henry from 1186 onwards, and subsequently his right-hand man when he became emperor; created Margrave of Ancona and Duke of Ravenna in 1195. For his career and background, Bosl, *Der Reichministerialität*, pp. 228–30, 588–98, who considered him, 'the most important of all imperial servants' (p. 228), and especially for his later career, Thomas Curtis Van Cleve, *Markward of Anweiler and the Sicilian Regency* (Princeton 1937).

[230]　Genesis 31:2. The reference is to Jacob and his father-in-law Laban.

own through the hereditary right of the queen, his wife,[231] and in addition that King Philip of France and Richard, the new King of England, and many other princes had received the sign of the Holy Cross and were about to follow our journey with a new expedition. He also told [us] what he had seen as he crossed Bulgaria, that, oh horror, the bodies of almost all the pilgrims of Christ that had been buried along the road there had through the inhuman savagery and insane stupidity of the Bulgarians been dug up, to the shame of the army of Christ. As David said: 'the dead bodies of thy servants they have given to be meat to the fowls of Heaven'.[232] In truth, only the body of the venerable Abbot of Admont was untouched; that it remained intact was through the wonderful power of God.

Meanwhile the columns of our companions left Philippopolis with all their baggage on the emperor's instructions, all but destroying that city by fire because of their hatred for the Greeks. During their journey some of them made a diversion to the town of Berrhoë, which they also consigned to the avenging flames after they had gathered enough plunder. They made a halt for some days at Constantia, while the Duke of Dalmatia and his escort returned [north] for a meeting with the Great Count of Serbia. But the latter was busy with his efforts to conduct a campaign in Bulgaria, and when the duke did not find him at the designated meeting place he sent a messenger to him. After the messenger's return he went back to his companions at Constantia, after which they all set off towards Adrianople. They straggled into Adrianople in several groups, but the army of Christ was finally reunited there on the feast of the blessed virgin Agatha.[233]

During this time the indefatigable Duke of Swabia made a fourth sortie from Adrianople, and captured the city of Arcadiopolis, which had been built by the Emperor Arcadius, but is popularly known as Argionopolis.[234] We found it deserted, lacking both warriors and foodstuffs, although some of our men discovered corn and wine there, which they carried back to their companions. However, on the holy night of the Purification of the Virgin Mary, an extraordinary sign was seen by all those who had marched out with the duke; for around the first watch of the night they all saw the sign of the Holy Cross, blood-coloured and of great size, shining

---

[231]   Henry II had died at Chinon in Touraine on 6 July 1189, and William II of Sicily on 18 November of that same year. William was childless, and the nearest legitimate heir was his aunt Constance, Henry VI's wife, whom he had already designated as the heir to the kingdom. However, there was a rival claimant in the late king's cousin, Tancred, who was crowned as King of Sicily in January 1190.

[232]   Psalm 78:2 (Vulgate), 79:2 (AV).

[233]   5 February 1190. According to the diary of Tageno, this rear detachment left Philippolis on 15 January 1190, arrived at Constantia (modern Costanitza) on 21 January, and was eventually reunited on 6 February, *Chronicon Magni Presbiteri*, MGH SS xvii.512 [see below p. 156].

[234]   Now Lüleburgaz, Eickhoff, *Friedrich Barbarossa im Orient*, p. 72. Arcadius, son of Theodosius the Great, was Roman Emperor in the East 395–408.

for some considerable time in the heavens.[235] As a result all those who served the Holy Cross and wore its sign were absolutely delighted. They gave thanks to the Lord, and that night they loudly and joyfully sang the *Kyrie Eleison* and other holy chants. When afterwards the imperial envoys had returned from Constantinople, they recounted that on that same day, following the night when this joyful sign had been seen, and because of the glorious reputation of the lord emperor, the Emperor of Constantinople released all the prisoners who had been held there for between two and five months in wretched captivity.[236]

The following day our men attacked the squadrons of the mercenary army of the Emperor of Constantinople, composed of Vlachs and Cumans. They fought with them and unexpectedly put them to flight, despite the absence of the duke. A few of our men, but a great many of the enemy, were taken prisoner; barely fifteen of our sergeants were killed, and one knight was also slain, Hugh of Teisbach.[237] The leader of the enemy forces then returned those of our men who had been made prisoner to the Duke of Swabia, on condition that his own men who were captives would also be released. This the duke did, and he also of his own volition returned the horses that the enemy had lost in the battle, while recovering his own horses. After this battle the Duke of Swabia returned to Adrianople. The division of the Bohemians, who were [even] more practised in war and plundering than the rest, along with a few others from the army, went in search of the foodstuffs they needed to a certain coastal town, where they seized horses and mules, wine and wheat, and other desirable commodities in abundance, and they returned with them to our men. The Bohemians also made a dangerous attack on an all but inaccessible marsh, to which a by no means small force of the enemy had fled with all their followers. The Bohemians brought back spectacular booty from there too. Our men spread out once more into various parts of Greece, in two divisions. The first of these forces, which was that of the Bishop of Würzburg and the counts of Salm, Wied and Spanheim, went towards the land of the Vlachs, capturing two towns that had been abandoned by the enemy and bloodily storming a third, where more than five thousand [of the enemy] were killed.[238] One of these cities was set on fire. The other force was led by the Count of Abenberg and Frederick, advocate

---

[235] 1 February.

[236] The text reads that these prisoners had been held *intra biennium vel quinquennium*, that is literally 'between two and five years'. But these captives were clearly members of the Crusade, and especially the envoys, the Bishop of Münster and his companions, referred to in Frederick's letter to his son, above, who had been arrested in the autumn of 1189.

[237] Teisbach, near Landshut in Bavaria (35 km south of Regensburg). The *Historia Peregrinorum*, p. 147, which places this battle somewhat earlier, immediately after the capture of Probaton (that is, at the end of November), suggests that a small force from the army was surprised, and it was the arrival of the duke to rescue it that led to the defeat of the Cumans.

[238] This was presumably the region near Thessalonica already attacked by Frederick of Berg, the Bishop of Passau and the Duke of Dalmatia [above, p. 83].

of Berg, who was always quite ferocious in fighting the enemies of the army of the Holy Cross. This column turned southwards, and after inflicting terrible slaughter returned with extensive booty.

While the kingdom of Greece was rocked by these tribulations, the imperial envoys, namely Count Berthold of Künigsberg, and the two Markwards (mentioned above), along with the previous envoys from the Emperor of Constantinople, the *pansebastos* and James,[239] were now sent for a third time to the most serene emperor. They arrived at Adrianople on 14 February, that is on the feast of the blessed martyr Valentine, bringing good news, namely that they were to be congratulated on carrying a real and genuine treaty of peace and concord between the glorious Emperor of the Romans and the Emperor of Constantinople. The terms of this agreement were as follows.

1. The Emperor of Constantinople willingly remitted in full all claims for damages with regard to the theft of property, the destruction of towns, the deaths of men and every [other] injury unexpectedly inflicted upon him.

2. And he would provide enough ships for the crossing from Gallipoli, or for the voyage of the glorious army of Christ and the life-giving Cross between Sestos and Abydos, namely seventy *vissiers* and a hundred and fifty [other] ships suitable for the safe transport of horses, and fifteen galleys, all fully equipped, so that with galleys of this type under his own control the invincible emperor might exercise guard over his army as he wished.[240] He would not, however, inflict any damage [with them] on any part of the empire of Greece, nor would he prevent any ships from entering Constantinople.

3. And that all the galleys that are stationed between Abydos and Constantinople are to remain tied up in port, and will not put to sea during this period, to remove any suspicion of treachery.

4. And that the land army of the Emperor of Constantinople will remain at four days' distance from the army of Christ and the Emperor of the Romans, while that army remains in the land of the Emperor of Constantinople.

5. And that the Emperor of Constantinople shall give to the glorious Emperor of the Romans, now and during the crossing, two towns near the coast where the expedition may rest, but the expedition is not to inflict any damage or harm on these towns or their inhabitants.

6. And to ensure that these promises are observed and maintained, the Emperor Isaac shall give to the lord emperor twenty-two carefully selected hostages

---

[239]   That is Eumathius Philokales and James the Pisan.

[240]   Vissiers were galleys specifically designed for the transport of horses, with stern ports for disembarking them, for which John Pryor, 'The Venetian fleet for the Fourth Crusade and the diversion of the Crusade to Constantinople', in *The Experience of Crusading: presented to Jonathan Riley-Smith on his Sixty-Fifth Birthday, i: Western Approaches*, ed. Marcus Bull and Norman Housley (Cambridge 2003), 103–23.

of the royal kin and of ducal rank: namely the lord Andronikos, the son of the emperor's brother John Angelos; six judges and six of the better men from the people of Constantinople, who were to be sent back unharmed after the glorious emperor and his whole army had crossed the straits; and in addition the lord Michael, son of the emperor's uncle the *Sebastokrator* John Dukas;[241] the lord Michael, son of another uncle of his, the lord Alexios Angelos; Manuel, a cousin of the emperor, son of *Stratobasilus*; the lord Alexios, son of his cousin the *Protostrator* Manuel Kamytzes; and a third Manuel Monomarkos, the *Sebastos*, the son of Joseph Bryennios; and the *Pansebastos Akolithon* Eumathius Philokales.[242] These were to remain with the lord emperor and march with him, and as long as he could march in safety as far as the towns of Philadelphia,[243] where they would then be released unharmed.

7. That if through the reluctance of the inhabitants the designated guardian, the *Pansebastos*, was unable to furnish food for the army, the columns of the army had permission to behave towards them as they saw fit, except that they were not to hand over their land to any foreign person.[244]

8. The Emperor of Constantinople also pardons all who have followed the Emperor of the Romans and served him, Greeks, Armenians and Latins, and grants them the full grace of his empire.

9. A mark of silver will be sold for five and a half *hyperpera*, and the *hyperper* will be exchanged for 120 *stamina*, with no difference being made between the old and the new *stamina*.

10. And that good markets will be set up for the army, both during its crossing and further on, as time and place shall make possible, that sales will be made to them at a fair price, as they should sell to the Emperor Isaac [himself], if he was making the crossing there. And this will be done without trickery or any dishonesty.

11. And that the Emperor of Constantinople will make reparations for the loss of goods suffered at Constantinople by the Bishop of Münster, Count Rupert and their companions, in accordance with the advice of the Lord Emperor of the Romans.[245]

---

[241]   Michael Dukas, the future ruler of Epiros (d. 1215).

[242]   This actually adds up to 19 hostages, not 22: the *Historia* later said 18 [below, p. 96]. The *Historia Peregrinorum*, p. 150, said there were 14; the *Chronica Regia Coloniensis*, p. 148, said 24.

[243]   The Latin has a plural here; presumably this meant the towns in the region of Philadelphia. The *Historia Peregrinorum*, p. 151, has 'as far as the town of Philadelphia'.

[244]   Brand, *Byzantium Confronts the West*, p. 186, suggests that this was aimed especially at the Serbs or Vlachs, presumably while the army was still on the European side of the Bosphorus.

[245]   A letter from the Armenian Catholicos to Saladin, included in the history of Bahâ' al-Dîn Ibn Shaddâd, suggested that Barbarossa had extorted large quantities of gold, silver

12. And that five hundred of the better men of the city and the empire shall, in the temple of the great and most holy church of God at St Sophia and in the presence of the universal patriarch Dositheus, swear [to observe] all these terms.
13. And the universal patriarch will add his own signature as confirmation of this present peace treaty.
14. And that the Emperor of Constantinople will set free all the men of the Roman empire who have been captured from the time when the war began, whether on land or sea, and whether they be pilgrim or merchant.

All the details of this pact were then confirmed on oath, so that the most victorious emperor and the whole army of the Holy Cross would promptly and within twenty days set off from Adrianople towards the agreed crossing of the Hellespont. While not doing any harm or setting fire to towns and villages, the oft-mentioned army of Christ had the right to levy wheat, barley and wine, without hindrance from any of the Greeks, up to the crossing of the Hellespont. They would, however, refrain from the unnecessary seizure of animals and clothing, and the killing of their people. Finally, to confirm this agreement and that the emperor and his men would faithfully observe the peace, an oath was requested to be taken by five hundred knights from the army, which they so swore at Constantinople. The agreement was formally concluded in the presence of his [*Isaac's*] envoys at Adrianople.

Moreover, the day after the arrival of the Greek envoys, there also arrived an envoy of the Great Sultan of Iconium, called Tokili, a wise and sensible man, who according to human judgement feared the Lord.[246] He came together with the imperial envoy, the knight Gottfried of Wiesenbach, who had previously been sent to the sultan by the most illustrious emperor.[247] Both of these men had spent eight wretched weeks as prisoners of the Emperor of Constantinople and had been stripped of their goods. The sultan described himself in his letter as 'great lord and ruler' of the Turks, Armenians and Syrians, and in it he greeted the lord emperor most affectionately, and promised him all sorts of advice, comfort and assistance against all his enemies, as well as excellent markets throughout the land under his rule. However, the present that this same sultan had sent to the lord emperor had been forcibly confiscated by the Emperor of Constantinople from the aforesaid envoys during the disputes that have been described above, although the aforesaid emperor promised to make reparation for this. On the third day after this, a heathen envoy arrived from the Malik, the son of the great sultan, who in

---

and precious textiles from Isaac, *The Rare and Excellent History of Saladin*, p. 114.

[246] Barbarossa had already been in touch with Qilij Arslan II in 1188, above p. 45. For the significance of this comment, see introduction, p. 6.

[247] For this earlier embassy, see above p. 75. Wiesenbach has several possible identifications: (1) a place 15 km east of Heidelberg in the Neckar valley; (2) near Gunzberg on the Bavarian/Swabian border; (3) Wissenbach near Luzern; and (4) Weissenbach in Styria.

his letter addressed to the most mighty emperor also steadfastly pledged his regard for and faithful service to him in the future.[248] But in accordance with the proverb that 'there is no more deadly plague than a friendly enemy', this man was weaving tricks in order to deceive and injure the most steadfast emperor and overthrow the unsuspecting Christian army, since 'the kings of the earth set themselves, and the rulers take counsel, against the Lord and against his anointed',[249] that is Christ, and the Christian people who were far from home for love of His Passion. After this, the hostages provided by the Greek emperor, who have been named above, and the guides for our road who had been promised, were dispatched from Constantinople to the lord emperor and arrived at Adrianople on Tuesday, 27 February, in the third week of Lent, in the year from the Incarnation of the Lord 1190. He received them kindly, and thereafter they were treated honourably. In their surrender, as 'in all (other) things, the Lord', who is blessed through the ages, 'did honour and exalt his people'.[250]

Let the wise reader be warned here that 'the eye of the Lord is upon them that fear him, upon them that hope in his mercy'.[251] Lo a little time before that arrogant Emperor of Constantinople had in his letters haughtily demanded his grace from the most victorious and always august Emperor of the Romans, even if quite unavailingly. He was a transgressor of his oath, who blocked our roads with bandits. Moreover, after pledging his faith to us that we might cross [the Bosphorus] peacefully and have ships for our passage, and proudly offering to provide distinguished hostages from among the chief men of his army, in the meanwhile he threw the envoys of the most serene emperor and of the army into chains, and foolishly exulted that all the pilgrims of Christ were trapped in his net, as he had sent all his ships far away to sea and he absolutely refused to allow the passage of the army of the life-giving Cross, offering vain and dishonest excuses. It was only after his lands had been utterly devastated and the terrible slaughter of his men that he set aside his customary pride and once more offered the most pious emperor a fleet of ships and supplies for the crossing, in accordance with his word and the other aforesaid terms of the agreement. Furthermore, he sent distinguished hostages from his blood-kin, and kept silence over all the damage that he had suffered. Having been like Pharaoh afflicted by heavenly chastisement,

---

[248]   Qutb al-Dīn Malikshāh (d. 1195). Malik = 'king' in Arabic. Following the dates given earlier, this envoy arrived on 16 February 1190. The *Historia Peregrinorum*, pp. 151–2, quoted what purported to be the text of this letter, adding 'rashly trusting these words, the emperor received the envoys and kept them with him'.

[249]   Psalm 2:2. The *Historia Peregrinorum*, p. 151, commented: 'Who is so wary, who so circumspect, that he would be able to discern the snares of so many ambushes, and escape unscathed from the traps set by so many treacherous men? The emperor had now indeed entered the land of scorpions, from whom he had nothing to fear face-to-face, for they strike one in the back.'

[250]   Sapientia 19:20

[251]   Psalm 32:18 (Vulgate); 33:18 (AV).

he requested that the journey of the people of God, that is of those signed with the Cross, whom he had thought to harass or indeed drive from the land, [now] be hastened;[252] for, giving thought to what was left of Bulgaria and thereafter to the city of Constantinople, he [now] made conciliatory requests.

The whole of the army of Christ favoured an attack upon this city, if the Emperor of Constantinople continued obstinately and determinedly to resist the most pious emperor, even if the latter did this reluctantly. This same emperor also sent letters and envoys to recruit galleys from Italy, Apulia and other coastal regions, while he held an army of more than 60,000 Serb and Vlach auxiliaries ready. But the Lord 'commandeth even the wind and the water', and stilled the danger that the war might continue.[253] One ought also to consider another factor: that, although our men found this delay made by the army of Christ in Greece over the winter tedious and burdensome, in fact this was caused by Divine clemency, which prevented us marching into the wastelands of Romania during the harsh winter season, in which both men and animals would have suffered through bad weather and lack of food.

Meanwhile, on the advice of the princes and of the more important men of the army, the lord emperor, who was always anxious to avoid disagreements among his various men and downheartedness among some, with pious and modest heart exacted an oath from all the knights of his army of due obedience and fealty, to last until six weeks after Antioch had been passed, so that the authority of the pentarchs or masters of fifty, which was unpopular, should lapse, and everyone should unquestioningly obey the orders of the lord emperor alone, for he was afraid that in that great enterprise the Lord would not dwell where there was disagreement, and thinking on the words of the Prophet: 'obedience is better than sacrifice'.[254] 'And there went out a decree from Caesar Augustus, that all the world – that is, the knights of the army – should be recorded.'[255] Each of the pentarchs made known the names and usual stations of their accompanying knights, and these were brought to the emperor. All this was done without delay at the command of the most wise emperor.

At that time the great steward of the Emperor of Constantinople, who had mustered a very large army to defeat the forces of the Vlachs, their public enemies, sent an embassy to request the lord emperor that, since he and his lord the Emperor of Constantinople were now joined together in peace and brotherhood, he would send the glorious army of the pilgrims of Christ to assist him in fighting against these Vlachs. On that very same day Kalopeter, the lord of the Vlachs, who was

---

[252]   Cf. Exodus 12:31–3.

[253]   Luke 8:25.

[254]   I Samuel 15:22. Cf. *Historia Peregrinorum*, p. 152: 'the emperor exacted an oath from everyone, which all took freely and unanimously … lest the inconstancy of some should create discord and dissension among the army'.

[255]   Luke 2:1: *describerentur*. In the Biblical context, this means 'taxed' (as in the AV), but literally 'written down' (in the tax registers).

called by his own men Emperor of Greece, earnestly entreated by letter the help of the pilgrims of Christ against the army of the Greeks; but both envoys sought the help of the lord emperor in vain and returned home. During our stay at Adrianople three distinguished knights who made a crucial contribution to the army of Christ passed from this earthly life: Gaubert of Aspremont, Count Simon of Spanheim and Reinold of Reifenberg. The army of the Holy Cross made no little lamentation over their deaths.

Thus, on the Thursday before the middle of Lent, that is 1 March, the renowned Duke of Swabia set out from Adrianople, as had been agreed and on the emperor's order, with his columns of Swabians and Bavarians, and on the following day, 2 March, the rest of the army with the lord emperor began the journey it wanted to the sea crossing, after spending fourteen weeks at Adrianople during the winter season. During this march both we and the animals suffered great misery in the week of the Lord's Passion because of the pouring rain. It was also at this time that the nobleman Poto of Massing fell ill and died on 16 March. Thereafter we celebrated Palm Sunday[256] at the city of Roussa, suffering greatly from this horrid rain, as a result of which the greater part of the army abandoned its carts and wagons because of the difficulty of the roads and loaded the baggage onto packhorses. Then, passing by the town of Brachol,[257] the whole army finally reached Gallipoli, the city where we were to make the crossing, on 21 March, the day before the Lord's Supper. On the holy day of the Lord's Supper the Duke of Swabia was the very first to make the crossing, which he did with great ceremony, and on Good Friday and Holy Saturday the remainder of his company, that is all the Swabians and the Bavarians, also made their crossing.

The feast of Easter now fell on 25 March, which was the Sunday of the Annunciation, and it happened that the clouds brought forth endless rain. Hence, 'making a virtue out of necessity', the whole army busied itself in praise of the Lord. We have heard, not without admiration, of a notable prayer, worthy of record, of a certain knight on this occasion. 'Lord Almighty,' he said, 'who once spoke through Moses to the people of Israel as they went to the Promised Land, now nevertheless speak with fatherly mercy to us through clear signs. For today You have mercifully sent this rain to chastise us and join us to Your service, for if the weather had been fair we would have postponed Divine service and concentrated on the work of crossing the sea. Similarly,' he said, 'in the deceit of the Venetians who have fled from us and in the storm that hit our port, a miracle has been worked through Your power, and the wickedness of the ancient enemy has been rightly punished through their diversion.' For when they were coming with ships laden with corn and other foodstuffs intended for Constantinople, they were forced by contrary winds towards the coast at Gallipoli. They had been told by Berthold and

---

[256]   18 March. Roussa = modern Keşan.

[257]   Modern Bolayir, in the middle of the peninsula between the Bosphorus and the Gulf of Saros, where the army reached the military road from Constantinople to Gallipoli (modern Gelibolu), Eickhoff, *Friedrich Barbarossa im Orient*, p. 79.

Markward, the envoys of the glorious emperor, that the forces of the Holy Cross were ready to make the crossing and awaiting their arrival with corn and other goods for us. However, they disregarded this advice and set sail for Constantinople, thinking to gain greater profit there; but at the command of Almighty God, 'who bringeth the wind out of his treasuries',[258] they were driven back by a storm that had arisen to the Gallipoli shore, from which they had secretly crept away, where they were held fast by our men, who relieved them of their cargoes of corn and the other merchandise that was needed for the army. Moreover, envoys of the Pisans arrived there, greeting the lord emperor with the proper submission and devoted loyalty, and asking solicitously after his welfare and that of the army of Christ. They also most devotedly offered him ships and galleys to besiege Constantinople.

On the second day of Easter, and on the two following days,[259] the rest of the army sailed across [the Bosphorus], and thus it happened that the whole army made the passage in six days, with joy and exaltation, and great glory, and entirely without danger. On the sixth day the invincible emperor sailed with the last people, escorted by five galleys full of warriors and other ships, while the Greeks blew trumpets. He was also accompanied by the eighteen hostages already mentioned, but he immediately sent thirteen of them back to Constantinople, keeping five of them with him until [reaching] Philadelphia. Thus from the crossing of the River Sava or Sowe, by which we entered the land under the rule of the Greeks, up until the crossing from Gallipoli, that is from Europe to Asia, thirty-nine weeks elapsed, during which we passed in great prosperity through Bulgaria and Greece.

At last, on 29 March, the whole army moved off from the crossing point, leaving behind the carts and wagons, and set out on its journey with pack animals and burdens, leaving ancient Troy on our left.[260] We had passed from the west to the east, that is to say, from Europe to Asia, and soon began to pass through the region of Romania. That part of Asia Minor which we now call Romania is divided into two different provinces, Phyrigia and Bithynia. We travelled for three days along mountainous and difficult roads and on the octave of Easter came to the city of Pegae, which is inhabited by Latins, where we camped by the River Diga. We rested there on the Sunday because we needed a market. Then on 4 April we crossed the great River Aveloica, not without difficulty, for we lost a knight and a boy, with some horses and donkeys, in the waters of that river.

Meanwhile, the Greeks with their customary treachery broke the peace agreement, and harmed those who were unwary with unexpected attacks. They killed some unarmed people and stole the goods of those they had murdered. Once

---

[258]   Psalm 134:7 (Vulgate), 135:7 (AV).

[259]   26–28 March 1190.

[260]   It is probable that the surviving Roman roads of Asia Minor had been rebuilt with narrower roadways unsuitable for wagons and carts, and with steps on some of the steeper gradients that would preclude wheeled traffic entirely, Haldon, 'Roads and communications', 140–1. 'Troy' was misidentified here. Ancient Troy was at Hisarlik, near Canakkale, further to the west, whereas the army appears to have set out from Lampsakos.

our men realised what had happened, they destroyed the bandits.[261] On 3 April Frederick, advocate of Berg, attacked their squadrons and slew more than sixty of them. In the next few days he fought bravely against them, and prevented them ambushing our men; however our men did generally observe the emperor's orders and observe the peace that had been agreed towards the inhabitants of that land, even though they did not deserve it.[262]

On 6 April we came to a castle, between the town of Ypomenon and the city of Archangelos, where we stopped.[263] On 9 April we came to Sycheron in the valley of Ascaratana, where we remained on the following day, where 'the army began to murmur'[264] about a market: however the governor of the city treacherously fled from the imperial presence. On 13 April we arrived at Kalamos, losing two knights in the mountains that lay in between. On 15 April, passing by the ruined city of Meleos, which contains the church of St Hermas, we came to the city of Agyos, where saints Cosmas and Damian were crowned with martyrdom, and there we stayed.[265] It was here, too, that the Emperor of Greece finally sent a tent and a golden goblet to the lord emperor, as he had indeed promised to him at their meeting. On 18 April we passed the city of Alos, and arrived at Philadelphia, which the Apostle and Evangelist St John mentions.[266] We had hoped that we

---

[261] The *Historia Peregrinorum*, p. 153, told a story of how one of the pilgrims, a citizen of Ulm in Swabia, found his brother murdered by the Greeks. He led out a party to find these bandits and discovered some of them hiding in a marsh. When his companions proved reluctant to attack and urged him to return to camp, he attacked the Greeks single-handedly, killing nine of them, while the sole survivor threw himself into the water to escape.

[262] The *Historia Peregrinorum*, p. 154, associates Count Ulrich of Kyburg with Frederick in these exploits, and then continues with the following story. 'Count Conrad of Dornberg had been sent out with his men one day to scout out the route. At the entrance to a certain valley he saw the tents of the robbers who had come to set ambushes for the pilgrims. Our men immediately charged them on horseback, uttering their war cries, and the robbers, who were resting and eating their dinner, immediately fled from their camp in terror, leaving behind horses, silver vessels and [other] spoil. Taking these, Conrad and his men returned joyfully to the camp.'

[263] The 'city of the Archangel' was the ancient monastery complex of St Michael near Ypomenon, near which the Nikean ruler John Vatatzes defeated the Franks in 1224, while some ruins 10 km southeast of the modern town of Manyas may mark the site of the castle. From here the army, which had been marching east-southeast, now turned south following the military road, Eickhoff, *Friedrich Barbarossa im Orient*, p. 85.

[264] Maccabees 11:39.

[265] Two brothers, Christian physicians, martyred during the persecution of Diocletian c. 303, whose cult was widespread in both eastern and western Christianity from the fifth century. However, the author may here have been in error, confusing Agyos with Aigai in Cilicia, Eickhoff, *Friedrich Barbarossa im Orient*, p. 93. Kalamos = modern Gelembe.

[266] Revelations 1:11 and 3:7. Alos may have been the ancient Sardis, as is suggested by the *Historia Peregrinorum*, p. 154. Philadelphia (modern Alaşehir) was the most important

might be given a good market by the governor and citizens of Philadelphia, in accordance with the promise given by the Emperor of Constantinople and his princes, but the citizens not only refused with rash pride to provide us with a suitable market and exchange, but some of the more impudent dared to exasperate our men with arrogant words. Thus what happened in that city was that each side bandied foolish insults back and forth, a riot suddenly erupted, the goods of some of our men were unexpectedly seized, and indeed a few were arrested and held prisoner in the city that night, although they were released next morning with a respect that was owed to fear. As a result the most serene emperor dispatched an envoy to the city to inquire what insane madness had provoked an outrage of this sort, from people who knew that the strength of the army of the Holy Cross and the steadfastness of the German knights was not only famous from long ago but had also recently been shown [once more] by a string of victories in Greece. The governor of the city and its region then came to his senses and along with the other leading men of the town purged himself through an oath on the Gospels of guilt from the offence charged against them. He claimed that certain foolish young men had babbled the reckless insults, and had similarly rashly provoked some of our men with arrows. He now offered appropriate satisfaction both to the lord emperor and to the glorious army for their insolence, adding also that all Christians should be moved to mercy for the said city, which had for a long time and single-handedly defended the cult and honour of the Christian faith by resisting the neighbouring Turks and other peoples; hence we would incur a much graver sin were we to destroy it than was involved in the destruction of Adrianople and Philippopolis. But meanwhile the division of the Bohemians and the knights of the Bishop of Regensburg had launched an attack on the city gate, where they wounded many of the citizens. The crossbowmen and archers of the army hit many men who were on the top of the walls with their arrows and sent them falling to the ground. But the gentleness of [our] imperial majesty recalled our men from what they had begun. Indeed, this most pious emperor with his customary benevolence not only did not punish the Greek hostages whom he had brought here [with him] for the dishonest breach of the promises given under oath, but he kindly and honourably sent them back to their homes.

Moreover, outside the city there was a bastion held by a band of Latin infantry, equipped with bows and scale armour [*phalerae*], expert warriors, who had for various reasons at different times ended up in Greece and Romania. They now joined the mighty army of the Holy Cross, and proved themselves thereafter alongside our men as fierce warriors against the Turks.

When we left Philadelphia on 22 April the citizens of that town launched some foolish attacks against the rear units of the army, without however doing

---

town still in Greek hands in western Asia Minor, where Isaac II had besieged the usurper Theodore Mangaphas the previous year, Eickhoff, *Friedrich Barbarossa im Orient*, p. 95.

any harm to our men or suffering it themselves.[267] The next day the Turks attacked the advance guard of the lord emperor: more than fifty of them perished. We then traversed some difficult mountains, with considerable trouble since the horses were for the most part weak and all the army's supplies, except for bread, had been eaten.

On 24 April we came to a ruined city called Tripoli the Lesser, which is thought by some to be Thyatira. The next day, in the Rogation period, we passed the destroyed city of Ierapolis, where St Philip the Apostle suffered, and a river that is called 'the lesser'.[268] Passing through a most fertile valley, filled with liquorice, cardamom, myrtle, figs and other plants, we now entered the Turkish area and came to the plain of Laodicia, where we found a good campsite and stayed for a day. This town is at the foot of a very high mountain, beyond which lies Ephesus. It is said that King Louis of France was defeated here, and also Bishop Otto of Freising.[269] This was the boundary of the land under Greek rule.

We think it worthwhile to make a brief note of the beliefs of the Greeks that differ from the faith of the universal Church, namely of the Holy Roman Church. They are in error in their belief about the Holy Trinity, since they teach that the Holy Spirit proceeds from the Father alone, and not from the Son, and is less important than the Father and Son. In the Eucharist they use leavened bread and not the Azyme,[270] and in that sacrifice or solemnity of the Mass they do not offer that reverence, care and compunction of the heart with which we, although sinners and unworthy, celebrate and use. They make no distinction between their priests and other clerics, apart from the bishops, and peasants, and [thus] show no respect for the Divine cult. They make no change to the chant or to the prayers from the

---

[267]   The *Historia Peregrinorum*, pp. 154–5, said that 500 cavalry from Philadelphia had followed the army, and suggests that the fighting was more serious than the *Historia de Expeditione* implies. 'The emperor and the others who were acting as the rearguard of the army with him met these advancing enemies manfully. Many of them were killed, and the others were defeated and scattered in flight, forced to return to Philadelphia with loss and shame.'

[268]   Tageno [below p. 157], or perhaps Magnus as he reworked Tageno, assumed that all these names referred to the same place: thus here the compiler of the *Historia* seems to be using another source, which correctly distinguished Tripoli (modern Yenice), on the River Maeander, from Ierapolis (modern Pammukale).

[269]   Mount Cadmos, which at 2,600 m is indeed 'a very high mountain', where Louis VII and Bishop Otto (the latter in charge of the rear column of the German contingent) took heavy losses during the Second Crusade, in December 1147 and January 1148.

[270]   Unleavened bread. The reference to the Greek belief that the Holy Spirit proceeded from the Father alone and not from the Son refers to Byzantine opposition to the so-called *filioque* clause inserted into the Latin version of the Creed; for which John Meyendorf, *Byzantine Theology. Historical Trends and Doctrinal Themes* (New York, 2nd ed. 1979), pp. 91–4, and for the origins of this dispute, Henry Chadwick, *East and West: The Making of a Rift in the Church, from Apostolic Times until the Council of Florence* (Oxford 2003), pp. 89–94, 183–92.

collect for the feast days during the year or the saints' days, apart from the [Biblical] readings and the Gospels. They anathematise all those who do not agree with their beliefs; they describe all Christians, whether spirituals or secular people in the popular idiom, as seculars, and they pour out arrogant prayers for their conversion. They describe themselves alone as spiritual and orthodox. They separated themselves a long time ago from the jurisdiction of the Holy Roman Church, and they make themselves subject in Divine matters only to their own patriarch, whom they describe as 'universal', giving this Greek Patriarch of Constantinople precedence over the two other patriarchs of Jerusalem and Antioch by name alone. Their priests and clergy are neither vowed to nor observe continence.

On 27 April we descended through a most desolate Turkish region towards a salt lake 'in a deserted land and in the waste',[271] incapable of supporting crops or human life. We found there flocks of sheep, goats and lambs, and herds of cattle, horses, camels and asses, numbering about five thousand, which belonged to nomadic Turks who on our arrival abandoned their tents of felt and fled, climbing up into the mountains.[272] But since we reckoned that they would show themselves peaceful towards us, we did not seize anything of theirs that we came across on our way, desirable and even necessary though it might be. That night, at the head of the lake, we found neither grass, nor plants nor boughs, and as a result many of the horses were suffering. From the next day, and during the days that followed, from 28 April up until 18 May we were beset by evils unheard of in past ages. We had hoped to be free of troubles and harassment in the lands of the Turkish lords, the sultan and his son the Malik,[273] since we had entered them peacefully as friends, and especially since imperial envoys had been sent to them three times within the last two years and had reported a clear and most kindly response to our requests for safe transit and provision of markets, as did envoys of theirs.[274] But quite unexpectedly and contrary to this agreement, they showed themselves not as friends but as most savage enemies, for the Turkish troops, both cavalry and

---

[271] Deuteronomy 32:10. From Laodicia the army marched more or less due east across the plateau of Aci Göl, past Lake Anava, Eickhoff, *Friedrich Barbarossa im Orient*, p. 107.

[272] The *Historia Peregrinorum*, p. 155, commented that: 'It is the custom of the inhabitants of that land who are called "wild Turks" (*silvestres Turci*) or Bedouins to do without houses and to live at all times in tents and to move with their flocks and herds from pasture to pasture. They are always prepared and ready to take up arms and go to war. An innumerable multitude of these now appeared from all sides to fight the pilgrims, and our men were henceforth taught by necessity to strive manfully for their own defence.'

[273] Qilij Arslan II, Sultan of Iconium (Konya) 1155–92, and his eldest son Qutb al-Dīn Malikshāh (d. 1195).

[274] An embassy from the sultan had arrived at Nuremberg in Christmas 1188, for which above p. 45, and the Bishop of Münster's embassy had been intended to negotiate with him as well as with Isaac Comnenos, although the bishop's arrest en route by the Byzantine emperor had prevented this contact.

infantry, even though they were in the service of the sultan and his son, harassed us unceasingly with attacks and missiles and prevented our men collecting fodder.[275] In this desperate situation all our men, insofar as they had arms, marched in their armour and manfully resisted the enemy. God however, 'seeing the affliction of his people',[276] remitted some of the anger that had so strongly burned upon us as a result of our sins, 'wishing to revive His people'.[277] At daybreak on 30 April the aforesaid Turks entered our camp after we had left, hoping to capture those people who had failed to march on because of their exhaustion. The emperor ordered smoke to be made, quite deliberately, and they were blinded; they were suddenly attacked by our men, and nearly three hundred of them were slain, either in the camp itself or on the steep mountain nearby.[278] Those who were left followed us on the very difficult road towards Sozopolis and kept a watch upon us.[279]

On 2 May the persecutors of the Cross of Christ once again started a battle, and our men, though hungry and greatly in need, slew up to three hundred of them. Both in this battle and in the earlier ones, the Duke of Swabia, the Duke of Merania, the Count of Kyburg, who killed seventeen men in a single day, the Count of Öettingen and Frederick, advocate of Berg, were distinguished by their steadfastness and valour. In this perilous situation the Bohemians also displayed their customary courage against the common enemy. Six of the latter put on servants' clothes over their armour and went out as though to gather fodder. Six Turks rushed out upon them like slavering dogs. While the Bohemians at first

---

[275] The problem, of which the Germans were clearly unaware, was that Qutb al-Dīn Malikshāh had during the winter of 1189/90 forced his elderly father to surrender much of his authority, and was not necessarily prepared to abide by any agreement his father may have made. Furthermore his disputes with his brothers had led to a breakdown in the stability of the Seljuk state, which would have made restraining attacks on the Crusaders difficult, even if the rulers had been so minded, Claude Cahen, *Pre-Ottoman Turkey* (London 1968), pp. 110–14; also Claude Cahen, *The Formation of Turkey. The Seljukid Sultanate of Rum: Eleventh to Fourteenth Century* (Harlow 2001), pp. 38–41.

[276] Exodus 3:7, and II Kings 14:26.

[277] II Maccabees 13:11.

[278] The *Historia Peregrinorum*, p. 156, makes sense of this problematic passage, saying that the emperor ordered the abandoned tents to be set on fire as a deliberate trap to lure the Turks into ambush. This author estimated the Turkish losses as five hundred men, and added that this was witnessed by the envoys of the sultan who, disguising their chagrin at the slaughter, pretended to be overjoyed, saying that the Turcomans were outside the sultan's jurisdiction and even sometimes dared to attack his forces. They claimed: 'O, how joyful would be the heart of the sultan, if he knew that they had suffered this reverse.' The army's camp on the night of 29 April was near the sources of the River Maeander.

[279] Sozopolis = modern Burglu, c. 1,250 m above sea level. The emperor John Komnenos had retaken this town from the Turks in 1119, and it had only been lost again c. 1180, Eickhoff, *Friedrich Barbarossa im Orient*, p. 113. In the split of the sultan's dominions in 1189/90, it had been assigned to his son and eventual successor Ghiyāth al-Dīn Kay Khusraw, Cahen, *The Formation of Turkey*, p. 39.

pretended to be afraid, they suddenly whipped out their swords and charged bravely against their attackers, killing all six of them and joyfully leading their horses back to the camp. Furthermore, there was one of our men on foot, who had by now eaten all his foodstuffs, and the only means of life left to him was a single loaf of bread. One of the Turks suddenly shot arrows at him, one of which penetrated through that loaf of bread and the sack placed over it and slightly wounded him. However, he immediately regained his feet, bent his bow and fired a well-directed arrow that struck the enemy through the heart. The Turk fell dead on the ground, and through Divine providence, or so it is believed, our man found nine loaves, and thus was provided with rations for the next ten days.

On 3 May, which was Ascension Day, more than thirty thousand Turks were massed in a very narrow pass through which we were to travel. This was where Manuel, the Emperor of the Greeks, had been defeated with a great army, and the Turks intended to annihilate us in the same way.[280] But 'the Lord turned the counsel of Achitophel into foolishness',[281] since the emperor was warned by the Holy Spirit and took another route. For we traversed with great difficulty a very high and steep mountain, accessible only to the mountain goats, guided by a Turkish prisoner who had promised to lead us by a short cut from this desert land to a more fertile area.[282] While we were amid the defiles of this mountain, the Turks once again attacked us from ambush, shooting arrows and throwing stones down on us from above, as a result of which the Duke of Swabia was wounded by a stone,[283] and

---

[280]   A reference to the Battle of Myriokephalon (1176).

[281]   II Samuel 15:31.

[282]   There is a fuller account in the *Historia Peregrinorum*, pp. 157–8: the emperor offered the prisoner his life if he would guide the army to safety; if he refused he would be immediately beheaded. The Turk agreed to help, and said that there was a choice of two routes, but one of these led into a desert region where they would inevitably perish [this was the military road towards Antioch in Pisidia]. If they followed him along the mountain road, this would, although difficult, lead them to water, and then they would reach the best route towards Iconium. The Turk led them, with an iron chain around his neck. His information turned out to be true, and in the mountains the Crusaders found some Turkish flocks from which they could relieve their hunger, but on the steep descent they lost some horses and many of their pack animals, which slipped over the precipitous drops. According to the *Chronica Regia Coloniensis*, p. 149, the Turk was one of two prisoners taken, one of whom was immediately killed, while the second was promised his life if he would guide the army, 'but he treacherously led them across a mountain that was three miles high'. The *Gesta Federici I Imperatoris in Expeditione Sacra*, p. 88, said that the guide was an emir who volunteered his services to the emperor, saying that the latter could cut off his head if he played him false. Eickhoff, *Friedrich Barbarossa im Orient*, pp. 116–17, suggests that the route the Crusaders took headed northwest, climbing through the mountains to c. 1,600 m. They then swung in a circle to the east, before turning southeast towards Philomelium along the old Roman road from Doryleum to Iconium.

[283]   The *Historia Peregrinorum*, p. 158, said that he lost a tooth; the *Chronica Regia Coloniensis*, p. 150, that he lost two teeth. The *Historia Peregrinorum*, p. 159, added that

some ten other knights were injured, one of whom, named Werner, was killed. Our men would not put up with this, and, valiantly climbing up the mountain on foot in the name of the Lord, they drove the enemy who were so cruelly threatening the emperor's army from there, killing more than sixty of them. Some of our men also seized camels, sheep and oxen in these mountains. That same day we came to a fertile lowland area, where without the emperor's knowledge many of the Turks, along with their wives and little children, were slaughtered.

On 5 May we knew for certain that the friendship and the gold of the sultan 'was turned into dross',[284] and that he and the Greeks had come to an agreement that, since they could not resist us in battle, they would destroy us with treachery. 'But the Lord freed us from all these things'.[285] For the envoys of the sultan and his son, who had met the lord emperor and the army of Christ at Adrianople, treacherously fled from us, on the pretext, so they claimed, of speaking with the emir,[286] taking Gottfried with them as a prisoner.[287] Once again, the deceit of the Turks seemed greater and greater.

On 6 May, which was the feast of St John 'before the Latin gate', our men were once again attacked from the rear by the Turks, more than twenty of whom were killed. Unfortunately, in the pursuit of these Turks, a distinguished knight, Frederick of Hausen, accidentally fell from his horse and died. He was buried beneath a large apple tree. The whole host mourned him as a key figure in the army.[288]

---

the emperor told his son that his wound was an honourable scar, showing that he had fought for the faith.

[284]   Isaiah 1:22.

[285]   Cf. Psalm 33:20.

[286]   The Latin text, as it stands, makes no sense. This translation reads *ammirato* for *admirando* in the phrase *quasi admirando locuturi*, an emendation suggested by Ian Moxon. The emir would presumably have been the commander of the Turks who were attacking the Crusade army, who is referred to somewhat later in the narrative, and whom the *Historia Peregrinorum*, p. 160, called the Emir of Philomelium.

[287]   Gottfried of Wiesenbach, for whom above, p. 92.

[288]   The *Epistola de Morte*, p. 175, adds that he broke his neck in the fall [below, pp. 170–1]. The *Historia Peregrinorum*, p. 159, called him 'a valiant and famous knight'. Hausen is near Bensheim in Hesse, c. 20 km east of Worms. Before the Crusade, Frederick had acted as an imperial agent, notably in the negotiations over the erection of the county of Namur into an imperial principality in 1184, Gilbert of Mons, *Le Chronique de Gislebert de Mons*, pp. 202, 231–2 [*The Chronicle of Hainaut*, pp. 111, 125–6]. Gilbert considered him 'a most virtuous knight (*probissimus miles*)', and considered him to be one of the *familiares* of the emperor, *Le Chronique de Gislebert de Mons*, pp 230, 272 [*The Chronicle of Hainaut*, pp. 125, 150]. He had also taken part in the fifth Italian expedition, *Mainzer Urkundenbuch* ii(2).615–16 no. 372–3 (July 1175). Frederick was in addition a noted poet (*Minnesänger*), Eickhoff, *Friedrich Barbarossa im Orient*, pp. 54–7. The *Historia Peregrinorum* added that on the same day the Turks, when they saw the valiant resistance of the Crusaders, offered through an interpreter to cease their attacks if the emperor paid them off with part of the

On 7 May we camped near the city of Philomelium,[289] to which we had made no threat and which we still hoped might be friendly. About the hour of Vespers the Turks, thinking that we were completely exhausted from hunger, launched a powerful attack on our camp, showering us with stones, darts and lances. However, the army of the life-giving Cross hastened manfully to meet their attacks, first the infantry and then the cavalry, so that 'two put ten thousand to flight',[290] and, if night and the mountains had not intervened, they all would have fallen to the edge of the sword. For as we later learned from the account of our enemies, 4,174 men, both cavalry and infantry, fell [there], and there were also six hundred [more] whom they said had undoubtedly been lost, but whose bodies were never found.[291] This battle took place under the leadership of the Duke of Swabia and the Duke of Merania.

We passed Philomelium on 8 May, and now hunger that was crueller than any enemy grew so strong in our army that an ox and a cow were sold for five marks, and sometimes even for nine, while a small loaf of bread was sold for one mark, moreover the flesh of horses and mules were consumed as if delicacies. Some people, albeit only a few, were made so desperate, or even ensnared by the devil, that they deserted to the enemy, abandoning their intention of [following] the sacred way and unmindful, alas, of the Christian religion.[292] By contrast some of those on foot were so worn down, both by their efforts and by hunger and sickness, and driven to the depths of despair, that when the army marched on they were quite unable to follow. Making the above-mentioned public symbol[293] and saying the Lord's prayer, they steadfastly sent their weeping companions away, and with great constancy of mind willingly prostrated themselves in the form of the Cross, awaiting their imminent death in the name of the Lord. And indeed, we had not moved very far away when the enemies who were following us beheaded them and rendered them martyrs of Christ.[294]

---

army's money, saying that it would be better to lose some of its treasure rather than all of it. The emperor responded 'ironically' that all he was willing to give them was one silver coin, which they could divide equally between them.

[289]   Now Akşehir, Eickhoff, *Friedrich Barbarossa im Orient*, p. 117.

[290]   Deuteronomy 32:30.

[291]   The *Historia Peregrinorum*, p. 160, said that 'about 5,000' Turks were killed. But the author of that text added: 'The more of them fell in battle, the greater their numbers seemed to grow as new ones arrived, like the hydra that was made more fruitful as its heads were cut off.'

[292]   Cf. *Historia Peregrinorum*, p. 161: 'Indeed some of our men, worn down both by hunger and the anxieties of war, were forced to apostatise, handing themselves over to the miserable servitude of [their] enemies. But better were those who suffered the pain of earthly death and [by doing so] gained perpetual freedom for themselves.'

[293]   i.e. the sign of the Cross.

[294]   This incident was also recorded by Arnold of Lübeck, *Chronica Slavorum*, IV.11, p. 135: 'And when men were unable to walk [further], they fell on their faces on the ground,

That night it happened that some of the imperial watchmen saw a memorable and manifest sign of Divine mercy on His army of pilgrims. During the first watch of the night they saw a column of snow-white birds fly three times over the entire army and then come near to the imperial tent, and then fly to the body of a certain poor man who was drawing his last breath. Spreading their wings they hovered in the air for a little while, but once he was dead 'and seeking the upper ether',[295] these birds suddenly disappeared from our sight.

On 9 May a great force of Turks attacked us, so that 'they filled mountains and valleys',[296] and our men pretended weakness. This made them even more savage, and on 11 May they made a [further] attack upon us, shouting. But our men suddenly swung round and killed two hundred of them, and on the mountain near the town of Firmin another fifty or more, that in addition to the sixty-four whom they had slain in the previous two days.[297] Furthermore, among the booty, horses and other things taken from them were sheaves of arrows and darts, on which they were very dependent.

On 12 May, which was the Vigil of Pentecost, we struggled along, hungry and fasting, amid dense swarms of Turks until nightfall, when we crossed over a very narrow bridge where there was barely room for us to go two by two. They could have done us a great deal of harm there, if Divine power had not prevented them. More than twenty of them were killed that day.

The holy day of Pentecost was celebrated on 13 May. We once again marched among the Turks, while hearing mass with the utmost devotion.[298] That day 'our master spared us'[299] from the attacks of the evil Turks. Our delicacies at that feast were the skins of cattle and the blood of horses, or for the rich horseflesh 'in weight or in measure'.[300] Bravery and steadfastness, as well as the utmost alertness,

---

so that they might receive martyrdom in the name of the Lord. The enemy, rushing upon them, slew them without mercy while everyone looked on.'

[295]   Vergil, *Georgics*, I.142.

[296]   After Luke 3:5.

[297]   Firmin = modern Ilgin. According to the *Historia Peregrinorum*, pp. 161–2, the Duke of Swabia led this attack, and the Germans killed a hundred Turks in battle, while others drowned in a nearby lake as they fled (this being before the separate battle on the mountain). The author adds that because of these two battles the army made only a short march on that day. From Firmin the road turned east-southeast, through steppe land over 1,000 m high, Eickhoff, *Friedrich Barbarossa im Orient*, p. 126.

[298]   The *Historia Peregrinorum*, pp. 162–3, adds that Bishop Gottfried of Würzburg preached a sermon that morning, promising the Crusaders eternal life should they be killed, and urging them to 'true penitence and confession'. 'After this address, the most steadfast emperor encouraged everyone and urged them on to the fight. Everyone immediately with one voice raised the battle cry in the German manner.'

[299]   II Kings 5:20.

[300]   Leviticus 19:35. The *Historia Peregrinorum*, p. 162, reported that: 'They pitched camp on the holy day of Pentecost in a barren place, lacking in pasture, but had no choice in the matter. For it was announced on good authority that the Malik was drawing near with five

flourished in the army. But, not undeservedly, 'the Lord chastened us sorely'[301] for the excessive feasting and drunkenness of almost all our people in Greece; however He did not hand us over to death. The deceit and dishonesty of the sultan and his son, from whom we had presumed too much, with the result that we had not furnished ourselves adequately with supplies, had through Divine punishment brought us unexpectedly to this miserable situation. Flour, if it was to be had in the army at all, was guarded and concealed as though it was gold. A little bowl of flour was sold for fourteen shillings [in money] of Cologne.

On the following day, that is 14 May, we marched with the newly created household knights,[302] and lo and behold the sons of the sultan, who had mustered three hundred thousand horsemen, drew up their battle lines and fought with us. But the lord emperor ordered our first line, commanded by the imperial marshal,[303] to charge them bravely. This was done, and they all turned in flight. Furthermore, a religious layman called Ludwig[304] saw a man who was riding a white horse and clad in a snow-white tunic coming to assist us, whom he believed to be St George; while others said that he was an angel of God who miraculously struck down the Turkish column with a single lance.[305] On the descent from the mountain where we

---

hundred thousand horsemen, seeking to meet our men in battle on the morrow. Therefore on the emperor's order all the chosen leaders and warriors of the army were summoned to meet in the emperor's presence; they remained in good spirits but were wretchedly clad. Indeed those who had previously lived delicately and in splendour, and who were accustomed to prepare for the solemn ceremonies of so sacred a day with baths and soft clothes, were now worn down by long fasting, experiencing uncomfortable hardships in dirt and rusty armour, and many of them who were now on foot cast away their hauberks every day.' Cf. here the letter from the Catholicos of Armenia reported in *The Rare and Excellent History of Saladin*, p. 117.

[301]   Psalm 117:18 (Vulgate), 118:18 (AV).

[302]   The army here turned almost due south towards Iconium (modern Konya).

[303]   Heinrich of Kalden, who was later to be one of the most trusted counsellors of the Emperor Henry VI and of the latter's brother, King Philip (of Swabia), and a leader of the German Crusade to the Holy Land in 1197. However, the *Historia Peregrinorum*, p. 164, said that the army was arranged in a triangular formation, in three squadrons (*acies*), the first led by the bishops of Münster and Würzburg, the second to the right rear by the emperor himself, and the third to the left rear by the Duke of Swabia, with the non-combatants placed between them.

[304]   He was identified by the *Epistola de Morte*, p. 176 [below. p. 171], as Ludwig of Helfenstein (near Geislingen in Swabia). He was thus the brother of Bishop Gottfried of Würzburg. The *Historia Peregrinorum*, p. 165, called him 'a certain powerful man in our army named Ludwig'.

[305]   According to the *Gesta Federici Imperatoris*, p. 92, the Bishop of Würzburg and several others claimed to have seen St George fighting for the Christians, while the later chronicle of James of Aqua, that expanded upon this, said that the emperor himself had had a dream of St George, ibid., p. 93. In his sermon the previous day the Bishop of Würzburg had urged the Crusaders to pray for the help of St George, *Historia Peregrinorum*, p. 163.

put to flight the first [Turkish] line, the troops of the lord emperor laid low about a hundred chosen men of the Turks. The lord emperor then steadfastly marched up another mountain that was held by two sons of the sultan and a great multitude of Turks, along with the royal trumpet, and he forced them into a shameful retreat. The Duke of Swabia pursued them too, and the infantry also drove them back manfully. Meanwhile, however, the great Malik was knocked off his horse by one of our knights, and one of his barons had his right hand in its mailed gauntlet cut off by a sword stroke. The Emir of *Crazzarat* then was alleged to have accused his lord the great Malik, or so we were told by a certain Armenian who deserted to us that day, saying: 'Have you not seen that we should not go near this army, whose strength is not human but Divine? For some of my most reliable knights reckoned that there were today seven thousand men in white, riding snow-white horses, at the head of that army, who all struck us most violently with the lances that they held in their hands, and forced us to flee. If there were so many white horses, how many horses do you think there were of another colour? What glory do you think will be gained from your most shameful flight today with your three hundred thousand men?'[306]

A certain emir of the Turks who was one of our hostages later said that the King of Galatia had been summoned by the sultan's son to bring help against us, that he had come with ten thousand armed men, and he had that day closely observed our forces, and noted the courage of both cavalry and infantry, and their fierce attacks on the many thousands of Turks. He said to [the] Malik, 'where are the treasures, all the arms and plunder that you said would be in your hands, part of which you promised to me? Those people whom you claimed were weak and all but dead, wasting away with hunger and lacking horses, have with unrivalled courage put more than three hundred thousand to flight. Has anyone seen two more contrary things to have happened? For these people are hastening inevitably to their deaths, but even though [they are supposed to be] dead, they are fighting back most steadfastly in battle.'

Since, after this victory was secured, we did not 'sing a hymn to God', 'we paid the appropriate penalty',[307] for after great heat and hardship, the army found itself at sunset in a sandy desert, split up by a dust storm and surrounded by enemies, wandering about here and there like bleating sheep. Finally, however, they found the standards of the army and made camp, but one without either water or grazing. As a result a great many of the horses perished, while the men were parched with thirst. Next morning we set off on our march as though half-dead; some people

---

[306] *Crazzarat* may have been Çankiri, to the northeast of Ankara, Cahen, *The Formation of Turkey*, p. 41. The *Historia Peregrinorum*, p. 164, reported a similar speech, adding that the great man who made it presented Qutb al-Dīn with the severed arm of the Turk. But the sense of what was said was altered, for according to the *HP* the emir then urged his lord not to fight the Crusaders, but rather to refuse battle and rely on hunger to destroy their army.

[307] Judith 16:15; II Maccabees 7:36.

drank their own urine, others the blood of their horses, while some chewed horse dung for moisture, and many ate plants from the earth, until we finally found some boggy ground where there was water. But since they were unable to find wood, reeds or straw on which we could cook horseflesh, many people made fires from the saddles of horses or from various sorts of tent, tunics or shirts.[308] On 15 May our horses were to some extent refreshed by these bogs, and we remained there too the next day, that is 16 May, but we lost almost sixty young boys there, killed by a Turkish attack.[309]

While we were there, the great Malik and his satrap sent an envoy to us, who said that if the emperor and the army gave them three hundred *centenarii* of gold, and the land of the Armenians,[310] then they would grant us safe passage, and would have a market set up three days later. The emperor responded with his customary good temper, saying: 'It is not our imperial law, nor should the army of the Christians and the knighthood of the life-giving Cross become accustomed to buying a royal passage with gold and silver, but with the help of our Lord Jesus Christ, for whom we are knights, a way shall be opened with our swords.'[311] The envoy then left, saying: 'If I do not return to you tonight, you should know for certain that tomorrow, before the third hour, the Turks will be fighting you with the utmost determination.' But since the army and its horses, as a result of what had happened earlier, were greatly in want, 'we began to be greatly sorrowful and very heavy'.[312] However, He who is 'a refuge in time of troubles',[313] who always wants to spare rather than to punish, inspired the hearts of the bishops to encourage the people, with fatherly and salutary warning, to beg for Divine help and to call upon

---

[308]   Cf. *Historia Peregrinorum*, p. 166, which said that horse and donkey flesh was cooked for the more important men, while the rank and file subsisted on herbs and roots; and also the letter from the Catholicos of Armenia reported by *The Rare and Excellent History of Saladin*, p. 117.

[309]   From this point onwards the *Historia* closely follows the diary of Tageno, see Güterbock, 'Il Diario di Tageno', pp. 254-64.

[310]   Cilicia, which had been settled by Armenian immigrants during the twelfth century, and was now a loose confederation of independent principalities, under the overall rule of the Roupenid dynasty, T.S.R. Boase, *The Cilician Kingdom of Armenia* (Edinburgh 1978), especially pp. 12–18 [see also below, note 344].

[311]   The *Historia Peregrinorum*, p. 167, added that the emperor said: 'nor does it seem proper that a price should be paid to obtain passage for the pilgrims of Christ'. Cf. Arnold of Lübeck, *Chronica Slavorum*, IV.12, p. 136: 'It is indeed unheard of that the Emperor of the Romans should pay tribute to any mortal person, for he is rather accustomed to exact tribute rather than to pay it. However, since our forces are exhausted, and to secure our passage in peace, I shall voluntarily pay you one penny, which is called a *manlat*. If you are unwilling to accept this and prefer to fight us, let it be known that we are most willing to do battle with you in the name of Christ, and we are willing for love of Him to conquer or be conquered.'

[312]   Cf. Matthew 26:37.

[313]   Psalm 9:10.

the name of St George the Martyr, who is indeed held in high regard throughout the Catholic Church, and who had appeared during our travails on several occasions to religious men, with hymns of praise and promises of fasting to the utmost of their ability.[314] To speak more plainly, they entreated God, with many sighs and tears, to give them the saint as their standard-bearer, champion and advocate. With our affairs appearing to be in a very dangerous situation, even the lord emperor was somewhat apprehensive, although he kept this to himself, about the next day's camp, which he intended to make in a wild animal park and orchard of the sultan. He said to the members of his household: 'If tomorrow, with the help of God, we are able to pitch our tents with any sort of security, it is no bad omen for our future peace.'[315]

The next morning, 17 May, we heard a solemn mass and one by one took most Holy Communion in the name of the Lord, through which the many weak and sick were strengthened, and then we set off, albeit rather late. The Turks, of whom there was an innumerable multitude, surrounded us in a half-moon formation, and greatly harassed us with their yelling and attacks. They remained with us until we arrived at our camp, but without inflicting any harm upon us, while they lost about sixty of their men. When we entered the royal park and its orchard, we found a great abundance of plants and water. That night we suffered from thunderstorms and unusual cloudbursts. When dawn arrived, the lord emperor drew up [the army in] two divisions; the first he entrusted to his son the Duke of Swabia, the second he himself commanded. He instructed the clergy and those knights who lacked arms, along with the rest of the common people, the baggage and pack animals, to march in between them. He also issued an imperial edict[316] that, if God should grant us the victory, nobody was to be allowed to search for booty until the enemy forces were stretched out on the ground and the city was in our hands. But while we were making preparations, an envoy of the sultan and his sons met us, 'seeking

---

[314]   The *Historia Peregrinorum*, p. 167, said that the emperor vowed to found a church dedicated to St George if the saint helped them to secure victory.

[315]   'After the envoys [of the sultan] had left, our men were extremely anxious, and there was disagreement in the emperor's presence as to what the best plan was. For it seemed safer to many to hasten from the land of the enemy towards Armenia, insofar as the army was still able to march, and to pass by Iconium without stopping, since it did not seem feasible that such a great city could be stormed by so few, and particularly since there were so many to fight us both within and without, and they were indeed hemming us in and besieging us every day in the open field, and we were scarcely able to protect ourselves. However, someone of a fiercer and hardier spirit urged to the contrary, saying that: "even if the enemy do not levy battle, we are so short of food that in my opinion we will not be able to march nor to live for very long. Armenia is still a long way away, a large number of our horses are failing, and we have now suffered for a long time from hunger and shortage and are ourselves weakened. It would be better for us to attack boldly and to fall honourably in battle rather than to suffer a slow and cowardly death because we are afraid".' *Historia Peregrinorum*, p. 167.

[316]   *Edictum exiit* is taken from Lucan, *Pharsalia*, II.1.

those things that were of peace'.[317] The emperor replied that if his own envoy was freed from captivity and returned to him, and diligent and wise ambassadors were sent who knew about and had powers to conduct such important negotiations, then they would find him in earnest in concluding a peace agreement. But after the envoy's departure, the emperor realised that all this was a trick, intended to create a disastrous delay. He ordered his son to set out on the march. When the duke, following his father's instructions, had marched steadfastly up to the gate of Iconium, the knight Gottfried was freed from his captivity and came out to meet him, saying: 'May the Lord bless you, go on confidently; "God has given this city into your hands",[318] and the land too.' For the sultan had gone out to meet the army with six hundred armed knights, although it is doubtful whether his intentions were good or evil, but when he saw the first squadron he and his men turned tail and fled, entering the citadel that overlooked the city. Almost all the townspeople, both rich and poor, also took refuge there, carrying with them vast stocks of gold, silver and precious textiles, as well as a plentiful stock of foodstuffs, and they shut up their horses, asses and cattle in their fortifications.

The most steadfast duke and his men stormed the outer gate of the city, despite the vigorous resistance of the Turks, who were with the help of God defeated.[319] They pursued them right up to the gate of the heavily fortified citadel, putting all those whom they found in the city to the sword. The duke thus captured the city and slew its citizens. [Meanwhile] a wonderful thing happened, in the following way. While the Duke of Swabia was indeed, with the help of an angel of the Lord, triumphing in the city, the emperor's division had remained for quite some time outside the gardens of the town, unaware of this, for it was surrounded by a vast horde of Turks whose attacks were so fierce that we who were there were expecting death to fall upon us at any moment. The bishops and many of the priests were offering the living Host to the High Priest,[320] wishing for the purposes of their office to place their stoles round their necks, to be covered over with that stole of immortality, saying gloriously with the Apostle, 'having a desire to depart and to be with Christ'.[321] [Then] a holy legion of most exceptional soldiers, to be compared in every respect with the legion of Theban martyrs, everyone united with the desire to shed their blood for Christ, stood there undaunted, so that no trace of weakness appeared, either in them or in their warhorses.[322] In their midst was that

---

[317]   Ibid., XIV.32.

[318]   Jeremiah 34:2.

[319]   The *Historia Peregrinorum*, p. 169, reported that first of all an advance party of the Germans was forced to withdraw amid a shower of missiles, but the duke then rallied his troops, telling them: 'return immediately to the fight, and let your courage be stimulated by the memory of that God for whom you have assumed the sign of the life-giving Cross'.

[320]   i.e. celebrating Mass.

[321]   Philippians 1:23.

[322]   The Theban Legion, led by St Maurice, were reputed to have been martyred *en masse* in Gaul by the Emperor Maximian (286–305) for their refusal to make pagan

glorious Emperor of the Romans Frederick, to whom no equal could be found in the whole world. Although he had often been victorious over most mighty lands, conquering Tuscany, Lombardy, Apulia and Burgundy, and had seen innumerable men laid low in warlike encounters, he is supposed to have shed some tears in this perilous situation, and said that: 'If the Christian army, that is today in such a tight spot for love of our Father in Heaven, should arrive safe in Antioch, I would be happy to suffer the loss of my imperial head, even though such a punishment is quite improper to be visited upon the person of an emperor.' After saying this, and with all those who were there shedding tears of joy in their desire for eternal reward and wonder at his mighty and invariable courage, this great emperor added: 'why are we hesitating, what is there to fear? May Christ rule [us], Christ be victorious, Christ command [us]'.[323] And although his efforts had greatly tired him, he was, like Judas Maccabeus, noble of heart. He first turned round his warhorse, and, with the others bravely accompanying him, he charged down on the enemy like a lion and put them to flight. Not one of them raised his hand against him but all turned and fled away from his presence. The sons of Belial lost about three thousand men, and if our knights had not been so weak from hunger the citadel would have been stormed that very night. However, the knights had for some two weeks been suffering from the appalling and unprecedented shortage of food.

The lord emperor then made his entry to the city with his army following behind him, and received a magnificent welcome from his son and his companions, and there the suffering of our bellies was to some extent relieved by the spoil taken from the enemy. Many of our men discovered grain pits filled with wheat and barley, and as a result the men and their horses were very greatly restored. Moreover there are those who claim that the booty gained in this city, in gold, silver, jewels and purple cloths, came to a value of more than a hundred thousand marks. For in the house of the great Malik 'there is treasure to be desired'.[324] It is said that what was found there was the dowry that the evil Saladin had given to him along with his daughter.

On the following day, that is 19 May, we began to praise the name of the Lord, since 'he giveth us the victory' over our enemies.[325] The mass said this: 'the love

---

sacrifices. St Maurice, the patron of Magdeburg cathedral and of the Bavarian monastery of Niederaltaich, was highly esteemed in Germany; see Maurice Zuffery, 'Der Mauritius-kult im Früh und Hochmittelalter', *Historisches Jahrbuch* 106 (1986), 23–58, especially pp. 48–53.

[323]   *Christus regnat, Christus vincit, Christus imperat*: the so-called *laudes regiae* or ceremonial chant used to honour medieval rulers.

[324]   Proverbs 21:20. The *Historia Peregrinorum*, p. 170, said that the plunder in the Malik's house alone was estimated to be worth 10,000 marks: 'And this had been sent there by Saladin for the work of hiring an army of mercenaries (*stipendiarii*) against us.'

[325]   I Corinthians 15:57.

of God is shed abroad'.[326] That office was therefore very much in accord with our joy and our vows; there was even a mention of Iconium in it.

After this the sultan and his sons, and the emirs, saw that 'they had dug a pit' for us 'into the midst of which they have fallen themselves',[327] and lamented. They sent their envoys to the lord emperor, begging that 'in the bowels of mercy' he respect the land and its people, and 'recompense no man evil for evil',[328] and in return they would show him every sort of honour that he desired in recompense for the harm that they had brought upon him. They added further that they would try in every way they could to assuage the anger of his imperial majesty.[329] Since therefore it was not the emperor's intention to hold up the journey of the life-giving Cross with any difficult negotiations, he discussed the matter with the princes and replied in this way:

'The sultan sent envoys to us, in accordance with the friendship that he has for a long time had with our empire,[330] invited us to his land, and promised us safe conduct and good markets for us and our army. Furthermore, other ambassadors from him and from his son [the] Malik came into our presence at Adrianople to promise us greater and more favourable benefits than those promised earlier, both to us and to those who entered this land with us. Instead, they have provided for us as a safeguard bows and arrows, swords and lances and every sort of weapon, they have offered us attacks and strange war cries, and instead of the provision of markets that we were promised in an appearance of faithful friendship the great Malik has attacked us and our army with all the courage and power of his race. "They have compassed me about like bees; they are quenched as the fire of thorns."[331] Nevertheless, in the name of our Lord Jesus Christ the Roman emperor and special advocate of the land of Jerusalem has penetrated the squadrons of the enemy in safety and put to flight the multitudes of your army, "our God hath given

---

[326]   Romans 5:5.

[327]   Psalm 56:7 (Vulgate), 57:6 (AV), also quoted by the *Historia Peregrinorum*, p. 170.

[328]   Luke 1:78, Romans 12:7.

[329]   'They [the sultan and Qutb al-Dīn] therefore sent envoys to the emperor, saying: "the sultan admits his fault and looks for your customary mercy. He does not despair of gaining pardon from you, since he was forced to this breach of long-standing agreements and good relations through evil counsel and pressure from his men, for he is now an old man, who is feeble and unwarlike. He begs you for peace and mercy, that your majesty might deign to spare for his sake the people of the city and his land. He promises a more secure peace and to furnish a market for horses and foodstuffs until you leave his kingdom. To guarantee these conditions, he is ready to provide most distinguished hostages, whomsoever you should wish, with the sole exception of his son the Malik."', *Historia Peregrinorum*, p. 170.

[330]   The diplomatic relations between Germany and the Seljuks went back at least as far as 1172, when Duke Henry the Lion of Saxony had been granted safe passage through Seljuk territory on his return from pilgrimage to Jerusalem.

[331]   Psalm 117:12 (Vulgate), 118:12 (AV).

the city into our hands".[332] But since the Roman emperor ought always to have as his companions "mercy and justice",[333] and prefers rather to spare than to wound, we have decided to impart this grace to you and your lords, that our peace may be upon you, provided that you give hostages into our keeping, so that we may leave your land in complete safety and with a good market.'

On hearing this, the envoys most joyfully reported it back to the sultan and his son. The latter put what had been proposed into effect within a short space of time, giving ten emirs and ten other great barons as hostages.[334]

The army left Iconium on 23 May,[335] and camped next to the royal park as before, where we found a market where things were sold, admittedly dearly, but sufficient for our needs. For there, according to my reckoning, more than six thousand horses and mules were sold, not counting asses, and the army was well supplied with bread and meat, as well as butter and cheese.

On 26 May we marched over a very broad plain and came to forty springs. The next day we arrived at a great lake that was fit to drink. There, since the Turcomans had still not all ceased to follow us, the lord emperor spoke to the hostages: 'If your Turks will not stop following us, and if a market is not provided for the army, as has been arranged, then you will certainly be put to death.' Afterwards we experienced very little harm from them. We then marched on, passing a great village where we saw many vineyards, but little water. We went on by a difficult road to another village called Pergos, where we found a good market and rested for a day.[336] Late in the day on 30 May we came to the fine town of Karaman, which is on the border between Licaonia and Cilician Armenia. Iconium is the capital of Licaonia.

If I should try to describe in full all the many troubles, oppressions, hunger and thirst, tricks and deceits, insults and attacks, that the army of Christ patiently endured, with a smiling face and without complaint, in the land of the Turks, for the sake of Christ and the honour of the life-giving Cross, 'though I speak with the tongues of men and of angels',[337] my efforts would only cause annoyance, since 'I have nothing to draw with and the well is deep'.[338] For I think that a full and proper description of so great an enterprise would, if they were still alive, leave the

---

[332]   Joshua 6:16.

[333]   Tobit 3:2.

[334]   Ibn al-Athīr suggested that the hostages whom Qutb al-Dīn gave to the Germans were 'twenty or so emirs whom he disliked', *The Chronicle of Ibn al-Athīr*, ii.375.

[335]   The *Historia Peregrinorum*, p. 171, said that the smell of the corpses encouraged this move.

[336]   Pergos = modern Kazimkarabehiv. The army was following the old Roman military road southeast from Iconium to Karaman. There were two possible routes that it could have taken from Iconium; it followed the more southerly of the two, Eickhoff, *Friedrich Barbarossa im Orient*, pp. 137–8.

[337]   I Corinthians 13:1.

[338]   John 4:11.

legendary Homer, the eloquent Lucan or the Mantuan poet himself placing their finger over their mouths as though speechless.[339]

And it happened that as the army of the life-giving Cross was moving its camp from Karaman, where it had to some extent recovered its strength, we came to a village of the Armenians. There we found crosses erected in the fields by the Christians, as a result of which our hearts were uplifted by great 'joy and gladness'.[340] We had neither seen nor heard for a long time anything of those who belonged to the glorious Christian religion. As we marched onwards, we climbed some mountains, barely accessible even to mountain goats, which we crossed with the utmost difficulty. Here we left the region held by the most treacherous Turks. The hostages provided by the sultan and his son then vehemently requested that they be sent back to their homes, adding indeed that the agreement specified that they should be released at this point. However, the princes utterly disregarded their pleas, rather the order was given that they be placed under stricter guard. While we faced the appalling difficulty of 'the height of the mountain',[341] the prince of Sibilia, a powerful and distinguished man, met the lord emperor, whom he welcomed with great respect, and insofar as he could he provided a market for the army. Sibilia is a very well-defended fortress and frontier district that he defends from the frequent attacks of the Turks.[342] On the descent from this mountain, the sons of 'the right hand of the most High'[343] pitched camp next to a large, shallow lake, where our beasts found good grazing. Then we stayed in a broad plain where there was excellent grazing and we rested there for two days. However, many of the people began to suffer so greatly from hunger here that as before they ate horseflesh, while even the princes and barons had remarkably little to put on the table during our passage through these mountain slopes.

As we were descending near this lake, which is called Selephica, we made our camp next to a stone bridge, and there the distinguished envoys of the lord Leo of the Mountains met the lord emperor on 7 June.[344] On behalf of their lord, as is the custom of their people, they showed a friendly disposition, ordering that we should be given every assistance from their people and land. The lord emperor welcomed them as men of worth, took their advice as to the route of the army, and learned from them that we were about to follow a very steep and difficult path. The

---

[339]   The Mantuan poet is Vergil.

[340]   Luke 1:14.

[341]   II Kings 19:23.

[342]   To be identified with modern Mauga Kalesi, where there are still the remains of a castle. Sibilia had been the seat of a bishopric in the early Middle Ages. Eickhoff, *Friedrich Barbarossa im Orient*, pp. 143–7.

[343]   Psalm 76:11 (Vulgate), 77:10 (AV).

[344]   The leader of this embassy was Nerses of Lamphron, Archbishop of Tarsus. Leo, the leader of the Roupenid clan, was the most powerful lord of Cilician Armenia, and was subsequently recognised as king of that region by the Emperor Henry VI and the papacy in 1197, ruling until his death in 1219.

most pious emperor felt fatherly sorrow for all his pilgrims, and so he ordered this information to be kept secret, to prevent the people being upset by the difficulty of the way and the lack of supplies if they heard of the labours that would beset them. For day after day, good things and happiness, and the abundance of a good market, were promised to us, but it all turned out very differently.

For on the following day, 9 June, we came with the utmost difficulty to the resting place. The usual formation of the army was not observed because of the extraordinary difficulty of the way, nor did the squadrons of the princes and of [their] companions wait [for others], but every single person tried to get in front of the others as best they could. That night the greater part of the army crossed a very high mountain that lay along the shore of the water mentioned above. The darkness of the night prevented them from seeing the many dangers of the narrow, rocky path, which in daylight terrified those following our route, and we gather from what they told us they were in a very difficult situation. For who would be so stony-hearted and stiff-necked not to dissolve into tears when he saw bishops and most distinguished knights carried in horse litters because of long-running bouts of illness, and a horse in front of, and sometimes after, his lord, whom he was carrying, on a very high, narrow and stony ridge, and menaced by a terrible fall to one's death? One could see there how praiseworthy and deserving of reward was the zeal of those men who are called squires, who carried their sick lords over this mountain 'in the sweat of their brow'.[345]

On the descent from that mountain we found an abundance of vegetables, and by having these for dinner there we recovered a little bit. It happened, however, that the lord emperor and those who were with him wished to avoid the dangers of the mountain that lay before their eyes, and so acting on the advice of the local people, when the rays of the morning sun began to shine, they descended towards the lakeshore. But this was no less hard work than faced those who descended by the mountain ridge. Indeed, so it is said, certain bishops and powerful princes abandoned their horses at various places where deadly danger threatened with the water to their right and the mountain cliff to their left, and crept along on their hands and feet like a four-footed creature. But all these things seemed delightful and pleasant to them for love of 'Him who orders the steps of man',[346] and with the desire for the Heavenly land for which they longed.

The vanguard that marched forth that day, 10 June, had made camp in the plain of Seleucia.[347] All the members of the army of the Holy Cross, both rich and poor, sick and those who seemed still healthy, were now toiling one and all because of the difficulty of the way, through rocky crags that were accessible only to the mountain goats and birds, and also the warmth of the sun and the raging heat. The emperor, who was unruffled by any danger, wanted to alleviate the dreadful

---

[345]   Genesis 3:19.

[346]   Psalm 36:23 (Vulgate), 37:23 (AV).

[347]   The diary of Tageno ended at this point, and from now on the account is once again independent.

heat and to avoid the mountain peaks by swimming across the fast-flowing river of Seleucia. But since, as the wise man says: 'nor should you struggle against the force of the river', that man who was wise in other matters tried in vain to pit his strength against the flow and 'the force of the river'.[348] Even though everyone warned him against this, he entered the water and was swept away by the flood. He who had so often escaped great dangers died miserably. We should be confident in the secret judgement of God what was intended by the death of this great man: 'Who shall then say, wherefore hast thou done so?'[349] For we are certain that one who stood forth as a knight of Christ and wore His Cross in warfare for Him and in the praiseworthy attempt to recover the land of the Lord, notwithstanding his sudden end, will undoubtedly find salvation. The other nobles who were with him hastened to his aid, albeit too late; however, they got hold of his body and brought it to the bank.[350]

Everyone was deeply upset by his death, and so keenly stricken by grief that some people, torn between fear and hope, finished their lives with him; others indeed despaired, and, seemingly thinking that God had abandoned His care of them, renounced their Christian faith and went over to the heathen. Hence appalling grief and lamentation, not unmerited given the death of such a great prince, lodged in every heart, so that they should rightly bemoan with the prophet, saying: 'the crown has fallen from our head; woe unto us, that we have sinned, for this our heart is faint'.[351]

The Duke of Swabia, a very distinguished prince and the most noble heir of his father, was now chosen and enthusiastically acclaimed by everyone as the leader of the Christian army. Taking the body of his father with him, he brought it to the city of Tarsus in Cilicia, where he laid his intestines to rest with great reverence.[352]

---

[348] Ecclesiastes 4:32; Psalm 45:5 (Vulgate)

[349] II Samuel 16:10.

[350] It was only in later sources that it was alleged that Frederick was rescued from the river while still alive and expired later, Hiestand, 'Barbarossa und der Kreuzzug', p. 107. The *Historia Peregrinorum*, p. 172, concludes with the words: 'And so, lamentably, the emperor was recovered but to the confusion and ruin of the army expired. O what a horrible and wretched mischance for the Christian people, through whose sins the pillar of law and faith was overthrown! O fatal and hateful river bed, in which the light of all honesty was extinguished! In a little stream the head and leader of the entire world was snatched away. Of whom … [*MS. ends at this point*]. For a comparison of all the various versions of Frederick's death, see Nicholson, *Chronicle of the Third Crusade*, p. 65 note 108.

[351] Lamentations 5:16–17.

[352] They followed the coast road, a journey of c. 90 km, to Tarsus, and from there the main body took the old Roman military road to Mamistra, Eickhoff, *Friedrich Barbarossa im Orient*, pp. 162–4. The separate burial of the intestines was a necessary measure to avoid the speedy decomposition of the corpse, and the appalling smells that would result, when refrigeration was not available. Cf. the death of the Landgrave of Thuringia in 1191, as described by the *Cronica Reinhardsbrunnensis*, MGH SS xxx(1).546–7. His intestines were buried at Acre, his flesh in Cyprus and his bones brought back to Germany. But such

Here the army of the Lord was divided. Some set off for Tripoli, which was [still] in Christian hands, while others marched towards Antioch under the leadership of the aforesaid Duke of Swabia. They arrived at the port of St Symeon on 19 June. They arrived at Antioch on 21 June, where the envoys of the lord Leo of the Mountains had also come, so as to meet the lord emperor, for they had not yet heard the news of his death, but when they were informed of this they were even more upset than other people.[353] There also the remainder of his corpse received a royal burial, as was fitting, in the cathedral church of St Peter, the prince of the Apostles, amid inconsolable lamentation.[354]

They intended to rest and recoup there after their great labours and lack of food and hunger pangs, but there was such widespread sickness and death there that scarcely anyone was spared, of whatever age or condition, for both noble and poor, young and old, were all struck down indiscriminately. Among those who were taken from us and buried there was Gottfried, the wise and venerable Bishop of Würzburg, whose diligence had guided the whole army of the Lord, along with other bishops and princes, whom it would take too long to name.[355] While he was still breathing, he instructed those of his *fideles* who were present at his deathbed that, after his death, they should cut off his right hand and carry it back to Würzburg, so that memory of him should not perish but always remain alive in that church, which he had adorned with that same hand in praise of the Divine name. Those who survived this great disaster and remained there with the Duke of Swabia, who had taken over the leadership of the knighthood of Christ from his mighty father, took ship and went to Ptolomais, also called Acre, where

---

division of the remains had long been usual practice for high-status burials in Germany; thus in 1002 the intestines of the Emperor Otto III had been interred at Augsburg, while the rest of his corpse was buried at Aachen, *Ottonian Germany. The Chronicon of Thietmar of Merseburg*, trans. David A. Warner (Manchester 2001), Bk. IV.51, 53, pp. 188–90.

[353]   Güterbock, 'Il Diario di Tageno', pp. 264–6, suggests that here the author misunderstood his source, which may be the account of Magnus, and the dates for the arrival at St Symeon and Antioch given here were those when the group, which included Tageno, who went by sea arrived, rather than for the main body of the army, which had anyway been delayed by the obsequies for the emperor. Those following the land route would not, anyway, have needed to travel via St Symeon. But the land route from Tarsus to Antioch is about 160 km over quite difficult terrain, and Duke Frederick was also unwell, Eickhoff, *Friedrich Barbarossa im Orient*, pp. 164–6.

[354]   According to the 'Itinerary of the Pilgrims' and Roger of Howden, Frederick's flesh was buried at Antioch, but his bones, which it was intended should be buried at Jerusalem, were eventually interred at Tyre, *Itinerarium Peregrinorum*, p. 302 = Nicholson, *Chronicle of the Third Crusade*, p. 66; *Gesta Regis Ricardi*, in *Gesta Henrici Secundi Regis*, ed. William Stubbs (2 vols, Rolls Series, London 1867), ii.89. Willibrand of Oldenburg inspected the marble sarcophagus that contained Frederick's remains in Antioch cathedral in 1212, *Itinerarium Terrae Sanctae*, c. 14, p. 214.

[355]   His death was also briefly noted by Arnold of Lübeck, *Chronica Slavorum*, IV.13, pp. 138–9.

the whole of the army of the Cross of Christ was reunited. There, however, both those who had first laid siege to this city, which the Turks had fortified and were defending fiercely, and those who arrived later were dying miserably. So great was the mortality that it seemed as if the human race was now coming to an end, but as the Prophet says: 'abroad the sword bereaveth, at home there is as death'.[356] An unparalleled disease and pestilence struck down absolutely everyone, so that those who had not finished their lives at Antioch and sought to delay their death sailed even though sick to Acre and died there, while those who had fallen ill while besieging that city similarly found their deaths. Among them was the Duke of Swabia, who had been the most ardent athlete of God and terror of the Saracens, who died along with other noble warriors in the holy struggle.[357] Some died slowly, others quickly, but all fell victim to the same fate and bowed to the same inevitable necessity. Among them was the venerable Bishop Diepold of Passau, who, born into a family of imperial blood, entered with the others on the way of all flesh.[358] The canons and clerics of his church died with him, some at Acre, while Tegno and his companions died at Tripoli.[359] Bishop Diepold died on 13 November. We have been unable to note down the dates of the deaths of the other princes, since such fatal days came one after another.

In the year of the Lord 1190 King William of Sicily, who piously assisted all the pilgrims setting out on the expedition to Jerusalem, died without heir. Since the royal line died out with him, as a result bitter dispute arose in the kingdom concerning the succession.[360] Some people put forward a certain Tancred, who derived his descent not from the royal house but from a private family. The Roman prince, Henry, to whom his father, the glorious emperor Frederick, had left the kingdom when he had set off with his army on the journey to Jerusalem, ought by right to have succeeded, because he had previously married the sister of this same Sicilian king.[361] He set out with his wife and those princes who had remained at home on a royal expedition to obtain the kingdom, which belonged to him by marital right, and to drive out its invader. Along the way on his journey to Apulia

---

[356]   Lamentations 1:20.

[357]   He died on 20 January 1191. The *Historia* says nothing of the tensions among the besiegers to which his arrival at Acre was alleged to have given rise, mentioned by the *Itinerarium Peregrinorum*, p. 334 (Nicholson, *Chronicle of the Third Crusade*, p. 100).

[358]   For the relationship of Diepold with the Staufen, see above notes 65, 68.

[359]   That is Tageno, Dean of Passau, and the other clergy of that church whose deaths were recorded by Magnus of Reichersberg [below, p. 166].

[360]   William II of Sicily actually died on 18 November 1189, aged 36.

[361]   Tancred was in fact a member of the royal family, for he was the illegitimate son of Duke Roger of Apulia (d. 1149), the eldest son of King Roger of Sicily, who had predeceased his father. He was thus the first cousin of William II. He was crowned king in February 1190. Henry VI's wife Constance was actually William II's aunt, not his sister, being the youngest child of King Roger, who was born shortly after his death in February 1154.

it was his intention to be promoted to imperial rank through papal anointing and blessing. There fortune favoured him, and he happily entered Tuscany without opposition and without bloodshed. Clement, who had formerly been known as Paul, Bishop of Palestrina, had died, and Henry and his wife received the blessing, the imperial crown and regalia from Celestine, formerly called Hyacinth, on the day after Easter, which was 26 March. For this same lord pope had only recently been elected; he had been first made deacon, and then, in the middle of Lent, on the Saturday called 'Thirst' [*Sitientes*] priest, and he had been consecrated as pope on Easter Day, that is on 25 March. On the day after he promptly and splendidly raised the king and queen to imperial rank. Among the other princes who were in the company of this same emperor, their lord, were Otto, also known as Conrad, Duke of the Bohemians, and Henry, the brother of Duke Leopold of Austria, [both of whom] had taken the sign of pilgrimage. But although they sought above all to fight for the King of Kings, they were however bearing arms for their lord the King of the Romans against the enemies of the empire, but they had no intention of withdrawing from their original design. Also on this expedition were the lord Archbishop Philip of Cologne, and the son of the former Duke of Saxony, Henry, also called Henry after his father, who was undertaking this service in the hope of recovering his father's rank, which the latter had lost some time previously when the Emperor Frederick had been fighting against the Lombards and he had refused him his help.[362] But I do not know what excuse he seized upon to return home secretly and without permission. Meanwhile, after his coronation, to begin with matters went well for the Emperor Henry, but he then laid siege to Naples, and during this siege, which lasted for a long time, he lost many of his princes, notably the Archbishop of Cologne and Duke Otto of Bohemia, as well as various others. He himself fell ill and was forced to retreat, along with those who had survived this epidemic unscathed and with the sick.[363]

It was not just, however, from the territory of the Roman Empire but from the other western kingdoms, namely France and England, that the kings, along with all the inhabitants of their lands, were signed by the mark of the Cross and roused to undertake the way of the Lord. Wishing indeed to hinder the fulfilment of this

---

[362] Frederick had deprived Henry the Lion of his duchy in April 1180, and had confiscated the imperial fiefs the latter had held, although Henry was allowed to retain his allodial land in Brunswick. The ducal title, and the eastern part of the region, was then granted to Count Bernhardt of Anhalt (d. 1212), while the western part was given to the archbishopric of Cologne. For Henry's refusal to aid the emperor in Italy (in 1176), see Jordan, *Henry the Lion*, pp. 161–4.

[363] The siege of Naples began in May 1191, and was eventually abandoned on 24 August. Archbishop Philip, who had played an important part in the diplomatic preparations for this expedition, died on 12 or 13 August, and Duke Otto on 9 September 1191; see Hubert Houben, 'Philipp von Heinsberg, Heinrich VI und Montecassino. Mit einen Exkurs zum Todesdatum Papst Clemens' III', *Quellen und Forschungen aus Italienischen Archiven und Bibliotheken* 68 (1988), 52–73.

praiseworthy intention, the enemy of the human race sowed dissension between these same kings, so that they fought prolonged campaigns against each other and postponed the cause of the Lord, which they ought to have undertaken against the enemies of the faith. Neither [of them] was willing to begin the journey without the other [doing so], nor would he give way to the other. Finally, they were led by zeal for God to pretend that no hatred lay between them, and they set out on the journey.[364] King Philip of France and the noble count of Flanders travelled through Italy with a great company and took ship at Genoa, intending to make the sea crossing; but since the harsh weather of autumn drove them back they were forced to remain at the city of Messina in Calabria for the whole of [the rest of] that year. King Richard of England was also diligent in all aspects of the business, and, accompanied by a vast army and its equipment, and with so much money that it was more than all his companions on the way of the Lord had, he set sail over the sea with many galleys, but he [too] was forced for the same reason as above to put into this same port of Messina and spend the winter there.[365]

Duke Leopold of Austria had also for a long time burned with desire to go on this pilgrimage, even though he had only recently returned home and despite the fact that he had been requested and summoned by his lord, the then King of the Romans Henry, to join his expedition. He preferred however to wage war for the Eternal King rather than a temporal one.[366] On the Assumption of St Mary [*15 August*], he set off on the road of Christian knighthood from Vienna. He went to Venice, and there took ship, proposing to sail via Illyria and Dalmatia. But he was beset by bad weather, a problem that, as was said above, is accustomed to become more dangerous in the autumn, which was then beginning, and was forced to land at the Dalmatian town of Zara. There he was forced to stay over the winter until the next spring, when he waited, along with others who had been held up for a similar reason, for a suitable time for their passage and the gentle spring wind for sailing. Once the springtime had arrived, both those who had suffered the tedium of delay for a whole year at Messina and the others at Zara started off once more on their journey, and they reached the port of Acre safely and without [further] hold-up. There were in the company of the illustrious Duke of Austria: Count Siegfried

---

[364]   They eventually set off on 5 July 1190.

[365]   The Anglo-Norman fleet arrived at Messina on 14 September, the King of France and part of his fleet two days later, although some of the French fleet managed to sail directly to the Holy Land.

[366]   Leopold had made a pilgrimage to Jerusalem in 1182 [see above, p. 15]. The *Continuatio Zwetlensis Altera*, MGH SS ix.544, explained that despite 'his most burning desire to bear arms alongside the other princes in this warfare of the Lord (*militia Domini*) against the enemies of the Cross of Christ', Leopold was unable to join the original expedition because his relations with his brother-in-law the King of Hungary had broken down because of his attempt to gain Styria and border disputes concerning that duchy.

of Moerl,[367] the freeman Dietmar, and a few of his *ministeriales*, namely Ortlieb von Winkel,[368] Hugo von Puchperg,[369] Heinrich von Mödling, Albert von Horn,[370] Albero von Zemling,[371] Berthold von Wormze, Rudwin von Gars, and one of the brothers of [the family of] Rodaun. None of these came home with him; all were overcome by the aforesaid fatal necessity and ended their days, apart from Count Siegfried who brought some sickness with him and fell ill. He stopped on the way and returned home in the following year.

The King of England was sailing with difficulty when he arrived at Cyprus, where a certain Isaac then ruled. He was called by the same name as he who had seized the kingdom of Constantinople after the death of Andronikos. When after the death of Manuel, who had ruled over these various principalities by himself, his empire was split up, and since everybody seized what he could, this man had usurped lordship over all of Cyprus for himself. The King of England was unable to suffer the insolence and cruelty that he was said to have exercised against poor pilgrims,[372] and so he carried off him and his wife into captivity, and he took this same island for his own use, making it subject to him, while he dispatched Isaac to the most formidable castle of Margab. This same King of England was indeed first and foremost in the whole of Christian knighthood, for he surpassed others both in his abilities and with all his wealth, and he treated them disdainfully, usurping lordship for himself over others. Nor indeed did he respect the King of France, holding him in contempt, although rightfully he owed him homage. Furthermore he despised the Margrave Conrad, the lord of Tyre, through whom that city was held for the Christians after the destruction of the land of the Lord, and through whom too the power of the Turks and of Saladin their prince was repelled. He also considered Duke Leopold, that most illustrious prince, as a coward, although he remained there [in the Holy Land], albeit not as gloriously as he ought to have done.

---

[367]   Count Siegfried II of Moerl and Kleeburg (d. 1194), son of Siegfried I, Count of Peilstein (d. 1175), of the Sighardiner family; cf. Chroust, *Quellen*, p. 97n.

[368]   He witnessed, alongside Duke Leopold, a gift by Count Sigiboto III of Herrnstein to the monastery of Gottweig (1183–90?), *Traditionsbuch Göttweig*, p. 535 no. 400, and a charter of Leopold for the monastery of Wittering in February 1187, *Urkundenbuch des Landes ob der Enns*, ii.410 no. 279 (for the date, *Regesten der Bischöfe von Passau*, i.278 no. 910).

[369]   *Regesten der Bischöfe von Passau*, i.282 no. 925 (1172 x 1188).

[370]   He witnessed a judgement of Duke Henry of Austria in favour of the monastery of Klosterneuburg in March 1171, *Urkundenbuch zur Geschichte der Babenberger*, iv.176 no. 840.

[371]   Before his departure, he sold his patrimony to the monastery of Wittering, with Leopold's permission, *Urkundenbuch des Landes ob der Enns*, ii.478 no. 332.

[372]   A similar charge of outrages against pilgrims was made against Isaac by Richard of the Temple, Nicholson, *Chronicle of the Third Crusade*, p. 179.

His unrestrained pride ended up causing him harm. Thus when this same king was striving with the whole immense strength of the Christian army in the siege of Ptolomais [Acre], using various war machines, they attacked it manfully and finally captured it by force, and made the Turkish garrison, seven thousand or more strong, prisoner. He then claimed lordship of this captured city for himself alone, refusing any share to his allies. He even repulsed the Margrave Conrad, who had been made king by general agreement, and it is said that the latter was murdered through his connivance. For two men with whom he had enjoyed friendly relations for some time had been sent by the Old Man of the Mountains to assassinate him, and when nobody had any suspicions concerning them they stabbed him with their daggers and killed him. These men, however, did not escape unscathed but paid the penalty that they richly deserved.[373]

When Acre had been captured and garrisoned by our men, Saladin refused to conclude an agreement for the redemption of the captive Turks. The King of England was enraged, and this aroused his fury to an even greater extent than usual, and he had them all slaughtered apart from a handful of nobles whom he kept as prisoners in the hope of another pact in the future. After all this had taken place, the knights of Christ were hastening towards Ascalon, which had also been garrisoned by the Turks and was opposing the Christians, when the Turks, terrified by the capture of Acre, left the town empty, and the Christians occupied it without a battle. However, the King of England allowed the enemy to regain it, to the disgust of the others. He did this because both men and money were in short supply, which meant that the town could neither be inhabited nor defended from attack and storm by its adversaries; he preferred therefore to abandon it by agreement in return for a money payment, before losing the place once again through the lack of a garrison adequate to defend it.

Meanwhile, unable to bear the arrogance of the King of England, from whom he should have expected service not contempt, the King of France returned home after the death of the Count of Flanders.[374] He journeyed through Italy, spoke at the Lateran with Pope Celestine, and then passed through Tuscany. The pope received him kindly, but earnestly encouraged him with pious admonishment to work for the liberation of the land of the Lord. He also gave him presents and the gift of holy blessing, as his dearest son and a beloved pilgrim, and granted him permission to leave with the kiss of peace. When he arrived at Milan, a city of Liguria, he met the Emperor Henry, who was making a slow journey home from Apulia, and they had discussions.[375] A cloud of dispute arose between them, which took some time

[373] For Conrad's murder, on 28 April 1192, see especially the so-called *Estoire d'Eracles*, c. 137, in Edbury, *The Conquest of Jerusalem and the Third Crusade*, pp. 114–15. This account, one should note, does not ascribe any blame to King Richard, and attributes the murder to a dispute between Conrad and the leader of the Assassins, the so-called Old Man of the Mountains, over the former's seizure of a ship belonging to the latter.

[374] Count Philip of Flanders died on 1 June 1191.

[375] In the first week of December 1191.

to dispel. The principal reason for this was that when the emperor's father had been in conflict with Philip of Cologne, the king had provided help to the latter, but through the mediation of the sensible men who wisely negotiated on each side the reason for this distrust was removed. The emperor granted him the kiss of peace, endowed him with appropriate gifts, honoured him thereafter as a glorious prince and his beloved friend, and allowed him to depart for his own kingdom with a suitable escort.

In the year following his return home, and after considerable effort, Duke Leopold obtained the duchy of Styria, which his cousin Ottokar, who had died without an heir, had assigned to him in his will, drawn up in the presence of the Emperor Frederick. Leopold and his son Frederick were most solemnly invested with this territory by the emperor's son Henry at Worms.[376]

King Richard of England, who wished to surpass everyone in glory and deserved the anger of all, remained trying to take the land and heredity of the Lord more actively than others and longer than the rest. In this same year from the Incarnation of the Lord 1192, I do not know whether from fear of the King of France, who had gone home before him, or through weariness with his pilgrimage, he made peace with Saladin and the Turks, fixing and confirming this for five years. He and his wife then set off for home by ship after the others. Blown by the winds, the sea journey was beset with peril, and finally they were driven to shore and forced to land at the city of Pola in Istria. There he abandoned his wife and his whole household to the uncertainty of the waves, while accompanied by only a handful of men he left the dangers of the sea behind and set off by land through Friuli. Although he wished to remain unknown, he was however recognised by many people, and along the way some of his men were captured and others murdered, while his goods were lost in Austria as he crossed the land of Duke Leopold. He was anxious to travel in secret, wishing to leave the land of a prince whom he had earlier gravely and frequently offended without being recognised, but caught by the judgement of God 'he fell into a snare'[377] of him whom earlier he wished to entrap. For Divine equity did not allow his arrogance to pass unpunished for long, but handed him over into the hands and power of those whom he himself had earlier treated with contempt and shamefully insulted. This was indeed by the just judgement of God, so that a man who, when his affairs were prospering, refused to honour those whom he could have known to be worthy of honour should be judged worthy now to be treated shamefully by them. Thus he had reached the neighbourhood of Vienna secretly and on foot, accompanied by only two companions, when he was discovered by spies [*exploratores*] in a

---

[376]   24 May 1192, according to *Chronicon Magni Presbiteri*, MGH SS xvii.519. Ottokar IV had died on 8/9 May 1192, so in fact the investiture had followed very speedily. The childless Duke Ottokar of Styria (who had been granted the ducal title by Barbarossa in 1180) had made his cousin Leopold his heir in 1186, Lechner, *Die Babenberger*, pp. 174–7, 190.

[377]   I Timothy 3:7, and 6:9.

tawdry inn and arrested by the men of the Duke of Austria.[378] Although this same illustrious Duke of Austria had many grievances to charge against him, and he now rightfully held him in his hand, handed over by Divine judgement, nevertheless he treated him decently and better than he deserved, and ordered him to be kept in his castle of Dürrenstein on the Danube. One reason for this was indeed that he had deemed him a coward at the siege of Acre, but in addition he had held prisoner Isaac the Prince of Cyprus and his wife, who belonged to his blood kin, and also that he was suspected of having had Conrad, the son of his aunt, murdered.[379] This same Conrad was a most noble prince and an invincible athlete of God, and on the advice of all the wise men who were present on the expedition of the Lord he was appointed King of Jerusalem, and he was given as his wife that woman who had previously been married to Humphrey, said to be king of that land.[380] I do not know how a divorce was secured between them, but Conrad was chosen by everyone, with only the King of England opposing this. After his death, an account of which was given earlier, Count Henry of Champagne, who had remained for a long time on that expedition at great expense, succeeded both to his wife and to the kingdom. The King of England was therefore held for a long time by Duke Leopold, for although he was sought by the Emperor Henry, because he had encouraged his sister's son, namely Henry, the former Duke of Saxony, against his lord in all sorts of ways, and also interfered in other imperial business, the duke would not immediately hand him over.[381] There were indeed some among those who were driven by envy of Duke Leopold who gave evil advice that the emperor should put an end to the affair. The duke was certainly told that the emperor, acting on the advice of certain wicked men, wanted to seize the king by violence and get him into his power. Finally these suspicions were dispelled and an agreement was made between them, that the king would be brought from Austria at the following Easter and handed over to the lord emperor at Nebduna, also called Speyer. We attach below a legal copy of the pact that was made between them:

---

[378] There were various different accounts of Richard's capture, but the German sources all dwelt on the embarrassing, demeaning and 'unkingly' aspects of his arrest while in disguise, see J. Gillingham, 'The kidnapped king: Richard I in Germany, 1192–1194', *Bulletin of the German Historical Institute, London* 30 (2008), 10–11.

[379] Leopold's mother was Theodora Komnena, niece of the Emperor Manuel, whom Duke Henry had married in 1148, Lechner, *Die Babenberger*, p. 149.

[380] Isabella, the younger daughter of King Amalric of Jerusalem (1163–74) had been married to Humphrey (IV) of Toron, but he was never king, and indeed had refused to be a candidate for the kingship when this was mooted in 1186. Nor was Conrad ever formally crowned as king, even though he functioned as such, for (as our author implies) the annulment of the marriage of Isabella and Humphrey was of dubious legality.

[381] Henry the Lion was actually King Richard's brother-in-law, having married his eldest sister Matilda in 1168. The author may be confusing him with his eldest son, also Henry, who if this passage was written after 1195 was by then the head of the Welf family. Alternatively, he knew that Henry the Lion had married a daughter of the King of England, and assumed that this king was Richard rather than his father Henry II.

This is the form of the convention or pact concluded between the lord Henry, Emperor of the Romans, and Leopold, Duke of Austria, concerning the safety and peace of the King of England and other matters. [1] I, Leopold, Duke of Austria, will give and present the King of England to my lord Henry, the Emperor of the Romans, on condition that this same king, as has been agreed, shall give to the lord emperor 100,000 marks of silver, of which I shall have half, as a dowry for the daughter of the brother of the King of England, who shall be brought as wife for one of my sons.[382] This daughter of the brother of the King of England should be made available for presentation to one of my sons, whom I shall choose, at Michaelmas. And half of the aforesaid 100,000 marks of silver, namely 50,000 marks of silver, is to be paid by the same date, of which my lord the emperor will receive half, and I the other half. The other half of this same 100,000 marks, namely the 50,000 marks that remain, is to be paid at the beginning of next Lent.[383] The lord emperor will similarly have half of this money, and I shall have [the other] half. And whatever part of all this aforesaid money that is less than the whole amount that shall be paid to the lord emperor within this deadline by which the whole sum ought to be paid, half of this shall be presented to me without bad faith. [2] My lord the emperor shall give two hundred hostages to me, [to guarantee] that if, after I shall have presented the King of England to him, he should die – may the Lord prevent this – while the aforesaid king remains in his power, this same king shall be presented to me without bad faith. But if it should happen that I should die before him, this same agreement is to be observed in every detail with one of my sons, whom I shall nominate for this, namely with the one who shall receive the daughter of the brother of the King of England as his wife, and if it should not be to him, the same agreement shall be observed with another of my sons. [3] Furthermore, the King of England shall give to the lord emperor fifty galleys, with crews, expenses and everything else belonging to them, and he shall place one hundred knights and fifty crossbowmen in these same galleys, and in addition he himself in person shall enter the kingdom of Sicily with the lord emperor, accompanied by another hundred knights and fifty crossbowmen, and he shall assist him in good faith to obtain that kingdom, until the emperor of his own free will gives him permission to depart. [4] And furthermore, that this same king shall faithfully execute and pay all this, he shall give to my lord the emperor as hostages two hundred of the best men of the lands under his jurisdiction, whom the lord emperor shall request of him. However, if in truth it shall happen to the lord emperor that one or more of these shall openly refuse him, in such a way that he clearly cannot have them, then the king shall give him as hostage or hostages in their place another or others, whom the lord emperor shall designate by name, with the exception of the sons of his sister and of Henry, former Duke of Saxony, and

---

[382]   Eleanor, the daughter of Geoffrey, the third son of Henry II, who had died in 1186, and his wife Constance of Brittany.

[383]   That is, 23 February 1194.

the son of his brother. [5] Those, however, to whom the lord emperor entrusts these same hostages to be guarded shall swear that, if the lord emperor should in the meanwhile die – may God prevent this – while these same hostages are in their power, they shall release these hostages unconditionally and without bad faith bring them to a place of safety. [6] Item, if the King of England discharges to the lord emperor all that he has promised, the lord emperor shall still retain these hostages in the meanwhile, until such time as the king shall grant me, the Duke of Austria, forgiveness in the pope's presence. If however the said king does not pay what has been promised to the lord emperor, the latter shall decide what he will do with the hostages of the king, as he wishes, provided that I, the Duke of Austria, have nothing to do with this. [7] The lord emperor shall have ten noblemen from his empire, whom I the duke shall select, swear that if the King of England fulfils all that he has promised, then his hostages shall be set free unconditionally. [8] Item, the lord emperor shall retain the King of England in his power in the meanwhile until the King of Cyprus and his daughter, who are prisoners of the king, have been freed. If however the King of Cyprus and his daughter have been freed from captivity, and anything has been given or exacted for their release, the lord emperor shall similarly retain the King of England in his power, until all that [has been paid] has been fully restored. [9] Item, if the King of England has within the present year, that is from the beginning of the present Lent up to the beginning of next Lent, neither paid the money nor given the hostages, or has done one but failed to fulfil the other, and after the deadline has passed it has in my opinion become clear to the emperor that the said king can provide neither the promised money nor the hostages, or has provided one but not the other of these, and, that being acknowledged, if the lord emperor is unwilling to offer the king to me, I shall be able to choose fifty of the aforesaid two hundred hostages, whom the lord emperor shall give to me, namely those who are boys and not knights, whom I wish to retain while the others are released, and the King of England shall be restored to my power. [10] If however it happens that the King of England should die while in the power of the emperor, the aforesaid two hundred hostages of the lord emperor shall be set free, unless the lord emperor has received anything of the aforesaid money, and of this I have not received my half; once this half is paid, these same hostages shall be set free. [11] After everything that is set out above has been fulfilled in good faith and without deceit, the lord emperor shall be held to observe a lasting peace and concord with the oft-mentioned King of England. Dated at Würzburg, on 14 February in the year from the Incarnation of the Lord 1193.

While the king was still being held prisoner in Austria, rumour flew round and spread to neighbouring kingdoms and the princes of those realms, and they wrote letters enquiring as to the truth of what had been done by the Duke of Austria, and concerning the unheard-of humiliation and captivity of this great and respected man. That, therefore, what we said above was suspected about the death of the Margrave Conrad was considered [actually] to be more likely, we think it proper to append below a copy of a letter from the King of France, who was acquainted with him while they were overseas, and to whom the matter was revealed more fully from that region:

> Philip, by the grace of God King of France, to his dearest friend the noble Duke of Austria greeting and the fullness of [his] sincere love. Since 'you have seen eye to eye',[384] and have heard how Richard, the most impious King of England, lived in the lands overseas and what he did there [so] perversely and against God and man, it is not unfitting to remind you of one of these. For we know indeed that you hold firmly in your memory that Richard had your and our dearest blood relative Conrad, Margrave and lord of Tyre, who stood right up until his final day as the defender and column of Christianity, without cause or any respect for what had gone before, cruelly murdered by the Assassins.[385] We therefore urge you, by all the arguments that we can muster, and we pray you from the depth of our heart that, having consideration for the mercy of God and with regard for whatever service that we can ever do for you, you hold the aforesaid Richard under strict guard, nor should you under any circumstances release him, until both you and we have spoken face to face with the illustrious Emperor of the Romans, or communicated through messengers from our presence.

[Report came] in that same year that Saladin had died a similar death at the hands of those who were called the Assassins, while he was seeking to inflict further bloodshed on the Christians.[386] ...

Since therefore repeated outbreaks of disease plagued them continuously and spared nobody from this great army, but struck them all down at random, while a similar or even more severe epidemic also ravaged their opponents, the adversaries of the Christian name, a truce was concluded between them, so that there would be peace confirmed for the space of three years from the following Easter,[387] and thereafter a further agreement would be negotiated for preserving the peace. However, as a wise man said, 'when one side has no use for peace, it will not last'.[388] For while, through the merit of Christ the champion, they were prepared indefatigably to endure every labour on his behalf, and did not fear sudden death, they agreed to this period of peace so that they might restore their strength and be the more ready to return once more to battle.

---

[384]   Isaiah 52:8.

[385]   Conrad's mother Judith was the granddaughter of the Emperor Henry IV, who was Barbarossa's great-grandfather. Any relationship with the Capetians was very distant.

[386]   Saladin died on 3 March 1193, but of natural causes, *Rare and Excellent History*, pp. 243–4. There seems to be some omission in the text of the *Historia* here.

[387]   28 March 1193. The truce had finally been agreed on 2 September 1192, Lyons and Jackson, *Saladin*, p. 360.

[388]   Ovid, *Heroides*, iv.89.

After the death of Saladin, it appears that there was dispute between his brother Saphadin and the sons whom he had had from his many wives. This Saphadin succeeded his brother in his position, and would not grant their father's inheritance to the sons of his brother; thus he quarrelled with them, and some of them sought the help of the Christians.[389]

King Richard of England was still held in captivity, but was allowed to go free, in return for the ransom, part of which had already been paid, although the remainder was still to be paid, and when noble hostages had been furnished.[390] These hostages included the son of the King of Navarre and the son of the Duke of Saxony, who was King Richard's brother-in-law.[391] These hostages were not only provided for the money, but also to ensure that the remaining terms of the treaty would be fulfilled.

Meanwhile both Tancred, who had claimed the kingdom of Apulia for himself, and his eldest son had died, leaving one other son surviving, who although he was no more than a small child still hoped to succeed his father on the throne.[392] This Tancred was indeed the son of Roger, but not from a legitimate union; for he had engendered him by a daughter of Count Rupert, whom he had alone loved for he had afterwards lawfully married her and granted him [*Tancred*] legitimacy.[393] However, the Emperor Henry, whose wife was now the legitimate heiress to this often-mentioned kingdom, had returned to this kingdom with a powerful force of knights, from the first invasion of which he had withdrawn when matters had gone awry. He brought with him a most mighty army, and organised the expedition both on land and sea, and he occupied with the strength of his majesty not just Apulia, but also Calabria and Sicily, including Palermo, the chief city of Sicily which Roger

---

[389]   Saphadin (Saif ad-Din al Adil) eventually took over Egypt in 1200.

[390]   Richard was handed over by Duke Leopold to the emperor at Easter 1193, but only eventually released in February 1194, as Henry sought to extort an even larger ransom, and indeed his eventual release only came when the emperor bowed to the pressure of his princes to honour his promises. Only the contemporary English sources discuss this episode in detail; not only the 'History' but also the other German sources say virtually nothing of this, perhaps through embarrassment at Henry's double-dealing, Gillingham, 'The kidnapped king', 17–26.

[391]   Richard was married to Berengaria, the daughter of the King of Navarre; the hostage was probably her brother Alfonso. The other hostage mentioned was Otto, the second son of Henry the Lion, the later Emperor Otto IV, who was seventeen in 1194.

[392]   King Tancred of Sicily died on 20 February 1194, his eldest son Roger having predeceased him a couple of months earlier, on 24 December 1193. His younger son William, then about seven or eight, was crowned king, under the regency of his mother Sybilla.

[393]   The account of Tancred's descent is confused. He was the illegitimate son (born c. 1137/8) of Duke Roger of Apulia, the eldest son of King Roger of Sicily, who predeceased his father in, probably, May 1149. His mother was a daughter of the Count of Lecce, but she and Duke Roger never married, even after the birth of their two children. C. Reisinger, *Tankred von Lecce* (Cologne 1992), pp. 8–12.

had lived in as the capital of these lands. He ordered Salerno, the most powerful city of Apulia, to be deprived of all its honour and glory and its inhabitants to be expelled, in punishment for it having previously injured the majesty of the imperial dignity.[394] For that city which had formerly provided its medicines as a help for other nations could [now] find nothing that might administer a remedy for its own ills.[395] These events took place in the year from the Lord's Incarnation 1194.

Among the other princes who took part in this expedition was the son of Duke Leopold, who was called by his father's name, and who, although he had not yet been dubbed a knight, nonetheless exercised the warrior's craft. However his father, that glorious prince the duke, and his brother Frederick remained at home.[396] The duke was spending the Christmas season in the March [of Styria], a region that he had recently acquired, and he held a solemn celebration of the feast itself in the castle of Graz. On the day after the feast he mounted a horse with an awkward disposition and rode across some light snow that was covered with ice. The horse that he was riding fell, and although he was a knight of vast experience in all the aspects of his craft he was unable to avoid this unfortunate accident, in which he broke his leg, in such a way that the bone was sticking through the flesh.[397] None of the methods tried by the doctors could heal this limb, and as his illness grew worse he was persuaded by their most urgent entreaties [to allow] his foot to be cut off. When therefore he realised that his end was inevitably approaching, and since he had been bound by the chain of anathema through a sentence of the supreme pontiff, he summoned the Archbishop of Salzburg, a close relative bound to him by ties of blood, and who also happened through Divine foresight to be not far away.[398] He humbly requested him both to mitigate the punishment of Divine wrath and to grant him absolution from that sentence. He surrendered himself totally to the advice and instructions of the archbishop, and making satisfaction, insofar as he could, with contrite heart, he died on 30 December 1194.[399]

---

[394] The citizens of Salerno had, after the failure of the emperor's first invasion of southern Italy in 1191, handed over the Empress Constance to Tancred (the latter had subsequently been persuaded to release her by Pope Celestine III).

[395] The allusion here was to Salerno's long-standing reputation as a centre for medical knowledge, for which see especially Patricia Skinner, *Health and Medicine in Early Medieval Southern Italy* (Leiden 1997), pp. 131–6.

[396] Frederick I, Duke of Austria 1194–8, and his younger brother, the future Leopold VI, duke 1198–1230. The latter witnessed two diplomas of Henry VI at Milan in June 1195 with the title of Duke of Styria, *Reg. Henry VI*, p. 184, nos 451–2.

[397] In other words, he suffered a compound fracture.

[398] Adalbert III, Archbishop of Salzburg 1183–1200, was the duke's first cousin, the son of his aunt Gertrude, his father's sister, and Duke Vladislav of Bohemia.

[399] The author of this section has not previously mentioned that Celestine III had excommunicated Duke Leopold (and imposed an interdict on his lands), for which Lechner, *Die Babenberger*, pp. 187–8.

His son Frederick, who succeeded him in Austria, as the noble heir of his father, and also in response to his father's admonition, allowed the hostages who were [still] detained to go free, and he remitted the money that he had received from the King of England, both what he had already received and what was still to be paid.[400] However, although the aforesaid Archbishop of Salzburg, through the authority of the legation conferred on him by the Roman pontiff, had in his presence granted him [*Leopold*] absolution, the Bishop of Passau, a venerable man of great wisdom, who was at that time acting as the trusted mediator between the two quarrelling heads of the world and was earnestly striving to bring them to peaceful agreement, on learning of his death did not let slip the opportunity granted to concern himself with these matters.[401] He had previously sought to secure the peace of his church and prevent the disturbance of persecution by concealing the news from his diocese that it had either already been placed, or was about to be put, under interdict. He finally removed all threat of ecclesiastical penalty, which the land had deserved because of its prince, and restored peace [to it]. Among other things that he arranged on his deathbed, the illustrious Duke Leopold took measures for his salvation, and he assigned Austria to his elder son Frederick, while he left the duchy of Styria to his other son, who had still not returned from the expedition, and he requested burial at the monastery of Grey Monks that had been founded by his grandfather in honour of the Holy Cross, where he had indeed envisaged undertaking a new life.[402] This was done.

Since we are describing the death of such an illustrious prince, the memory of whom ought always to be cherished, we have made a digression from our purpose, but now we ought to return to the story that we had begun to tell. One should not pass over in silence that before the victory of the invincible Emperor Henry, as a certain wise man says: 'tears at first are followed by better fortune',[403] for that mighty conqueror changed the sad beginning that occurred at the siege of Naples for a joyful conclusion.[404] For after capturing Campania, Apulia, Calabria and Sicily, and making all their cities and fortresses subject to him, as well as the inhabitants of those lands who had fought against him, he returned home in triumph. He brought back with him to Germany the greater and better men, to prevent them establishing their power again, and he ordered that they be kept safe under strict guard in his extremely powerful and strongly defended castle of Trifels.[405] I

---

[400]   For Richard's letter of thanks to Archbishop Adalbert, Magnus of Reichersberg, *Chronicon*, MGH SS xvii.523.

[401]   Wolfger of Ellenbrechtskirchen, Bishop of Passau 1191–1204.

[402]   Margrave Leopold III had founded the Cistercian monastery of Heiligenkreuz in the Wienerwald in 1133, with monks from Morimond, Lechner, *Die Babenberger*, p. 128.

[403]   Ovid, *Metamorphosis*, VII.518.

[404]   The author here refers to the failure of Henry's first south Italian expedition in 1191, which was abandoned after the failure of the siege of Naples in August of that year.

[405]   On the River Queich, in the diocese of Speyer, where King Richard of England had been held for a time.

have included the names of some of these people: the Archbishop of Salerno and the count his brother, Roger of Trebisacce, Geoffrey of Carbonara, Geoffrey de *Marran*, William de *Boglyn*, the nobleman Roger, Robert of *Cathanea*, Tancred of Tarsia, the queen – the wife of King Tancred – the wife of the son of Tancred who was the daughter of Isaac, the Emperor of the Greeks, William the son of Tancred and his brother, Margaritus, Count Roger of Avellino, Peter the son of the Prince of Sorrento, the Count of Carinola, Eugenius and a number of others.[406]

In the year of the Lord 1195, all the princes had returned home worn out by their labours and short of funds, while those who had been fighting for Christ, both rich and poor, had also returned, leaving the land of the Lord in need, with Count Henry of Champagne as its only guardian and defender, and even he doubted whether it could be defended and considered abandoning it.[407] Hence 'the Lord stirred up his spirit once more',[408] touching the hearts of his faithful German subjects through the venerable Archbishop Conrad of Mainz, who unceasingly encouraged them to come to the help of the land of the Lord with the word of preaching.[409] He urged the Emperor of the Romans himself, the bishops, all the princes, both dukes and margraves, the nobles, barons and men of every sort and condition to go to the help of the aforesaid land, and he encouraged them to meditate unceasingly on the nature of the Lord's Passion. All without exception heard this encouragement both avidly and devotedly, so that nobody was held back by love for their dear ones

---

[406]   The Sicilian hostages are identified and discussed by E.M. Jamison, *Admiral Eugenius of Sicily. His Life and Work* (London 1957), pp. 347–9. The surnames left in italics cannot be certainly identified, but the first six names listed appear all to be noblemen from Calabria. Nicholas, Archbishop of Salerno 1182-1222, and his brother Count Richard of Ajello were the sons of Matthew of Salerno, the chancellor of the kingdom of Sicily, and Tancred's principal supporter (who died in 1193). Margaritus of Brindisi and Eugenius were both Greeks, the former the commander of the Sicilian fleet, the latter an important financial official. Roger of Castelvetere, lord of Taurasi, had been appointed as Count of Avellino by Tancred c. 1190 (he was married to the daughter of the previous holder, also called Roger, who had died in 1183). Count Richard of Carinola, in the principality of Capua, had joined Henry when he had invaded the kingdom in 1191, but subsequently changed sides and was then captured by Henry's supporters in the autumn of 1192. Unlike the male hostages, Queen Sybilla and her daughters were held in the nunnery of Hohenburg in Alsace. However, her son, the young king, William III of Sicily, did not have a surviving brother.

[407]   Count Henry of Champagne had joined the siege of Acre in 1190, and after the murder of Conrad of Montferrat he had married the latter's widow, Isabella, and become the de facto ruler of the kingdom of Jerusalem. He was, through his mother, the nephew of both Richard I and Philip II of France. He died after falling out of a window at Acre in September 1197 [see below, pp. 190–1].

[408]   II Chronicles 36: 22.

[409]   Conrad of Wittelsbach, Archbishop of Mainz 1161–5, driven from his see because of his support for Alexander III, subsequently cardinal and Archbishop of Salzburg 1177–83, and Archbishop of Mainz once more 1183–1200.

or their possessions; not the father because of his wife and children, nor duke, margrave or count was mindful for the glory of his land. No archbishop, bishop, abbot, prior, nor any sort of cleric, nor layman, was so attached to or mindful of 'their pleasant houses'[410] that they could be prevented from undertaking this road of pilgrimage. Even those who could properly serve the worship of God at home through fasting, vigils, prayer, domestic concerns, and the sustenance of the poor considered however that these domestic endeavours were not equal to the labours of the holy road, and, putting from their mind all the toils of the Christian struggle, they unhesitatingly left them all behind. For where the faith is assailed by idolaters, heretics and false Christians, and the name of Christianity is defended by the true Christian and the confession of the true faith is shown through hand and tongue, I think that nothing can be compared to this action of Christian profession; for abandoning thought of self and property, they proclaim the Christian name, in circumstances where Christians ought not to be silent, saying with the prophet, 'I believed therefore I have spoken'.[411]

The first person to undertake this vocation was undoubtedly Henry, the Roman Emperor himself, who, even though he did not yet undertake the journey because of the rebellions that had arisen in those lands that he had recently gained through conquest, nonetheless burned with an inner desire to come to the aid of the knighthood of Christ.[412] There joined with him the archbishops of Mainz and Bremen, the Bishop of Hildesheim, who was also at that time acting as imperial chancellor, and who was then too managing the emperor's affairs in the whole of Apulia, Calabria and Sicily, as well as the bishops of Halberstadt, Verden, Zeitz, Regensburg and Passau, with a huge following; and dukes, margraves and counts, with every noble, *ministerialis* and ordinary knight whom they could enlist in their following. All were moved by the Spirit of God to undertake this vocation.[413] Moreover the Duke of Brabant, Duke Henry of Saxony, who was rather known as the Count Palatine of the Rhine, Duke Frederick of Austria, the Duke of Merania, the Duke of Carinthia, and the landgrave, as well as margraves and counts whom

---

[410]　　Micah 2:9.

[411]　　Psalm 115:10 (Vulgate), 116:10 (AV).

[412]　　According to the *Annales Marbacenses*, p. 65, Henry received the Cross in secret from the Bishop of Sutri on Good Friday 1195. Soon afterwards he announced that he would support a force of 1,500 knights and 1,500 sergeants in the Holy Land for one year, *Chronica Regia Coloniensis*, p. 157.

[413]　　Hartwig II, Archbishop of Bremen 1184–1207; Conrad of Querfurt, Bishop of Hildesheim 1194–8 and Bishop of Würzburg 1198–1202 (for his role as regent of Sicily in 1195–6, Jamison, *Admiral Eugenius*, pp. 146–54); Gardulf of Harpke, Bishop of Halberstadt 1193–1201; Bishop Rudolf of Verden 1189–1205; Berthold II, Bishop of Naumburg-Zeitz 1186–1206; Conrad III, Bishop of Regensburg 1187–1204, who had taken part in the Third Crusade; and Bishop Wolfger of Passau (for whom above note 401).

it would take too long to list here, hastened to set out on this road.[414] The Duke of Bohemia, Henry, who was also bishop of that land, took the Cross, along with many of his men, and made preparations for the journey, on which he was anxious to embark, but like the Roman Emperor he was prevented from this by the actions of various persons and through a number of problems that arose with regard to Saxony. He had not, however, in any way abandoned his intention, despite the postponement, but he died during this delay, and thus the journey of those who had planned to go with him was interrupted.[415] Some of the counts and vassals from Hungary also proposed to go, but their king, Bela, who needed their assistance, kept some of them at home – apart from those who had taken the Cross on the order of the pope – and they laid down the sign of the Cross that they had previously assumed.[416]

The Emperor Henry took the advice of all the princes and decided to travel by sea, since those who had previously journeyed through Hungary, Greece and Turkey had failed in all they had attempted. Those who had formerly attempted this journey were Conrad, King of the Romans, and Louis, King of the French, and most recently the Emperor Frederick. But Henry and his princes decided that it would be easier and more practical to journey by sea, since the lands of Apulia, Sicily and Calabria were now under the rule of the Roman emperor, although others preferred to take a different route. This dispute among them about which way to take lasted for some time, and the Saxons refused to follow the emperor. The latter, however, took advantage of the opportunity that presented itself, while they were discussing the choice of route. Since the queen (through whom the aforementioned lands belonged to him) had now presented him with an heir, the emperor wished to secure through the common assent of the princes of the empire that he might transmit this empire to the next heir as if by hereditary right, and to secure this he sought the agreement of all the princes that the election which had always taken place and ought to take place should be replaced by hereditary right.[417] At first he appeared to be making some progress in this, but after he had

---

[414]   Henry I, Duke of Brabant 1190–1235; Henry, the eldest son of Henry the Lion, the former duke of Saxony (deposed in 1180), who married Agnes, the daughter of the Count Palatine Conrad in 1194, and succeeded his father-in-law on the latter's death in November 1195; Duke Berthold of Merania, who had taken part in the Third Crusade (and who died in 1204); Ulrich II of Spanheim, Duke of Carinthia 1181–1202; and Herman I, Landgrave of Thuringia 1190–1217, whose elder brother Ludwig III had died while in the Holy Land in 1190.

[415]   He died on 15 June 1197.

[416]   Bela III of Hungary died in April 1196. He had himself taken the Cross, but appears to have been reluctant to allow his subjects to join an army led by others.

[417]   Cf. the *Annales Marbacenses*, p. 68: 'The emperor held a court at Würzburg around the middle of Lent, in which many people received the sign of the Cross. At that same court the emperor wished to confirm with the princes a new and unheard-of decree for the Roman Empire, that in the Roman realm, as in France and other kingdoms, the [future]

persuaded them all to make this change to the dignity of the Roman principate, the Saxons refused to accept what everyone else had agreed, and although he wished to add the lands that had been conquered (and which have so often been mentioned) to the empire, not even this could assist him nor persuade them to agree. Even though he also agreed to allow all the ecclesiastical princes the right of succession to the moveable property of their predecessors after the death of the latter, and whereas previously this moveable property had been adjudged to the royal fisc now it would come without contradiction into the power of those who succeeded, and he decreed that this be embodied in a royal privilege and promised to confirm it, he still did not get his way.[418]

Hence, after failing to succeed in this, the emperor returned through Italy to Apulia.[419]

---

kings would succeed him by hereditary right'. His son, the future Frederick II, had been born on 26 December 1194, at Jesi in the March of Ancona.

[418] Other sources, notably the *Chronica Regia Coloniensis*, p. 159, suggest that the opposition was led by Archbishop Adolf of Cologne. The princes eventually agreed to elect Frederick as king, but not to agree to the empire becoming hereditary.

[419] Henry set off for Italy at the end of June 1196, *Annales Marbacenses*, p. 68.

The History of the Pilgrims[1]

The prologue for the *History of the Pilgrims* commences.

Often and for a long time, O venerable man, I have weighed my own abilities and 'how they refuse to bring what they ought to completion',[2] and that paucity of skill has previously dissuaded me; but finally your order had forced me to set this in motion. Although some say, perhaps ironically, that I 'have dreamed in Parnassus',[3] I deem it more tolerable, however, to expose my muse among those who charge [me] with presumption or to the teeth of detraction rather than to disobey your order by continuing to remain silent. And if in this little work the beauty of song or the arrangement of words does not caress the ears of the reader, the importance of the subject can at least be set against the poison of an uncultivated pen. I intend, insofar as my ability to explain allows me, to write about this subject briefly and succinctly, so that I shall seek out the unvarnished truth about the journey of our pilgrims and the deeds they accomplished, without the addition of any invention or the insertion of any tales. It is especially proper to explain among other matters how both Frederick, the most Christian and most invincible Emperor of the Romans, a man of great experience imitating Charles in his valour,[4] and his most distinguished son, the illustrious Duke of Swabia, an heir not unworthy of the uprightness and name of his father, like two shining beacons and bastions of the Christian faith under the banner of the life-giving Cross, striving bravely and in proper fashion, were the guides and leaders of the army of Christ, so that they now rightly enjoy the payment of eternal reward in Heaven and that on earth their reputation is rendered more celebrated to those who come after them. For Thou, lord God, along with them, 'hast led forth the people which Thou has redeemed',[5] thus Thou would not allow either the untrustworthiness of the Greeks nor the deceits and battles of the Turks to prevail over them. It was indeed a miracle, not of human power but of Divine virtue, that the people of God, though so few, having triumphantly entered through the passes and bounds of Greece, should subdue almost all that land and bring it to surrender; afterwards they passed through all sorts of anxieties and many different tribulations, which the following history will explain each in its own place. Finally 'the snare of the fowler is broken'[6] and they stormed Iconium, defeating six

---

[1]   Translated from *Quellen*, pp. 116–30.

[2]   Horace, *Ars Poetica*, v. 38.

[3]   Persius, *Saturarum Prologus*, v. 2.

[4]   Charlemagne, King of the Franks 768–814, the first medieval emperor, from 800, who was considered a model for all his successors.

[5]   Exodus 15:13.

[6]   Psalm 123:7 (Vulgate), 124:7 (AV).

hundred thousand Turkish cavalry. A little while earlier, as if secure and glorying in their triumph over them, the enemy was saying: 'I have pursued mine enemies and overtaken them' [and] 'I will divide the spoil; my lust shall be satisfied'.[7] But finally the Divine commandment ordained differently, as the course of events afterwards proved.

Sometimes by reading about the brave deeds of men of old, this helps the audience of our own day and incites their courage. Indeed, what is more worthy of record and better suited to edification than to recall the labours of pilgrims and those fighting for the Holy Cross, the men who in our times have experienced so many travails and such dangerous wars for the name of Christ, and [in doing so] have left such examples of courage and steadfastness to be imitated? For 'narrow is the way which leadeth unto life',[8] and since 'he rejoices in the patience of suffering',[9] those who are faithful to Christ and have chosen with devoted and intrepid heart to suffer hard and bitter things for His sake may expect the reward of eternal life. And truly happy is he whose soul is not dulled by the fear of labour nor is deterred by bodily discomforts, but who is rather encouraged by such examples. For sometimes He 'who is the true vine, and purges his branches, that they may bring forth more fruit',[10] examines those He loves on the road of adversity, and is accustomed to summon them to their reward through bitter tribulation and labour.

Therefore, to proceed with this work of history in the proper order, one should first explain the nature and gravity of the crisis that roused so many distinguished warriors to make their pilgrimage against the evil race of the Turks.

In the year from the Incarnation of the Word 1187 the sins of men decreed that 'the Lord made a way for his anger'[11] over the holy city and the whole kingdom of Jerusalem, so that their wretched grief and wailing could equal the lamentations of Jeremiah. It was not through any act but by Divine judgement that almost the whole of Christianity overseas was given over to destruction and ruin; for 'there was no truth in the Land',[12] faith and justice were shut out, it flourished as the root and nursery of all evil, 'greed undermines the hearts of men, and turns them away from the path of truth'. For, according to the poet, 'blind love of gold does not force mortal breasts to hear';[13] thus, while a seven-year peace had been previously established between the kingdom of Jerusalem and Saladin and confirmed on oath by both sides, it happened that within that same period companies of merchants, which are called in the vernacular 'caravans', who were subject to Saladin, were travelling from Aleppo to Babylon with uncountable merchandise of great value,

---

7   Psalm 17:38 (Vulgate), 18:37 (AV); Exodus 15:9.

8   Matthew 7:14.

9   Lucan, *Pharsalia*, IX.403.

10   John 15:1–2.

11   Psalm 77:50 (Vulgate), 78:50 (AV).

12   Hosea 4:1.

13   Here three similar but separate lines from the *Aeneid* are conflated: *Aeneid*, I.349, III.56–7, IV.412.

accompanied by several emirs.[14] The soldiers and allies of Rainald, who was the stepfather of Prince Bohemond of Antioch, acting treacherously and in defiance of the truce, captured these various companies and laid rapacious hands on them and their money just as they liked, as 'young lions that roar after their prey'.[15] Because he was weighed down by debts to others, Rainald was shamefully consumed by greed for money, and he preferred shamelessly to commit the crime of perjury rather than respecting the aforesaid truce and heeding Saladin's requests that he restore his plunder. Thus he kept the booty for himself and consigned the men to imprisonment, to the shame and dishonour both of himself and of the whole land. Saladin therefore immediately sent an embassy to King Guy asking that, in accordance with the laws and customs of the Christians, he have the case heard by the barons and men learned in the law at his royal court to decide whether the booty should be returned or retained. Even after he was unable to secure this, he was [still] willing to forego any legal complaint and abandon any compensation for the stolen money if his men who were being held in prison were immediately granted their freedom. But when this too was refused to him and his envoys returned empty-handed, he was extremely annoyed. From that time onwards he undoubtedly sought an opportunity to attack the kingdom of Jerusalem, and he mustered a very great and powerful army from the different nations of the Saracens.

Fear stalked the land, and the stability of the kingdom of Jerusalem also began to be weakened through a dispute that developed between the king and Count Raymond of Tripoli. The origin and cause of this was as follows. The king was a foreigner, an immigrant from the nation of Poitou, of middling rank but a knight of handsome appearance and valiant in war. When the queen cast her eyes upon him, she yielded to her nature as a lover and a woman and married him, against the wishes of the count and the other princes.[16] Thence it happened that through hatred of the

---

[14]   Here Babylon was used, as it often was in medieval Latin, to refer to Cairo, or in a more general sense Egypt.

[15]   Psalm 103:21 (Vulgate), 104:21 (AV). Rainald of Châtillon had become Prince of Antioch through his marriage to the widowed Princess Constance in 1153, her son Bohemond III at that stage being only an infant. But, after his capture by Nur-ed-Din in 1161, Rainald had spent many years in prison, during which time his wife had died. Soon after his release in 1176 he married Stephanie of Milly, the heiress of Oultre-Jordain, from which lordship he had conducted a series of raids against the Muslims. See especially Bernard Hamilton, '"The Elephant of Christ", Reynald of Chatillon', *Studies in Church History* 15 (1978), 97–108.

[16]   The story that Sybilla herself was responsible for her marriage to Guy was also told by Ernoul, the earliest continuator of William of Tyre, but was contradicted by William's own account, which made clear that the choice was made by Baldwin IV; see Bernard Hamilton, *The Leper King and his Heirs. Baldwin IV and the Crusader Kingdom of Jerusalem* (Cambridge 2000), pp. 150–8. The Lusignans were, in fact, the most powerful noble family in Poitou, even though Guy was a younger son. While Count Raymond III of Tripoli ruled his own independent state, he was also through his marriage to the widowed Princess of Galilee a vassal to the King of Jerusalem, as well as first cousin to Baldwin IV.

king the count joined himself in friendship to Saladin. However, the barons and leading men of the kingdom, together with the Templars and Hospitallers, anxious in such a crisis to safeguard the defence of the land quickly sought to negotiate a beneficial peace [between them]. Meanwhile ten thousand Turks had secretly gathered between Tiberias and Mount Tabor, and were observing from their place of ambush the journey of those men who were travelling to the count to negotiate the peace, news of which had already come before them. The count had found out about the ambush laid by the Turks and immediately sent word to those who were preparing to come to him, warning them of the trap. The latter were however rash and overconfident, and despite the warning travelled along the planned route, where they were ambushed by the Turks, who rushed upon them from all sides. A fierce battle began, in which our men, although they had rashly entered the fight, stained their swords with a great deal of Turkish blood that day; but eventually the Turks, who were much more numerous, prevailed. Roger the Master of the Hospitallers fell in that battle, along with many others, though not without inflicting great slaughter among the enemy.[17] Those who had been able to escape came to the count and through their mediation peace was established between the king and him; the count then sent a message to Saladin repudiating their aforesaid friendship and alliance. Saladin [then] entered the land with a vast force of Saracens and through hatred of the count besieged Tiberias. Meanwhile the king and his army mustered at the springs of Sephoria, and despite the persuasion of the count they then marched out and pitched camp in a place that was known locally as *Marscalcia*.

O matter of wonder, O terrible presage of the approaching disaster! That night in the patriarch's tent, where the Holy Cross was, during the office of Matins it happened that there was read, quite by chance, 'the ark of the Covenant was taken by the Philistines in battle and carried off'.[18] Thus the hearts of all those who heard this and understood were immediately struck with fear, since as the poet says: 'fear [is] the gloomiest of augurs in perplexity'.[19] When morning came Saladin hastened to meet the king with a vast army and offered battle. The Turks bravely made ready for the fight, fiercely provoking our men to fight with trumpets and arrows. The division of the Templars was at the forefront of the battle, and casting their spears they spurred their horses and boldly charged the Turkish squadrons.[20] However, after they had slaughtered a host of enemies, they resumed their formation but were unable to withdraw, for they were surrounded on all sides by swarms of Turks, and

---

[17]   The Battle of Cresson, May 1187. For other, fuller, contemporary accounts, the Old French Continuation of William of Tyre, in Edbury, *The Conquest of Jerusalem and the Third Crusade*, pp. 31–4; a papal letter of September 1187, based on a report by the Master of the Temple, in ibid., pp. 156–7; Nicholson, *Chronicle of the Third Crusade*, pp. 25–6; and the *De Expugnatione Terrae Sanctae per Saladinum*, in Ralph of Coggeshall, *Chronicon Anglicanum*, ed. J. Stevenson (Rolls Series, London 1875), pp. 211–17.

[18]   Probably I Samuel 4:11.

[19]   Statius, *Thebaïs*, III:6.

[20]   *Cunei*, literally 'wedge-shaped formations'.

almost all of them were cut off by them and trapped. On seeing this catastrophe the Count of Tripoli and a few of his men threw down their arms and fled to Safed.[21] The Turks, who had lit fires round the army of the king, saw that the army was now suffering wretchedly from the heat and thirst and they pressed more boldly, launching unceasing attacks on our men and threatening them from all sides. Finally God permitted the Holy Cross and the king to be captured and victory was granted to the Turks. Some of the Christians were wretchedly put to death immediately, while others were kept in chains for lengthier torment, but once the victorious battle was concluded they were brought to Saladin and on his order were slain with the edge of the sword. After this dreadful massacre, and once Saladin had slain Rainald, about whom we made mention above, with his own hand, he returned triumphantly to Tiberias, and with the bravest and more outstanding men of the kingdom slain in the recent battle he was easily able to force the surrender not only of that place but also of Acre, Ascalon and almost all the land of Jerusalem.

Meanwhile, by the command of God who [even] in his anger knows [that] 'I have remembered with mercy',[22] and lest what was left of Christianity in those parts should completely perish, it happened that Conrad, Margrave of Montferrat, should be sailing as a pilgrim from Constantinople to worship at the Holy Sepulchre. He was of the Italian nation, and a blood relation of the most serene Emperor Frederick, a man both clever and valiant, wisely trained in matters warlike through long practice in the use of arms. When he had already almost sailed into the port, he saw that the city of Acre and all the land around it had recently been sacked and occupied by the Turks. He ordered a change of course and sailing before the wind he reached Tyre. The citizens, who had been deprived of the protection of a ruler and governor, welcomed him enthusiastically and made themselves and their city subject to his protection and guidance. The Count of Tripoli, who was now suspected by some of treachery, left Tyre and went to Tripoli, where not long afterwards, or so some people say, he fell victim to a lethal dose of poison, although according to others he ended his life in disgust and anguish because of the evils and desolation of the land.

Saladin then came to Tyre, bringing with him Margrave Rainier of Montferrat, whom he had captured in the war, since he hoped through him to force his son Conrad to an immediate surrender of the city.[23] O how admirable, that with 'pious impiety'[24] he judged the love of God to be preferable to the love of a father! Saladin was unable to weaken the constancy of this man in return for the freedom of his

---

[21]   A castle in northern Galilee, built c. 1101 in the earliest days of Crusader settlement: the surviving remains on this site are those of the rebuilt thirteenth-century castle, Hugh Kennedy, *Crusader Castles* (Cambridge 1994), p. 40.

[22]   Psalm 97:3 (Vulgate), 98:3 (AV)

[23]   Conrad's father, who had been captured at Hattin, was Margrave William: here the author of the *HP* seems to have copied a mistake in the *Historia de Expeditione* [above, p. 63 and note 157], where William and his eldest son Rainier (d. 1182) were confused.

[24]   Ovid, *Metamorphoses*, VIII.477.

father, nor to influence him either with threats or promises. He therefore departed to deal with the matters that required his attention with regard to the kingdom and the cities that had just been conquered. He ordained 'satraps and judges' in them,[25] appointing emirs to rule over them. A short time later he returned to Tyre with a great army and for almost two months he fiercely besieged it by land and sea. The citizens were now hemmed in by assault from without and suffering from shortage of food within, for they now had nothing except hazelnuts through which to sustain themselves. Eventually the citizens cunningly seized an opportunity to do battle, and they launched a night attack with the few ships that they had on those who were blockading the city at sea. They captured some of Saladin's ships, damaged and sank others along with their crews, and they brought the defeated archpirate as prisoner back into the town amid tumult and great rejoicing.[26] When those who were besieging the city on land heard the noise of the naval battle, although they did not then know of the disaster that had befallen their men, they gathered themselves for a simultaneous attempt to storm the city with their siege-engines and an assault. The Turks broke through the outer defences and were now destroying part of the inner walls while they were also climbing up the main city wall. However, Conrad, a great-hearted man experienced in warfare, encouraged his men and led them out to battle, calling upon God [for help]. He immediately and valiantly charged the enemy, making a fierce and noisy attack, and through the power of God he overcame their resolution with his victorious hand. Three hundred of the Turks met with a well-merited death there; the rest turned in flight and they burned their camp and the siege-engines they had built to capture the city. Our men were rewarded with booty and rejoiced in the lord who had thus secured a double triumph, 'raising up the horn of safety',[27] and saving both the city and its people. Moreover Hugh of Tiberias, the stepson of the aforementioned Count Raymond, made a sortie from Tyre with a column of troops and came to Arsuf, which he stormed and plundered.[28] The Turkish garrison was slain, the emir who was the governor of the town was captured, and Hugh returned joyful and victorious. Saladin was much upset by this, but as he was haughty of mind he played down the defeat for a time. He departed [northwards] and apart from the two cities of Antioch and Tripoli and a handful of

---

[25]   Esther 3:12.

[26]   The 'archpirate' was presumably Fâris al-Dîn Badrân, the commander of Saladin's naval squadron blockading Tyre, the defeat of which, on 30 December 1187, the sultan's biographer ascribed to the failure of the sailors to keep a proper watch at night, *The Rare and Excellent History*, p. 79. For another account of this naval battle, see the letter of the Templar official Terricus to Henry II of England, Edbury, *Conquest of Jerusalem and the Third Crusade*, p. 166.

[27]   Lucan, *Pharsalia*, 1:69.

[28]   Hugh was one of the four sons of Eschiva of Bures by her first husband; she subsequently married Raymond of Tripoli in 1175.

castles he captured the rest of that land and its fortresses, and almost all 'the land was silent in his sight'.[29]

* * * *

Once the rumours of the dreadful tidings had spread, to be greeted with horror, and news reached the Roman See of the disaster and destruction of the kingdom of Jerusalem, the Roman pontiff was filled with paternal affliction at this great loss for Christendom, and he vehemently lamented. After discussion and sensible advice he felt it necessary, because of this crisis, to send a legation to the kings and princes, and in particular to the invincible Emperor of the Romans, Frederick, on which mighty and most excellent man the hope and trust of Holy Mother Church now depended mightily, as its guardian and champion in remedying this injury.[30] The legation was directed universally to all suitable men accustomed to arms who were described by the name of Christian, inviting and earnestly advising them through Apostolic authority, either in writing or through preaching, to take part in the liberation of the Holy Sepulchre for remission of [their] sins.

The envoys of the Holy and Apostolic See travelled to Germany by the direct route and were eagerly and kindly received by the emperor at the city of Strassburg, sited on the River Rhine, where the emperor was then holding a court to deal with the business of the empire, to which the territorial princes had been summoned.[31] It is believed that it was not by chance but by Divine command that this great host of important men had gathered there, so that a happy beginning was made there to the expedition to Jerusalem, which was subsequently more fully discussed and promoted at the court of God and the pilgrims held at Mainz, which will be discussed below. The next day, with the bishops and other princes sitting alongside the emperor, and with a great crowd of knights and citizens also gathered there, the legates called for silence and began to sow the word of God in the ears of those present, encouraging them to [take part in] the expedition to Jerusalem. In response to their preaching, founded as it was on the gracious sweetness of eloquence, only one single knight among so many thousands was so consumed by devotion that he took the Cross there and pledged himself to undertake the journey.[32] However, the Bishop of Strassburg, Henry by name, a man experienced and wise in both religious and secular matters, saw and lamented that this exhortation had failed to rouse all but a very few hearts from their stubborn slumber. It was as if he had heard from

---

[29]   I Maccabees 1:3.

[30]   This ignores the often very difficult relations between Frederick and the papacy, especially under Urban III (pope 1185–7), for which see especially I.S. Robinson, *The Papacy 1073–1198. Continuity and Innovation* (Cambridge 1990), pp. 499–505.

[31]   December 1187.

[32]   The *Annales Marbacenses*, p. 58, named him as Siegfried, 'a rich and valiant' knight, who was one of the *ministeriales* of Count Albrecht of Dagsburg.

on high: 'Open thy mouth wide and I will fill it'.[33] He seized the opportunity to speak and won over all his audience through a persuasive display of Ciceronian eloquence, which went like this:

'O distinguished knights; it is an extraordinary thing! Courage and innate steadfastness have given you a great reputation for military activity, and have rendered you more famous [for this] than other peoples. We wonder greatly, and it is a matter for amazement, that in this great crisis your devotion to God has grown so shamefully cold and sluggish, and that you have forgotten your customary courage as if you were lazy and degenerate. Some pantomime or theatrical play has entertained you and enticed away your hearing, and the words of God have stirred up no response within you, as though you find them too difficult and hard to understand. O what grief! Charity has frozen in the hearts of all. For shame! "They are all gone aside, they are all together become filthy, there is none that doeth good".[34] There is no one who has been stirred by the injury to his Saviour, so that once again it has been possible to say: "I have trodden the winepress alone, and of the people there was none with me".[35] What would happen if somebody saw his earthly lord suffer injury through destruction or disinheritance? If you did not take up arms on his behalf you would undoubtedly be considered shameful and disgraced. How much more do we owe to Him, all [of us] under one head, namely "the members of Christ":[36] [we owe] what we are, that we exist, and we have all received what we have from His plenitude. But the shoots are not coming forth from the tree; the branches of the vine do not give heed to the goodness. To weep with those who are weeping is a matter of piety, yet the grief and desolation of the land of Jerusalem does not move you to tears, though what we have just heard inclines every faithful soul to bitterness and "the cup of desolation".[37] Need requires a friend, and lo, once again, He is suffering, so that He calls on and tries his [friends]. He invites you to furnish your help; He who for your redemption took on human form, was fixed to the Cross, and worked on earth for your salvation. This is the land of the Lord's inheritance, where His feet stood, from where first through the Prophets and then by the Apostles the first plantation of our faith was propagated in the world. And when God should be glorified "in all places of His dominion",[38] that place is especially worthy to be regarded with veneration, for it happened that the Son of God consecrated it by the deliberate touch of his presence to secure our redemption. May He therefore put grief in your hearts, may He move and incite you to revenge, because the mother and nurse of your faith, the holy city of Jerusalem, is in thrall to the profane rites of the pagans, and the worship

---

[33]   Psalm 80:11 (Vulgate), 81:10 (AV). For the bishop, see *History of the Expedition*, note 46.

[34]   Psalm 13:3 and 52:4 (Vulgate), 14:3 and 53:3 (AV).

[35]   Isaiah 63:3.

[36]   I Corinthians 6:15.

[37]   Ezekiel 23:33.

[38]   Psalm 102:22 (Vulgate), 103:22 (AV).

of the Christian religion has been destroyed and wiped out therein. For if, may this not happen, there is no one who helps or consoles her from all those dear to Him, what will happen in the future apart from the plantation of Christianity being gravely maimed and the shoots of paganism becoming spread more widely? If on the other hand someone were to encourage you to theft or some other sort of crime, by promoting evil he would easily find many accomplices for this iniquity, whereas God has gained only one from all these knights to fight for him. Think therefore, distinguished knights, how happy, how favourable and excellent is this sort of warfare, what fruitful work [it is], the reward for which is remission of sins, what indeed God promises and offers to His pilgrims.'

After these words the devotion of all, which had previously seemed to be sleeping, was roused. Pious tears welled up from contrite hearts. Many counts and barons, and many thousands of both knights and footmen, hastened together to receive the sign of the Cross. In a short time news of this spread far and wide, and roused all sorts of far peoples. Although the emperor had already privately decided that he wished to make the pilgrimage, as a man of wide-ranging circumspection, however, he still pretended [that he had not], waiting until a larger group of the princes and other men took the Cross without retraction, since with their help and involvement he would be able more easily and effectively to forward the business of the expedition. Thus expressly to arrange matters for the pilgrims with wise and necessary planning, he summoned a court to meet at Mainz in the middle of Lent, which [day] then fell on 27 March. This was rightly called the 'court of God'.

Meanwhile Henry, Cardinal Bishop of Albano, a religious man distinguished by his knowledge of letters and his delightful eloquence, had been sent by the Apostolic See as legate for the same purpose, since he was a distinguished preacher. He went first to the emperor, as was proper, by whom, as was fitting, he was received kindly and with due ceremony. He realised, after some private enquiry and discussion, that the latter looked favourably on the business of the pilgrimage, and rejoicing in the Lord he travelled around Germany, 'casting the seed', that is the Word of the Lord, 'into good ground',[39] and in a short space of time he recruited many for the expedition's journey to Jerusalem. He then travelled to Philip, the most serene King of the French, and King Henry of England, who were at that time in dispute, and through his persuasive speech he convinced them to make peace. Both they and many of the leading men from each kingdom received the sign of the Cross. Then he decided to return to Germany to attend the aforesaid 'court of God', the time for which was now approaching.

When the appointed time for the court had arrived, the most serene emperor and many archbishops, bishops, dukes, margraves, counts and barons gathered at the place designated, along with innumerable pilgrims and a host of other people. The city of Mainz rejoiced to be chosen and named as the site for discussing this matter so conducive to the common good and welcomed them as its guests. The court was celebrated with great ceremony and religious observance, so as to find favour

---

[39] Mark 4:26. For Henry of Albano, *History of the Expedition*, note 35.

and veneration from everyone. Among those present there was Bishop Gottfried of Würzburg, a man of prudence and eloquence, who was admirable and widely esteemed for his probity and other innate good qualities. He too was a pilgrim of the life-giving Cross, and, as a distinguished sower of the Divine Word, he gained the good opinion of his hearers through a persuasive and pleasing sermon, and he preached well and effectively, advancing many good arguments, to encourage them towards the way [of the Cross].[40] For the most Christian emperor himself, his illustrious son the Duke of Swabia, many bishops and princes along with other high-ranking men took the sign of the Cross from his hand there and bound themselves on oath and in public to undertake the journey. Many other people burned with devotion to undertake this enterprise, and all these great men were determined to make war against the hateful people of the Turks; [indeed] it was as if they were already in sight of the enemy, and imagined that they were already fighting them. As a consequence of the news of these great military preparations, the Christians became justifiably and increasingly joyful, while the Saracens were struck with terror and dread. All the pilgrims were very pleased by the presence of the duke; for thereafter, as his deeds will testify, not only was he highly distinguished by both birth and character, but in many dangerous military situations and while suffering great tribulations on behalf of the army of Christ, he often, indeed always, called forth his courage to do great deeds, and through his valour he won golden opinions from everyone. The emperor saw and rejoiced that the knighthood of Christ was so fruitfully increased, but he issued a decree that forbade anyone on foot, or who lacked capacity in the use of arms, also anyone who could not finance themselves for the journey for at least two years, from undertaking the way of pilgrimage with him, since a weak and unwarlike crowd was customarily more of a hindrance than a help to such a difficult expedition.[41] He explained to the rest that such an arduous operation required some pause and delay to make preparations for the journey. Thus it seemed to the emperor, after taking advice from the princes in private, that the proposed expedition should be put off for a year from Easter, which was approaching; the pilgrims should then muster at Regensburg on 23 April, that is, the feast of St George. Everyone was in full agreement to this. Once these arrangements had been settled, everyone was given permission to return home.

Since the most serene emperor and Saladin had for a long time been friends, sending a succession of envoys and gifts to each other,[42] the emperor thought it necessary for the reputation of his throne to send the latter an embassy with a

---

[40]   His preaching at the Mainz assembly was also noted by Arnold of Lübeck, *Chronica Slavorum*, IV.7, p. 128. For Gottfried, see *History of the Expedition*, note 47.

[41]   The English *Itinerarium Peregrinorum* said that Frederick insisted that all participants have the means for one year's absence, Nicholson, *Chronicle of the Third Crusade*, p. 55.

[42]   Saladin had sent an embassy to Frederick in 1173, *Chronica Regia Coloniensis*, p. 124; the emperor had dispatched his own ambassador to Egypt two years later, a report from whom was preserved by Arnold of Lübeck, *Chronica Slavorum*, VII.8, pp. 264–77.

declaration of war to initiate hostilities between them, unless Saladin returned the Holy Cross that had been taken in battle from the Christians, along with the land of Jerusalem that he had made subject to his yoke. The task of leading the embassy to Saladin was undertaken, at the emperor's request, by Count Henry of Dietz.[43] In addition, the emperor sent other embassies to King Bela of Hungary, to confirm the provision of markets, safe conduct along the way and a secure peace between the two of them, to the Emperor Isaac in Greece and to the Sultan of Iconium, with whom he had already long ago established good relations and friendship through an interchange of envoys, gifts and messages. The King of Hungary responded speedily and favourably to the request of the emperor and pilgrims concerning this matter. The chancellor and envoys of the Emperor of Constantinople then arrived and came into the presence of the most serene emperor, who received them kindly, at Nuremberg, where they conducted negotiations for the aforesaid peace.[44] They received sworn security from the distinguished Duke of Swabia and the other princes and great men who were present there, and in return they bound themselves on oath to him to secure a comprehensive peace treaty. They suggested that important and high-ranking envoys should be sent to Constantinople to receive fuller assurances from them there and to confirm the peace more fully. Amid other terms of the treaty that were agreed was this clause in particular: that the pilgrims might be allowed to take fruit from the trees, vegetables from gardens, wood to make fires provided houses were not damaged, and fodder and straw for the needs of their horses. Other clauses dealt with the provision of markets according to the resources of [particular] regions and the exigencies of the season. The following distinguished envoys were chosen to carry out this embassy after discussion between the emperor and the princes; namely the Bishop of Münster, Count Rupert of Nassau and Count Henry of Diez the younger.[45] And thus the aforesaid chancellor and his colleagues were bid a generous and honourable farewell by the emperor and returned to Greece. In addition to this, it had happened that a little while earlier other envoys had arrived,

---

The *Annales Stadenses*, MGH SS xvi.350, suggested that an envoy from Saladin arrived at Frederick's court in 1185.

[43]   This embassy was not mentioned by the *History of the Expedition*, but is confirmed by the *Chronica Regia Coloniensis*, p. 140. Henry of Diez was one of the emperor's closest and most loyal supporters, who had played a particularly prominent part in his Italian expedition of 1174–8, and was a frequent witness of his charters [see above, p. 23]. However, what purport to be the texts of this letter and of Saladin's response, reproduced in the *Itinerarium Peregrinorum* and several other English sources, are forgeries, part of the propaganda of the upcoming Crusade, *Das Itinerarium Peregrinorum*, pp. 280–8, c. 18 (English translation, Nicholson, *Chronicle of the Third Crusade*, pp. 49–54); Ralph of Diceto, *Opera Historica*, ed. W. Stubbs (2 vols, Rolls Series, London 1876), ii.56–7. See H.E. Mayer, 'Das Brief Kaiser Friedrichs I. an Saladin von Jahre 1188', *Deutsches Archiv für Erforschung des Mittelalters* 14 (1958), 488–94.

[44]   End of December 1188; see the *History of the Expedition*, above, p. 45 and note 55..

[45]   For these men, see *History of the Expedition*, note 59.

deceitfully making all sorts of promises of friendship on behalf of the sultan [of Iconium], not only with regard to markets and to security on the road but also for the continuation of the long-standing love [between them] and to show the emperor every mark of respect, which, so they said, the sultan would like to do in person. But, as events afterward proved, the message that the sultan had sent to the emperor was empty and faithless, and bore no relation to the truth. So what actually befell him was well deserved, for subsequently, after his deceit had been revealed, he received an appropriate recompense for the treachery he had perpetrated; [and] his lying and deceitful promise rightly rebounded to his detriment and ignominy. However, the emperor rashly believed in this vain promise, and he who had formerly been circumspect in all things and was usually adroitly on his guard was now heedless and was deceived by the lying words of the aforesaid envoys. After receiving them kindly and keeping them with him for a long time and looking after them more carefully than the others, he allowed them to go, sending back along with them a man named Gottfried, on a mission of peace and friendship to the sultan.[46]

As the starting date for the pilgrimage approached, 'the sower of the tares' and 'the kindler of all evils',[47] the devil, stirred up dissension and disrupted the peace between the King of the French and the King of England. For this reason both they and many others involved in conflicts now set aside the journey proposed. Some others chose to travel by ship, abandoning the intention to travel by land, which seemed to be more difficult and dangerous. Some indeed took the opportunity to make their excuses and, steeped in sin, they turned back, but 'no man having put his hand to the plough and looking back is fit for the kingdom of God'.[48] The most Christian emperor, however, great of heart as he was, remained nevertheless determined to undertake the journey, thinking it proper and suitable if he might make recompense in this holy service for the frequent successes by which he had earlier been distinguished, with a worthy 'fulfilment of his courageous endeavours'.[49] Thus, as had been arranged, on 23 April the pilgrims mustered at Regensburg.

The Bishop of Münster, Count Rupert of Nassau and Henry the younger of Dietz, who had been sent on the aforesaid embassy to Constantinople, had already gone on ahead, taking with them a hundred knights and with many other people in their train. After crossing Bulgaria and Macedonia with considerable difficulty, they arrived at Constantinople, where they stayed for some time, awaiting the return

---

[46]   Gottfried of Wiesenbach, who in October 1189 was dispatched on a further mission to Constantinople and Iconium; for which the *History of the Expedition*, above, p. 75 and notes 197, 247.

[47]   Cf. Matthew 13:25; II Maccabees 4:1.

[48]   Luke 9:62.

[49]   Ecclesiasticus 50:11 (Vulgate), a quotation copied from the *History of the Expedition* [above, p. 37]. A very similar phrase was used about Frederick and the Crusade by Arnold of Lübeck, *Chronica Slavorum*, IV.7, pp. 127–8: 'he directed the strength of his forces to attack the enemies of the Cross of Christ, thinking that this was a good fulfilment for his struggle'.

of the Emperor of Constantinople, who was then absent. When the emperor did return they came into his presence, and his demeanour was cheerful, as if he was overjoyed by the coming of the pilgrims. O unheard-of wickedness! O monstrous treachery! However, in the words of Claudianus, 'he learned the arts of injury and deceit, how to conceal the intended menace and cover his treachery with a smile'.[50] The envoys were therefore mistakenly cheerful and returned to their lodgings. Why had the crafty emperor pretended to show a cheerful countenance to the envoys of peace and good faith, when, showing himself 'a stone of stumbling and a rock of offence'[51] to all Christendom, he was plotting their destruction? The next day the envoys were arrested on his order, plundered, assaulted, and finally wretchedly marched off, brought under armed guard and subject to all sorts of fearful threats, to a place of torment and thrown into prison. Thus the ancient rights of envoys and of hospitality were shamefully dishonoured at the expense of innocent and peaceful men to secure the favour and grace of Saladin. This most wicked emperor had only recently given audience in friendly fashion to their embassy. He ought at least first to have paid attention to that pagan saying that 'it is worse to cast out a guest than not to receive him'.[52]

Meanwhile the most serene emperor Frederick, who knew nothing of this wicked act, had gone down the river by ship from Regensburg into Austria, while his army with its horses and carts marched by land. He had a town called Mauthausen, sited on the bank of the Danube, completely destroyed by fire as a punishment, since its inhabitants had arrogantly presumed to extort an unjustified toll from the pilgrims crossing [the river]. After the army had arrived at Vienna, Duke Leopold of Austria, who was famous and renowned among everyone as a beacon of generosity, made admirable efforts to provide for the pilgrims, both by furnishing them with a market and through happily making gifts from his own property.

[The account of the Crusade continues thereafter.]

---

[50] Claudianus, *In Rufinum*, I, lines 98–9: the translation is that of Maurice Platnauer, in the Loeb edition (Cambridge, MA, 1922), p. 33.

[51] I Peter 2:8.

[52] Ovid, *Tristia*, V.vi.13.

The Chronicle of Magnus of Reichersberg[1]

In the year 1189 a very strong and valiant army of the Christians was mustered from many kingdoms and different regions, and set out on the way of the Holy Sepulchre. The lord emperor and his son the Duke of Swabia, with many princes from the kingdom, bishops, dukes, margraves and counts, along with a huge multitude of [other] people, set off to travel through Hungary and Greece, immediately after the season of Easter, which fell on 9 April. The emperor travelled by ship down the Danube, and arrived at Passau on the first day of Rogations, that is on 15 May. Diepold, the lord Bishop of Passau, along with certain of his brother canons, namely the greater and more distinguished men of the chapter of Passau, manfully joined this journey and the emperor's enterprise both for the sake of the Lord and for the redemption of his soul, choosing this path not because he sought temporal wealth, for he left many possessions behind, but knowing that he would receive life everlasting in the Heavenly Jerusalem once this life was over. In this same year the aforesaid bishop sent a letter from Greece, the text of which is as follows.

'Diepold, by the grace of God humble minister of the church of Passau to the friend of his heart Leopold, illustrious Duke of Austria, [wishing him] salvation and sincere regard. We wish to communicate to you the joyful and sweet tidings of our heart, and we [also] want to notify your diligence of all the unfortunate events that have befallen our army. You would wish to know that on entering Bulgaria we sustained many injuries at the hands of the Bulgarians, since they wounded many of our men with javelins. So whenever we captured any of them we had them hanged. Coming to the city of Nish, we encountered there the Great Count of Serbia, who met us in state. The lord emperor received him honourably and had long discussions with him, giving him worthy gifts, while he too received great things from him. Similarly all the princes were overwhelmed with wine, mead and animals by the count. We then moved on to the first of the passes, where we sustained serious losses to our baggage. A certain worthy knight from Halle was killed here. In these regions most of the army fell sick, some with tertian fever, others with quartan, while some were indeed suffering with

---

[1] Translated from *Magni Presbiteri Chronicon*, ed. Wilhelm Wattenbach, MGH SS xvii.509–17. Magnus died in 1195, and so his chronicle represents contemporary testimony to the Crusade of Frederick Barbarossa, but its particular importance in this context is that he copied within his own work the contemporary Crusade diary of Tageno, Dean of Passau cathedral, whose death at Tripoli late in 1190 he recorded [see the introduction, pp. 3–5, for a fuller discussion]. In this translation, Tageno's diary will be printed in larger type, and what appears to be the work of Magnus himself in smaller size.

dysentery. The second pass, which was strongly defended by nature, was strengthened further by rocks and wood, and a great crowd of looters and robbers had gathered there. This had been arranged by the Duke of Branchevo, who had treacherously gone in advance of us. But the Duke of Swabia, who commanded the first battle line, did them great damage. Then the division subject to us and the Duke of Merania, which was the middle one, charged them, inflicting wounds on some, and the greater part of their equipment was captured. Around the hour of Vespers, we and the aforesaid Duke of Merania were guarding the flanks of our group, and we were riding with only about a dozen knights when suddenly two sons of one of the counts of that province, with at least a hundred companions, launched a vigorous and daring attack upon us, and fought with us for a long time with swords and spears. But with the help of God we put them to flight, leaving more than forty wounded concealed in hiding places. We gathered up some twenty-four of these people and tied them to the tails of our horses. We brought them back to our camp and ordered them to be strung up by their feet. At Stralitz we found hardly any men left, since by the order of the Duke of Branchevo the men of that province had gone up into the mountains and taken their supplies with them. Here the army suffered greatly through a shortage of wine. In the third pass, which was so fortified that it threatened to make the passage of our men difficult, we sustained no setback. Although the scouts of the Duke of Swabia spotted more than five hundred well-armed Greeks there, as soon as the latter saw the leading knights of the duke they immediately turned tail and fled. In that place the suffering of the army was entirely relieved through an abundance of bread, wine and fresh fruit, and the division of the lord emperor joined us. At Circuviz a certain Hungarian count named Lectoforus, who had gone before us on an embassy to the Emperor of Constantinople, returned to us with an envoy from the King of the Greeks. The aforesaid king proudly and arrogantly described himself as Emperor of the Romans, an angel of God and the source of our faith. He conveyed his grace to our emperor, saying that he had learned from messages from the kings of France and England, and the Duke of Brindisi,[2] that the lord emperor had entered Greece with the intention of extinguishing his line and that he wished to transfer rule over the Greeks into the power of his son the Duke of Swabia. Moreover he said that the treaty of friendship that he had heard had been concluded between the emperor and the Great Count was suspicious and very much against his interests. He added also that the lord emperor should send hostages to him to secure his agreement to the army's crossing of the Bosphorus,[3] and once he swore to do this then he would grant a market [for the army]. He said furthermore that he wanted half the land which our army conquered from the

---

[2]   Who this might be is a good question, since no such official can be identified. Was this Margaritus of Brindisi [below note 8], the Sicilian admiral, who was himself a Greek, or was this perhaps a reference to Tancred of Lecce, the future King of Sicily, whose county was in southern Apulia not far from Brindisi?

[3]   *Bracchium*, i.e. the 'Arm of St George'.

Saracens to be assigned to him. Although the lord emperor and the princes were extremely annoyed when they heard this, in the circumstances they responded politely and wisely, saying that when they had secured the return of his envoys, who were at this time robbed of their possessions, shamefully exposed to the insults and mockery of the envoys of Saladin, treated shamefully and cast into a squalid prison where they were suffering cruelly, then they could look favourably upon this request, provided that it was in accordance with the honour of God and the empire. We then marched on to the town of Philippopolis, which we found empty of men but full of wine, corn and other valuable supplies. At that time the brother of the King of the Greeks was six miles away from us with a great army, but when one day our men incautiously approached them they put them to flight, and they did not appear in these parts again. Thereafter the King of the Greeks, his brother and their army continually tried to trick us, and delayed us more and more.[4] However, by the grace of God and through a great deal of effort and ingenuity we recovered our envoys, only barely clothed. And then at first the king promised us that we would make the crossing during the winter season, if we would give hostages to him that the peace of the land be respected, and he pledged the other things that had been sworn at Nuremberg. The lord emperor saw that all these offers were fraudulent, and he had no wish to agree to them, both because his envoys had been treated quite dreadfully and shamefully, and since he had no wish to entrust either himself or the army of the holy pilgrimage to the deceitful oaths of these people. And so while at first he spoke humbly so as to recover his envoys, once they had been restored to him he spoke in an imperial fashion. If the King of the Greeks would give as hostages his son, his brother and uncle, on whose advice he and all of Greece depended, and he could travel through the land and make the crossing of the Bosphorus in peace and safety and have good markets, then in response he would have whomever the latter wanted to choose from his army swear that he had entered his land with no evil intent or ulterior motive. We still have no idea how the king will respond [to this offer]. We can scarcely explain to you what joy there was among us on the day when the envoys were restored to us, for more than three thousand chosen knights rode out at least six miles on their war horses with lance and shield, and as a result the chancellor and great men of the Greeks were absolutely terrified, since they feared that ambushes had been prepared for them. But when the Duke of Swabia and the other nobles realised this they immediately put down their shields and received them kindly, explaining that this was a custom of the Germans, and that it had been done to welcome those rescued and for the glory of the Greeks. Then after taking care of the Greek envoys, they brought our envoys to the lord emperor with great rejoicing, with some chanting "You have come, desired ones";[5] others crying out, *Hiute herre din tach*. The lord emperor came out from his lodging,

---

[4]   The Greek commander, Manuel Kamytzes, was a cousin on his father's side, rather than the emperor's brother.

[5]   *Advenisti desiderabiles.*

embraced the bishop and count and received them with many tears, saying: "I give thanks to God, 'for this my son was dead, and is alive again; he was lost and is found'".[6] The following day the bishop tearfully informed the princes of the circumstances of his captivity, so that they too were moved to tears. Then the Greek envoys finished the business of their legation, and the lord emperor gave them a crisp response, in the terms described above, saying that he would be satisfied with nothing without the aforesaid hostages. As a result the Greeks were greatly disturbed. Since, however, the King of the Greeks had sent letters to the lord emperor on three occasions, but had neither called him by name nor described him as emperor, in the presence both of the Greeks and of our princes he addressed them in a suitably imperial manner and speech.

"We cannot be more astounded and we have been made very angry that our brother has been accustomed to omit our name in his letters, for this name, which is Frederick, is well known to many kings, princes and provinces. His predecessor, Manuel of pious memory, was careful to use our name in his letters, even when we were enemies one to another, nor did he make any attempt to impair the dignity of our majesty. I behaved in the same manner to him. For indeed our predecessor Charles of famous memory, happy in victory, obtained royal rule over Rome, from which it has been passed on to our times without interruption for more than five hundred years. And we ourselves, through the agency of God and free election by the princes, have now gloriously enjoyed power at the head of the Holy Roman Empire for almost thirty-eight years. For in the city of Rome, which is known as the lady and head of the world, we received the crown and rule over all of Christianity from the altar of St Peter, prince of the Apostles, and were solemnly anointed with the oil of majesty by the lord Pope Adrian, the successor to St Peter, before our fellows, and our name is held to be famous and glorious because of this. We have therefore explained this because perhaps your lord is ignorant of our name and rank. You should know that in future we will not accept his letters unless the appropriate protocol of name and majesty is expressly included within them, for we have called him, and we do call him, by his name. Your lord calls himself holy: a holiness that is extraordinary when he suddenly consigns to prison and torments with life-threatening hunger and nudity holy, decent and religious men and after having received them kindly and with the kiss of peace as trustworthy ambassadors, in the mouth of whom no evil or dishonesty is to be found. God distance ourselves from such holiness."

On hearing this, the Greeks withdrew. What more? The whole of Macedonia right up to the walls of Constantinople is subject to our orders and obeys our will. The cities and castles are in our hands, nor is there anyone who dares complain on hearing our name. The Vlachs are our allies. The Armenians are our loyal subjects. Our lord the emperor intended to spend the winter at Philippopolis, the Duke of Swabia at Berrhoë. The army was divided up between three locations. The Greeks are calling us heretics. Their clerics and monks are making life very difficult for

---

[6]   Luke 15:24, from the parable of the prodigal son.

us both through words and deeds. You should know, however, that we are well supplied, and that our companions are all safe and well. On 29 September our men were threatened by the most awful smell because of the countless bodies at Philippopolis. On 5 November the lord emperor left Philippopolis and went to Adrianople. Those who remained at Philippopolis enjoyed a remarkable abundance of foodstuffs. Dated 11 November.'

That the sequence of the history about which we are writing should be brought more clearly to the notice of posterity it is desirable to insert here a letter explaining this history, written in the regions across the sea and sent to our lands – hence it has come to our attention. This reads as follows.[7]

'It happened that some years after the death of the Emperor Manuel of Constantinople Andronikos undertook rule there. He punished those who had committed treason, so that he blinded some, drowned others, and condemned some to perpetual prison or sent them into exile. This led Andronikos Angelos and his sons to fear him, since they had been involved in the death of the Emperor Alexios, so they fled and arrived most fearfully in Acre. And after the aforesaid Andronikos Angelos was dead, two of his sons fled back to the feet of Andronikos, and were immediately blinded. The other two, who did not trust in the mercy of Andronikos, fled to Saladin. And after they had stayed with him for a time, one of them was led by love of his homeland to return to Constantinople. And after Andronikos had spared him, and helped him in many ways, an oracle was consulted and the emperor and [his] logothete heard that the throne would pass to the said Isaac, and on the logothete's persuasion they decided that he ought to be blinded. But when the logothete came to him with the imperial order, and he had been warned by his words, he had no hesitation about killing him. Isaac [then] hastened to St Sophia and proclaimed to the people: "I have killed your enemy." The people followed him and he was acclaimed emperor, and he inflicted a most cruel and extraordinary revenge on Andronikos, to whom he had sworn as his lord. But in the aforesaid crisis, when Andronikos was savagely treating those who were traitors to him, the kings of Sicily and Hungary had risen up [in arms] against him, and the whole people was conspiring against him, Andronikos was forced by grief and anxiety to look to the advice and help of Saladin. And that he might recall their old friendship and agreement, and the benefits that the latter had conferred upon him, and that in order to conclude a similar alliance he insistently urged him that he might do homage to him, since he was [now] emperor, and [in return] he would be ready to bring help to him when urgently needed, if he had the resources and Saladin requested this. Furthermore they joined together and then swore to this agreement, that if Saladin succeeded in occupying the land of the men of Jerusalem with his advice and assistance, then Saladin would keep some land for himself, but would leave Jerusalem and all the coastal area apart from

---

[7]   Brand, 'The Byzantines and Saladin', p. 181, discusses the authenticity of this letter, and suggests that it was a genuine letter, probably written at Tyre in summer or autumn 1188 under the instructions, or within the circle, of Conrad of Montferrat. On the other hand, Harris, *Byzantium and the Crusades*, pp. 129–31, regards this as merely another piece of Frankish anti-Byzantine propaganda.

Ascalon free, on condition however that he would hold it from the aforesaid emperor, and that they might acquire Iconium and the land of the sultan, and the land as far as Antioch and the territory of the Armenians would belong to the aforesaid emperor, if they could gain it. But since death prevented Andronikos from putting this agreement into effect, after the aforesaid Isaac had become emperor he confirmed this same treaty through the best and most noble men whom he had, and with the affixing of his gold seal, since he both hated and feared the Latins. He [also] recalled his brother, whom Saladin had honoured and endowed, but while the latter was travelling through Acre the Count of Tripoli and the Prince of Antioch, since they had inklings about this treaty and had been warned both by their own subjects and by some of the more noble Saracens, whose relations Saladin had had strangled, arrested him and bound him most tightly with iron chains.

After being informed by his envoys that the news of this was undoubtedly true, the aforesaid Emperor Isaac reminded Saladin, as his most beloved vassal [*homo*], of the aforesaid treaty, and instructed him to attack the eastern Christians who were the bitter enemies of them both in force. He would attack them as best he could from the other side and strive to free his brother from prison, and once complete victory had been gained each would rejoice in their share of the land, as agreed in the treaty. But when Isaac sent eighty well-armed galleys to help Saladin, Margaritus launched a most powerful attack upon them at Cyprus.[8] Saladin however suddenly and unexpectedly invaded the land of Jerusalem with a vast host, and as has often been told, and as I say weeping, God allowed him to defeat all our Christian forces. He illegally placed almost all the land under his own rule, with nobody [now] to defend it, he had, shamefully, crosses dragged through the streets, he polluted the Sepulchre in the presence of the Saracens, and he forced virgins, married women and infants into exile in foreign lands that will be permanent unless God in his mercy summons them back. Made quite unbelievably exultant by this victory, he sent envoys to the emperor and gave him information by letter so that he [too] might rejoice in his victory, and he sent him an elephant, fifty Turkish saddles, a phial of balsam and a hundred Turkish bows, with quivers and arrows; he returned [also] a hundred Greek prisoners to Greece. He gave him [too] 1,050 Turkish or Turcoman warhorses, and infinite treasure and other things that he knew to be more valuable. The emperor was delighted with these gifts, showed the envoys as much honour as he could, and granted them one of the best palaces in the middle of Constantinople to stay in for their time there, something which he had never or rarely been known to do for any Latin envoys, and he renewed the aforesaid alliance and oaths. And when these honoured envoys took their leave of him, the emperor sent his own envoys with them, namely Sovestot, Aspion and Constantius, the latter an elderly man fluent in the Saracen language, and he sent a golden crown for Saladin with them, saying: "I send this to you since to my mind you are, with my help and God's consent, rightly a king," and he sent him forty top-quality breastplates, four thousand iron plates, and five thousand swords, all of which he had had from the King of Sicily, and twelve samite and two golden cloaks, and two imperial tunics and three

---

8   Margaritus of Brindisi, the commander of the Sicilian fleet, subsequently Count of Malta, and one of the Sicilian nobles taken as a prisoner to Germany in 1195.

hundred beaver skins. He sent Saphadin, the brother of Saladin,[9] six bolts of samite and two imperial tunics, and six bolts of samite and an imperial tunic to each of the three elder sons of Saladin. But when these envoys had arrived by sea at Acre, Saladin had been wretchedly defeated before Tyre, and using the arrival of the envoys as an excuse he fled to Acre on the day of the Epiphany, and meeting the ambassadors and wishing to greet them he summoned all his princes and friends, and his sons, and in the presence of his scribes he renewed the aforesaid treaty and [his] oaths, and treated the envoys with great honour, and he diligently enquired of them concerning the situation of the emperor, about the war with the Vlachs and about the other wars of other princes. The envoys kneeled and thanked him for the honour granted to the emperor's brother, and they kissed his knee, saying: "Through you he has been saved and freed from the hands of the Latins, who were holding him in prison on your account."

There was a delay when Saladin heard of the particulars [*consignatio*] and of the arrival of the Latin princes, and he promptly started to mull over plans for their destruction. He sent the envoys back to the emperor, and with them he sent twenty Latin warhorses, a casket a cubit long filled with precious stones, another casket of the same length full of balsam, three hundred ropes, studded with perforated [precious] stones of great size, and a chest full of aloes and a tree of wood with green arms and branches, which is much more precious, and a hundred follicles of musk, twenty thousand bizantii, a baby elephant and a little beast that makes musk,[10] an ostrich and five leopards, thirty quintals of pepper and other things without number or measure, and a vessel of solid silver that could hold twenty measures of wine, full of most strong poison. When Saladin wanted to prove [the effects of this] in the presence of the envoys, he summoned a Latin Christian and ordered him to open the container in the middle of a square, a long way from the Saracens, and when the man did open it he immediately fell dead. [Saladin also sent] six thousand moggia of poisoned flour, and three thousand moggia of wheat, similarly poisoned, and he sent a mosque to him as he had promised, instructing him to hold it in veneration.'[11]

In this same year lord Philip, provost of the church of Reichersberg, installed a water fountain in the cloister of the brothers, after a long and difficult passage [of the water] from a place called Lind, doing this through his own efforts and the help of some of the faithful from outside [the cloister]. Then, taking into account his own weakness, since he was no longer able to rule because of old age, he resigned this same provostship into the hands of Archbishop Adalbert of Salzburg on 28 August.[12] He was indeed a good and gentle man, and devoted to the religious life, so that from his youth he had devoted his

---

[9] Saif ad-Din al-Adil (d. 1218).

[10] Presumably a musk deer, obtained from central Asia.

[11] For this mosque, *The Rare and Excellent History of Saladin*, p. 121, which also gives the text of a letter from Isaac to Saladin, written in August/September 1189, assuring him that Barbarossa's army would be no threat to him. German sources took the darkest view of the alliance of Isaac and Saladin: the Lauterberg chronicler even claimed that Saladin had sent the Byzantine ruler 800 Turkish archers to help him stop the Crusaders, *Chronicon Montis Sereni*, MGH SS xxiii.161.

[12] Adalbert III, Archbishop of Salzburg 1183–1200.

life completely to God; he had lived in the abbey of Reichersberg for more than fifty years without dispute, obeying his masters, always busy with fasting and vigils, and devoting his efforts to copying sacred books carefully with his own hands. After him, on 30 August the brothers elected in his place the lord priest Gerloch, who was educated in the discipline from boyhood by Master Gerhoh of happy memory, and ordained to the priesthood in the abbey of Reichersberg.[13] At the provost's own request and that of the lords of the Salzburg chapter, he was with the permission of his brothers made an associate of the chapter of the church of Salzburg and its lords.

On 15 January 1190 that part of our army that had wintered at Philippopolis followed the lord emperor to Adrianople, and it came to Constantia on the day on which was sung 'The pains of death have surrounded me', that is on 21 January.[14] It met the emperor at Adrianople on 6 February. An envoy from the Emperor of the Greeks arrived on 14 January, bringing to our lord emperor a brief and final draft of the peace treaty. Envoys from the sultan and his son [also] came to the lord emperor at Adrianople on 17 February, carrying a favourable message. On 24 March our pilgrims suffered a bitingly cold and unbearable storm at Adrianople. Envoys were then sent out to explore a safe route to the Bosphorus. On 27 February the Greek hostages whom the emperor had sought from them arrived. On 1 March the Duke of Swabia led his column forth from Adrianople. The next day the emperor and his army marched out. On 4 March they crossed the River Reina, with great difficulty, and that day was Sunday, when 'Rejoice Jerusalem' was sung.[15] On 8 March terrible thunder was heard, and the clouds poured forth unusually heavy rain, making the road difficult for both men and horses. On Palm Sunday, 18 March, there was weeping and great sadness, since the horses were suffering from a severe shortage of corn. On the Day of the Lord's Supper Ainwicus of Hagenau died; he was buried at Roussa.[16] They [then] arrived at Gallipoli for the crossing of the Bosphorus. The Duke of Swabia and his division were the first to cross the Bosphorus, on Good Friday, 23 March. The lord Bishop of Passau, the Duke of Merania and their following crossed on 26 March, and entered the first parts of Romania. On 28 March, which was a Wednesday, the lord emperor crossed, after the passage of all the pilgrims. On 29 March, having left behind the carts and wagons, they set off on their journey with pack animals, and for two days they had a difficult march, beset by shortage. On the third day they entered a valley where the men were restored by wine and food, and the horses by excellent grazing. On 2 April they crossed the River Diga, and on the following day the River Analonica, with great labour

---

[13]   The celebrated theologian Gerhoh was provost of Reichersberg 1133–69.

[14]   *Circumdederunt me gemitus mortis.*

[15]   *Laetare Ierusalem*: the fourth Sunday in Lent [see above p. 43]. The River Reina was probably the modern Iskenderköy-Bach, near Karakasim, Eickhoff, *Friedrich Barbarossa im Orient*, p. 78.

[16]   Thursday, 24 March.

and damage to equipment; they had a low-lying and muddy path.[17] On 7 April they joined the road that comes from Constantinople. Then, faced with crossing one of Romania's desert regions, they furnished both men and horses with seven days' supplies. On 9 April they entered the valley of Ascarata, and here a large part of the army began to complain because of [the absence] of a market. On 14 April they came to the castle of Calomon, which they found empty. On 21 April they arrived at Philadelphia. Then they crossed a certain mountain with great difficulty, since the greater part of the horses were failing, and all the supplies apart from bread had been eaten. Then they came to Tripoli the Lesser, which is called in Greek Ierapolis, and in the Apocrypha Thyatira, where Philip the Apostle had suffered. They found this to have been deserted by the Turks; and they crossed the water that is called 'the Lesser' there and entered the land of the Turks. These received them cheerfully and with all humanity, and provided as best they could a market for the army. They then went on to the plain of Laodicea, which is situated at the foot of a particularly high mountain, beyond which is Ephesus; here they found a good market. It was said that Louis, the former King of France, was defeated by the Turks here, and [also] Otto, lord Bishop of Freising, during the expedition of King Conrad. They then entered a certain most desolate place in Turkey, descending through horrible salty land to a lake of salt pans. There they found flocks of sheep, goats, lambs and kids, and herds of oxen, horses, camels and asses, numbering at least 5,000 head. All these were the animals of the Turks, who at our arrival abandoned their tents and felt huts and fled up into the mountains. But since we thought that they would behave peacefully towards us, we took none of the animals found on our road, desirable or indeed necessary though these might have been. That night at the head of the lake they found neither plants, nor grass nor trees. The following morning all sorts of evils unknown to the ages beset us. For the Turks harassed both horse and foot with javelins and attacked them unceasingly. However, on 29 April God, wishing to spare His people, held back the wrath that had burned so greatly upon us because of our sins. When the aforesaid Turks entered the camp that they had left to gather up the things that the people had abandoned there through exhaustion, the emperor cleverly ordered smoke to be made, and they then launched a sudden attack on the enemy while the latter were blinded and they killed almost three hundred of them. They then followed a very difficult route to Sozopolis, while the remaining enemy kept them under observation from the mountains. On 2 May they slew up to three hundred more of the enemies of the Cross of Christ, but our men were suffering great want. On 3 May more than thirty thousand Turks had gathered in a very narrow pass, through which our men were to cross – this was the place where the Greek emperor Manuel was defeated and his mighty army destroyed – their intention was to slay our men in the same way. But 'the

---

[17]   Reading *lutosa*, 'muddy', for *butosa*, although the latter could have been derived from *butinnosus*, 'swampy'.

Lord turned the counsel of Achitophel into foolishness',[18] since the emperor was warned by the Holy Spirit, and had the army cross a certain very high mountain, where more than a thousand horses perished. Everyone remembered that day in which they crossed this high and difficult mountain. On descending from the mountain they found a wide plain and numerous flocks. The next day the Turks surrounded them, and attacked them fiercely day and night with arrows and hit-and-run charges. On 4 May hunger gripped the army in earnest, and the envoys of the sultan treacherously fled from them, after making Gottfried a prisoner. Then we knew for certain that the gold of the sultan, that is his friendship, 'was turned into dross',[19] and that he and the Greeks had come to an agreement that they would destroy us by treachery, since they could not resist us in battle. 'But the Lord freed us from all these things.'[20]

On 7 May, thinking that we were completely exhausted from hunger, the Turks launched a powerful attack on our camp, showering us with stones, darts and lances. However, the army of the life-giving Cross hastened manfully to meet their attacks, so that 'two put ten thousand to flight',[21] and, if night and the mountains had not intervened, they all would have fallen to the edge of the sword. And as I speak truly, more than five thousand Turks fell there, both horse and foot, through the leadership of the Duke of Swabia and the Duke of Merania. On 10 May our men heard the trumpet of the sultan and they saw his banner, as a Turkish guide whom they had taken prisoner informed them. On 11 May the Turks attacked them in full force, so that 'they filled mountains and valleys',[22] and our men pretended weakness, so that they were made even more savage, and they made a [further] attack on them, shouting. But our men suddenly swung round and killed two hundred of them, and on the mountain near the town of Firmin another fifty or more. On 13 May, when it was the holy day of Pentecost, God spared us. The following day, which was 14 May, the sons of the sultan, who had mustered three hundred thousand horsemen, drew up their battle lines and fought with us. But the lord emperor ordered our first line to charge them bravely. This was done, and they all turned in flight. Next morning, marching as though half-dead, they found water in some boggy ground, and their horses were somewhat refreshed in these marshes. There the great Malik and his satraps sent an envoy [through whom] they said that if the emperor and the army gave them three hundred *centenarii* of gold, and the land of the Armenians, then they would grant them safe passage, and would have a market set up three days later. The emperor responded with his customary good temper, saying: 'It is not our imperial law, and the army of the Christians and the knighthood of the life-giving Cross should not be accustomed to buying a royal passage with gold and silver,

---

[18]   II Samuel 15:31.

[19]   Isaiah 1:22.

[20]   Cf. Psalm 33:20.

[21]   Deuteronomy 32:30.

[22]   Cf. Luke 3:5.

but with the help of our Lord Jesus Christ, for whom we are knights, a way shall be opened with our swords.' The envoy then left, saying: 'If I do not return to you tonight, you should know for certain that tomorrow, before the third hour, the Turks will be fighting you with the utmost determination.' But since the army and its horses, as a result of what had happened earlier, were greatly in want, 'we began to be greatly sorrowful and very heavy'.[23] However, He who is 'a refuge in time of troubles',[24] who always wants to spare rather than to punish, inspired the hearts of the bishops to encourage the people, with fatherly and salutary warning, to beg for Divine help and to call upon the name of St George the Martyr, who is indeed held in high regard throughout the Catholic Church, and who had appeared during our travails on several occasions to religious men, with hymns of praise and promises of fasting to the utmost of their ability. They entreated God, with many sighs and tears, to give them the saint as their standard-bearer, champion and advocate. With the situation now seeming to be at a crisis, even the lord emperor was somewhat apprehensive, although he kept this to himself, about the next day's camp, which he intended to make in a wild animal park and orchard of the sultan. He said to the members of his household: 'If tomorrow, with the help of God, we are able to pitch our tents with any sort of security, it is no bad omen for our future peace.'

The next morning, 17 May, we heard a solemn mass and one by one took most Holy Communion in the name of the Lord, and then we set off, albeit rather late. The Turks, of whom there was an innumerable multitude, surrounded us in a half-moon formation, although they did not greatly harass us with their yelling and attacks. They remained with us until we arrived at our camp, but without inflicting any harm upon us, while they lost about thirty of their men.[25] When we entered the royal park and its orchard, we found a great abundance of plants and water. That night we suffered from thunderstorms and unusual cloudbursts. When dawn arrived, the lord emperor drew up [the army in] two divisions; the first he entrusted to his son the Duke of Swabia, the second he himself commanded. He instructed the clergy and those knights who lacked arms, along with the rest of the common people, the baggage and pack animals, to march in between them. He also issued an imperial edict[26] that, if God should grant us the victory, nobody was to be allowed to search for booty until the enemy forces were stretched out on the ground and the city of Iconium was in our hands. But while we were making preparations, an envoy of the sultan met the emperor, 'seeking those things that were of peace'.[27] The emperor replied that if his own envoy was freed from captivity and returned to him, and diligent and wise ambassadors were sent who knew about and had powers to conduct such important negotiations, then

---

23 Cf. Matthew 26:37.
24 Psalm 9:10.
25 The *Historia* changes this to 'about sixty'.
26 Lucan, *Pharsalia*, II.1.
27 Ibid., XIV.32.

they would find him in earnest in concluding a peace agreement. But after the envoy's departure, the emperor realised that all this was a trick, intended to create a disastrous delay. He ordered his son to set out on the march. When the duke, following his father's instructions, had marched up to the gate of Iconium, the knight Gottfried was freed from his captivity and came out to meet him, saying: 'May the Lord bless you, go on confidently; "God has given the city into your hands",[28] and the land too.' For the sultan had gone out to meet the army with six hundred armed knights, although whether his intentions were good or evil is unknown, but when he saw the first squadron he and his men turned tail and fled, entering the citadel that overlooked the city. Almost all the townspeople, both rich and poor, also took refuge there, carrying with them vast stocks of gold, silver and precious textiles, as well as a plentiful stock of foodstuffs, and they shut up their horses, asses and cattle in their fortifications.

The aforesaid duke and his men pursued them right up to the gate of the heavily fortified citadel, putting all those whom they found in the city to the sword, boys and women too. [Meanwhile] a wonderful thing happened, in the following way. While the Duke of Swabia was indeed, with the help of an angel of God, triumphing in the city, the emperor's division had remained for quite some time outside the gardens of the town, unaware of this, for it was surrounded by a vast horde of Turks whose attacks were so fierce that those who were there were expecting death to fall upon them at any moment. The bishops and many of the priests were offering the living Host to the High Priest, wishing for the purposes of their office to place their stoles round their necks, to be covered over with that stole of immortality, saying gloriously with the Apostle, 'having a desire to depart and to be with Christ'.[29] [Then] a holy legion of most exceptional soldiers, to be compared in every respect with the legion of Theban martyrs, everyone united with the desire to shed their blood for Christ, stood there undaunted, so that no trace of weakness appeared, either in them or in their warhorses. In their midst was that most glorious and invincible Emperor of the Romans Frederick, to whom no equal could be found in the whole world. Although he had often been victorious over most powerful lands, conquering Tuscany, Lombardy, Apulia and Burgundy, and had seen innumerable men laid low in warlike encounters, he is supposed to have shed some tears in this perilous situation, and said that: 'If the Christian army, that is today in such a tight spot for love of our Father in Heaven, should arrive safe in Antioch, I would be happy to suffer the loss of my head, even though such a punishment is quite improper to be visited upon the person of an emperor.' After he had said this, and with all those who were there shedding tears of joy in their desire for eternal reward and wonder at his mighty and invariable courage, this great emperor added: 'why are we hesitating, what is there to fear? May Christ rule [us], Christ be victorious, Christ command [us]'. And although his efforts had greatly tired him, he was, like a greater Judas

---

[28]   Jeremiah 34:2.
[29]   Philippians 1:23.

Maccabeus, noble of heart. He first turned round his warhorse, and, with the others bravely accompanying him, he charged down on the enemy like a lion and put them to flight. Not one of them raised his hand against him but all turned and fled away from his presence. The sons of Belial lost about three thousand men, and if our knights had not been so weak from hunger the citadel would have been stormed that very night. However, the knights had for some two weeks been suffering from the appalling and unprecedented shortage of food. After his victory, the lord emperor then made his entry to the city with his army following behind him, and received a magnificent reception from his son and his companions. There the hunger of the army was to some extent relieved by the spoil taken from the enemy. Many of them found grain pits filled with wheat and barley, and as a result the men and their horses were very greatly restored. Moreover there are those who claim that the booty gained in this city, in gold, silver, jewels and purple cloths, came to a value of more than a hundred thousand marks. For in the house of the great Malik 'there is treasure to be desired'.[30] It was said that what was found there was the dowry that the evil Saladin had given to him along with his daughter. On the following day, that is 19 May, we began to praise the name of the Lord, since 'he giveth us the victory' over our enemies.[31] The mass said this: 'the love of God is shed abroad in our hearts'.[32] That office was therefore very much in accord with our joy and our vows; there was even a mention of Iconium in it, namely in the prophecy taken from the Acts of the Apostles, which on that day of fasting is repeated four times over in all the church.[33]

After this the sultan and his sons, and the emirs, seeing that 'they had dug a pit' for us 'into which they had fallen themselves',[34] lamented. They sent their envoys to the lord emperor, begging that 'in the bowels of mercy' he respect the land and its people, and 'recompense no man evil for evil'.[35] They added further that they would try in every way they could to assuage the anger of his imperial majesty. Since therefore it was not the emperor's intention to hold up the journey of the life-giving Cross with any difficult negotiations, he discussed the matter with the princes and replied in this way:

'The sultan sent envoys to us, in accordance with the friendship that he has for a long time had with our empire, invited us to this land, and promised us safe conduct and good markets for us and our army. Furthermore, other ambassadors from him and from his son came into our presence at Adrianople offering us greater and more favourable benefits than those promised earlier. But those who have entered this land with us have seen what has been offered to us as

---

[30] Proverbs 21:20.
[31] I Corinthians 15:57.
[32] Romans 5:5.
[33] Acts 14:1–5.
[34] Psalm 56:7 (Vulgate), 57:6 (AV).
[35] Luke 1:78, Romans 12:7.

a safeguard: bows and arrows, swords and lances, and every sort of weapon, along with attacks and strange war cries, and instead of the provision of markets that we were promised in an appearance of faithful friendship the great Malik has attacked us and our army with all the courage and power of his race. "They have compassed me about like bees, they are quenched as the fire of thorns."[36] Nevertheless, in the name of our Lord Jesus Christ the Roman emperor and special advocate of the land of Jerusalem has penetrated the squadrons of the enemy in safety and put to flight the multitudes of your army, "our God hath given the city into our hands".[37] But since the Roman emperor ought always to have as his companions "mercy and justice",[38] and prefers rather to spare than to wound, we have decided to impart this grace to you and your lords, that our peace may be upon you, provided that you give hostages into our keeping, so that we may leave your land in complete safety and with a good market.'

On hearing this, the envoys most joyfully reported it back to the sultan and his son. The latter put what had been proposed into effect within a short space of time, giving ten emirs and ten other great barons as hostages.

The army left Iconium on 23 May, and camped next to the royal park as before. There we found a market where things were sold, admittedly dearly, but sufficient for our needs. For more than six thousand horses and mules were sold there, not counting asses, and the army was well supplied with bread and meat, as well as butter and cheese. On 26 May they marched over a very broad plain and came to forty springs. The next day they arrived at a great lake that was fit to drink. There, since the Turcomans had still not all ceased to follow us, the lord emperor spoke to the hostages: 'If your Turks will not stop following us, and if a market is not provided for the army, as has been arranged, then you will certainly be put to death.' Afterwards we experienced very little harm from them. We then marched on, passing a great village where we saw many vineyards, but little water. They went on by a difficult road to another village called Pergos, where finding a good market they rested for a day. Late in the day on 30 May we came to the fine town of Karaman, which is on the border between Licaonia and Cilician Armenia. Iconium is the capital of Licaonia. If I should try to describe in full all the many troubles, oppressions, hunger and thirst, tricks and deceits, insults and attacks that the army of Christ patiently endured, with a smiling face and without complaint, in the land of the Turks, for the sake of Christ and the honour of the life-giving Cross, 'though I speak with the tongues of men and of angels',[39] my efforts would only cause annoyance, since 'I have nothing to draw with and the well is deep'.[40] For a full and proper description of so great an enterprise would, if they were still alive, leave the legendary Homer, the eloquent

---

[36] Psalm 117:12 (Vulgate), 118:12 (AV).

[37] Joshua 6:16.

[38] Tobit 3:2.

[39] I Corinthians 13:1.

[40] John 4:11.

Lucan or the Mantuan poet himself placing their finger over their mouths as though speechless.

It also happened that as the army of the life-giving Cross was moving its camp from Karaman, where it had to some extent recovered its strength, they came to a village of the Armenians. There they found crosses erected in the fields by the Christians, as a result of which our hearts were uplifted by great 'joy and gladness'.[41] They had neither seen nor heard for a long time anything of those who belonged to the glorious Christian religion. As they marched onwards, they climbed some mountains, barely accessible even to mountain goats, which they crossed with the utmost difficulty, and there they left the region held by the most treacherous Turks. The hostages provided by the sultan and his son then vehemently requested that they be sent back to their homes, adding indeed that the agreement specified that they should be released at this point. However, the princes utterly disregarded their pleas, rather the order was given that they be placed under stricter guard. While 'the height of the mountain'[42] posed them appalling difficulty, the Prince of Sibilia, a powerful and distinguished man, met the lord emperor, whom he welcomed with great respect, and insofar as he could he provided a market for the army. Sibilia is a very well-defended fortress and frontier district that he defends from the frequent attacks of the Turks. On the descent from this mountain, the sons of 'the right hand of the most High'[43] pitched camp next to a large, shallow lake, where our beasts found good grazing. Then we stayed in a broad plain where there was excellent grazing and we rested there for two days. However, many of the people began to suffer so greatly from hunger here that as before they ate horseflesh. Even the princes and barons had remarkably little to put on the table during our passage through these mountain slopes. As they were descending near this lake, which is called Selephica, they made their camp next to a stone bridge, and there the distinguished envoys of the lord Leo of the Mountains met the lord emperor on 7 June. On behalf of their lord, as is the custom of their people, they showed a friendly disposition, ordering that we should be given every assistance from their people and land. The lord emperor welcomed them as men of worth, took their advice as to the route of the army, and learned from them that we were about to follow a very steep and difficult path. The most pious emperor felt fatherly sorrow for all his pilgrims, and so he ordered this information to be kept secret, to prevent the people being upset by the difficulty of the way and the lack of supplies if they heard of the labours that would beset them. For day after day they were promised good things and happiness, and the abundance of a good market. But it all turned out very differently.

For on the following day, 9 June, we came with the utmost difficulty to the resting place. The usual formation of the army was not observed because of the

---

[41] Luke 1:14.

[42] II Kings 19:23.

[43] Psalm 76:11 (Vulgate), 77:10 (AV).

extraordinary difficulty of the way, nor did the squadrons of the princes and of [their] companions wait [for others], but every single person tried to get in front of the others as best they could. That night the greater part of the army crossed a very high mountain that lay along the shore of the water mentioned above. The darkness of the night prevented them from seeing the many dangers of the narrow, rocky path, which in daylight terrified those following our route, and we gather from what they told us they were in a very difficult situation. For who would be so stony-hearted and stiff-necked not to dissolve into tears when he saw the most distinguished bishops carried in horse litters because of long-running bouts of illness, and a horse in front of, and sometimes after, his lord, whom he was carrying, on a very high, narrow and stony ridge, and menaced by a terrible fall to one's death? It was a miserable spectacle there. How praiseworthy and deserving of reward was the zeal of those men who are called squires, who carried their sick lords over this mountain 'in the sweat of their brow'.[44] On the descent from that mountain we found an abundance of vegetables, and by having these for dinner there they recovered a little bit. It happened, however, that the lord emperor and those who were with him wished to avoid the dangers of the mountain that lay before their eyes, and so, acting on the advice of the local people, when the rays of the morning sun began to shine they descended towards the lakeshore. But this was no less hard work than faced those who descended by the mountain ridge. Indeed, so it is said, certain bishops and powerful princes abandoned their horses at various places where deadly danger threatened with the water to their right and the mountain cliff to their left, and crept along on their hands and feet like a four-footed creature. But all these things seemed delightful and pleasant to them for love of 'Him who orders the steps of man',[45] and with the desire for the Heavenly land for which they longed. The vanguard that marched forth that day, 10 June, had made camp in the plain of Seleucia, and there was great joy among the people, since they had escaped many dangers and the task which they had in hand was going well. The Lord had now visited them with His mercy and freed them from all anxiety.[46]

However, their joy was suddenly changed into lamentation, their music alas into mourning and their song into weeping. This was because on that day in Seleucia the crown fell from our head, and the glory and splendour of the Roman empire perished. For on 10 June, so it is said, a Sunday, our most august Emperor Frederick, the most fortunate among almost every king, suddenly at about the hour of Vespers ended his days and paid his debt to death. He was in the second year of his pilgrimage, the fourth [sic] year of his reign[47] and the thirty-fifth of his imperial rule. All the pilgrims who were following him lamented and shed tears inconsolably. Then as it is written, 'smite the shepherd and the flock of sheep will be dispersed', so it was in our army. For the head having been struck

---

[44]   Genesis 3:19.

[45]   Psalm 36:23 (Vulgate), 37:23 (AV).

[46]   The account of Tageno ends at this point.

[47]   Actually the thirty-ninth.

down and lost, that is the leader of the people, the army was to a large extent scattered and overthrown, since their hands were made loose through grief. The greater part of the army followed the emperor's son the Duke of Swabia and the other princes, and after a day of mourning for the emperor arrived at Curcas on 14 June, and from there some people went by sea. They came to the port of St Simeon on 19 June. They arrived at Antioch on 21 June with the main body of the army; and there too the bones of the emperor were first buried by his son the aforesaid duke before the altar of St Peter. However, while they were at Antioch and expecting good things from God, lo a dreadful calamity struck them. For as a result of our sins and by the secret judgement of God that army of chosen knights was overcome by death, so that every day multitudes fell victim to a raging disease, so many that there was no one to bury them. Bishops and clergy, princes and a vast multitude of chosen knights there followed their prince in death. The very few of this great army who escaped that disease and death finally arrived at Acre round about the feast of St Michael,[48] with the Duke of Swabia and the handful of princes who were left. There they found those who while also being on pilgrimage for the Lord's sake had crossed the sea by ship, and for more than a year had worn themselves out in vain besieging this city. There the Duke of Swabia, the prince in whom those few who remained seemed to have placed what little hope they had, was struck down by the death that comes to all, and made his end on 20 January, at the beginning of the third year [of the expedition]. He and his men followed [in the footsteps of] those who had died earlier. In this way and in this unfortunate manner that great and chosen army which had set off with the Emperor Frederick of holy memory, and which was numbered at more than 80,000 men, was all but completely destroyed within a brief space of time, for within two years, indeed really within the space of a single year, it was consumed by hunger, disease and death, and alas achieved nothing of note. Alone among the greater princes the Bishop of Regensburg and the Duke of Merania returned to their homeland, before the interminably prolonged siege of Acre was finished. Indeed signs and wonders were not lacking at this time that perhaps foretold and announced this great enterprise, as was also the case with that great enterprise which took place in earlier years under King Conrad.[49] For in the seven years before this expedition took place the faithful people frequently flocked with great veneration to the tombs of many saints throughout almost all the Roman world because of the miracles that took place there, which the Lord was thought to have performed through his saints, or so it was believed. In our region, namely in the city of Salzburg, the people thronged to the tomb of the blessed Bishop Virgilius, wishing to discover what wonders might be performed through him and through the other holy bishops who lay there. Similarly in the city of Passau [they went] to the tomb of the blessed Bishop Pilgrim and to the tombs of the other bishops of that place.[50]

---

[48] 29 September.

[49] That is the Second Crusade of 1147–9.

[50] Virgilius, Bishop of Salzburg 749–84, an Irishman by birth, and a rival of St Boniface, whose missionary activities led him to be known as the 'Apostle of the Carentanian Slavs', see Ian Wood, *The Missionary Life. Saints and the Evangelisation of*

Diepold, the venerable lord Bishop of Passau, took as guide his predecessor of holy memory the lord Reginbert, formerly bishop of that same church of Passau, and, following the Lord who is the way, the truth and the life, he took the Cross, along with his brother canon, that is six of the more important and distinguished members of the chapter of Passau. For the redemption of his soul, he set out on the journey of holy pilgrimage with the lord Emperor Frederick of holy memory. Although he was of most noble birth, indeed related by blood to great princes and to the imperial family,[51] and furthermore still youthful, he was not however afraid bravely to pledge his soul for the liberation of the earthly Jerusalem, insofar as this was within his power, that he might be promised eternal life in the Heavenly Jerusalem. This he has received and now enjoys in Heaven, along with the holy confessors and priests of the Lord. Having already donned one robe,[52] he gained his reward at the end of his second year of pilgrimage when on 3 November [1190] he surrendered this earthly flesh and rendered up his blessed soul to Heaven.[53] He was buried at Acre. All his brothers who had followed him as their father from their own land to the land of eternal promise had gone before him to the Lord. Their names were these: the archpriest Burchard, a freeman of Chambe; Udalrich, provost of Andacher and archpriest; Meginhalm of Passau, parish priest of that city and archpriest; Markward, provost of St Andrew; Rüdiger of Aheim; Conrad, who was prior among them; and a man of greater rank and dignity but their companion on the journey, the lord Tageno, dean of the church of Passau.[54] He was the man who noted down with pious care every stay that they made during their journey, and full of charity he committed to writing, for the memory of posterity and for all who want to know, the sequence of events, the labours and troubles of his brother clerics and of the army of God while they lived and as they went on their pilgrimage for the Lord. He died and was buried at Tripoli, and in his record [memoria] he diligently wrote down what

---

Europe 400–1000 (Harlow 2001), pp. 145–8, 168–9; Pilgrim, Bishop of Passau 971–91, rebuilt the cathedral of that city.

[51]   He was the son of Count Diepold II of Berg and of Gisela, daughter of Berthold III of Andechs-Merania (d. 1151), the grandfather of the Duke of Merania who took part in the Crusade.

[52]   *decoratus iam una stola*, i.e. taken the Cross.

[53]   The *Historia* said that he died on 13 November [above, p.118]. Interestingly, while the necrology of the abbey Melk also gave the date as 13 November, those of the canons of Diessen and Pernegg both recorded his death on 3 November. Was Magnus following one of the latter? *MGH Necrologia Germania* i *Dioceses Augustensis, Constantiensis, Curiensis*, ed. Ludwig Baumann (Berlin 1886–8), i. 29; v *Diocesis Pataviensis pars altera: Austria Inferior*, ed. Adalbert R. Fuchs (Berlin 1913), 558, 566.

[54]   Tageno the dean, Burchard of Chalme, Meginhalm the parish priest and Master Rüdiger were among the witnesses to a donation to the cathedral of Passau, 1187 x 1189, in *Die Traditionen des Hochstifts Passau*, ed. Max Heuwisser (Quellen und Erörterungen zur Bayerischen Geschichte 6, Munich 1930) pp. 257–8 no. 716. All of these appeared as witnesses in the charters of Bishop Diepold, as did Udalrich, provost of Andacher, from 1183 onwards (for him, *Regesten der Bischöfe von Passau*, i, nos 893, 900, 919, 922, 927, 932, 938). Markward, provost of St Andrew, witnessed a charter in July 1188, ibid., no. 922.

he saw and endured on that same expedition, from the departure of Bishop Diepold from Passau, which took place on 16 May, until the army of the Christians arrived at Antioch on 21 June of the following year. He sent back a copy of this text to us, which has also been faithfully copied for the [appropriate] years in this little book.

In this same year, that is 1190, the King of France, the King of England, the Count of Flanders, and Duke Leopold of Austria, the son of the Emperor Frederick's paternal uncle, left their homelands in the autumn, each with their own army, that they might come to the aid of the Christian Church in the east that was now [so] wretchedly ruined. At this same time the king of the Romans set off with his army for Apulia, to fight against those who had rebelled against him there.

A Letter Concerning the Death of the Emperor Frederick[1]

Believing that your holiness is desirous to receive details of what was done by the emperor, of 'that which we have looked upon and our hands have handled',[2] without any improper admixture of falsity, we have been at pains to write to you with the utmost brevity.[3]

The discretion of your sanctity should know therefore that after having been honourably received by King Bela of Hungary and having been kindly and humanely treated by him, no sooner had we entered the kingdom of Greece than we fell into the hands of thieves and robbers, for no trust is to be placed in the Greeks. For contrary to the common law of not maltreating envoys they imprisoned the Bishop of Münster and Count Rupert. We marched with great difficulty through the regions of Bulgaria, and after a long time on the road we first captured and sacked the city of Philippopolis, and then destroyed the famous citadel of Berrhoë, putting the whole of the surrounding region to the sword. We also captured the noble city of Adrianople and the towns around about, while the Duke of Swabia captured the impregnable city of Dimotika, killing a vast number of the inhabitants of the town. A fortress called Maniceta was destroyed by our knights and a few [others] from the army.[4] Some six thousand Greeks perished there through fire and sword, many other fortresses were captured and there was a great massacre of the Greeks. When, however, they were perished with hunger, suitable hostages were received from the Emperor of Constantinople, and our envoys were returned to us, along with those whom the sultan and his son had sent to us, who had [also] previously been detained. We crossed the Arm of St George during the feast of Easter, with both people and goods in excellent condition. But afterwards what had been sworn and promised to us by the aforesaid emperor was never observed.

We then marched through the region of Philadelphia until we came to Laodicia, with the troops of the army of Christ mustered in arms every day. As we travelled on the sixth day before Rogation Day, we suffered terrible losses among the horses through lack of water and grazing, and through a day's march that was much

---

[1]   Translated from *Quellen*, pp. 173–8.

[2]   I John 1:1.

[3]   Chroust suggests that the addressee of the letter was probably one of the German bishops rather than the pope, as one might assume, *Quellen*, p. xcviii.

[4]   Moniac in the Rhodope Mountains. This was also named in the *Historia Peregrinorum*, p. 147, but not in the *Historia de Expeditione*.

longer than normal.[5] On the following Sunday we came to the source of the River Maeander, and while we were there envoys of the sultan and his son [arrived], who brought great presents for the lord emperor, and promised us an absolutely secure peace, pledging their faith unequivocally to this. However, we discovered a large force of Turks drawn up against us who had been sent to put us to death; but through the help and guidance of God and under the banner of the Holy Cross we put them to the sword at dawn the next day, which was the first of the Rogation days, and we slew a great many of them.[6] That same day we passed through the extremely narrow defiles of the mountains on the way to Sozopolis. During our difficult journey through this region, we once again killed a great host of Turks on the eve of the Ascension of the Lord.[7] And since we now were aware of the number of horses that had been killed or wounded, we did not find crops or grazing because of the cold, and we were beginning to suffer from hunger – nor did we get any helpful advice from the envoys of the sultan – we were forced by necessity to turn away to the left from the royal road that the Emperor Manuel customarily used to travel, because it ran through a desert region and took a very lengthy route to Iconium, entirely overlooked by mountains.

On Ascension Day, climbing to the tops of the mountains through which our journey lay, we travelled through very steep hills and along a very narrow path, which seemed to offer men little hope, and with the utmost difficulty and suffering great losses of both men and equipment we descended that same day down to the plain of Philomelium. For the Turks had completely surrounded the army on all sides, like a crown, and attacked it. The Duke of Swabia, with the Duke of Merano, the Margrave of Baden, other nobles and the archers, stayed in the rear to protect those who went in front, who having sent their horses on ahead had to descend on foot. The attacks of the Turks, with arrows, slingshots and stones, were so heavy that our men became split up and were placed in a situation of great danger. The Duke of Swabia was wounded; one of his upper teeth was completely knocked out and he lost half of a lower one. But although many of our knights were wounded, only one was killed. Many of the pack animals were lost along with the money, clothing and equipment [they carried]. However, a great many of the Turks were killed. The strength of the Turks increased from day to day, more than one would believe to be possible, for we now encountered the Governor of Philomelium and his army, the Governor of Gradra and his army and the Governor of Firmin and his army, along with a great number of others. Through the days that followed we fought against all these combined forces from morning to evening, but God always placed victory in our hands, even though many of our men were wounded and many of the horses were killed. On the Sunday after Ascension Day Frederick of Hunlith fell from his horse while pursuing them and died from a

---

5   27 April 1190.

6   30 April.

7   2 May.

broken neck.[8] We made camp the following day at Philomelium. Around Vespers the Turks attacked our camp there; they had already seized booty from some of our huts (*hospitia*) when we put them to flight, and more than six thousand Turks were slain, and among these three hundred and seventy-four of the best men from the whole of Turkey were killed, while none of our men perished, although many horses were killed. And 'the mountains broke forth with the noise of lamentation',[9] and night divided us one from another. Famine had now got us in its grip, both wine and flour were totally exhausted, and I and others were eating horseflesh. The horses were also suffering from hunger, since we found neither corn, nor crops nor grazing, and the Turks hemmed us in day and night with such a large force that nobody was allowed to venture outside the camp. Note that on the fourth day before Pentecost we killed a great host of them.[10]

After the holy day of Pentecost we found the Malik, the son of the Great Sultan, and his forces disposed against us and the multitude of Turks [numbered] some forty thousand horsemen, who filled the earth like locusts.[11] We raised up at our head the victorious eagles in the name of Christ against them; nor did we feel weakness from either hunger or wounds, and even though we had only some six hundred mounted men under the sign of the life-giving Cross we defeated them and put them to flight. The Malik, son of the sultan, was thrown from his horse there, and four of his most distinguished princes were killed, along with many others. Something else happened here that is worthy of record: for on that same day St George was seen by Ludwig of Helfenstein to ride before some of our squadrons, giving aid to our army. Ludwig publicly attested to this, under oath and in accordance with his religious duty as a pilgrim, in the presence of the emperor and of the army.[12] Indeed, the Turks afterwards told us that they had seen squadrons clad in white garments and with white horses.

This same day, after pursuing the Malik who had fled towards Iconium, we arrived at our lodging around nightfall, having won this great and glorious victory, but we found no water there, and there were men, horses and animals with nothing to eat or drink, and we began, to some extent anyway, to fear for our lives. For almost all of the horses who had up to then remained to us were [now] dead, from hunger or from the length of the journey. So we set out at the crack of dawn, since we were only about a mile away from Iconium, and as we got nearer we found water, where we remained for the whole of that Wednesday.

---

[8]   Both the *Historia de Expeditione* and the *Historia Peregrinorum* call him Frederick of Hausen, *Quellen*, pp. 79, 159. See above, p. 103 note 288.

[9]   Wisdom 17:18; cf. Isaiah 44:23.

[10]   9 May.

[11]   Cf. Judith 2:11: 'who covered the face of the earth like locusts'; and also Judges 6:5.

[12]   The *Historia de Expeditione* called him simply 'a religious layman called Ludwig' [above, p. 106 and n. 304]; the *Historia Peregrinorum* 'a certain powerful man in our army called Ludwig', *Quellen*, p. 165. Both agree that this incident took place on 14 May.

The following day we stationed ourselves next to a most pleasant walled garden next to the city of Iconium, where we also destroyed two most noble palaces of the sultan. And since we were in a situation of most deadly danger, because we were suffering desperately from hunger and now had scarcely five hundred knights who still had horses, and no means of either advancing further or retreating, we were forced by our situation to divide our forces into two parts, and on the sixth day after Pentecost we marched out to make a frontal attack to capture the city.[13] It seems extraordinary and incredible to say this, but with the help of God the Duke of Swabia, along with six others, seized the city at sword point and slaughtered its inhabitants. Meanwhile the lord emperor remained outside, fighting the other Turks who were attacking us in the rear, and although they had about two hundred thousand horsemen he fought them with 'the power of the Highest' and put them to flight.[14] It is worth noting that the city of Iconium is about the same size as Cologne. After ransacking it for booty, we stayed there from the Friday until the next Wednesday, until the sultan, who had taken refuge with his men in the citadel, was constrained by fear of death to surrender twenty hostages of our choosing. These we afterwards held as prisoners, since he did not observe the faith that he had pledged.

We then raised camp on the next Sunday and set off by the shortest route towards Karaman, where we stayed on the Friday, namely 1 June. And 'during the silence of the night' there was a great earthquake, which we thought was [the noise of] the army of the Turks charging upon us. Now we think that it was a presentiment of what was going to happen to the lord emperor. For when we set off forthwith on our march, we went towards the [River] Saleph. We discovered the way across the mountains to be extremely steep and difficult, and we were only able to reach the Saleph with terrible loss of equipment. We arrived there on a Sunday, which was the vigil of the feast of the Apostle Barnabas.[15]

The lord emperor had crossed these valleys and mountains through a short cut: and on this same day he traversed this fast-flowing river and reached the other side in safety. He had lunch there, and, after the many and terrible exertions that he had undergone in the previous month and more, he decided to bathe in that same river, for he wanted to cool down with a swim. But by the secret judgement of God there was an unexpected and lamentable accident and he drowned.

We carried his remains with us with proper reverence until we arrived at the most renowned city of Tarsus. Marching onwards towards Antioch, we have however suffered from a great loss of our equipment and we have laboured for six weeks on end with food in very short supply, for we could not obtain supplies to buy.

We have been at pains to write to you, albeit briefly, about our dangers, hoping for relief hereafter through the mercy of God.

---

[13]	18 May.

[14]	Luke 1:35.

[15]	10 June.

The Chronicle of Otto of St Blasien
1187–1197

This chronicle, one of the main sources for German history at the end of the twelfth century, was written c. 1209–10, and intended as a continuation to the Chronicle of Bishop Otto of Freising, from which the author frequently quoted. The attribution to Otto of St Blasien comes in a fifteenth-century manuscript, one of only four medieval manuscripts known. The strong Swabian bias of the text supports this attribution. Its presumed author, Otto, subsequently became Abbot of the monastery of St Blasien (in the Black Forest) in 1222, but died a year later. The account of German history at this period is generally favourable to the Staufen, or perhaps more accurately to the imperial authority, irrespective of who wielded it; hence the view of Otto IV as ruler in 1208/9 is similarly favourable to that of the earlier Staufen emperors. Otto of St Blasien was particularly interested in the Third Crusade, but he also provided quite a lengthy, if not always entirely accurate, account of Henry VI's conquest of the kingdom of Sicily, and showed an interest in Parisian theological study in his own time. One should, however, note that dates are sometimes given a year in arrears, and that a number of important events have been misplaced. Indeed, despite the chronicle's annalistic format, Otto's chronology is often very dubious. Thus the Treaty of Konstanz was recorded two years after the event, while Count Richard of Acerra, whose death was reported during Henry VI's successful invasion of the kingdom of Sicily in 1194 (itself misdated), was in fact only captured and executed two years later. Similarly, the account of the brutal repression of conspiracy on Sicily, which Otto suggests took place immediately after the conquest, refers to events which actually took place in 1197. Otto also conflated the conquest of 1194 and the subsequent German Crusade of 1197, of which he left a vivid, if often disapproving, account. Nevertheless, despite such chronological uncertainty, this is an important and often informative source concerning Germany at the end of the twelfth century.[1]

---

[1]   The passages below have been translated from *Ottonis de Sancto Blasio Chronica*, ed. A. Hofmeister (MGH SRG, Hanover 1912), pp. 41–70, chapters 29–42. It should be noted that the more recent edition, by F.-J. Schmale, *Die Chronik Ottos von St Blasien und die Marbacher Annalen* (Ausgewählte Quellen zur Deutschen Geschichte des Mittelalters 17, Darmstadt 1998), simply reproduces the Latin text from the edition of Hofmeister, albeit with a German translation and improved notes appended.

(29) At this time Baldwin, king of the people of Jerusalem, died, leaving as heir to the kingdom a nubile daughter – for he lacked a son.[2] Through sin it was 'divided against itself' and rightly 'brought to desolation',[3] and it was trampled underfoot by the pagans, since no good had come from rule being in the hands of a woman.[4] For each of the great men (*principes*) of the kingdom was eager to rule it, and sought to marry the girl and obtain the hereditary kingdom with her, if he lacked a wife, or if he was already married to join her to his son, or if lacking a son to marry her to a near relative. For this reason great hatred arose among them, which brought the kingdom to disaster. She herself, spurning the native inhabitants, chose rather Count Guy of Ascalon, a foreigner of handsome appearance and notable for his manly courage; and with the approval of the patriarch and the knights of the Temple she married him and conferred the kingdom upon him. The rest of the magnates were greatly annoyed by this, and in particular the Count of Tripoli, who thought it unworthy to recognise him as king, since he was a stranger. After receiving a bribe, he invited the Saracens into the kingdom, and he betrayed various castles and towns to them as he strove to obtain Jerusalem. Those who had often brought banditry to the kingdom gained the support through bribery of some of the knights of the Temple, as well as some of the greater men of the kingdom, to prevent them resisting by force those who were 'exercising banditry',[5] and by so dissimulating they very quickly obtained for themselves a great part of the region.

(30) In the year from the Lord's Incarnation 1187, Saladin, the King of the Saracens, who was living at Damascus, took notice of the most wicked conduct of the Christians, and considering them to be riddled with discord, envy and avarice decided that this was a suitable moment to set about gaining all of Syria and Palestine. He raised a vast army of Saracens drawn from the entire east and engaged in battle against the Christians. He ravaged the whole of Palestine with fire and sword, and stormed many castles and towns, killing or capturing the Christians there, and importing Saracens to live there. Hence the king of the people of Jerusalem, as well as Prince Rainald of Antioch and other magnates among the Christians, raised a great army, and with the Cross of the Lord preceding the army they hastened to meet Saladin and do battle with him. They were defeated by him, many Christian warriors were killed and, O horror, the Cross of the Lord was captured. The Christians were put to flight; the king and the most illustrious Prince Rainald, along with many other Christians, were captured and taken to Damascus,

---

[2]   Otto's account was inaccurate in several respects, not least that Queen Sybilla was Baldwin IV's sister, not his daughter, and she married Guy de Lusignan in 1180, some years before her brother's death.

[3]   Luke 11:17.

[4]   Cf. Judith 16:7, and Otto of Freising, *Chronice sive Historia de Duabus Civitatibus*, ed. Adolf Hofmeister (MGH SRG, Hanover 1912), V.29, p. 255.

[5]   Cf. Judges 9:25.

where this same king and the aforesaid prince were beheaded for confessing the true faith.[6]

Made bold by this victory, the pagans ravaged the whole region, and captured or destroyed all the towns of the Christians apart from Tyre, Sidon, Tripoli and Antioch, and a few other towns and very strong and impregnable castles.[7] Acre had already been captured. It is a port and had formerly been, and is [now] 'a unique and special refuge of the Christians'.[8] They laid siege to Jerusalem, and, after destroying the churches round about, notably Bethlehem and that on the Mount of Olives, and many others [too], finally the Christians were forced to leave by an agreement, and Jerusalem was captured. The holy places of our redemption were profaned by the pagans who now lived there. I consider that one ought not to pass over in silence an incident that occurred while Jerusalem was under siege. The pagans attacked and captured one of the towers, killing many Christians, and Saladin's banner was raised there. As a result the citizens grew desperate and ceased to defend the rest of the walls, and that very same day the city was about to fall, with its people facing extermination 'with the edge of the sword'.[9] Seeing this, a certain German knight, 'summoning audacity from desperation',[10] encouraged those around him and making a valiant attack on the enemy stormed the tower. The pagans within it were slain, and he cut down the staff of Saladin's banner and threw the standard into the mud. By doing this he restored the confidence of the citizens, and he brought them back to defend the walls as quickly as possible. After the city was surrendered on terms, as was mentioned, the pagans did respect the Sepulchre of the Lord, though [only] 'for the sake of profit'.[11] This lamentable desolation of the Holy Land took place in the year from the Lord's Incarnation 1187, in the eighty-eighth year from the coming of the Franks, when that same land was liberated from the pagans by Duke Godfrey. And so Saladin overcame Palestine and wretchedly undermined the Church beyond the sea, and that region has now for many years been groaning under its subjection by the pagans.

In this same year Pope Urban died, and Gregory VIII succeeded, the 174th in line. When he received the awful news of the destruction of the land beyond the

---

[6]   The inaccuracies in the above account are obvious, not least in that Rainald of Châtillon was executed on the evening of the Battle of Hattin, while far from being put to death Guy de Lusignan was later ransomed and died on Cyprus in 1194. In this section Otto employs the 'historic present', which has here been rendered as a past tense.

[7]   In fact Sidon surrendered to Saladin on 29 July 1187, though Otto was correct with regard to the other three cities named.

[8]   Cf. Otto of Freising, *Chronica,* VII.30, p. 357, where a very similar phrase was applied to Edessa, when Otto described its capture.

[9]   Exodus 17:13.

[10]   Cf. *Gesta Francorum*, II.23, which in turn followed the translation by Hegesippus of Josephus, *De Bello Iudiaco*, III.9.

[11]   Otto of Freising, *Chronica*, VII.2, p. 310, describing Jerusalem before 1099, though Otto himself copied this passage from Ekkehard of Aura.

seas, he imposed penance on the whole Church to placate God, and he sent out cardinal bishops and priests as legates to all the lands subject to the Church on this side of the sea, lamenting the disaster with paternal affection, and informing the sons of Mother Church that, 'mindful of the breasts'[12] through whose milk the ancient church in Jerusalem was nourished, they should bring help to their suffering mother. He strengthened their manly resolve, and called them to witness, by receiving the Cross in remission of sins. He manfully encouraged them through the word of preaching that they bring glory to themselves as servants of the Cross, and avenge the disgrace of the Cross, which was being held captive by the pagans, in praise and glorification of Him who was crucified.

(31) In the year from the Lord's Incarnation 1188, the Emperor Frederick celebrated a general court at Mainz in the middle of Lent, and there, with the storms of war quieted over the whole of Germany and peace everywhere regained, he dealt with matters of state. Legates of the Apostolic See came to this meeting, where in the name of the lord pope and the whole Church they lamented the destruction of the Church overseas, which they made known both orally and through written documents, and they requested the protection of the Roman Empire for its assistance. After consultation the emperor pledged himself to bring aid, and he and his son Frederick, Duke of the Swabians, received the Cross of pilgrimage in remission of their sins. He announced publicly that he would avenge the injury to the Cross, and he inspired many of the magnates of the kingdom, along with a multitude of others of various classes and ages, to follow his example and enlist in this same matter. After this had taken place at the court the cardinals went out to preach in different parts of the empire and they urged and persuaded many to 'leave father and mother, wife and children and lands' in the name of Christ, and 'take up His Cross and follow' him on the expedition overseas, and they gathered an innumerable army.[13] The emperor informed them all that the time for departure would be May of the next year. The poor were [each] at least to possess three marks for their expenses, the richer were to gather funds as best they could. He forbade under pain of anathema the needy, who had less than three marks in weight, from undertaking the journey, for he did not wish the army to be hampered by a crowd of unsuitable people.

While these events were taking place in the Roman empire, the pope sent cardinals from his side to Louis [*sic*], the King of the French, and Richard, King of the English, encouraging them to take the Cross and undertake the same endeavour, and he enlisted many people from the aforesaid kingdoms in this same knighthood.[14]

At this time the men of Cologne devoted all their efforts and resources to the fortification of their city and surrounded it with a most formidable wall. This

---

[12]   Song of Solomon 1:3 (Vulgate).

[13]   Mark 10:29 and 8:34; Matthew 16:24.

[14]   Kings Philip of France and Henry II of England took the Cross in January 1188; Richard only became king on the death of his father on 6 July 1189.

roused the suspicions of the emperor and was displeasing to him. He threatened them with punishment unless they demolished their fortifications, and fear of him forced them to breach the wall in four places.

In these days envoys of the Sultan or King of Iconium came to the emperor to renew their treaty, although this was a piece of deceit, and on behalf of their lord they offered him free passage all the way through Cilicia to his army, provided that he came in peace.[15] For through Cilicia the emperor and his army would have been able to cross the land of the sultan, whose capital was Iconium, and thus the pagans, fearful for their own land, preferred to seek peace by treaty rather war, although events turned out very differently from what was hoped.

(32) In the year from the Lord's Incarnation 1189, the Emperor Frederick celebrated his general court at Pentecost at Pressburg in the march of Hungary, where he mustered the army of pilgrims for the warfare of Christ, after handing over the regalia to his son King Henry. He divided the income from his estates among his sons, along with the rights attached to them, as he saw fit. After thus appropriately settling all his affairs, he said farewell and led his army towards the east, to fight against Saladin, the King of the Saracens and all the enemies of the Cross of Christ. He was accompanied by his son of the same name, the Duke of Swabia, the Margrave of Meissen with the Saxons,[16] and many other princes and bishops, along with a most numerous army, equipped with everything that was needed for war. As he marched through Hungary, he was generously provided with many gifts by the King of Hungary, who also furnished the army with foodstuffs: quantities of flour, wine and meat. He crossed into Bulgaria, but there the inhabitants denied him 'the king's high way',[17] and he took it by force. A host of those who fought against him were killed, and he had many of those who were captured hanged from the trees on either side of the highway. Thus he showed that he was visiting the Sepulchre of the Lord not with the wallet and staff but with lance and sword, and so after crossing Bulgaria he passed into Greece. The Greeks behaved even worse than the Bulgarians, refusing the army the supplies needed for life, for on the order of the Emperor of Constantinople they denied the knights of the Holy Sepulchre a free market to buy foodstuffs, and took refuge in their fortresses, taking with them everything from the surrounding areas. Caesar was annoyed to suffer such treatment from Christians, and gave the army permission to plunder, and issued an edict to treat the Greeks as if they were pagans, for so they had shown themselves by their actions. As a result the army was let loose, and it captured the very rich city of Philippopolis by storm, and after obtaining extensive booty destroyed it. He similarly stormed the very strong fortress of Dimotika, and the terror that this induced led many castles and towns of the Greeks to surrender to him. By conquering this wealthy province and giving it over to plunder, he

---

[15]   Cf. Genesis 42:11.

[16]   Perhaps Dietrich, the brother of Margrave Albrecht, who later succeeded him as margrave (1195–1221).

[17]   Numbers 21:22.

forced the rest of the Greeks to allow him an unopposed passage. These events took place towards the end of the month of August. The emperor then summoned the princes and on their advice decided to spend the winter in Greece, and after making all the land round about subject to himself he fortified a mountain that was difficult of access for the safe keeping of his army. He called it *Chunigsberg* in the German language. There he remained in security 'against the face' of the city of Constantinople,[18] having all the supplies that were needed by the army brought there from the neighbouring towns. He overcame Greek cunning through Roman power and German resolution, and he remained there throughout the winter until Easter of the following year, while the Greeks and their emperor 'fled from before his face'.[19]

(33) In the year from the Lord's Incarnation 1190 Pope Clement III died, and Celestine III succeeded him, the 175th in line.[20]

In this same year Duke Leopold of Austria and the army of the men of Cologne, along with many others from the Lower Rhineland, after receiving the Cross, set sail from Brindisi and travelled to Acre, where King Richard of the English and King Louis [*sic*] of the French had previously arrived with a well-equipped force. They joined the Pisans, who with an Italian army were already besieging the city, and attacked it with all their forces, while Saladin devoted all his efforts to bringing help to those besieged.

In this same year King Henry, son of the Emperor Frederick, raised an army, crossed the Alps and entered Italy. Reaching the City, he was gloriously received by Pope Celestine, and on the holy day of Easter he and his wife were crowned by the pope, with the acclamation of all the Romans, and his name was entered as the 95th emperor from Augustus.[21] He gained the agreement of the Romans by satisfying their avarice with extravagant bribes, and he promised to hand over to them the castle of Tusculo, which had formerly stood as a bastion of the empire against all their attacks; by doing this he in no small way dishonoured the empire. The Romans immediately poured forth from the City, and on Good Friday they utterly destroyed the castle, overthrowing its walls and towers, and afterwards consuming it by fire. This was done in revenge for the defeat that they had sustained at the hands of [Arch]bishop Christian of Mainz in a former war.[22]

Meanwhile the Emperor of Constantinople, being unable to resist the power of the Caesar Frederick, made satisfaction to him for what had previously occurred, and, when peace had been agreed, he provided the army with a plethora of foodstuffs and restored good relations. After they had been reconciled and the

---

[18]   I Maccabees 16:6. Frederick spent the winter of 1189–90 at Adrianople, c. 150 km from Constantinople.

[19]   Cf. Psalm 88:24 (Vulgate), 89:23 (AV)

[20]   Celestine was elected on 30 March 1191; Clement III died a few days earlier.

[21]   The imperial coronation actually took place on Easter Monday, 15 April 1191.

[22]   In 1167, described by Otto in c. 20.

emperor had concluded a treaty, ships were prepared with great care, and after Easter he and his army crossed the Hellespont.

(34) Thus while Henry was being numbered among the western emperors, the Emperor Frederick marched eastwards with the troops of the Germans, and he and his army entered Asia. His march went well for a time, and everyone throughout Romania was obedient to his will.

However, the Sultan or King of Iconium broke the treaty. Approaching the emperor with his army, he had the foodstuffs and other supplies throughout Cilicia taken into the fortresses, and he refused to allow a market for the army, behaving most treacherously like a 'barbarian or Scythian'.[23] As a consequence a great famine broke out in the army, and forced them to eat many of the mules, asses and horses, food to which they were unaccustomed. Furthermore, the rear columns and foragers of the Christian army were harassed by frequent raids from the pagan troops hanging on their flanks and acting like bandits. They killed a number of our men. They very often revealed themselves drawn up in ordered ranks on horseback as though ready to do battle with our men, but then retreated for they refused to come to close quarters. Despite this harassment and the shortage of food and everything else under which the army was labouring, the emperor kept to his peace treaty with the sultan and prevented the army from ravaging and plundering, for he believed that what was being done was either without the sultan's knowledge or against his wishes. But once he was informed by his scouts that these actions were committed on the direct order of the sultan, and that the latter had thus betrayed him, he was enraged and declaring the sultan to be a public enemy he allowed the army to take revenge by giving over Cilicia, Pamphylia and Phrygia to slaughter and destruction, ravaging everywhere by fire and sword, while the pagans, although they appeared ready for battle, invariably took flight. This plundering restored the army, and the emperor now directed his march towards Iconium, the sultan's capital and the principal city of Cilicia, upon which he launched an attack with unheard-of speed. This city had a very large population; furthermore it was most strongly fortified with strong walls and high towers, had an impregnable citadel situated in its midst, and had been stocked with all the supplies needed to undergo a siege, while all the region round about had been stripped bare of foodstuffs, so that when the emperor arrived there he would be unable to sustain his troops for any length of time. But through God's help matters turned out quite differently to what the pagans had hoped. For before the third hour of the day the emperor launched a surprise and very heavy attack, many of the pagan warriors were killed, and by the ninth hour he had forced his way into the city. Vast numbers of all ages and both genders were slaughtered 'with the edge of the sword'.[24] The sultan-king and his nobles fled to the citadel. Having gained control of the city, that very same day he laid siege to the citadel. Seeing that the forces of the Germans were utterly victorious, that they had the support of Divine power, and that all those who

---

23   Colossians 3:11.
24   I Samuel 22:19.

resisted them suffered instant death and awful slaughter, the sultan learned from this dangerous trial that he had to surrender. He sought a truce from the emperor, and in a spirit of belated penitence asked that he might be allowed to speak to him. This being granted, he came down from the citadel with his men and surrendered to the emperor. He gave hostages and was reconciled to him – and the city of Iconium and his kingdom were restored to him.[25]

(35) After this had taken place, and with the army enjoying rich spoils, the emperor struck camp and left Iconium in triumph. The princes of the Armenians 'flowed from everywhere to him',[26] and in particular Leo, the most noble prince of the Christians of this area, who lived in the mountains. They received him joyfully, and they rendered him proper thanks for his arrival and for the defeat of the pagans, and he set off with great rejoicing and glory towards Tarsus, which is notable as the birthplace of the Apostle Paul. For 'the Land was silent in his sight'.[27] But 'God is terrible in his doing towards the children of Men', while 'the set time' had not yet 'come to have mercy upon Sion'.[28] The Emperor Frederick had showed himself to be a most strong anchor for the bark of Peter, but, after so many and great successes, the rope of our hope now broke, and God did not allow this bark, shaken and flogged in the midst of the storms of this world, yet to be rendered pure. For as the mighty Caesar Frederick marched near Tarsus, he entered a certain river, through which part of the army had already crossed, in the hope of cooling down, for it was extremely hot and he was a good swimmer. But the sudden cold extinguished his natural heat and he was drowned, and this emperor who was victorious on land and sea ended his life with a wretched death. It is said by some that this happened in the River Cydnus, in which Alexander the Great had done something similar, but not at the expense of his life. For the Cydnus is very near to Tarsus.[29] He died in the thirty-eighth year of his reign, and his thirty-fifth as emperor, in the year from the Lord's Incarnation 1190. The entire army of the Christians was irretrievably downcast by his death and fell into heartfelt lamentation, for if the emperor had lived he would have made the whole of the east fear him. His intestines and the rest of his flesh were buried at Tarsus, while his bones were brought to Antioch, where they were most solemnly interred with royal ceremonial.

Then his son Frederick, Duke of the Swabians, the noble heir of his father,[30] the glory of the Christian army and its only hope, generously distributed his father's

---

[25] The *Historia de Expeditione Friderici* and other accounts suggest that the negotiations were carried on through envoys, and that Frederick and Qilij-Arslan did not in fact meet in person.

[26] Daniel 13:4 (Vulgate).

[27] I Maccabees 1:3 and 11:52.

[28] Psalms 65:5, 101:14 (Vulgate); 66:5, 102:14 (AV).

[29] This story was taken from Orosius, but Frederick drowned in the River Saleph (Calycadnus), not the Cydnus.

[30] Cf. Otto of Freising, *Chronica*, VI.19, p. 280.

treasure to the army, consoled his troops who were prostrated by grief, restored it and led it from that fatal place, and led it unscathed to Antioch. But there, with its head already cut off by the death of the emperor, plague immediately spread through its whole body. Both rich and poor fell prey as one to this disease, and the greater part of the army was consumed by unlucky death and was buried in Antioch and the regions round about. With almost all of this great army unexpectedly destroyed through Heavenly judgement, Duke Frederick led the rest to join the other Christians who were striving to besiege Acre, and was ceremoniously welcomed by them. But after he had been there only a little while, he was struck down by fever and taken off by premature death. He was buried there amid great lamentation. So that noble and renowned imperial valour both of father and son, the hope of the entire Church, 'melted away as waters which run continually',[31] so that the lamentation of Jeremiah can appropriately be used for this calamity, where he bewails in his Threnodies the sons of Sion, for these sons of Sion are now the pilgrims to the Sepulchre of the Lord. He says: 'The precious sons of Sion, comparable to fine gold, how are they esteemed as earthen pitchers, the work of the hands of the potter?'[32] For if they had lived, and, with their army, prepared with such care and arrayed with such valour, had joined the forces at Acre to form one body, what people, what region, what king, however brave, or even the power of the many kings of the east, would have been able to resist the power of Italy, the ardour and knowledge of war of France, and above all the courage and endurance of Germany and the indomitable leader of its kingdom? But 'there is no wisdom, nor counsel nor understanding against the Lord'.[33] 'Except the Lord build the house, they labour in vain that build it: except the Lord keep the city, the watchman waketh but in vain'.[34] Thus 'Thou shalt arise and have mercy upon Sion', O Lord, when and how and by whom You wish, and when 'the time to favour her is come'.[35] Since, if it should be made free by human valour, with Your permission, Frederick would have obtained the title of victory. Therefore since, in accordance with Your will, he has given this sacrifice of his blood in honour of the Holy Sepulchre and Your Holy Cross, would that the sacrifice of his life as a pilgrim has pleased You, and You have deigned to associate his soul with the spirits of the blessed in the Celestial Jerusalem. Amen.

(36) So Acre was besieged by the Christians, under the command of the kings of the French and English, Duke Leopold and the rest of the princes. It was fiercely attacked from land and sea by all sorts of war engines, catapults and trebuchets. The Pisans, Genoese and Venetians attacked from the ocean, since they were accustomed to ships and to 'do business on great waters'.[36] Meanwhile the

---

[31]   Psalm 57:8 (Vulgate), 58:7 (AV).
[32]   Lamentations 4:2.
[33]   Proverbs 21:30.
[34]   Psalm 126:1 (Vulgate), 127:1 (AV).
[35]   Psalm 101:14 (Vulgate), 102:13 (AV).
[36]   Psalm 106:23 (Vulgate), 107:23 (AV).

King of the French received an ill-omened messenger informing him that his own kingdom had been invaded, and so he abandoned the siege, and left along with many others, loving rather an earthly than the heavenly kingdom. He crossed the sea and went home via Apulia. But the admirable King of England, Duke Leopold and the remaining mighty warriors put their hands to the Lord's plough and did not look back[37] until they had rendered the territory of Acre fruitful with the corpses of the pagans.

Saladin, however, devoted every effort to rescue those who were in Acre. He mustered his army and tried to break the siege by the Christians. But on hearing of Saladin's arrival the Christians surrounded themselves with two very broad and very deep ditches, having two gates built above the moat to allow them to make sorties, if chance presented itself, and to bring in foodstuffs from round about to continue the siege. Therefore, after raising a very powerful army, Saladin led his troops against Acre, and besieged the Christians who were [themselves] besieging the city. He established a castle on a certain hill not far from the city, which allowed the citizens to send a smoke signal to him when they were attacked by the Christians. Thus he assisted them from outside, and he attacked the Christians with arrows, bolts and all sorts of missiles. The Christians, however, often drew up their columns and advanced outside the ditches, wishing to fight him in open combat, but he always retreated and declined battle. Finally, despite Saladin's presence they attacked the city with all their forces and stormed it. They slaughtered all the pagans, both men and women, whatever their age or condition, with the edge of the sword, while Saladin was watching. He retired, grief-stricken. A few of the more important people were kept as prisoners.[38]

Once the city was captured, the King of the English ordered his banner to be raised on a tower as a sign of triumph, quite arrogantly claiming responsibility for the victory for himself alone. It was for this reason that as he was passing through the city and saw the banner of Duke Leopold flying from a tower that the latter had taken with his men, knowing that it was not his own, he asked whose it was. He was told that it belonged to Duke Leopold of the Austrians, and that the latter had taken possession of that part of the city. On learning this, he became extremely angry, and he ordered that the banner be thrown down from the tower and trodden into the mud. Furthermore he added further injury by insulting the duke verbally. In addition, he excited the hatred of everyone there against him by distributing most of the booty that had been acquired through the efforts of everyone to his own men, thus depriving the rest [of their fair share]. For since he was the outstanding soldier among them all, he wished to arrange everything in accordance with his wishes and despised the other princes. However, these events led the German and Italian knights to become totally exasperated with the king, and they would have

---

[37]   Cf. Luke 9:62.

[38]   In fact Acre surrendered in July 1191; most of the prisoners were massacred over a month later, after Richard I failed to come to an agreement with Saladin.

'withstood him to his face',[39] had not this been prevented by the authority of the knights of the Temple. However, detesting English dishonesty and refusing to be subject to the King of the English, they boarded their ships and went home, along with Duke Leopold. The king and his men remained there further, fighting every day with the pagans.

The citizens of Jerusalem and all those who had escaped from the pagans from the other towns and villages congregated in Acre, and fortifying that town with great care they established it as a bastion for the Christian army and a seat of battle against the pagans. They divided it up among various authorities, providing quarters for the Templars, Hospitallers and the canons of the Lord's Sepulchre with a seat for the Patriarch, and they often marched out with the army to fight with the pagans. They recovered many of the cities and castles that they had lost, and resisted the pagans manfully. As the King of the English was going home, they chose Count Henry of Champagne as king, giving him the widow of King Guy,[40] and so, having mustered, 'growing by number every day', 'they fought the Lord's battles joyfully',[41] and many from the lands this side of the sea sailed together to their help.

But these words are enough on this subject, so let our pen return to our empire.

(37) In the year from the Lord's Incarnation 1190 [*sic*] the Emperor Henry and his wife were, as has previously been described, crowned by Pope Celestine.[42] Then, desiring to take possession of Apulia and Sicily after the death of William, and taking her with him, he led his army into the Campania, where he found the whole country in rebellion against him. For on William's death a relative of his, descended from Roger, a man called Tancred, had with the consent of all the barons and cities of Sicily tyrannously set up his own government in that land, which has from antiquity been the mother of tyrants, seizing the name of king and violently resisting the emperor. While he lived he steadfastly deprived him of his wife's inheritance. The emperor thus laid siege to the rebellious city of Naples in the Campania, ravaging all the land round about with fire and sword. During his return from his expedition across the sea the King of France came to him and made an alliance, then honourably taking his leave he went back to France. With his army attacked by pestilence and having gained no advantage, the emperor planned [himself] to return home. It was then that the empress was captured by some of the barons of Apulia who were related to her, and was held for a time in captivity under extremely careful guard. With this lamentable beginning the emperor despaired of obtaining Apulia, and he returned across the Alps, to await better times in future; first however he complained to the pope about his wife's

---

39 Galatians 2:11.

40 Rather he married Isabella, her half-sister, King Amalric's younger daughter, the widow of Conrad of Montferrat. Queen Sybilla had predeceased her husband in 1190.

41 I Maccabees 3:2.

42 See above, c. 33.

imprisonment. The pope was angered by those who had presumed to do this and laid an anathema upon them, placing the whole land under interdict, and forcing the release of the empress from her captivity. Afterwards she returned north of the Alps and was restored to the emperor, who filled with indignation looked forward to the day when he could take his revenge. On his return north of the Alps the Emperor Henry granted the duchy of Swabia to his brother Conrad. This Conrad was a man of fierce and coarse nature, although quite generous at heart, but on that account seeking after great things and always committing crimes, so he spread fear among people near and far.

(38) At this time, namely in the year 1191 [*sic*], King Richard of the English was returning through Hungary from the expedition overseas, and accompanied by only a small escort he entered the lands of Duke Leopold. Remembering the injuries that he had inflicted upon this same duke at Acre, he was much afraid of him, and so he abandoned his royal state, wishing to cross his lands speedily and secretly, in the guise of an ordinary person. Needing to eat, he turned aside to a little inn near Vienna, having sent away all but a few companions. To avoid being recognised, he busied himself in work fitting for servants, and was himself helping to cook chickens, turning the spit with his own hand, but he forgot that he was wearing a valuable ring on his finger. By chance a man from the duke's household, who had been with him at Acre and had seen and taken note of the king there, happened to leave the city and entered the tavern that was distinguished by its royal cook. He spotted the ring and recognised him. Concealing this knowledge, he hastened back to the city and informed the duke, who happened to be there, of the king's presence – which news made the duke extremely happy. So the duke and a large band of knights immediately mounted their horses and hastened there, and he arrested the king as the latter was holding a roasted chicken in his hand. Mocking him for the menial work with which he had been busy, he took him back to the city, and kept him under the strictest guard, thus with a fitting reward 'repaying him as he deserved'.[43] However, many people criticised the duke for this deed, thinking it to be sacrilege to have done this to one who was a pilgrim to the Holy Sepulchre, and were in haste to denounce him – although this disapproval was of little benefit to the captive king.

Hearing of the capture of the King of the English, the emperor sent envoys to the duke, ordering him to hand over the king, and, once the latter had been handed over at Worms, he ordered him to be taken away and laden with chains, treating him thus to make him wish to be ransomed. Many of the leading men of his realm arrived to visit him, and they brought all sorts of treasure for their lord.[44]

---

[43]   Esther 16:18 (Vulgate). The king's arrest took place on 21 December 1192.

[44]   Richard was briefly held prisoner at the castle of Trifels, but thereafter largely at Worms and Speyer, where he was clearly granted a degree of conditional liberty, not least to negotiate between the emperor and a group of rebel princes from the Lower Rhineland. Otto referred to the court held at Worms in June 1193, where the terms of the ransom were agreed. For details of Richard's stay in Germany, and of the English magnates who joined

Duke Leopold was however excommunicated by the pope for his capture of the pilgrim king. This was to prevent anybody else similarly daring to kidnap pilgrims to the Holy Sepulchre and discouraging them from going to help the Church overseas. Finally, after giving some thousands of measures of gold and silver from his ransom to the emperor, and more gold and silver to Duke Leopold to secure his agreement, and confirming on oath that he would live in peace and be reconciled with them, he was released from captivity and, with this payment, returned to his homeland.[45] I shall not describe the huge weight of precious metal that the ransom provided, lest anyone should consider it so incredible as to be a falsehood. One ought however to know that the contents of the treasuries of all the churches of England were brought together, and the ransom was for the most part composed of chalices, crosses and other sorts of ecclesiastical valuables. After receiving this huge sum the emperor gave generous gifts to his knights, and sent a large army of paid troops to Apulia under the command of the steward Markward of Anweiler and Bertold of Künigsberg, and through their efforts many castles and cities surrendered to him.[46] Berthold was killed there, being hit by a missile from a catapult. Tancred having in the meanwhile died, the leading men of that land conspired together against the emperor, refused to surrender and drove all the German foreigners from their cities.

(39) In the year from the Lord's Incarnation 1193 [*sic*] many pilgrims from the lands this side of the sea took the Cross and looked to the Church for help with their passage. In this same year the Emperor Henry raised an army, crossed the Alps by the 'second route',[47] passed through [northern] Italy and Tuscany and invaded Campania. During this march Richard of Acerra, a very powerful count, was captured by Diepold of Roggatart [*Rocca d'Arce*?] and was handed over to the emperor at Capua. The latter rightly loathed him because of the capture of the empress, and he had him hanged from a gallows with his head downwards.[48]

Then he either attacked and destroyed, or received the surrender of, all the cities of Campania and Apulia. Burning with anger, he stormed Salerno, Barletta, Bari and many other very strong cities and there seized vast plunder; nor was there any city or fortress which could resist his attack. The army of pilgrims which was preparing for the expedition across the sea crossed the Alps with him and marched along with him for a while, greatly reinforcing his troops. After imposing his rule over all of Apulia and Campania, he marched with his troops into Calabria, plundering that province, and then crossed over to Sicily. He sent the marshal,

---

him there, Hans Eberhard Mayer, 'A ghost ship called *Frankenef*: King Richard I's German itinerary', *English Historical Review* 115 (2000), 134–44.

[45] He was formally released at Mainz on 4 February 1194.

[46] For them, see above 'History of the Expedition', notes 118 and 229.

[47] The Splügen Pass between Chur and Chiavenna.

[48] Count Richard of Acerra was the brother-in-law and principal supporter of King Tancred, commanding his army on the mainland of south Italy. But Otto's chronology was in error here, since he was only captured and executed in 1196.

Henry of Kalden, to carry the war into the area round Catania, where without delay he encountered and attacked the powerful army which had been drawn up there ready for battle by the leading men of that land. He gained the victory, and a huge number of men were killed. He pursued the fugitives into the city and stormed it. The bishop, who had been a leader of the rebellion, and many noblemen were captured, and the city was set on fire. The marshal did not spare its churches, and he set fire to and tragically destroyed the church of St Agatha, killing a great multitude of all ages, both men and women, who had taken refuge there. He then returned in triumph to the emperor, bringing his noble prisoners with him.[49]

The [Sicilian] nobles were absolutely desperate, and treacherously plotted to murder the emperor. In order to fulfil this plan, they surrendered themselves and all their property into his power. The emperor received their pledges of loyalty and treated them decently, and he escaped their plots, albeit only just. Once he had realised their deceit, he decided to overcome their plot by one of his own, even though it was dishonourable to punish treachery by treachery. Hence he summoned the known conspirators, and they (little suspecting) gathered at this court. They were all arrested and thrown into prison where he had them put painfully to death with hideous tortures. He deprived the archpirate Margaritus, one of the country's most powerful barons, and Count Richard, a man of great leaning, of their eyes. He had one person convicted of treason skinned alive, and he ordered that a man who aspired to the royal crown should have a crown fixed to him by iron nails.[50] He had some people tied to a stake, surrounded by a pyre and cruelly put to death by burning, and others fastened to the ground with stakes through their bodies. By these actions he struck fear into all the nations round about, not only on this side of the ocean but on the other side as well; all were absolutely terrified by his severity.

(40) In the year from the Lord's Incarnation 1194 the emperor directed his forces against the city of Palermo on the far side of Sicily, which was not only the site of the capital and archbishopric of Sicily but was also the place where its kings' treasury was up to this time stored. After setting up [siege] castles facing it, it was his intention to storm the city. He ordered his troops to break into the great royal garden, which was surrounded on all sides by a wall and filled in a charming way with all sorts of beasts – these animals were consumed to supply his army. The citizens were greatly afraid of the emperor's anger and without a fight held out their hands in surrender, seeking peace terms and offering to surrender themselves and all their property. He agreed to this, the city was surrendered and he received

---

[49]   This account appears to confuse what happened in 1194 with the later rebellion in 1197, after which we know that the Bishop of Catania, Roger Orbus (Bishop 1195–1206), was imprisoned and his brother blinded.

[50]   The latter may have been Jordan Lupinus, Count of Bovino. These executions probably took place in June 1197, and Margaritus of Brindisi, the former commander of the Sicilian fleet, and Count Richard of Ajello, who had been prisoners since Christmas 1194, were blinded shortly afterwards.

them back into his grace. Imperial banners were displayed on all the towers, and on the appointed day the emperor, in full regalia, was welcomed by the citizens in a procession. He allowed his army to take its leisure in all sorts of pleasant activities and, free from care, to enjoy the extraordinarily rich booty; meanwhile he took pleasure in all sorts of splendid shows and entertainments on the parade ground.

Finally, the whole city was prepared for his triumphal entry, decorated with great expense and labour by the citizens, filled with carpets and garlands of all sorts of flowers, valuable decorations, the squares both inside and outside the city permeated by the smell of frankincense and myrrh and other expensive scents. The emperor and his army remained some way outside the city, and so the citizens went out in groups arranged according the differences of rank, class and age, the nobles in their own party, the older men in order of age, and the younger and stronger, then the young people not yet old enough to grow beards or to serve in war, adorned with every sort of clothing and trappings for their horses. They went to meet the emperor in the order of their rank, each and every one of them applauding in time with the music from the various instruments. The emperor meanwhile, with no small effort, drew up his army in the proper military manner. He absolutely forbade all indiscipline among the Germans, threatening that those who disobeyed him would have their hands cut off. He paraded his troops with their armour glittering superbly, slowly marching two by two along the road towards the city. He himself then made a glorious state entry into the city, followed by the princes, with everyone properly acclaiming him with the *laudes*; and when the crowd who stood in the squares saw the emperor then, as is the custom of that land, they prostrated themselves face downwards on the ground in front of him. So he was received as king and established his peace. He was given many gifts by the citizens, most excellent horses with golden saddles, and reins and trappings and other things of gold, silver, silk and jewels, with all of which he generously rewarded his army. First he gave royal gifts to the princes, then he showed himself most generous to the knights who deserved reward, and thus he bound all of them in a variety of ways to his service.

A huge sum of gold and silver was then discovered in the royal treasury which he sent to the public treasury at Trifels and from this he greatly enriched a number of other imperial palaces. For he found there the riches of Apulia, Calabria and Sicily, lands which are very rich in metals, a glorious collection of precious stones and all sorts of gems. He also took with this infinite treasure Tancred's wife, daughter and son, and the latter's fiancée, the daughter of the Emperor of Constantinople, and, bringing the captive nobles with him, he celebrated a wonderful victory. Thus after having conquered Samnium, Apulia and Calabria, Henry, that most warlike of emperors, reduced all of Sicily and Sardinia to obedience. He dismissed the army of pilgrims, honouring it with many gifts, and dispatched with it from his own forces to help the Church across the sea five hundred stipendiary knights, paid for from the public treasury. These sailed from Siponto and Brindisi across the Mediterranean and landed at Acre where they were joyfully received by the Christians. With their help the Christians recovered many castles and, after both sides had met in a number of battles and the Christians had invariably been victorious, they forced the pagans to ask for peace. As a result, when the peace was concluded, the pagans energetically fortified the cities and castles which they held, and above all Jerusalem, which they rendered impregnable, surrounding it with a double wall and very deep ditches, and building an antemural [fortification]. They granted safe conduct to Christians wishing to see the Lord's Sepulchre, but the pope forbade anyone to take advantage of this favour, lest the pagans profit from the gifts of the Christians, and bound those who transgressed his prohibition with the bond of anathema.

[*A paragraph was here inserted, quite unconnected with what went before, concerning the leading Parisian scholars of the day.*]

(41) The year from the Lord's Incarnation 1195. The Emperor Henry went to Taranto where there were ships laden with an abundance of every sort of provision which had been sent across the sea by the army of the Christians. He decided to send the noble captives back to Germany, sending them before him to await his triumphant return, and he ordered them to be guarded at suitable places. He ordered that the son of King Tancred, who was just a boy, be brought to Regensburg and deprived of his eyes, and then consigned to perpetual captivity in the castle of *Amiso*.[51] When he came to adulthood, he abandoned transitory matters and, so it is said, sought those eternal with good works, eager for Heaven since he was unable to attend to earthly affairs. For having been forcibly removed from the active life, he studied the contemplative, which is the more meritorious.[52] The emperor betrothed his fiancée, the daughter of the Emperor of Constantinople, to his brother Philip, and sent the Apulian queen, Tancred's wife, whose name was Sibilia, and her daughter under guard to the nunnery of Hohenburg in Alsace. He dispatched the archpirate Margaritus and Count Richard, the empress's [*sic*] relative, who had, as said, been deprived of their eyes, to be held in perpetual chains at Trifels.[53] And so, completely victorious both by land and sea, the mighty emperor returned home to Germany.

Duke Welf died. Also, Leopold, duke of the east [*dux Orientalis*], suffered a wound in his shin, and because of the unbearable pain his lower leg was cut off,

---

[51]   Probably Hohenems, in the Voralberg.

[52]   However, the *Gesta Innocentii Papae Tertii*, c. 25, MPL ccxiv, col. xlvii (written c. 1210), said that he died while still a child. He may still have been alive in May 1202, when his arrest was mentioned by the pope in a circular letter to the people of Sicily, with no reference to him being deceased, *Die Register Innocenz' III. 5 Pontifikatsjahr 1202/3*, ed. O. Hageneder et alii (Vienna 1993), pp. 67–70 no., 37, at p. 68.

[53]   Here Otto has confused Count Richard of Ajello with Queen Sibilia's brother, Count Richard of Acerra, who was put to death in 1196, and whose execution he had mentioned earlier. Furthermore Tancred and Sibilia had three daughters who were sent with her to Germany, and subsequently released after Henry's death.

but his illness grew worse and he finished his life painfully. At this same time the aforesaid King Richard of England was killed by an arrow while besieging a castle, and his brother John succeeded him as king.[54]

(42) In these days a third overseas expedition was organised that encouraged many princes from our lands, along with a lot of other people, to make the journey to Jerusalem. Conrad, the venerable Archbishop of Mainz, and the chancellor Conrad, Bishop of Würzburg, both men of distinction, acted as their leaders.[55] Among those on this expedition were Duke Frederick of Austria, the son of Leopold, intending to do this for the salvation of his father's soul. He died on the way, but it is to be hoped suffered only a temporal death, not that of the soul.[56] His brother Leopold succeeded him as duke. Furthermore Henry, Count Palatine of the Rhine, the son of Duke Henry of Saxony, maternal nephew to the King of England and brother of the Emperor Otto, along with the Duke of Brabant and Louvain,[57] and many other distinguished barons, took the Cross with a strong following, and, desiring to follow Christ[58] they sailed to the help of the Church across the sea, where they found many men from the first expedition. They joined together and attacked the pagans, ravaging much of their land daily with fire and sword, and recovering some of it. They besieged the castle of Toron, which was most strongly fortified, both by nature and man-made defences. They would have captured this, had not 'the holy hunger for gold'[59] weighed more in the minds of some people than desire for Christ. For, so it is said, certain of the knights of the Temple had been bribed by the pagans, and they and a few others persuaded the chancellor Conrad, who was taking a leading part in this siege, to raise the siege in return for a most weighty sum of gold. Hence they withdrew, and so because of this castle Christ was sold to the pagans, as he had once been to the Jews. Nor did they gain any benefit from the treasure that had thus been gained, just as Judas did not from the thirty pieces of silver. For these men who had been corrupted by money were bribed by the pagans with counterfeit gold, actually base metal the surface of which was gold-coloured, and for this they received 'an everlasting reproach'.[60] Furthermore, if this castle had been captured and remained in Christian hands it

---

[54]   Otto here conflates the death of various prominent persons over a period of several years. Welf VI died on 15 December 1191. Duke Leopold V of Austria died on 31 December 1194, after being injured in a riding accident [above, p. 129], and Richard I died on 6 April 1199, while besieging the castle of Chalus in the Limousin.

[55]   Archbishop Conrad set off for the Holy Land in January 1197, *Monumenta Erphesfurtensia*, p. 198.

[56]   He died on 16 April 1198; his remains were brought back to Austria and buried next to his father at Heiligenkreuz.

[57]   Henry I, Duke of Brabant 1190–1235.

[58]   Cf. Matthew 16:24: 'If any man will come after me, let him deny himself and take up his cross and follow me.'

[59]   Vergil, *Aeneid*, III.57.

[60]   Jeremiah 23:40.

would have greatly diminished the power of the pagans in that region. Nor was this left without vengeance. Would that this was like the paternal scourge,[61] but Divine severity did not allow this to go unpunished. For no sooner had this same Conrad the chancellor gone home, crossing the vastness of the sea and returning to his see of Würzburg, than he conspired against the kingdom. He built a castle on the Sankt Maria Berg in that city and came out in open rebellion, and much of the property of his church was laid waste. He was then murdered by some of the *ministeriales* of that church, whom he had waged war against and gravely injured, and he was buried in that same church.[62] However, it is said of him that various marks of flagellation were found on his body, through which his penitence and austere way of life were shown.

But let us return to the matter in hand. The army of the pilgrims at Acre was so shocked by the way of life of the Templars, Hospitallers and the other barons of that land, and greatly disliked their trade with, and the way in which they were, to some extent anyway, secretly friendly with, the pagans, and so they cast off their authority and guidance, and began to act independently under their own leadership. They had many fights with the pagans, both in open battle and in raids, in which they were usually victorious, and they strove to perform great deeds. When the people of that land saw that the army of the pilgrims was fighting so fiercely and prospering in the fulfilment of their vow, they grew more afraid of their diligence than of the evil intentions of the pagans, and (so we have heard from those who were present on this expedition) they started to plot and formed a conspiracy with the pagans to kill them all by craft. For they were afraid that, if the pilgrims prevailed over the pagans, they would drive them out of their homeland and forcibly seize it for themselves, and it was for this reason that they plotted to kill or enslave them. For 'seeking their own, not the things which are Jesus Christ's',[63] they were happy to remain in the coastal region, which is extremely fertile, because of its overflowing fruitfulness, and held Jerusalem and the Sepulchre of the Lord to be of little value. Hence, for a long time great armies have accomplished little, and 'Jerusalem will be trodden down by the gentiles'.[64] Thus it was that King Henry was standing with his associates in the window of a most high tower at Acre and, so it is said, was discussing with them how with the help of the pagans he might arrange the death of the pilgrims, when he was exposed to Divine judgement, into which 'it is a fearful thing to fall',[65] and through the wish of God he fell from

---

[61]   Cf. Hebrews 12:6: 'the Lord ... scourgeth every son whom he receiveth'.

[62]   Bishop Conrad was murdered on 29 October 1202 by Heinrich and Bodo of Ravensburg, the nephews of the imperial marshal Heinrich of Kalden; see *Chronicon Montis Sereni* (Lauterberg), MGH SS xxiii.170. For discussion, see Jan Keup, 'Reichsministerialen und Bischofsmord in staufischer Zeit', in *Bischofsmord im Mittelalter*, ed. Natalie Fryde and Dirk Reitz (Göttingen 2003), pp. 293–7.

[63]   Philippians 2:21.

[64]   Luke 21:24.

[65]   Hebrews 10:31.

the window in which he sat leaning out so carelessly. With his body smashed to pieces, he gave up the ghost; thus 'the counsel of the forward carried headlong',[66] and the plot they had arranged miscarried.

---

[66]   Job 5:13. Henry of Champagne died on 10 September 1197: despite what Otto says he was never formally crowned King of Jerusalem.

An Account of the Seaborne Journey of the Pilgrims Heading to Jerusalem Who Captured Silves in 1189[1]

Following the example of the wise custom of the Ancients, who were at pains to record their deeds through the adornment of writing, so that they did not escape the notice of posterity, I have decided to give a simple account of the many different events that took place on the seaborne journey of the pilgrims who were heading to Jerusalem.

Thus in the year from the Incarnation of the Lord 1187, after the land of promise was destroyed by Saladin, King of Egypt, with its cities captured and its inhabitants slain or prisoners, the trumpet of preaching along with an indulgence issued by Apostolic authority spread through Christian lands and moved a huge number of people to remedy this wretched disaster. Among these, it was pleasing to some people to undertake the forthcoming path of their pilgrimage[2] across the vast wastes of the sea in order to avenge this offence.

Leaving Bremen with eleven ships, well provided with warriors, arms and provisions, we set off on our journey from Blexen at the ninth hour on 22 April in the year from the Lord's Incarnation 1189. But the next day we left one ship [aground] on a sandbank to follow after us. However, we made sail and on 24 April arrived in England at a place called Lowestoft. The following day we sailed past the Thames in a storm and carelessly entering the port of Sandwich we lost three of our ships which ran onto the sandbanks, the men and equipment being saved.[3] Two of these ships were utterly destroyed, the third was repaired.

We made a delay of twenty-two days there, during which time we salvaged the ship that had been lost. People joined us here and elsewhere, but for various reasons some went on ahead while others followed later. We purchased a ship in London to replace a vessel that had been lost, and, after fitting it out, we set off

---

[1] Translated from Charles W. David, *Narratio de Itinere Navali Peregrinorum Hierosolymam Tendentium et Silviam Capientium*, in the *Proceedings of the American Philosophical Society* 81 (1939), 610-42. The MS. has no title, and the various modern editors have each provided their own: this is the title devised by David. The notes below make extensive use of those by David.

[2] David reads this phrase as *peregrinationis incolarum*, 'the pilgrimage of the inhabitants', whereas Chroust, *Quellen*, p. 179 emends this to *peregrinationis suorum*, which makes more sense, and which reading I have followed.

[3] These sandbanks were the Goodwin Sands, a notorious hazard for sailing ships.

from the port of Sandwich on 19 May and came to Winchelsea; but we were then delayed by contrary winds and it was only on the fourth day that we arrived at the harbour of Yarmouth.[4] There we found some of our companions, and the next morning we left England and set off towards Brittany, but, with the wind dropping and sometimes blowing in the wrong direction, we bobbed up and down at sea for six days. On the sixth day a stormy wind blew us off course and forced us to sail to a little island inhabited by poor Bretons, which is called Belle Ile by the French and *Wechele* by the Bretons. Within those six days, we celebrated Pentecost at sea with devotion and more than usually solemn masses.[5]

We spent eight days next to this same island, and on the ninth day when the wind was strong enough we made sail and continued until nightfall. We then lowered our sails, to avoid carelessly running aground if land should appear. The ships were tossed by the force of the winds all night long. It should be noted that we were going the right way, passing Saint-Mathieu, which is a peninsula of Brittany, stretching out into the sea,[6] and we passed through heavy seas because of the violence of the winds, until we met the pilots for the entry into La Rochelle.[7] Let it be known also that we sailed round both coasts of Brittany, [a land] which has nine bishoprics, in three of which they use the Breton language, which is common to no other people, while the rest share the speech of the Gauls. Brittany is part of the kingdom of the French, and borders Anjou and Poitou.

Remaining for one day at La Rochelle, at dawn we unfurled our sails and set out on the waves, but, with the winds proving variable and taking us in different directions, we passed nine days tossing on the deep. Nor ought one to omit that during one night when there was dreadful thunder and lightning, at the height of our ordeal many of our company saw two candles burning for a long time.[8] Furthermore, one should add that a huge multitude of fish, six or seven feet long and resembling sturgeon, very often passed our ships at high speed, with all their bodies out of the water.[9] On the ninth day we entered harbour, near a castle of the King of Galicia called Gozón and the town of Avilés.[10] It should be noted that during the aforesaid nine days we left Gascony, the kingdom of the Aragonese, the kingdom of the Navarrese and the kingdom of Spain on our left-hand side, and

---

[4]   Yarmouth on the Isle of Wight, on the south side of the Solent; this would seem to have been on 24 May. Chroust (wrongly?) suggested Portchester rather than Winchelsea.

[5]   Pentecost fell on 28 May.

[6]   Pointe-Saint Mathieu, 20 km west of Brest; the fleet would have passed this before coming to Belle Ile, south of Quiberon Bay.

[7]   The translation of this last phrase is problematic: Chroust rendered it 'when we were guided by two pilots on the entry into La Rochelle', *Quellen*, p. 180, but David did not like this reading.

[8]   David suggests that this was St Elmo's fire.

[9]   Clearly dolphins or porpoises.

[10]   They thus entered Luanco bay, west of Cap de Peñas, and some 20 km west of Gijon.

we were now in the kingdom of Galicia. It should be remembered that there are five kingdoms of the Spanish, namely those of the Aragonese, of the Navarrese, and of those people who are specifically called the 'Spanish', of which the capital is at Toledo, as well as those of the inhabitants of Galicia and Portugal.[11] The sea surrounds these kingdoms on every side except one; all of them are bounded by the Breton sea through which we came, and they have frontiers facing the Saracens, who live on the side away from the sea; and thus those who wish to go to the furthest of these, that is the kingdom of the Portuguese, must cross through all of them.

On the tenth day, leaving the ships in harbour, we travelled to San Salvador, a city that lies six leagues from the port. There we found a church filled with many things worthy of great veneration and relics of the saints, which at the time of ... persecution[12] were translated through fear of the enemy from Jerusalem to Africa, then to Hispalis, which is now called Seville, from Hispalis to Toledo, and from Toledo to Oviedo, which is now called by the name of San Salvador. Note that we have seen nothing on the coast of Galicia except steep cliffs, the whole region is very mountainous, and therefore infertile and unsuitable for vines. Chickpeas are the main crop.

On the eleventh day, we returned to our ships, and at dawn on the thirteenth day we put to sea once again. On the fourteenth, which was the vigil of St John the Baptist,[13] and on the feast itself a strong wind filled our sails, and on the evening of that holy day we arrived at the harbour of the Tambre, which is a river flowing through Galicia. There we left our ships and went back on a long day's journey to the church of St James, which we had now passed beyond.[14] What with going there and returning, and a delay in harbour waiting for a wind, we passed some eight days.

We boarded ship around midday on the Octave of St John, and at noon the next day we saw Portugal close by.[15] Then with a favourable wind blowing we entered the port of Lisbon at dawn on the third day. This port is at the mouth of the Tagus, which flows from Toledo and enters the sea there. The river is as wide as the Elbe near Stade. Note that near Lisbon, three of our miles away, is a castle called Sintra, where mares conceive from the wind. The horses that are born are extraordinarily

---

[11]   The five kingdoms are therefore Aragon, Navarre, Castile, Leon and Portugal.

[12]   There is a space in the manuscript here; David conjectured that the author had access to a written account of the Oviedo relics, and left a space for a word that he could not read.

[13]   23 June.

[14]   The Tambre estuary is to the south of Cape Finisterre. The port was presumably either Muros on the north side of the estuary or Noyas on the south side. From the former it was just over 40 km to Santiago de Compostella, from the latter somewhat less.

[15]   12 July.

speedy, but live for no more than eight years.[16] Lisbon, which is large and very rich, was captured by our pilgrims forty-four years ago, along with the castles round about, and made subject to the rule of the King of Portugal. That region is very fertile and healthy, surrounded by hills but well furnished with valleys.

Here we found forty-four ships, and we had eleven. The ships from our empire and from Flanders had arrived some four or five weeks before us, and on their voyage beyond Lisbon they had stormed a fortified town named Alvor, subject to the lordship of Silves, and we were reliably informed that, sparing neither age nor sex, they slew some 5,600 people.[17] Galleys from Lisbon accompanied them until they reached the Straits [of Gibraltar] and then they returned. They informed us that they were making a good voyage, and they brought back some captive Saracens. However, we were recruited to join in besieging Silves by the request of the King of Portugal, who was advancing upon it with a large army.[18] We remained in harbour for eleven days, with thirty-six great ships, and one galley from Tuy, a town in Galicia, which had joined up with our squadron, along with many ships from Lisbon. We set out around Vespers on the eleventh day, and sailed continuously, but slowly, for three days and nights. On the afternoon of the third day we saw the town of Alvor, which our men had captured and destroyed, overlooking the sea, as well as other abandoned places whose inhabitants had been killed at Alvor. Not far from there we entered the harbour of Silves, finding the land there ideal for agriculture. All the inhabitants, however, fled to Silves. Silves lies about one German mile from the sea by land, but by river the way is more winding and longer.[19]

Our men fanned out through the lands of the enemy with great enthusiasm but little care, and hence two men from Bremen who had foolishly become separated from the others were slain by ten Saracen cavalrymen, who were the only ones we saw in all that land. They were carried back to where the fleet lay, and they were buried there by our men. Our ships were anchored in the estuary, not far

---

[16]   Sintra is actually 17 miles (27 km) from Lisbon: the author clearly means the long German mile, to which he refers by name slightly later, equivalent to about four English miles. The legend about the mares of Sintra was also recounted by the earlier *De Expugnatione Lyxbonensi*, ed. C.W. David (New York 1936), pp. 92–3, and was ultimately derived from several classical sources.

[17]   Cf. *Chronica Regia Coloniensis*, p. 143.

[18]   Or perhaps, 'who was preparing a large army', depending on whether *properantes* should be emended to *preparantes*, as Chroust, *Quellen*, p. 182. The king was Sancho I, 1185–1211, the son of Afonso Henriques, the founder of the kingdom of Portugal. According to Ralph of Diceto, *Opera Historica*, ii.65–6, the king agreed with them that they might have whatever booty they gained at Silves, provided that they left the city itself to him, and the Portuguese contributed thirty-seven galleys and various pinnaces (see below) to the expedition.

[19]   Actually about 6½ miles (10 km) by road, and 7½ miles (12 km) if sailing up the River Arade.

from the sea, and our men burned the villages [nearby] and brought back what little plunder they found. That night we sent a *sagittina* from Lisbon to the leader of the Portuguese forces, who had gone before us by land, and whose camp then lay some four miles away from us.[20] The following day a ship with pilgrims from Brittany joined us. The leader of the Portuguese troops arrived around Vespers of the same day with a small escort, having left his army in camp. After we had discussed what we should do, it was his wish that we should move on to capture Dardea, for he had little hope of us taking Silves, since this was the capital of the kingdom and was extremely strong.[21] We, however, preferred to trust faithfully in the Lord, and we decided to undertake the more important operation, with which decision he concurred. The next day we sailed our ships towards the city, and fixed our anchors in a place from which we could see it, but the shallowness of the water prevented us going further. The leader of the army took station ahead of us with his men and with the galleys that had accompanied us. That night they lit many torches in the city, and we did the same. Our people were very joyful, and not deterred even though they saw that the place was extremely strongly fortified. At dawn on the following day we armed ourselves and approached the city with skiffs, and we pitched camp so that it was well within double bowshot of the wall.

The situation of Silves is as follows. In size it is not very different from Goslar, but it had many more houses and some very fine mansions. It is surrounded with walls and ditches, with not even a little hut to be found outside the walls. Within it there were four sets of fortifications. The first of these was a large town in the valley, which they call *arrabalde*.[22] The city on the hill, which they call *al-medina*, has another fortress extending into the valley, descending to the watercourse and to the river, which is called the Arade (another river flows into this called the Odelouca), and there are four towers above the watercourse, to ensure that the upper town is well supplied with water, and this fortification is called the *couraça*.[23] The entry by the gates was so crooked and twisting that it was easier to cross the wall than to enter through the doorway. Under the first castle there was what they called the *alcazar*. There was a great tower in the *arrabalde*, and this guarded the road to the *al-medina*, which has a wall with overhead cover (*muro testudinato*); thus from it one can see what is going on outside the wall of the *al-medina*. Those attacking the wall can be shot at from the rear from the tower, and vice versa. This is called

---

[20] A *sagittina* (pinnace?) was a small, fast craft; cf. Geoffrey Malaterra, *De Rebus Gestis Rogerii Comitis Siciliae et Calabriae*, ed. E. Pontieri (Rerum Italicarum Scriptores, 2nd ed., Bologna 1927–8), IV.2, p. 86, where at the siege of Syracuse in 1085 Count Roger sent out 'a very swift *sagita*' to reconnoitre the enemy's fleet. This vessel must have gone upriver, and perhaps up the tributary River Odelouca, to meet the Portuguese army.

[21] More properly Silves was the provincial capital of the Algarve, though it had been the capital of a small independent kingdom a century or more earlier. Dardea has not been identified.

[22] From the Arabic *al-rabad* (suburb).

[23] 'The breastwork.'

the *albarrana*.[24] It should be noted that these names are generic, and not proper names; for wherever there are similar arrangements in a city of that land, whether by the Christians or by the pagans, they have these names. The Saracens living in Spain are called Andelucians, while those in Africa are the *Mucimiti* or *Maximiti* or the *Moedini*, while those who are in Morocco are the *Moravidi*.[25] It should also be noted that in the wall of each fortress were towers that were so close to each other that a stone could easily be thrown from one turret to a third. In various places the towers were twice as close [as elsewhere].

As soon as we arrived on that day, some ten horsemen rode out of the city and galloped about near the walls, as if to provoke our people, who paid no attention to the orders of our leaders and rashly charged at them, but they were attacked by darts and stones from the wall. They both inflicted and suffered wounds, and with the fortunes of war in doubt they retreated. However, we pitched our tents closer [to the wall] and took a decision that we would make an attack in the morning, preparing ladders to scale the walls. At dawn therefore mass was solemnly celebrated, and the people most devoutly took communion, and then having armed themselves everyone advanced to the wall with the ladders, carrying them over the moat, paying no attention to the depth of the water, and came to the wall. The men who were in the bastions threw rocks for a little while, but then suddenly with the aid of God, 'who saves those who trust in Him',[26] they turned tail and fled up to the fortifications above. Our men, having set up their ladders there, pursued them. But since they had fled in good time few were killed, while the others took refuge in the fortress, for while our men were in armour they lacked this, and therefore easily escaped. However, many were suffocated in the gateway because of their great haste [to escape]. Their bodies were thrown outside the wall, for they were unwilling to bury them within the walls – I don't know why. We were then also informed that their king had had the men who had begun the flight beheaded. So therefore we took possession of the lower town, which our men had attacked from one side and the Portuguese from the other, and for [the rest of] that day and night we remained quietly in the city.

At dawn the next day, which was the feast of Mary Magdalene,[27] mass was said and communion taken, and our men armed themselves and left the city, leaving the galley crewmen within. Carrying ladders with them, they made an attack on the upper city, the enemy's strongest point, sited on the mountain and surrounded by a deep and steep-sided ditch. Our men pressed on and after lengthy efforts managed to set up the ladders, but they were hampered by the depth of the ditch and driven back by incessant missile fire, although many of those in the bastions

---

[24]   From the Arabic *al-barrānīya*, meaning an external tower or a watchtower.

[25]   Phonetic versions of the Arabic *Masmūdah* (the tribe within which the Almohad movement had begun): *Muwahhidūn* (followers of one God, the religious designation of the Almohads); and Almoravid.

[26]   Daniel 13:60.

[27]   22 July.

were wounded by the arrows showered on them by our men. The hopes of the latter were thus frustrated and they were therefore very upset. Without taking proper advice, they set fire to the parts of the town they had captured, insofar as they were able to do this since the building materials used were such that, when one house was ablaze, the flames did not spread to others, for they had roofs of tile, walls of clay covered with plaster, and little wood. We [also] set fire to five galleys and other vessels that had been taken within the walls for fear of the enemy, and [then] returned to the previous camp.

But that same day, after we had taken heart and our warlike resolution returned, we pitched our camp next to the wall of the captured part of the city. Over the next few days we built wooden machines, towers, ladders and all sorts of devices to take the city. Meanwhile, too, the army of the Portuguese that was taking part in the siege of the city with us grew stronger. The King of Portugal arrived on the Octave of Mary Magdalene,[28] and his army followed slowly behind with its baggage. The next day, which was a Sunday, the Saracens hanged three Christians whom they had previously captured by the feet from the tower called the *albarrana* in sight of our men and struck at them with swords and lances until they were dead. They did this because two days earlier some Englishmen in our ranks had slain a Saracen before the eyes of those who were besieged. We sorrowfully lamented the death of our men, but were by this roused to wage war more fiercely. The Portuguese army was [further] strengthened at this time, and the city was blockaded on every side. Nor did we slacken our efforts in any way, [being busy] either making siege equipment, or shooting and being shot at by arrows or with machines.

At dawn on the Sunday that was the feast of Sixtus, Felicissimus and Agapetus,[29] we from the German kingdom pushed a siege engine, which we call a battering ram, forward to the walls of the *couraça*, between two towers, so that we might dig a hole through the wall. This siege engine was most stoutly built, constructed with great beams, its roof made from ships' rudders, and covered with felt, earth and plaster. However, the Saracens threw down from above a huge wad of linen, and oil and fire, and burned up the engine, and they were able to do this especially since it was heavy and could not easily be pulled backwards. Then the pagans rejoiced that day and our own men were cast down. The curse of dissension also arose, with some, especially the Flemings, wanting to withdraw, while others wished to hold those parts of the city that had been captured. The following day our siege engine hit these same towers so many hard blows that one of them fell down and lay partly in ruins. Meanwhile two engines of the king, albeit small ones, greatly harmed the people within the city. The next night a certain Moor came out, bringing with him two standards that they had within. At dawn the next day we rejoiced, for the Moor had pledged to surrender the city, specifically once the *couraça* was captured. On the vigil of St Lawrence,[30] a certain knight from Galicia who had come with us as

---

28   29 July.

29   6 August.

30   9 August.

the pilot of one of our ships went to that part of the wall that had been damaged by our machine and, despite the danger from the defenders of the tower, pulled out a cornerstone and [then] returned. Encouraged by such bravery, our men set to work undermining the tower, and what is wonderful to say is that, although the Saracens still manned it above, they were not hindered either by the rubble [falling] from the structure or by the hail of arrows. They stayed busily digging away at it until Vespers, but when night fell they grew very afraid and withdrew, thinking that the Saracens, whom they heard nearby, were tunnelling through the wall towards them. The next morning they set fire to the beams that had supported the tunnel and brought down part of the tower. Then, once the fire had gone out and they had regained their courage, they once again began to tunnel, wishing to undermine the stonework of that tower on each side by the same method. Fires were once again lit, and such a large part of the tower then collapsed that our men placed a ladder there and climbed one by one up to the ramparts. A host of the enemy manned these battlements, but the Lord gave strength to our men and struck fear into them, so that they all fled as one, while the king and his men who were looking on from the other side of the hill were overjoyed and gave voice to their great admiration of our people. Thus through the excellence of the Mother of God rather than our own valour, the Saracens abandoned four very strong towers and the ramparts [around them]. They shot many crossbow bolts and threw spears [at us], but they slowly withdrew to the *al-medina* along the wall by which they had safe passage from each side of the *couraça*. After enough of our men had gained entry, they forced the pagans to flee to the upper fortress. The wall was then destroyed in two places and the rubble removed, and the well on which the pagans were relying was filled up with stones and earth and [thus] blocked. So that evening our men, although exhausted and some of them wounded, returned rejoicing together to their camp.

The next day we began to dig in the ground in two places to make a tunnel towards the wall of the *al-medina* and to undermine it. Our men toiled on that work through that day and the following night, but on the third day[31] the Saracens made a sortie and destroyed the houses under which they were digging. The fire spread to the beams by which the tunnel was supported and our men fled from the diggings, but many of the enemy received mortal wounds from our archers, so the effort expended on our work was amply compensated by their losses. Meanwhile the Flemings began to tunnel through the wall of the captured part of the city, which however led up to one of the towers of the *al-medina*, so that through this tunnel in the wall one might approach the tower; but the Saracens became aware of this and drove them from the works during the night. They demolished [part of?] the wall and made a clear space between it and the tower. What had not been done during the night, they finished the next day, to ensure that they could not be harmed in this way.

It should be noted that many people now fled to us at various times from the fortress, in order to save their lives; and to encourage others to leave too we did

---

[31]   12 August.

not harm them in any way. On the vigil of the Assumption of the Virgin Mary,[32] the Saracens attacked us and our men in that sector were drawn up ready for battle when one of the Saracens jumped off the wall and fled to our men. He was extremely thirsty and begged for water, and was so parched that he buried almost his whole face in it in his eagerness to drink. He told us that a great many of the enemy were dying of thirst, for they had only a little water in their wells up there, and it was very salty.

On the day after the Octave of St Lawrence,[33] our entire army armed itself and approached the wall on every side, carrying ladders, and for a long time they struggled as hard as they could to raise these, but were driven back by a storm of heavy objects thrown down, which dashed our hopes. However, a number of the enemy were killed or wounded by our archers. Some of our men started to fill up the ditch on the northern side of the *al-medina* with boughs, but fire was hurled down from above and they were burned up. Nor is it to be wondered if the climb up to the wall was difficult for on one side was the foot of the mountain and a vast ditch, while on the other the packed houses made the way narrow. This setback struck fear into the Portuguese, especially since they lacked food for themselves and fodder for their horses, and so they started to ask both the king and us for permission to withdraw. The king indeed seemed ready to depart; but our men took a collective decision to continue the attack on the enemies of Christ, and informed the king of this. The king took counsel and valiantly agreed to remain with them; and so with spirits once again restored we strove more energetically to capture the city.[34]

Four siege engines were set up on the northern side, one of ours and three of the king's, and the enemy built four of their own to oppose our four. Meanwhile we also began to dig underground, but [began] a long way from the fortress, to avoid our work being sabotaged as previously. The pagans realised this, and opening their gates they made a sortie to destroy the tunnel, but our men hastened forward and suffering serious losses on both flanks the enemy retreated. They [then] made a second sortie at dawn on the Octave of the Assumption.[35] This time our men failed to stop them and they took station outside the walls and they stamped the ground to find out if it sounded hollow, since they were afraid that the tunnel had already reached the wall, although in fact it was still quite a long way away. Some of them were also digging in an effort to find the tunnel that way. A few of our men took up arms to drive them back, and making an attack on them they slew some, while many fell to our missiles. Our men pressed on right up to the entrance gate, so that if all our men had been in arms and ready they would easily have forced a way in through the gate. However, our men returned rejoicing at their victory.

---

[32]   14 August.

[33]   18 August.

[34]   The manuscript is damaged at this point. The reading *resumptis animis* is a conjecture of David, omitted by Chroust, *Quellen*, p. 188.

[35]   22 August.

A great deal of trouble and dispute arose on the vigil of St Bartholomew.[36] The Portuguese king and his men proposed an immediate withdrawal, but our men managed to secure, with difficulty, that he remained for another four days. Meanwhile our men began to tunnel from a pit where grain was stored, which was in soft ground near the wall. The king was pleased with this tunnel, and on the feast of St Bartholomew this man who had been of a mind to withdraw once again began to work with a resolute heart. Work on the tunnel was thus increased, but when our men were getting close to the wall the Saracens themselves breached the wall to send a tunnel out towards ours; when they encountered our men they fought a long battle with them. They eventually forced our men to retreat with fire flooding [through the tunnel], the materials for which they had [earlier] prepared;[37] but, albeit with difficulty, the entrance into our tunnel was blocked. Nevertheless, they made a hole between our tunnel and the wall, and [thus] prevented our men getting close to the wall. They also dug another long trench inside the wall and next to it, since they believed that we intended to use the tunnel to gain entrance to them under the wall – the plan was actually to undermine the wall. We were kept busy digging for a long time, and every day there was fighting in the tunnel with the pagans, who were similarly trying in all sorts of ways to hinder our undertaking. Finally, on St Giles's Day the men of the king shouted up to those on the wall, offering the chance to negotiate the city's surrender.[38] Many Saracens also then deserted and came over to us. The tunnel had struck fear into them and they said that they were suffering from thirst.

As a result the pagans met with the king, to negotiate a surrender of the city and its citadel and that they might leave in safety with their goods. The king strove to get the pilgrims to agree to this, but he did not succeed. He promised ten thousand gold coins for their consent, and then twenty thousand, which we accepted; but [then] on account of the delay that there would be in handing this over thereafter, since it would have had to have been brought from his own land, we refused. Then we agreed that the Saracens might leave, each with one garment, and we would have all their movable property and the king the city. The pagans were forced to accept this agreement, since they were weak from thirst and the tunnels were bringing them ever closer to defeat, for the great tower that they called *Burge Marie*, that is 'the tower of Mary', was in ruins thanks to the tunnel, which was now close to the wall.

On 3 September the lord of the city, named *Albainus*,[39] came out, he alone riding, with the rest of his men following on foot; however, our people most

---

[36]   23 August.

[37]   Does the phrase *igneo copioso fluvio*, literally 'with a copious fiery flood', suggest that the Muslims were using 'Greek fire' (naptha), the medieval version of napalm?

[38]   1 September.

[39]   David, p. 628n, on the basis of an Arabic source, identifies him as Aisa ben Abu Hafs, who was the son of one of the early disciples of Ibn Tūmart, the founder of the Almohad sect.

shamefully plundered some of them, in defiance of the treaty, and beat them. As a result there was bad feeling between the king and our people. As night fell we closed the gate to prevent more pagans leaving, and our people entered from the other side, although a few had earlier gone in by this main gate, and they were with the pagans throughout the night, and the pagans were shut in their houses. Some indeed were tortured to make them reveal where their money was, in defiance of the treaty. The next morning they were led out more kindly from the three gates, and then we saw for the first time how weak they were, for they were extremely thin and could barely walk. Many were crawling; others were helped by our men, while some were lying in the squares, either dead or barely alive, and there was an awful smell from the bodies of both men and of brute animals in the city.

Some Christian prisoners were brought out, hardly breathing: they told us that in the previous four days each of them had only had as much water as could be held in the head of a sheep, and some less than that, and nobody had been given water at all unless they were willing to fight, and even then not much – they had shared this with their wives and children. Nor had fresh bread been made because of the lack of water; they had been eating figs – hence most of the corn was still in store. At night the prisoners had lain naked on the cold flagstones in an attempt to generate moisture and thus live. The women and children had eaten the damp earth. And one should note that before we arrived there had been four hundred and fifty prisoners at Silves, and we found barely two hundred alive.

When the city was surrendered there were some 15,800 inhabitants of both sexes. From the day when the siege was begun until the day on which the city was captured six weeks and three days had passed.[40] Furthermore Silves was more strongly fortified than Lisbon, ten times richer and had grander buildings. The Portuguese indeed claimed that there was no more strongly fortified city in all Spain, and none so troublesome to the Christians.

One should also know that all the while the siege was going on the Portuguese neither worked nor fought, but poured scorn upon us, saying that we were working in vain and that the fortress was impregnable. They also encouraged the king to withdraw and tried in all sorts of ways to persuade us to abandon the siege. Indeed the majority of our people became discouraged and wanted to leave, but God mercifully and wonderfully kept us there for so happy an outcome. When we first arrived our army was 3,500 strong, or a few less, composed of men of every sort and age.[41] The king's forces had a large number of cavalry, infantry and galley crewmen, and also with him were religious knights of three types: the Templars, Jerusalemite knights who carry swords on belts, marry wives, and wage constant

---

[40]   21 July–3 September. The narrator was here entirely correct.

[41]   A similar number is given by Ralph of Diceto, *Opera*, ii.66, and as David points out, p. 630n, is entirely credible. With 55 ships, it would give an average of 64 men per vessel.

war against the Saracens, living however according to the Rule.[42] Then there were the knights from the Cistercian Order, who have this indulgence: that they may eat meat three times a week, but only once a day and one dish while they are in their house, but while on a military expedition they may eat like other men. Their headquarters are at Calatrava in the kingdom of Castile and at Evora in the kingdom of Portugal, but Calatrava is the mother house and Evora the daughter.[43] Some of those from Jerusalem were from the Temple, some from the Holy Sepulchre and some from the Hospital; and each has an income in that land.[44]

Once the city was captured only we Franks held it, and nobody else was allowed entry. All the movable property belonged to us, as in our original agreement, but since the Portuguese were incessantly badgering us about the division we gave part to them, to be allocated according to the judgement of the king. Once the city was taken, the king then strove to secure the grain from us for his share, this being more abundant and of greater value than anything else. Although we had forbidden anything to be taken out of the city, so that we could divide up the booty inside, some of our men, and particularly the Flemings, secretly sold wheat outside the walls to the Portuguese. The king was greatly angered by this – indeed he claimed that it would have been better not to have captured the city than to lose it through lack of bread; and in the commotion our men carried off the plunder before the division between the Portuguese and ourselves was made, acting without the permission of our leaders and against the terms of the agreement. Hence, to avoid the king's threats escalating into damaging disputes, we surrendered the city to him while it was still full of wealth, requesting him, as was proper for his royal majesty, to share it with us, having consideration both for our hard work and for our losses. The king, however, took it all for himself and distributed nothing to

---

[42]   The reference was to Templar *confratres*, rather than full brothers of the order; for these *The Rule of the Templars,* translated J.M. Upton-Ward (Woodbridge 1992), p. 36, c. 69.

[43]   The indulgence with regard to eating meat, on Wednesdays, Fridays and Sundays, was granted by Alexander III in his bull confirming the foundation of the Order of Calatrava in September 1164, *Patrologia Latina* 200, cols. 310–12 no. 273, addressed to 'the brothers of the Order of Calatrava living according to the Rule of the Cistercians'. For the role of the Cistercians in the creation of the order, see especially Joseph O'Callaghan, 'The affiliation of the Order of Calatrava with the Order of Cîteaux', *Analecta Sacri Ordinis Cisterciencis* 15 (1959), 161–93, especially 178–91 [reprinted in J. O'Callaghan, *The Spanish Military Order of Calatrava and its Affiliates* (London 1975)]. The suborder of Evora was later known as the Order of Avis.

[44]   The Holy Sepulchre never possessed a military order of its own, although it was often bracketed with the Templars and Hospitallers, as in the will of Alfonso I of Aragon in 1131 (for which Elena Lourie, 'The will of Alfonso I, "el Batallador", king of Aragon and Navarre: a reassessment', *Speculum* 50 (1975), 635–51). The author would thus seem to have been correct in his earlier statement, that members of three military monastic orders were present: the Temple, the Hospital and the Order of Calatrava and its Portuguese subsidiary.

us. Thus the pilgrims who had been so badly treated took their leave of him in a less than friendly fashion. Moreover, before the city was captured he had, on our urging, vowed the tenth part of all its land to the Holy Sepulchre, in order to compensate the latter through this gift for our delay in serving it; but after the taking of the city he did not fulfil his vow.[45]

On the Vigil of the Virgin Mary we took ship, and slowly went [downriver] towards the sea.[46] The king remained there for six days arranging matters, garrisoning the city with many knights and appointing the leader of his troops [as governor], then he returned home. We made some delay at the port, both for the division of the spoils and to repair two of our ships that had been damaged. Meanwhile the prince of the royal forces appointed a Flemish cleric to the bishopric of Silves, and some of the Flemings remained there with him.[47] He also requested, through the bishop, that the pilgrims accompany him to go to besiege a town one day's march away, which both pagans and Christians called St Maria de Faro, but he was unable to secure general agreement to that.

These are the castles that Christianity recovered through the acquisition of Silves: Carphanabel,[48] Lagos, Alvor, Portimão, Monchique, Montegudo, Carvoeiro, São Bartolomeu de Mussiene, and Paderne. All these were subject to the lordship of Silves, and we left them utterly deserted, although strong and well built. Some of their inhabitants had been slain by those who went before us at Alvor, but the greater part had fled to Silves. Albufeira surrendered itself to the king for fear of us: he brought what was of value there to Silves. Note that it is seven days' journey from Silves to Lisbon, and between these two places there had been no safe habitation for either Christians or Saracens, because of the raids of both sides, but now the Christians were able to live safely in this most fortunate land for as long as they possessed Silves. And one should note that eight days after the surrender of the city the greater part of the wall that our men had undermined, and where the Saracens had fought with our miners, collapsed.

We left the port of Silves on the vigil of St Matthew,[49] leaving St Maria de Faro and Tavira on our left. On St Maurice's day[50] we arrived at the Guadalquivir, which

---

[45]　For the growing tensions between northern Crusaders and the Portuguese, Stephen Lay, 'Miracles, martyrs and the cult of Henry the Crusader in Lisbon', *Portuguese Studies* 24 (2008), 7–31, especially 22–9. Lay discusses this passage on pp. 22–3; my translation differs somewhat from his.

[46]　7 September.

[47]　According to Ralph of Diceto, *Opera*, ii.66, the main mosque of Silves was converted to become the cathedral, and dedicated to the BVM, on the feast of her nativity (8 September). Ralph confirms the appointment of the Fleming as bishop; subsequent documents show his name to have been Nicholas.

[48]　David, p. 633n, suggests that this name, otherwise unidentified, may refer to Cape St Vincent.

[49]　20 September.

[50]　22 September.

flows through Seville. Seville is a very large and most wealthy city, two days from the sea. Cordoba is located three days from Seville on this same river. It is ... days from Silves to the River Guadiana,[51] and there are these towns which have cultivatable land: Faro, Loulé, Cacela, Tavira, Mértola and Serpa, which we might have taken with ease, and we would have left that land, which was called the Algarve,[52] entirely in the hands of the Christians, if the hatred of the king and the accursed haste of some of our men had not prevented this. From the Guadiana to Seville, two days' journey, the land is totally infertile and deserted. There is however one town on the seacoast, named Saltes, but for fear of the pilgrims the inhabitants abandoned it and fled to the mountains, to a castle called Huelva, which is on the road leading inland from the Guadiana to Seville, on which there are also the strong fortresses of Niebla and *Fealcazar*.[53] From Seville on the road towards the Straits are the towns of Jerez, Rota, Cadiz and Algeciras. From the Guadalquivir to Tarifa, which is the town next to the head of the Straits, it is a day and a half. On the right beyond the sea we left behind us Africa, a very good but flat land, [leading] to the Straits. The first town which occurs [there] is Fedala, which is opposite St Maria de Faro; then there is *Labu*,[54] Anaphe,[55] Salé, Azemmur, Masina, Arzila and Tangier, which is at the head of the Straits. Marrakesh, the metropolis of Africa, is in that flat land, but five days' distance from the sea. From the head of the Straits towards the interior begin the high mountains, and that mountainous land is called Ghomāra or Barbary, and it continues to Mecca where Muhammad is buried.

It should be known that, suffering endless problems with the winds, we were tossed about at sea for a long time. We were finally forced by the violence of the winds to make land at Cadiz, for the wind was blowing very strongly from the east. The inhabitants had deserted the town after certain Saracens who had been besieged at Silves had come to them after the fall of the city, making them even more afraid of us. However, the prefect of the town brought presents to us, begging that we spare the place, and he promised that next day he would surrender to us twelve Christian captives and as much money as he could raise. On the appointed day he produced only four prisoners, and he seemed to be putting forward spurious reasons for the delay in releasing the others. Although our men allowed him to depart unharmed – this was on the feast of saints Cosmas and Damian[56] – they then burned the houses, destroyed the walls, cut down the vines and fig trees, and that day they did everything they could to destroy the city.

---

[51]   The numeral has been omitted in the manuscript.

[52]   From the Arabic *al-Gharb*, 'the west'.

[53]   Not securely identified, but perhaps Aznalcázar, 24 km southwest of Seville.

[54]   Unidentified; perhaps the Wadi Sebu, a river that enters the Atlantic at al-Mahdīya, 28 km north of Rabat, but the sense suggests a town rather than a river.

[55]   Now Casablanca.

[56]   27 September.

Cadiz was an extremely wealthy town, inhabited only by merchants, sited on an island which is separated from the land by an arm of the *al-Bahr* sea. There is another small island, which is linked to the other by a narrow causeway in the sea leading to the town.[57] The town had five forts, each free-standing, with walls and towers, and most pleasant dwelling places; and Saracens from both Africa and Spain customarily went there three times a year for the exchange of merchandise, since it was more or less in between the two.

The following night we set off, but no sooner were the sails unfurled than we were hindered by adverse winds, and as sailors customarily do we skilfully avoided the contrary wind by sailing in a different direction. Thus we crossed over to the southern shore of the Straits on the feast of St Michael.[58] But since the greater part of the fleet was still struggling against the wind, we put in to Tarifa, anchored there and planned to attack the town. All those who were following did the same as we did. We saw many horsemen and infantry on shore who were ready to defend the coast, while the women fled to the mountains. Our men armed themselves and entered the skiffs. But since not everybody was agreed about the attack, and particularly since a great storm had blown up, while we were [still] waiting for three ships which were lagging a long way behind, we raised anchors and set sail on the evening of the same day, and went through the Straits, from which we could see high mountains on either side.

Opposite Tarifa on the other side of the sea is Cacir Mucemuthe, and between these two castles lies the usual crossing from Africa to Spain and vice versa. The Straits have a width of two of our miles and are six in length, so far as we were able to calculate.[59] On the following day at the [eastern] end of the Straits we left behind on our right a most opulent city of Barbary, to which all the Christian merchants come bringing their trade goods, and in particular the Genoese and Pisans frequent this place.[60] The berths for the galleys of the King of Morocco are also there. Also, on the left at the narrowest point of the crossing we passed by Algeciras, a good town, and the castle of Gibraltar.

Then we entered the wide expanse of the sea, and we passed at speed on our left these cities: Malaga, Almuñécar, Almería, Cartagena, Alicante, Denia, Valencia, Burriana, Oropesa and Peñíscola. Near *Betaienia* is Murcia.[61] And it should be known that this is a very long journey, which we only accomplished through five

---

[57]   Medieval Cadiz was on the island of Léon, with the smaller island later known as San Pedro at the southern end. *Al-Bahr* ('the sea') was the Arabic term for the Mediterranean, which was considered to begin at Cadiz.

[58]   29 September.

[59]   The author was once again using the long German mile, for which above note 16. *Cacir Mucemuthe* was the author's phonetic version of *Kasr Masmūda* (al-Kasr al-Saghīr), which under the Almohads was the chief embarkation port for Spain.

[60]   This must be Ceuta.

[61]   The identification of *Betaienia* is questionable. David, p. 641n, mentioned two possibilities, neither of which he found very convincing, that it referred either to Beniajan,

days and five nights of continuous and very fast sailing. It should be known that we saw nothing except very high cliffs.

On crossing the sea, one first encounters flat land, and then in a brief space of time Evora and the Ebro, a very broad and important river flowing into the sea, on which is sited *Corduba* [?] [and?] Tortosa,[62] which lies towards the mountains, two of our miles from the sea. This city first became Christian when it was captured by the Pisans and Genoese, at the same time as Lisbon was captured by our men.[63] Catalonia begins here, a most fertile land, distinguished by innumerable castles. Tarragona is a day's journey away from Tortosa: it was once a great city but is now small, although it has an archiepiscopal see of great rank. Then, a further day away is Barcelona, which is the capital of the county of Catalonia, and from there it is six days to Narbonne, then two to Montpellier, and three more to Marseilles. And it should be noted that afterwards we saw in Marseilles and Montpellier merchants who had been in the cities of the Saracens as we passed by, and they saw us and said that all the Saracens were so frightened by our passage that they would not have defended any of their cities had we approached them, but were rather preparing themselves for flight.

---

a village to the east of Murcia, or to the Wādi'l-abyad ('the White River') or River Segura, on which Murcia stands.

[62] The reading *Corduba* is uncertain. The author was well aware that Cordoba was in southern Spain on the Guadalquivir. This may refer either, as David suggests, to an alternative name for Tortosa, or as Chroust, *Quellen*, p. 196, believed, the island of Buda at the mouth of the Ebro.

[63] It was captured by the Genoese and Count Raymond Berenguer IV of Barcelona in December 1148. See *Annali Genovesi di Caffaro e de'suoi continuatori,* i, ed. L.T. Belgrano (Fonti per la storia d'Italia, Rome 1890), 86–9. Tortosa lies about 20 km from the mouth of the Ebro.

Frederick I's Imperial 'Land Peace' (issued at Nuremberg, 29 December 1188)

This edict survives in a number of copies, two of them written very soon after it was promulgated, and in addition it is quoted verbatim in the early thirteenth-century chronicle of Burchard of Ursberg.[1]

Frederick by the grace of God Emperor of the Romans and always Augustus.

First, therefore, we make a general proclamation concerning arsonists; that if a free man, freedman, *ministerialis*, or person of any condition whatsoever that may be, commits arson, in a conflict [*werra*] of his own, for a friend, relation or for whatever other reason, he shall immediately be held subject to the judgement of imperial outlawry. Here shall be excluded those who capture castles openly in a declared war, and if they burn here a suburb or stable or other building lying nearby. And judges are excluded who happen to exercise the penalty of burning against malefactors owing to the requirements of justice.

If anybody should commit arson in the duchy of any person, the latter shall pronounce him outlaw and then shall render justice to him as an outlaw by his own authority. Margraves, palatine counts, landgraves and other counts shall do the same; nor shall it be permitted to any of them to absolve such a person, with the exception of the lord emperor. In addition, whosoever knowingly receives an incendiary in their home, and renders help and advice to them, shall make restitution for the injury that has been caused, according to his means. He shall pay to the judge and to the lord emperor ten pounds, in the money of the district in which the arson was committed, to recover his grace. If however anyone wishes to prove or show himself to be innocent of this crime, he shall purge himself with [the help of] two truthful men in the presence of a judge. If anyone shall have charged somebody that he has received an incendiary, and then shall wish to lodge a complaint against someone else, then this shall not be permitted to him unless he has first sworn the oath concerning calumny. In addition, the lord emperor shall not absolve any outlaw from his sentence of outlawry unless this person has first made recompense to the injured party for the damages, and unless this is done with the agreement of the judge.

---

[1] *Burchardi Praepositi Urspergensis Chronicon*, ed. O. Holder-Egger and B. von Simson (MGH SRG, Hanover 1916), pp. 65–9. Also in *Die Urkunden Friedrichs I (1180–90)*, ed. H. Appelt (MGH Diplomatum Regum et Imperatorum Germaniae, x(4), Hannover 1990), 275–7 no. 988, from which this translation has been made.

An outlaw who has incurred this sentence of outlawry for arson shall be notorious to everyone. If he refuses to make satisfaction, the diocesan bishop shall cast him out from the communion of the Church of God and from the faithful of Christ; and he shall render him outcast. Nor shall he absolve him until he has made restitution for the damage [he has done]. And conversely, if a bishop shall have excommunicated someone, after citing them in the proper form and in accordance with justice, and he has informed a judge of this, the judge shall condemn him with a declaration (*bannum*) of outlawry, nor shall he free him from this until he makes satisfaction in the bishop's presence for those things for which he was found guilty.

But if he shall be freed from his outlawry in the aforesaid way and wishes to be obedient to his bishop, he shall first abjure arson. Then it shall be up to the judgement of the bishop what penalty he imposes upon him, either of visiting the Lord's Sepulchre or the abode of St James the Apostle.[2] If however the outlaw shall desire to be freed [from his outlawry] in the way that has been described, he shall swear to the lord emperor to depart the bounds of his empire for a year and a day.

If anyone has not been absolved from both his outlawry and his excommunication within a year and a day, he shall be deprived of all right, honour and legal status; he shall never be admitted to give evidence or plead in court concerning another person, and he shall be deprived in perpetuity of all feudal right (*omni feodali iure*).

Item, if, during a military expedition (*reisa*) by any lord, there shall be anybody who, with this same lord whose expedition this is, commits arson, as often happens, that lord whose expedition this is shall swear, over relics, that this was not done through his knowledge, will or instruction; he shall abjure the crime and the man shall never be received by him [henceforth]. But if he then receives the man before the latter has made satisfaction, he shall be held responsible for making restitution for all the damage that his man has committed.

Item, if it shall happen that a lord takes lodgings by force in a village, and by chance it occurs that a house is burned, and he to whom the damage shall be done, accuses the lord that what took place did so on his order or wish, let him first take the oath concerning calumny. Then the lord shall purge himself, on his own recognition, that what happened was not done through his wish, order or with his knowledge, and he shall make good the damage to the injured party.

Item, if an incendiary shall be captured, and wishes to deny in the presence of a judge that he has committed arson, unless he shall be notorious throughout the province, the judge shall only sentence him to the loss of his head if he can convict him with seven suitable witnesses. But if he is notorious no further testimony is required, and he should immediately be beheaded.

Item, if the castellans of any lord coming down from the castle of their lord shall start a fire, while their lord is absent from the province, the castle of the lord

---

2   Santiago di Compostella, in northwest Spain.

shall not be burned down because of this, but the goods of the arsonists shall be burned, wherever they shall be found outside the castle. After the return of the lord, if that lord shall wish to retain the arsonist and not dismiss him, then his castle shall similarly be burned down.

Item, if somebody who has been outlawed for arson shall flee to any house from which he cannot be taken unless the house is burned down, nobody shall be deemed to be guilty of arson on account of this fire, but the perpetrator shall make restitution for the fire.

Item, if an arsonist shall flee in panic to a castle and to the lord of that castle, who shall be either his lord, his vassal or blood relation, that lord need not hand him over to those who are pursuing him, but shall help him to go from the castle into a forest or to some other place where he shall seemingly be safe. However, if he shall be neither lord, nor vassal nor relation, then he shall immediately hand him over to his pursuers, or he shall share the same guilt with him.

We also decree and we firmly sanction by this same edict that whoever intends to bring harm to somebody else, or to injure that same person, should announce this to them by a reliable messenger, giving at least three days' warning. But if the injured party wishes to deny that he has been warned, this same messenger, if he is still alive, shall at a designated time and place make an oath to the contrary, on behalf of his lord. If the envoy is dead, the lord shall swear to the contrary, accompanied by two truthful men, to avoid being subject to the penalty for breaking faith.

We add [further] sanctions to these: that whosoever shall have given a truce to anyone, unless there is an exception and limitation, by which its observance shall be qualified or it shall not be valid, cannot ever proclaim its end before the specified date of termination. If he should do this, he shall be judged as a breaker of faith.

Item, whoever shall harm any messenger to him that is sent to proclaim defiance shall breach his faith, and he shall forfeit all the rest of his *honor*,[3] and in future nobody shall proclaim their defiance to him.

We decree that the sons of priests, deacons and peasants shall not in any way assume the belt of knighthood, and those who have already assumed it shall be expelled from knightly rank by the judge of the province. And if any lord of these people shall have attempted to retain a person in knightly rank against the prohibition of a judge, that lord shall be condemned to a fine of 10 pounds [payable] to the judge, while the serf shall be deprived of all right to knighthood.

---

[3]   This ambiguous word could have a wide range of meanings, including 'lordship' or 'property', but also 'right', 'privileges', 'social rank', or indeed 'honour/reputation', see J.F. Niermayer, *Mediae Latinitatis Lexicon Minus*, ed. C. Van der Kieft (Leiden 2001), pp. 495–8. Here it would seem to have the implication of rank or status, and law-worthiness, while in the *History of the Pilgrims* it was used, for example, as 'mark of respect', *Quellen*, p. 128 [above p. 146].

Item, if any count shall appoint deputy judges, he shall pay 30 pounds to the emperor and the deputy judge shall pay 10 pounds.

We also decree that, if anyone shall cut down vines or apple trees, he shall be subject to the outlawry and excommunication applicable to arsonists.

That however this so serviceable ordinance shall remain valid for all time and shall remain inviolate for the purpose for which it has been issued, we order that it be included among the laws of our predecessors the emperors and kings and be preserved [there] in perpetuity. If anyone should presume to dare to act contrary to it, their penalty shall be the wrath of Almighty God and of us in perpetuity. Fiat, fiat, Amen.

Done in Nuremberg, in the presence of our princes and by their advice and counsel, in the year from the Incarnation of the Lord 1187 [*sic*], sixth of the indiction, 29 December.[4]

---

[4]   The date of this edict has been debated, but the indiction number would fit with 1188, and Frederick is known to have been in Nuremberg at the end of that year. Furthermore Burchard of Ursberg states that this was promulgated after Frederick had taken the Cross, which he did in March 1188.

Bibliography

Primary Sources

[*Die*] *Admonter Briefsammlung*, ed. Gunther Hödel & Peter Classen (MGH Die Briefen der deutschen Kaiserzeit vi, Munich 1983).

Albert of Aachen, *Historia Ierosolimitana*, ed. Susan B. Edgington (Oxford 2007).

Annales Casinenses, MGH SS xix.303–20.

Annales Magdeburgenses, ed. Georg Heinrich Pertz, MGH SS xvi.105–96.

Annales Mellicenses, ed. Wilhem Wattenbach, MGH SS ix.479–535.

Annales Marbacenses qui dicuntur, ed. Hermann Bloch (MGH SRG, Hanover 1907).

Annales Pegavienses, ed. G.H. Pertz, MGH SS xvi.232–70.

Annales Reicherspergenses, and *Chronicon Magni Presbiteri*, ed. Wilhelm Wattenbach, MGH SS xvii.439–76, 476–523.

Annales Stadenses, ed. Johannes M. Lappenberg, MGH SS xvi.271–379.

Annales Stederbergenses, ed. G.H. Pertz, MGH SS xvi.197–231.

Annali Genovesi di Caffaro e de' suoi continuatori, i, ed. L.T. Belgrano (Fonti per la storia d'Italia, Rome 1890).

Arnoldi Chronica Slavorum, ed. Johannes M. Lappenberg (MGH SRG, Hanover 1868).

Burchardi Praepositi Urspergensis Chronicon, ed. Oswald Holder-Egger & Bernhard von Simson (MGH SRG, Hanover 1916)

Chronica Regia Coloniensis, ed. Georg Waitz (MGH SRG, Hanover 1880).

[*The*] *Chronicle of Ibn al-Athīr for the Crusading Period, from al-Kāmil fi'l-ta'rīkh, Part 2, The Years 541–589/1146–1193: The Age of Nur al-Din and Saladin*, translated by D.S. Richards (Crusader Texts in translation 15: Aldershot 2007).

Chronicle of the Third Crusade. A Translation of the Itinerarium Peregrinorum et Gesta Regis Ricardi, translated by Helen J. Nicholson (Crusader Texts in Translation 3: Aldershot 1997).

Chronicon Fratris Salimbene de Adam, ed. Oswald Holder-Egger (MGH SS xxii, Hanover 1905–13).

Chronicon Montis Sereni, ed. Ernst Ehrenfeuchter, MGH SS xxiii.130–226.

Le Chronique de Gislebert de Mons, ed. Leon Vanderkindere (Brussels 1904)

[English translation, Gilbert of Mons, *The Chronicle of Hainault*, translated by Laura Napran (Woodbridge 2005)].

D.R. Clementi, 'Calendar of the diplomas of the Hohenstaufen Emperor Henry VI concerning the kingdom of Sicily', *Quellen und Forschungen aus italienischen Archiven und Bibliotheken* 35 (1955), 86–225.

[*The*] *Conquest of Jerusalem and the Third Crusade*, trans. Peter W. Edbury (Crusader Texts in Translation 1, Aldershot 1996).

Continuatio Gerlaci Abbatis Milovicensis [to the Annals of Vincent of Prague] *1167–98*, MGH SS xvii.683–710.

Continuatio Zwetlensis Altera, MGH SS ix.541–4.

Cronica Reinhardsbrunnensis, ed. Oswald Holder-Egger, MGH SS xxx(1).490–658.

[*The*] *Crusades. Idea and Reality 1095–1274*, translated by Louise and Jonathan Riley-Smith (London 1981).

De Expugnatione Lyxbonensi, ed. C.W. David (New York 1936)

De Expugnatione Terrae Sanctae per Saladinum, in Ralph of Coggeshall, *Chronicon Anglicanum*, ed. J. Stevenson (Rolls Series, London 1875), pp. 209–62.

Geoffrey Malaterra, *De Rebus Gestis Rogerii Comitis Siciliae et Calabriae*, ed. E. Pontieri (Rerum Italicarum Scriptores, 2nd. ed., Bologna 1927–8).

Germania Sacra iii(3), ed. Albert Brackmann (Berlin 1935).

Germania Sacra ix(3), ed. Theodor Schieffer (Göttingen 2002).

[*Das*] *Geschichtswerk des Otto Morena und seiner Fortsetzer*, ed. Ferdinand Güterbock (MGH SRG, Berlin 1930).

Gesta Episcoporum Leodensium, ed. J. Heller, MGH SS xxv.1–129.

Gesta Federici I. Imperatoris in Expeditione Sacra, in *Gesta Federici I. Imperatoris in Lombardia*, ed. Oswald Holder-Egger (MGH SRG, Hanover 1892), pp. 74–98.

Gesta Francorum et aliorum Hierosolimitanorum, ed. Rosalind Hill (London 1956).

Historia Ducum Veneticorum, MGH SS xiv.72–97.

Itinerarium Peregrinorum, in Hans Eberhard Mayer, *Das Itinerarium Peregrinorum. Eine zeitgenössiche englische Chronik zum dritten Kreuzzug in ursprünglicher Gestalt* (MGH Schriften 18: Stuttgart 1962), pp. 243–357.

[*Die*] *Jüngere Hildesheimer Briefsammlung*, ed. Rolf de Kegel (MGH Die Briefen der deutschen Kaiserzeit vii, Munich 1995).

[*The*] *Letters of St Bernard of Clairvaux*, translated Bruno Scott James (London 1953).

Mainzer Urkundenbuch ii *Die Urkunden seit dem Tode Erzbischof Adalberts I (1137) bis zum Tode Erzbischofs Konrads (1200), Teil II, 1176–1200*, ed. Peter Acht (Darmstadt 1978).

Monumenta Erphesfurtensia, Saec. XII, XIII, XIV, ed. Oswald Holder-Egger (MGH SRG, Hanover 1899).

Narratio de Itinere Navali Peregrinorum Hierosolymam Tendentium et Silviam Capientium, ed. Charles Wendell David, in *Proceedings of the American Philosophical Society* 81 (1939), 591–676.

Necrologia Germania (MGH), i *Dioceses Augustensis, Constantiensis, Curiensis*, ed. Ludwig Baumann (Berlin 1886–8), ii *Dioecesis Salisburgensis*, ed. S. Herzberg-Fränkel (Berlin 1904), v *Diocesis Pataviensis, Austria Inferior*, ed. Adalbert Fuchs (Berlin 1913).

O City of Byzantium: Annals of Niketas Choniates, translated H.P. Magoulias (Detroit 1984).

Ottonian Germany: The Chronicon of Thietmar of Merseburg, translated David A. Warner (Manchester 2001).

Ottonis Episcopi Frisingensis Chronice sive Historia de Duabus Civitatibus, ed. Adolf Hofmeister (MGH SRG, Hanover 1912).

Ottonis et Rahewini Gesta Friderici I. Imperatoris, ed. Georg Waitz and Bernard von Simson (3rd. ed., MGH SRG, Hanover 1912).

[English translation, *The Deeds of Frederick Barbarossa by Otto of Freising and his Continuator Rahewin*, trans. C.C. Mierow (New York 1953)].

Ottonis Sancto Blasio Chronica, ed. Adolf Hofmeister (MGH SRG, Hanover 1912).

[*Die Chronik*] *Ottos von St. Blasien und die Marbacher Annalen*, ed. F-J. Schmale (Ausgewählte Quellen zur Deutschen Geschichte des Mittelalters 17, Darmstadt 1998).

Quellen zur deutschen Verfassungs-, Wirtschafts- und Sozialgeschichte bis 1250, ed. L. Weinrich (Darmstadt 1977).

Quellen zur Geschichte des Kreuzzuges Kaiser Friedrichs I., ed. Anton Chroust (MGH SRG, n.s. V, Berlin 1928; reprint Munich 1989).

Ralph of Diceto, *Opera Historica*, ed. W. Stubbs (2 vols., Rolls Series, London 1876).

[*The*] *Rare and Excellent History of Saladin*, translated by D.S. Richards (Crusader Texts in Translation 7: Aldershot 2002).

[*Die*] *Regesten der Bischöfe von Passau* i *731–1206*, ed. Egon Boshof and Franz-Reiner Erkens (Munich 1992).

Regesten der Bischöfe von Strassburg i *Bis zu Jahre 1202*, ed. Paul Wentzcke (Innsbruck 1908).

[*Die*] *Regesten des Kaiserreiches unter Heinrich VI. 1165–(1190)–1197*, ed. Gerhard Baaken, after J.F. Böhmer (Regesta Imperii IV(3), Cologne 1972).

Regestum Innocentii III Papae super Negotio Romani Imperii, ed. Friedrich Kempf (Rome 1947).

[*Die*] *Register Innocenz' III 5 Pontifikatsjahr 1202/3*, ed. O. Hageneder et alii (Vienna 1993).

Richard of S. Germano, *Chronicon*, ed. C.A. Garufi (Rerum Italicarum Scriptores, Bologna 1938).

Roger of Howden, *Gesta Regis Henrici Secundi*, ed. William Stubbs (2 vols., Rolls Series, London 1867) [although Stubbs ascribed this work to 'Benedict of Peterborough', Howden's authorship is now proven].

The Rule of the Templars, translated J.M. Upton-Ward (Woodbridge 1992).

Die Traditionsbücher des Benediktinerstiftes Göttweig, ed. Adalbert Fuchs (Fontes Rerum Austriacum, 2 Abteilung Diplomataria et Acta 69, Vienna 1931).

[*Die*] *Traditionen des Hochstifts Passau*, ed. Max Heuwisser (Quellen und Erörterungen zur Bayerischen Geschichte 6, Munich 1930).

[*Die*] *Urkunden Friedrichs I*, ed. Heinrich Appelt (5 vols., M.G.H. Diplomatum Regum et Imperatorum Germaniae, x, Hannover 1975–90).

Die Urkunden Friedrichs II. 1212–1217, ed. Walter Koch (MGH Diplomata Regum et Imperatorum Germaniae xiv(2), Hannover 2007).

[*Die*] *Urkunden Heinrichs des Löwen, Herzogs von Sachsen und Bayern*, ed. Karl Jordan (MGH, Weimar 1949).

[*Die*] *Urkunden Konrads III. und seiner Sohnes Heinrich*, ed. F. Hausmann (M.G.H. Diplomatum Regum et Imperatorum Germaniae, ix, Vienna 1969).

Urkundenbuch des Hochstifts Hildesheim und seiner Bischöfe i *Bis 1221*, ed. K. Janicke (Leipzig 1896).

Urkundenbuch des Landes ob der Enns, ii, ed. Erich Trinks (Vienna 1856).

Urkundenbuch für die Geschichte des Niederrheins, ed. Theodor J. Lacomblet (4 vols., Düsseldorf 1840–58).

Urkundenbuch zur Geschichte der Babenberger in Österreich, iv *Ergänzende Quellen 976–1194*, ed. Heinrich Fichtenau and Heide Dienst (Vienna and Munich 1997).

William of Newburgh, *Historia Regum Anglorum*, in *Chronicles of the Reigns of Stephen, Henry II and Richard I*, ed. R. Howlett (4 vols., Rolls Series, London 1884–90), i.1–408, ii.409–500.

Willibrand of Oldenburg, *Itinerarium Terra Sanctae*, in *Itinera Hierosolymitana Crucesignatorum (saec. xii–xiii)*, ed. Sabino de Sandoli (4 vols., Jerusalem 1978–85), iii.195–249.

Württembergisches Urkundenbuch, ii (Stuttgart 1858).

Secondary Literature

Michael Angold, *Church and Society in Byzantium under the Comneni 1081–1261* (Cambridge 1995).

Benjamin Arnold, 'German bishops and their military retinues in the medieval Empire', *German History* 7 (1989), 161–83.

Benjamin Arnold, *Princes and Territories in Medieval Germany* (Cambridge 1991).

Erwin Assmann, ,Friedrich Barbarossas Kinder', *Deutsches Archiv für Erforschung des Mittelalters* 33 (1977), 435–72.

Malcolm Barber, *The New Knighthood. A History of the Order of the Temple* (Cambridge 1994).

T.S.R. Boase, *The Cilician Kingdom of Armenia* (Edinburgh 1978).

Karl Bosl, *Der Reichsministerialät der Salier und Staufer* (MGH Schriften 10: Stuttgart 1951).

Charles M. Brand, 'The Byzantines and Saladin: opponents of the Third Crusade', *Speculum* xxxvii (1962), 167–181.

Charles M. Brand, *Byzantium Confronts the West 1180–1204* (Cambridge, MA, 1968).

Claude Cahen, *Pre-Ottoman Turkey* (London 1968).

Claude Cahen, *The Formation of Turkey. The Seljukid Sultanate of Rum: Eleventh to Fourteenth Century*, translated by Peter M. Holt (Harlow 2001).

Henry Chadwick, *East and West: the Making of a Rift within the Church, from Apostolic Times until the Council of Florence* (Oxford 2003).

Robert Chazan, 'Emperor Frederick I, the Third Crusade and the Jews', *Viator* 8 (1977), 83–93.

Franck Collard, '*Timeas Danaos et dona ferentes*. Remarques à propos d'un épisode méconnu de la troisième croisade', in *Chemins d'Outre-Mer. Études sur la Méditerranée médiévale offertes à Michel Balard* (2 vols., Paris 2004), i.139–47.

Yves Congar, 'Henri de Marcy, abbé de Clairvaux, cardinal-évêque d'Albano et légat pontifical', *Analecta Monastica* v (*Studia Anselmiana*, fasc. 43, Rome 1958), 1–90.

Peter Csendes, *Heinrich VI* (Darmstadt 1993).

Gérard Dédéyan, 'De la prise de Thessalonique par les Normands (1185) á la croisade de Frédéric Barbarousse (1189–90) : le revirement politico-religieux des pouvoirs arméniens', in *Chemins d'Outre-Mer. Études sur la Méditerranée médiévale offertes à Michel Balard*, i.183–96.

Ekkehard Eickhoff, *Friedrich Barbarossa im Orient: Kreuzzug und Tod Friedrichs I.* (Tübingen 1977).

Josef Fleckenstein, 'Friedrich Barbarossa und das Rittertum: zur Bedeutung der großen Mainzer Hoftage von 1184 und 1188', in *Festschrift für Heinrich Heimpel zum 70. Geburtstag 1971* (3 vols., Göttingen 1972), ii.1023–41.

J.B. Freed, *The Counts of Falkenstein. Noble Self-Consciousness in Twelfth-Century Germany* (Transactions of the American Philosophical Society 74(6), Philadelphia 1984).

John Gillingham, 'The kidnapped king: Richard I in Germany, 1192–4', *Bulletin of the German Historical Institute, London*, 30 (2008), 5–34.

F. Güterbock, 'Il Diario di Tageno e altre fonti della terza crociata', *Bullettino dell'istituto storico italiano per ile medio evo* 55 (1941), 223–75.

John Haldon, 'Roads and communications in the Byzantine Empire: wagons, horses and supplies', in *Logistics of Warfare in the Age of the Crusades*, ed. John Pryor (Aldershot 2006), 131–58.

Bernard Hamilton, '"The Elephant of Christ", Reynald of Chatillon', *Studies in Church History* 15 (1978), 97–108.

Bernard Hamilton, *The Leper King and his Heirs. Baldwin IV and the Crusader Kingdom of Jerusalem* (Cambridge 2000).

Jonathan Harris, *Byzantium and the Crusades* (London 2003).

Eva Haverkamp, 'What did the Christians know? Latin reports of the persecution of the Jews in 1096', *Crusades* 7 (2008), 59–86.

Peter Herde, 'Das staufische Zeitalter', in *Unterfränkische Geschichte* i *Von der germanischen Landnahme bis zum hohen Mittelater*, ed. Peter Kolb and Ernst-Günter Krenig (Würzburg 1989), 333–66.

Peter Herde, 'Die Katastrophe vor Rom im August 1167. Eine historisch-epidemioligische Studie zum vierten Italienzug Friedrichs I. Barbarossa', *Sitzungsberichte der wissenschaftlichen Gesellschaft an der Johann-Wolfgang-Goethe-Universität Frankfurt am Main* 26 (1991), 139–66.

Rudolf Hiestand, ,Precipua tocius christianismi columpna: Barbarossa und die Kreuzzug', in *Friedrich Barbarossa: Handlungspielräume und Wirkungsweisen des staufischen Kaisers*, ed. A. Haverkamp (Vorträge und Forschungen 40: Sigmaringen 1992), pp. 51–108.

Rudolf Hiestand, ,Antiocha, Sizilien und das Reich am Ende des 12. Jahrhunderts', *Quellen und Forschungen aus italienischen Archiven und Bibliotheken* 73 (1993), 70–121.

Rudolf Hiestand, 'Kingship and Crusade in twelfth-century Germany', in *England and Germany in the High Middle Ages: in honour of Karl J. Leyser*, ed. Alfred Haverkamp & Hanna Vollrath (Oxford 1996), pp. 236–65.

Hubert Houben, 'Philipp von Heinsberg, Heinrich VI und Montecassino. Mit einen Exkurs zum Todesdatum Papst Clemens' III', *Quellen und Forschungen aus Italienischen Archiven und Bibliotheken* 68 (1988), 52–73.

B.U. Hucker, *Kaiser Otto IV* (MGH Schriften 34: Hanover 1990).

Evelyn M. Jamison, *Admiral Eugenius of Sicily. His Life and Work* (London 1957).

Edgar N. Johnson, 'The Crusades of Frederick Barbarossa and Henry VI', in *A History of the Crusades*, ed. Kenneth Setton, ii *The Later Crusades, 1189–1311*, ed. R.L. Wolff and H.W. Hazard (Madison 1969), 87–122.

Karl Jordan, *Henry the Lion* (Oxford 1986).

Hugh Kennedy, *Crusader Castles* (Cambridge 1994).

Jan Keup, 'Reichsministerialen und Bischofsmord in staufischer Zeit', in *Bischofsmord im Mittelalter*, ed. Natalie Fryde and Dirk Reitz (Göttingen 2003), pp. 273–302.

Thomas R. Kraus, ,Studien zur Frühgeschichte der Grafschaft von Kleves und die Enstehung der rheinische Landesherrschaft', *Rheinische Vierteljahrsblätter* 46 (1982), 1–47.

Karl-Friedrich Krieger, 'Obligatory military service and the use of mercenaries in imperial military campaigns under the Hohenstaufen Emperors', in *England and Germany in the Middle Ages: in honour of Karl J. Leyser*, ed. Alfred Haverkamp & Hanna Vollrath (Oxford 1996), pp. 151–68.

Stephen Lay, 'Miracles, martyrs and the cult of Henry the Crusader in Lisbon', *Portuguese Studies* 24 (2008), 7–31.

Karl Lechner, *Die Babenberger. Markgrafen und Herzoge von Österreich* (6th ed., Vienna 1996).

Karl Leyser, 'Frederick Barbarossa and the Hohenstaufen polity', *Viator* 19 (1988), 153–76 [reprinted in K.J. Leyser, *Communications and Power in Medieval Europe. The Gregorian Revolution and Beyond* (London 1994), pp. 115–42].

Elena Lourie, 'The will of Alfonso I, "el Batallador", King of Aragon and Navarre', *Speculum* 50 (1975), 635–51.

M.C. Lyons & D. Jackson, *Saladin, the Politics of the Holy War* (Cambridge 1982).

Hans Eberhard Mayer, 'Das Brief Kaiser Friedrichs I. an Saladin von Jahre 1188', *Deutsches Archiv für Erforschung des Mittelalters* 14 (1958), 488–94.

Hans Eberhard Mayer, 'A ghost ship called *Frankenef*: King Richard I's German itinerary', *English Historical Review* 115 (2000), 134–44.

John Meyendorf, *Byzantine Theology. Historical Trends and Doctrinal Themes* (2nd. ed., New York, 1979).

Peter Munz, *Frederick Barbarossa. A Study in Medieval Politics* (London 1969).

Alan V. Murray, 'Zum Transfer von Zahlungsmitteln bei Kreuzzugsexpeditionen. Überlegungen zur Logistik des Kreuzzuges Kaiser Friedrichs I. (1189–90)', in *Transfer. Innovationen in der Zeit der Kreuzzüge* (Akten der 4. Landauer Staufertagung, 27–29. Juni 2003), ed. V. Herzner & J. Krüger (Speyer 2006), pp. 25–37.

Alan V. Murray, 'Finance and logistics of the Crusade of Frederick Barbarossa', in *In Laudem Hierosolymitani: Studies in Crusades and Material Culture in Honour of Benjamin Z. Kedar*, ed. I. Shagrir, R. Ellenblum & J. Riley-Smith (Aldershot 2007), pp. 357–68.

J.W. Nesbitt, 'Rates of march of Crusading armies in Europe: a study in computation', *Traditio* 19 (1963), 167–82.

Dimitri Obolensky, *The Byzantine Commonwealth. Eastern Europe, 500–1453* (London 1971).

Joseph O'Callaghan, 'The affiliation of the Order of Calatrava with the Order of Cîteaux', *Analecta Sacri Ordinis Cisterciencis* 15 (1959), 161–93 [reprinted in J. O'Callaghan, *The Spanish Military Order of Calatrava and its Affiliates* (London 1975)].

Marcel Pacaut, *Frederick Barbarossa* (London 1970).

John Pryor, 'The Venetian fleet for the Fourth Crusade and the diversion of the Crusade to Constantinople', in *The Experience of Crusading: presented to Jonathan Riley-Smith on his Sixty-Fifth Birthday*, i *Western Approaches*, ed. Marcus Bull and Norman Housley (Cambridge 2003), 103–23.

Jonathan Phillips, *The Second Crusade. Extending the Frontiers of Christendom* (New Haven 2007).

Christoph Reisinger, *Tankred von Lecce* (Cologne 1992).

Timothy Reuter, '*Episcopi cum sua militia*: the prelate as warrior in the early Staufen era', in *Warriors and Churchmen in the High Middle Ages. Essays Presented to Karl Leyser* (London 1992), pp. 79–94.

Jonathan Riley-Smith, 'The Templars and the Castle of Tortosa in Syria', *English Historical Review* 84 (1969), 278–288.

Bernd Schütte, *König Philip von Schwaben. Itinerar, Urkundenvergabe, Hof* (MGH Schriften 51, Hanover 2000).

Tilmann Struve, 'Renovatio imperii', in *Europa in Construzione. La Forza delle identità, la ricerca di unità (secoli IX–XIII)*, ed. G. Cracco, J. Le Goff, H. Keller and G. Ortalli (Bologna 2006), pp. 73–107.

Bernhard Töpfer, ,Kaiser Friedrich I. Barbarossa und der deutsche Reichsepiskopat', in *Friedrich Barbarossa: Handlungsspielräume und Wirkungsweisen des staufischen Kaisers*, ed. A. Haverkamp (Vorträge und Forschungen 40: Sigmaringen 1992), pp. 389–433.

Thomas Curtis Van Cleve, *Markward of Anweiler and the Sicilian Regency* (Princeton 1937).

Robert L. Wolff, 'The Second Bulgarian Empire. Its Origin and History to 1204', *Speculum* 24 (1949), 167–206.

Heinz Wolter, 'Der Mainzer Hoftage von 1184 als politische Fest', in *Feste und Feiern im Mittelalter*, ed. Detlef Altenburg, Jörg Jarnut and Hans-Hugo Steinhof (Sigmaringen 1991), pp. 193–9.

Maurice Zuffery, 'Der Mauritiuskult im Früh und Hochmittelalter', *Historisches Jahrbuch* 106 (1986), 23–58.

Index

Acre 35, 117–18, 120, 122, 140, 154, 165,
    181–3, 187–8
Adalbert III, Archbishop of Salzburg
    1183–1200 129, 155
Adalbert, Count of Dillingen 50–1,
Adalbert of Grumbach 23, 28n, 55,
Adalbert of Hildenburg 23–4, 28n, 55,
al-Adil 128, 154
Adolf III, Count of Holstein 15, 52
Adrianople 80, 85–6, 88, 90, 92–3, 95, 98,
    103, 112, 152, 156, 161,
Alexios II, Komnenos, Byzantine Emperor
    1180–2 63
Alexius III Angelos, Byzantine Emperor
    1195–1203 153–4
Almohads 198
Alvor (Portugal) 196, 205
Andronikos Komnenos, Byzantine
    Emperor 1182–5 61, 63, 121, 153
Antioch 26–7, 35–6, 153, 164–5, 175,
    180–1
Armenia / Armenians 17–18, 74, 108, 114,
    117, 152–3, 158, 162–3
Arnold (of Altena), Bishop of Osnabrück
    1173–91 22, 28n, 48, 57n, 65
Arnold of Hornberg 54, 83–4
Arnold of Lübeck, chronicler 11, 27–30,
    47n, 104n, 108n.
Assassins 127
Audita Tremendi, papal bull (1187) 5,
    37–40

Baldwin, Bishop of Utrecht 1178–96 14
Baldwin V, Count of Hainaut 14, 20,
Bela III, King of Hungary 1173–96 15, 47,
    58–61, 63, 79–80, 87, 133, 145,
    169, 177
Belgrade 59
Bernhard of Anhalt, Duke of Saxony
    1180–1212 15, 119n

Berrhoë, 71, 88, 152, 169
Berthold, Count of Neuenburg 51, 65
Berthold IV, Duke of Merania 23, 49n
Berthold V, Duke of Merania 21, 49, 62–3,
    65–6, 73–4, 82–3, 101, 104, 132,
    150, 156, 158, 165, 170
Berthold III, Margrave of Vohburg 49, 65,
Berthold of Künigsberg 54, 87, 90, 95–6,
    185
Bohemians 65, 89, 98, 101–2
Bohemond III, Prince of Antioch 1160–
    1201 18, 26, 137, 153,
Bosphorus, crossing of 17, 90, 95–6, 156,
    179
Branchevo 59, 69,
    Duke of 64, 149–50
Bremen 72, 193, 196
Bulgaria 60–70, 74, 81, 146, 149, 169, 177,
Burchard, Abbot of Ursperg, chronicler
    10, 12, 209
Burchard IV, Burgrave of Magdeburg 53
Burchard, Count of Wöltingerode 52

Cadiz 206–7
Calatrava, knights of 204
Celestine III, pope 1191–8 72, 119, 122,
    129, 178, 183–4
Charlemagne 135, 152,
Christian, Count of Oldenburg 52
Clement III, pope 1187–91 17, 44, 119,
    141, 178
Cologne 176–8
    chronicle of 11
    customs of the *ministeriales* of 19
    money of 58
Cono (Conrad), Count of Duras 20, 55
Cono (Conrad), Count of Falkenstein 28n,
    51.
Conrad (of Wittelsbach), Archbishop of
    Mainz (d. 1200) 14, 16, 131, 189

Conrad (of Querfurt), Bishop of
    Hildesheim 1194–8 and Würzburg
    1198–1202 132, 189–90
Conrad, Bishop of Regensburg 1187–1204
    48, 65, 80–1, 132, 165
Conrad (of Dornberg), Burgrave of
    Nuremberg 28n, 51, 85
Conrad, Count of Öttingen 50, 101
Conrad, Margrave of Montferrat 8, 121,
    124, 126–7, 139–40,
Conrad III, King of Germany 1138–52 1,
    13, 26, 133, 165,
Constance, Empress and Queen of Sicily
    (d. 1198) 118–19, 178, 183–4
Constantinople 96, 140, 153, 178
Cumans 81, 84, 89
Cyprus 63, 121, 154,

Diepold (of Berg), Bishop of Passau
    1172–90 5, 7, 9, 22, 28n, 48, 54n,
    61n, 65–6, 69n, 74, 80, 83, 89n,
    118, 149–52, 156, 165–7
Dietrich, Count of Hochstaden 56
Dietrich, Count of Wied 50, 89
Dimotika 28, 81, 169, 177
Disease 27–8, 127, 163–5, 181

Engelbert, Count of Berg 23, 50, 59
Eucharist, 99

Famine 104–8, 111, 114, 158, 171, 179
Florenz III, Count of Holland 23, 28n, 49,
    65, 82
Frederick, advocate of Berg 7, 28n, 53, 66,
    82–3, 97, 101
Frederick I, Barbarossa, Emperor of
    Germany 1152–90 33, 44–8,
    57–62, 64–5, 67–76, 78–80, 82,
    84–5, 87–8, 94, 96, 98, 101–3,
    107–16, 139, 141, 143–7, 149–52,
    156, 158–64, 169, 176–80
    and Crusade discipline 47, 58, 64–5,
        86, 103, 176
    and Crusade preparations 18–21, 44,
        143–5, 176, 209–12
    death of 26, 115–16, 164, 172, 180
    Italian expeditions of 18–19, 21–4, 27

negotiations with Byzantium 16–17,
    45–6, 61, 64, 69–71, 75–9, 84–5,
    87, 89–98, 145, 150–2, 156, 169,
    178–9
negotiations with Sultan of Iconium
    15–16, 45, 92–3, 100, 108, 112–13,
    145, 158–62, 172, 179–80
relations with Hungary 15, 47, 58–60,
    79–80, 87, 145,
Frederick, Count of Abenberg 50, 59, 89,
Frederick, Duke of Austria 1194–8 123,
    130, 132, 189
Frederick, Duke of Swabia (d. 1191) 24,
    26–9, 46, 48, 65–6, 71, 73, 81, 85,
    88, 95, 101–4, 109–11, 116–18,
    135, 144–5, 149–52, 156, 158–9,
    169–70, 172, 176–7, 180–1
    death of 118, 181
Frederick of Hausen 103, 170–1.

Gallipoli 90, 95–6, 156,
Gaubert of Aspremont 52–3, 68, 95
Gebhard, Count of Dollnstein 28, 51,
[St] George 106, 109, 144, 159, 171
Gerard, Count of Looz (Lon) 56,
Gottfried (of Helfenstein), Bishop of
    Würzburg 1186–90 6, 43–4, 64–5,
    117, 144
Gottfried, Duke of Brabant 55
Gottfried of Wiesenbach 15–16, 75, 92,
    103, 110, 158–60
Gregory VIII, pope 1187 37–41, 175–6
Greek fire 68
Guy of Lusignan, King of Jerusalem (d.
    1194) 34, 137–9, 174–5

Haimo, Archbishop of Tarentaise 1171–
    1211 46, 57, 65
Hartwig of Utlede, Archbishop of Bremen
    1184–1207 20, 57
Hattin, battle of (1187) 138–9, 174–5
Henry (of Horburg), Bishop of Basel
    1180–91 48, 65
Henry (of Hasenburg), Bishop of
    Strassburg, 1181–90 43, 141–3
Henry of Marcy, Cardinal Bishop of
    Albano 1179–89 41–3, 143

Henry, Count of Champagne (d. 1197) 124, 131, 183, 190–1
Henry II, Count of Diez 15, 145,
Henry III, Count of Diez 46, 52, 76, 145–7
Henry, Count of Kuick 24, 50
Henry, Count of Namur 14
Henry, Count of Saarbrücken 23, 50,
Henry, Count of Salm 52, 89
Henry, Count of Sayn 24, 49, 66–7
Henry, Count of Spanheim 49–50
Henry, Count of Vöhringen 51
Henry, Count Palatine of the Rhine 132, 189
Henry, Duke of Brabant 1190–1235 132, 189
Henry III, Duke of Limburg 1167–1221 55
Henry the Lion, Duke of Saxony 1143–80 14–15, 23, 30, 52n, 124–5
Henry VI, Emperor 1190–7 2, 5, 13, 15, 47, 50n, 54n, 56n, 70–2, 87–8, 118–19, 122–9, 173, 178–9, 183–8
Henry II, King of England 1154–89 44, 55, 87, 143,
Henry of Kalden, imperial marshal 28, 74, 106, 185–6
Herman (of Katzenellenbogen), Bishop of Münster, 17–18, 46, 48–9, 61, 65, 69, 71–2, 76, 80, 91, 145–7, 169
Herman, Margrave of Baden 28n, 49, 65, 170
Hospitallers (Knights of St. John) 5, 35, 138, 190
Humphrey (IV) of Toron 34, 124

Ibn al-Athīr, Muslim chronicler 16n, 27
Iconium 109–13, 135, 159–62, 171–2, 179–80
Isaac II Angelos, Byzantine Emperor 1185–95 30, 45, 49, 60–7, 69–71, 75–6, 78–80, 82, 84, 87, 90–2, 97–8, 145–7, 150–5, 169, 177–9
Isaac Komnenos, 'Emperor' of Cyprus 63, 121, 124, 126,
Isabella, Queen of Jerusalem 124, 183n
Isenrich, Abbot of Admont 7, 49, 67, 88

James the Pisan, Byzantine envoy 69n, 75n, 87, 90

Jerusalem, city 33, 36–7, 175–6, 188, 190
John Dositheus, Patriarch of Constantinople 1189–91 72, 77, 92
John Dukas, Logothete of the Drome 16, 67, 145, 151

Kalopeter, Bulgarian ruler 64, 84–5, 94–5
Karaman 162, 172

Laetare Jerusalem (fourth Sunday in Lent) 43–4, 156
Leo, Prince (later King) of Armenia 114–15, 163, 180
Leopold V, Duke of Austria 1177–94 2, 15, 35, 46–7, 120–1, 123–6, 147, 149, 167, 182–5,
  death of 129, 188–9
  excommunication 130, 185
  ministeriales of 121
Leopold VI, Duke of Austria 1198–1230 129–30, 189
Lisbon 195–6, 203
Liudolf, Count of Hallemund 28n, 52
Lombard League 13
Louis VII, King of France 1137–80 99, 133, 157
Lucius III, pope 1181–5 17
Ludwig, Count of Lohra 56
Ludwig, Count of Pfirt 56
Ludwig III, Landgrave of Thuringia 1172–90 24, 57, 116n
Ludwig of Helfenstein 106, 171

Magnus of Reichersberg, chronicler 4–5, 9
Mainz, Council of (1188) 13, 44–5, 141, 143–4, 176
Manuel Kamytzes 91, 151
Manuel Komnenos, Byzantine Emperor 1143–80 63, 102, 152, 157
Margab, castle of 36, 121
Margaret, Queen of Hungary 58
Margaritus of Brindisi, Sicilian admiral 131, 150n, 154, 186, 188
Markets 17, 25, 85–6, 91, 96, 98, 100, 113–14, 146, 150, 157, 162–3, 177, 179
Markward of Anweiler, *ministerialis* 82, 87, 90, 185

Markward of Neuenburg, chamberlain 46, 71, 76, 87, 90, 95–6
Martin, Bishop of Meissen 1170–90 48, 65, 67
money and coinage 18–21, 58–9, 91, 106,
Mühlhausen, abbey 1–2,
Myriokephalon, battle of (1176) 102, 157

Niketas Choniates, Byzantine chronicler 25–6, 30–1,
Nish 61–2, 64–5, 67, 75, 149

Otto (II) (of Andechs), Bishop of Bamberg 1177–96 22, 47
Otto of Babenberg, Bishop of Freising 1137–58, chronicler 6, 77n, 99, 157, 173,
Otto (of Berg), Bishop of Freising 1184–1220 47
Otto (of Henneberg), Bishop of Speyer 1188–1200 55–6
Otto, Count of Bentheim 49
Otto, Count of Geldern 57
Otto (Conrad), Duke of Bohemia 1189–91 119
Otto, Margrave of Meissen 1156–90 14
Otto of St. Blasien, chronicler 9, 173–90
Ottokar, Duke of Bohemia (King 1198–1230) 55
Ottokar, Duke of Styria (d. 1192) 63, 123

Peter (of Brezey), Bishop of Toul 1165–c.1192 48, 57, 68
Philadelphia 60, 64, 91, 96–9, 157, 169
Philip (of Heinsberg), Archbishop of Cologne 1167–91 14, 20, 119, 123
Philip, Duke of Swabia, later King of Germany 1198–1208 20–1, 24, 188
Philip II Augustus, King of France 1180–1223 6, 44, 46, 55, 63, 119–23, 127, 143, 146, 150, 167, 176, 178, 181–3
Philip, Count of Flanders 1168–91 6–7, 55, 120, 122, 167,
Philippopolis 65, 69, 71–2, 74, 76, 79–80, 82–4, 86, 88, 98, 150–2, 177,
Philomelium 104, 170–1,
Pisans 6, 96, 178, 181

poison 81–2
Poppo, Count of Henneberg 28n, 50, 65,
Poto of Massing, Bavarian nobleman 54, 95.

Qilij Arslan, Sultan of Iconium 1155–92 26, 45, 92, 100–1, 103, 109, 112–13, 145–6, 156, 158–63, 170–2, 177, 179–80
Qutb al-Dīn Malik, son of Qilij Arslan 92–3, 100–1, 103, 107–8, 111–13, 156, 158, 161–2, 170–2

Rainald of Chatillon, Prince of Antioch and lord of Oultrejordain 34, 137, 139, 174–5
Raymond III, Count of Tripoli 1150–87 34, 137–40, 153, 174,
Reichersberg, abbey 155–6
Reinhold of Reifenberg, Franconian nobleman 55, 95
Regensburg 47, 144, 147, 188
Richard, Count of Acerra 173, 185, 188n
Richard I, King of England 1189–99 2, 6, 9, 29, 44, 119–28, 130, 146, 150, 167, 176, 178, 181–5, 189
    capture of 123–4, 184,
    ransom 124–8, 184–5
Roger, Bishop of Cambrai 1179–91 6, 56
Rudolf (of Zähringen), Bishop of Liège 1167–91 12, 28, 48, 65,
Rupert, Count of Nassau 16–17, 52, 61, 65, 71, 91, 145–7, 169

Saladin 7, 33–8, 111, 121, 123, 127–8, 136–41, 144–5, 150, 153–5, 161, 174–5, 177, 182, 193
Salem (Salmansweiler), abbey 7–8
Sancho I, King of Portugal 1185–1211 196, 199, 201–5
Santiago de Compostella 195, 210

Second Crusade 18, 157, 165,
Sibilia (Armenia) 114, 163,
Sicily, kingdom of 63, 87–8, 118–19, 125, 128–9, 183–8
siege engines 181, 199, 201
Siegfried, Count of Libenau 28n, 51

Siegfried, Count of Moerl 120–1
Silves (Portugal) 9–10, 196–205
    description of 197–8
    surrender of, 202–3
Simon, Count of Spanheim 50, 89, 95,
Simon, Count of Tecklenburg 24, 57
Sofia 67–8
Sozopolis 101, 157, 170
Stephen Nemanja, zupan of Serbia 17,
    61–3, 75, 83, 149
Stralitz 62, 150
Sybilla, Queen of Jerusalem 137, 174,
    183n

Tageno, Dean of Passau 3–5, 7, 26, 28,
    118n, 149n, 166
Tancred, King of Sicily 1190–4 88n, 118,
    128, 131, 150n, 183, 185, 187
Tarsus 116, 172, 180
Templars 35, 138, 174, 190, 203–4
Theban Legion 110, 160
Trajan's Gates 67–8
Trifels, castle of, 130, 187–8
Tripoli 35, 118, 139–41, 175
Tokili, Turkish envoy 6, 92
True Cross 138–9, 174

Tyre 35, 72, 139–40, 154, 175

Ugrinus, Bishop of Raab 1174–1203 48, 80
Ulrich, Count of Kyburg 24, 50–1, 97n,
    101
Ulrich of Lutzelenhard, Swabian nobleman
    8
Urban III, pope 1185–7 22, 175

Venetians 95–6, 181,
Vlachs 60, 65, 84, 89, 94–5, 152, 155

Walram, Count of Nassau 46, 76,
Werner of Boland, *ministerialis* 71–2
William II, Count of Jülich 56
William II, King of Sicily 1166–89 63,
    118,
William III, King of Sicily 1194 128, 188
William, Marquis of Montferrat 63, 139,
William of Newburgh, English chronicler
    29
Willibrand of Oldenburg, pilgrim 27
Wolfger (of Ellensbrechtskirchen), Bishop
    of Passau 1191–1204 53n, 130,
    132.